W9-BCI-307

LEARNING DISABILITIES

Educational strategies

LEARNING DISABILITIES

Educational strategies

BILL R. GEARHEART

Professor, School of Special Education and Rehabilitation,
University of Northern Colorado,
Greeley, Colorado

THIRD EDITION

Illustrated

The C. V. Mosby Company

ST. LOUIS • TORONTO • LONDON 1981

A TRADITION OF PUBLISHING EXCELLENCE

Cover photograph by Richard Benkof.

THIRD EDITION

Printed in the United States of America

The C. V. Mosby Company
11830 Westline Industrial Drive, St. Louis, Missouri 63141

Library of Congress Cataloging in Publication Data

Gearheart, B R
Learning disabilities.

Includes index.
1. Learning disabilities. I. Title.
LC4704.G4 1981 371.9 80-39700
ISBN 0-8016-1768-5

GW/D/D 9 8 7 6 5 4 3 2 02/B/230

Preface

In this third edition of *Learning Disabilities: Educational Strategies,* the essential content of the second edition has been retained, in updated form, but important additions have been made. These additions are designed to reflect significant change and growth in the field of learning disabilities.

On a national basis, university training programs have improved and state certification requirements have been upgraded; learning disabilities teachers and specialists have increased in number, along with a parallel increase in their level of knowledge and competence. There has been a generalized move toward efforts to improve academic performance and concern with a broad range of language abilities and disabilities. There has also been a much needed increase in programming at the secondary level. Learning disabilities teachers and consultants have come to realize that students at all levels are referred for assistance on the basis of educational and academic difficulties and that measurable improvement in academic areas must be the major goal of special education programs for the learning disabled.

This evolving awareness does not dictate an abrupt change in direction but rather, for some, a change in emphasis. It does not mean that all we believed to be true in the recent past is no longer true. It does not mean that we have discovered "the way" to teach learning disabled students. The fact that learning disabilities is an "umbrella" term including a variety of learning difficulties and thus dictating a variety of approaches has been verified with even more certainty. This new awareness does mean that the only effective procedure is extensive, broad-range assessment, individualized educational planning, and a carefully orchestrated team approach designed to produce maximum improvement in the educational/academic efforts of the student. It also means that special educators must attend more to the role of the regular classroom teacher (in providing assistance to the learning disabled student) and provide more direct assistance to these highly important team members.

Because of the diverse nature of the educational needs of learning disabled students and the confusion that may result when we consider only one type of learning disability, teachers and teacher trainees need to understand the historic roots of learning disabilities and how they affect present programming. Thus the first chapter of this text is a description of how the field of learning disabilities evolved to its present state of development. Chapter 2 includes a discussion of the manner in which we determine the existence of learning disabilities (the assessment/identification sequence), a consideration of the assessment guidelines directed by Public Law 94-142, and a review of placement alternatives that should be considered when it is determined that a student requires additional specialized educational assistance. The final chapter of the first section includes a consideration of the wide range of areas in which a disability may occur and how these relate to what is known (or hypothesized) regarding the manner in which normal learning takes place.

Section Two, composed of six chapters, includes a summary of the major approaches that have been used to assist students with learning disabilities. Although, in practice, teachers may often use some combination of these various approaches, for purposes of initial consideration they are considered as separate approaches. Discussion of each approach includes some consideration of theoretical rationale, major advocates of such an approach, and practical, methodologic implications.

The final section, Chapters 10 through 12, emphasizes educational methods that are of value in assisting the learning disabled student to improve basic skills (reading, mathematics) and to apply basic skills in the various academic areas. Since publication of the second edition of this text, considerable expansion in secondary school programs for the learning disabled has taken place, and some of the more important information made available by experience at this level is also reviewed. This final section is important for those who will become learning disabilities specialists, but it is equally important to regular classroom teachers who have such students in their classrooms.

In total, this text should provide the reader with solid knowledge as to how the field of learning disabilities began and the variety of methods and approaches that may be required to assist students whom we call learning disabled. It should provide the basis for an informed decision as to whether the reader wishes to proceed further in the direction of training to be a teacher of individuals with learning disabilities. In addition, it should provide some "how-to-do-it" knowledge for those readers who may not, for any of a variety of reasons, take additional methods courses in learning disabilities.

Bill R. Gearheart

Acknowledgments

Many professional colleagues have provided indirect assistance in the preparation of the third edition of this text; however, certain individuals provided specific contributions, suggestions, or guidance. James DeRuiter and Judith Gilbert read specific chapters of this edition and made suggestions for change and improvement. I greatly appreciate their assistance. George Marsh III wrote a chapter on contributions from the field of medicine that appeared in the second edition, and many of his ideas were used in Chapter 8 of this edition. The continuing value of his earlier efforts is acknowledged with gratitude. Finally, Carol Kozisek Gearheart contributed to a very great extent through her comments on each chapter and support throughout the entire process of revision. Her assistance and encouragement are appreciated more than words can adequately express.

Bill R. Gearheart

Contents

SECTION ONE

LEARNING DISABILITIES: A CONCEPTUAL FRAMEWORK

1 Introduction, 3

Historical background (pre-1960s) of programs for students with learning disabilities, 4
Learning disabilities: the birth of a name (1963 to the present), 8
A learning disabilities definition, 9
More controversy, 10
Characteristics of students with learning disabilities, 14
Summary, 16

2 Identification, evaluation, and program planning, 19

Referral or screening: how we focus on students who may need special assistance, 19
The assessment process, 23
The individualized educational program (IEP), 25
The placement decision: a question of alternatives, 27
A residential setting or a separate special school, 27
Special (self-contained) classes, 27
Resource rooms, 28
Itinerant teacher program, 31
Consultive or special materials program, 31
The actual placement decision, 32
A summary of assessment and program planning considerations that have been greatly influenced by Public Law 94-142, 32
Tests used in the identification of learning disabled students and in planning educational remediation and intervention, 33
Measures of intelligence, 34
Measures of academic functioning, 36
Other tests used for identification and program planning, 37
Assessment of Children's Language Comprehension (ACLC), 37
Auditory Discrimination Test, 38

Basic Concepts Inventory (BCI), 38
Bender Visual-Motor Gestalt Test, 39
Boehm Test of Basic Concepts (BTBC), 39
Colored Progressive Matrices, 39
Developmental Test of Visual-Motor Integration (VMI), 39
Developmental Test of Visual Perception (DTVP), 39
Goldman-Fristoe Test of Articulation, 39
Goldman-Fristoe-Woodcock Test of Auditory Discrimination (GFW), 39
Harris Tests of Lateral Dominance, 39
Illinois Test of Psycholinguistic Abilities (ITPA), 40
Meeting Street School Screening Test (MSSST), 40
Memory-for-Designs Test (MFD), 40
Motor-Free Test of Visual Perception, 40
Picture Story Language Test (PSLT), 40
Purdue Perceptual-Motor Survey, 40
Southern California Sensory Integration Tests (SCSIT), 40
Standardized Road Map Test of Direction Sense, 40
Templin-Darley Tests of Articulation (TDTA), 41
Other assessment procedures, 41
Summary, 41

3 The development of normal learning abilities, 45

The nature of learning, 46
Major learning theories and theorists, 47
Behaviorism, 48
Neobehaviorism, 49
Cognitive theorists, 50
The development of cognitive structures as viewed by Jean Piaget, 51
The sensorimotor period, 52
The period of preparation and organization of concrete operations, categories, relations, and numbers, 54
The period of formal operations, 55
The conditions of learning—an integrated view, 56
Five major categories of learned capability, 57
Eight basic types of learning, 59
Signal learning, 59
Stimulus-response learning, 60
Chaining, 60
Verbal association, 60
Discrimination learning, 61
Concept learning, 62
Rule learning, 63
Problem solving, 64
Summary of Gagné's contributions, 64
Summary, 65

SECTION TWO

MAJOR APPROACHES AND TECHNIQUES FOR TEACHING THE LEARNING DISABLED

4 Perceptual-motor approaches, 73

Gross motor skills, 74
Fine motor skills, 74
The basic beliefs of perceptual-motor authorities, 75
Newell C. Kephart, 76
  Perceptual-motor match, 76
  Motor bases of learning, 77
  Basic movement generalizations, 79
  Purdue Perceptual-Motor Survey, 79
  Conclusion, 81
Gerald N. Getman, 82
  The Getman visuomotor model, 82
  Conclusion, 85
Raymond H. Barsch, 85
  Ten curriculum guidelines, 86
  Conclusion, 86
Bryant J. Cratty, 86
  Examples of gross movement as a learning modality, 87
  Conclusion, 88
A. Jean Ayres, 88
  The Southern California Sensory Integration Tests (SCSIT), 88
  Conclusion, 90
Marianne Frostig, 91
  Developmental Test of Visual Perception and related remediation, 91
  Conclusion, 93
Carl Delacato, 93
  Ontogeny recapitulates phylogeny, 94
  Concerns about the Delacato approach, 96
  Conclusion, 96
Summary, 98

5 Approaches used with hyperactive students, 101

Definitions and characteristics, 101
Hyperactivity—causal hypotheses, 103
Major approaches for reducing hyperactivity, 105
The environmental control approach, 106
  Alfred Strauss and Laura Lehtinen, 107
  William Cruickshank, 110
The use of biofeedback to reduce hyperactivity, 113
Summary, 114

6 Multisensory systems, 117

Kinesthetic and tactile learning, 118
The major multisensory approaches, 119
  The Fernald simultaneous multisensory (VAKT) approach, 120
  The Orton-Gillingham structured multisensory approach, 131
Multisensory approaches—variations and adaptations, 135
  The AKT modality blocking approach, 135
Variations and motivational techniques for use with the Fernald approach, 136
  A motoric/linguistic method, 137
  The apples, bananas, and candy approach, 138
Summary, 140

7 Language-development-related approaches, 143

Helmer Myklebust, 146
  Five levels of learning, 149
  A multidimensional approach to learning disability planning, 153
  Multiple states of readiness, 154
  Major principles for remediation, 154
  Visual and auditory dyslexia, 155
    Visual dyslexia, 156
    Auditory dyslexia, 156
  Other concepts growing out of Myklebust's efforts, 157
Samuel Kirk, 160
  Representational level functions, 162
  Automatic level functions, 162
  Interpretation of the ITPA, 163
Summary, 164

8 The role of medicine and medical specialists in the field of learning disabilities, 167

Medical specialists and allied health care professionals, 168
Pharmacotherapy: great promise and a number of problems, 170
Diet-related treatment, 175
  Food and food additive allergies, 175
  Orthomolecular medicine, 177
  Hypoglycemia and the narcolepsy complex, 178
  Summary: diet-related treatments, 179
Basic brain research, 179
Summary, 183

9 Behavior modification and learning disabilities, 187

Types of behavioral change, 187
Specifying goals and behavioral objectives, 188
Operant conditioning, 189
Contingency management and contingency contracting, 191
Behavioral modeling, 191
Principles for implementation, 192
Illustrative case studies, 194
Recommendations for practitioners, 199
Summary, 201

SECTION THREE

TEACHING APPROACHES FOR READING, ARITHMETIC, AND LANGUAGE DIFFICULTIES FOR GRADES K THROUGH 12

10 Reading methods for students with learning disabilities, 205

Basic controversies in how to teach reading, 206
  Significant findings of Chall's study, 207
Major reading approaches, 210
  Basal reader approach, 211
  Linguistic approaches, 212
  Language experience approach, 214
  Individualized reading approach, 216
  Phonic components in reading approaches, 216
  Reading approaches—a summary, 220
Reading approaches for students with learning disabilities, 220
  Basic guidelines for remediation, 220
Specific approaches to be considered, 225
  Major approaches (previously described), 225
  Color-coded phonetic approaches, 225
    Informal color-coding system, 226
  DISTAR program, 226
  Montessori-related approaches, 227
  Open Court Correlated Language Arts Program, 229
  Programmed instructional systems, 230
    Programmed reading approach, 230
    Individually Prescribed Instruction, 231
  Rebus approaches, 232
Summary, 234

11 Teaching arithmetic and written language to students with learning disabilities, 237

Learning disabilities that affect arithmetic, 237
Teaching approaches for use when arithmetic difficulties relate to learning disabilities, 238
  A diagnostic-remedial approach, 238
  Other teaching ideas, 244
  Piaget and the development of arithmetic and mathematical skills, 246
Arithmetic and learning disabilities—an evolving issue, 247
Learning disabilities and written language disorders, 249
  Handwriting disabilities, 249
    Methods for developing handwriting skills, 250
  Spelling disabilities, 252
  Written expression, 254
Summary, 256

12 Secondary school programs for the learning disabled, 259

The nature of the secondary school and the secondary school student, 259
Accommodation and compensatory teaching: a variety of procedures, 263
Secondary programming: a tutorial emphasis, 265
Special modified programs, 266
  Work-study programs, 266
  Alternative schools, 267
Summary, 268

APPENDIXES

A Pupil Behavior Rating Scale, 273

B Alaska Learning Disabilities Ranking Scale (ALDRS), 280

C Chart of normal development of motor and language abilities, 286

Glossary, 288

LEARNING DISABILITIES

Educational strategies

SECTION ONE

Learning disabilities: a conceptual framework

Section One is designed to introduce the reader to the basic concepts, unique nomenclature, and historical roots of the subarea of special education called learning disabilities. Chapter 1 provides a summary of the manner in which this newest area of specialty within the field of special education has grown, with emphasis on the role of key individuals and the federal government. In addition, continuing problems with the controversial "umbrella" definition are considered in some detail.

Chapter 2 includes a discussion of identification, evaluation, and program planning, plus a brief review of various tools commonly used in assessment of learning disabled students. Chapter 3 provides a review of the manner in which leading authorities believe *normal* learning takes place, as a basis for further consideration of the atypical learning patterns of learning disabled students. In composite, these three chapters should prepare the reader to better understand the various approaches considered in Section Two.

Courtesy St. Louis Art Museum.

chapter 1

Introduction

LEARNING DISABILITIES! This term, as used to describe the problems that some specific student may be experiencing, is welcomed by some parents, but may lead to despair for others. Potential reasons for these differing reactions are many; some parents may have been expecting the words "mental retardation," while others may have been convinced that their child was only "lazy." Some parents may have heard positive, encouraging comments about the success of programs for the learning disabled; others may equate all learning disability programs with those for severely brain-injured students. Although the term *learning disabilities* is commonly used in educational circles today, much misinformation remains on the part of many educators and much of the general public. Physicians are becoming more knowledgeable, but they too may be the source of incomplete information or misinformation.

Why does such confusion exist? Are there any solid answers to the many questions that may be asked in this field? Is there hope for a more reliable information base with regard to learning disabilities? And most important of all, can we really help learning disabled students? These and many other questions will become apparent to the reader as we proceed to introduce the exciting, confusing, sometimes frustrating field of learning disabilities.

In the introductory section (Chapters 1 through 3), we will consider the preceding questions and try to provide acceptable answers. In many instances there are a variety of possible answers, and in keeping with our primary purposes we will try to objectively review and briefly assess a broad range of opinions and points of view. In reviewing the work of authorities who have proposed educational strategies to assist the learning disabled, every effort will be directed toward objective analysis and comment.

In Section Two (Chapters 4 through 9), we will consider a broad view of learning disabilities, which will include the work of Fernald, Orton, and Strauss and Lehtinen as early efforts to serve some of those we now call learning disabled children, although these early attempts did not relate to a large number of children who were in need of assistance. Prior to the 1960s, only those children who were sufficiently different to be called brain injured or neurologically impaired, aphasic or severely language impaired, or who fit into a particular school district's plan for remedial reading were eligible to receive the badly needed special programs and services. Even *these* children were often denied services if their behavior was too unusual, and such denial of educational service was considered perfectly proper and "legal" at that time. Children with serious remedial reading problems were sometimes called dyslexic, but this simply meant that severe reading problems existed, with a tendency to reverse symbols and produce mirror writing.

Then, early in the 1960s, events took place that radically changed the educational prospects of learning disabled students. These events, which directly related to the learning disabled, combined with advocacy efforts on behalf of all handicapped students and supported by the work of the pioneers mentioned previously, led to an educational movement that became a virtual streamroller. The "learning disabilities wave" crested in the late 60s and early 70s, and continues with great strength today. This movement, how it evolved, the people who made it happen, and the results, in terms of present-day programs, are what this text is all about.

In this chapter, the historical development of the present field of learning disabilities will be explored. Definitions of learning disabilities will be provided, with discussion of the implications of these definitions to further illuminate the scope of the topic. Characteristics of learning disabled children will be enumerated, even though such listings can prove misleading if improperly interpreted.

In succeeding chapters, a discussion of assessment procedures and a consideration of how normal children learn will provide further information on which to base our pursuit of a better understanding of learning disabilities. In order to provide a general basis for the content of the remainder of this text, we will consider the events that led to this special education bombshell of the 60s.

HISTORICAL BACKGROUND (PRE-1960s) OF PROGRAMS FOR STUDENTS WITH LEARNING DISABILITIES

Some reviewers of the history of learning disabilities recognize the work of Franz Joseph Gall, a Viennese physician, as among the earliest that might be readily traced to what we presently call learning disabilities. Wiederholt (1974) takes this point of view, and notes that Gall, in 1802, published a description of a theoretical construct in which he related specific brain activities with identifiable parts of the brain. Gall had worked with adults who had brain injuries resulting from a variety of causes. These patients developed language disorders immediately following known injuries, and Gall believed he could relate specific areas of damage to what we now call asphasia. He described patients who, after their brain was damaged, were unable to express feelings and ideas in spoken language. Somewhat later, Gall became connected with phrenology (a system that allegedly could predict personal characteristics through knowledge of the shape and character of protuberances of the skull) and was soon discredited. For this reason, he lost much of his influence in the field, but certain of his followers (who rejected phrenology) carried on his work (Head, 1926).

By 1900, the efforts originated by Gall and his followers had led to a great deal more interest in such topics as the differing functions of the two sides of the brain, the extent to which brain trauma could lead to language dysfunction, and other related topics. Instead of accepting the idea that individuals were either generally intelligent (capable of learning normally), or to some degree mentally retarded, it was now understood, for example, that brain lesions on specific parts of the brain could cause predictable loss to specific brain functions. These and related efforts led to what might be considered a "branching" in the then recognized field of mental deficiency. Some of the research that related to mental deficiency continued down the path of more generalized subnormal mental functioning. Other research was directed toward greater understanding of the brain injured, a path that eventually led to efforts that were the forerunners of the present-day field of learning disabilities.

Gall's early efforts in 1802 were paralleled by other efforts which became part of the base of another strand of the developing field of learning disabilities. In *Visual Perception: The Nineteenth Century* (1964), William Dember gives accounts of contributions in the field of visual perceptual problems as early as 1801. It appears that research in visual perception was under way throughout most of the nineteenth century. Then, in 1895, James Hinshelwood, a Scottish opthalmologist, published a report on visual perceptual problems, which he called word blindness. His report of severe defects in visual memory documented severe reading difficulty (word blindness) in children with normal intelligence. Two British investigators, James Kerr, a physician, and W. P. Morgan, an ophthalmologist, reported in 1896 separate but similar cases of individuals with severe reading problems, despite normal intelligence. Thus another type of learning problem, which later became a part of learning disabilities, was substantiated.

Although there are some exceptions, most of our present emphasis in the field of learning disabilities is on youngsters of school age. In contrast, the early research in aphasia was primarily with adults, although efforts in the area of word blindness (later called dyslexia) were made regarding school-age children. The aphasia-related research dealt with abilities that had been developed but were lost. Word blindness research related to children who could not learn to read despite the presence of normal intelligence and the ability to accomplish many other learning tasks with relative ease.

Hinshelwood, who first reported on word blindness in 1895, published in 1917 a detailed description of methods for teaching students with this condition. His method (possibly the first description of how to teach "learning disabled" students—though he did not call them that) included three major steps: (1) teaching the student to "store" the individual letters of the alphabet in the visual memory part of the brain, (2) teaching the student to spell words out loud, thus developing, through auditory memory, the ability to retrieve the entire word, and (3) transferring this auditory retrieval to the visual memory center of the brain. His methods were based on his understanding of brain functioning, and he was pragmatic enough to note that "no amount of argument can decide the question as to the best method of instruction in these cases. The test of experience alone can definitely settle this point" (Hinshelwood, 1917, p. 107).

Hinshelwood based his teaching suggestions on theories of brain functioning that he had formulated in his lengthy investigations of word blindness. These theories are now recognized to have been inaccurate, but many of his teaching ideas have been of considerable value. The fact that he recognized the existence of students who had potential to learn, despite their extreme difficulties with reading, and proposed educational strategies designed to remediate their underlying disabilities was a most important step. Although others had provided written descriptions of such problems, he was among the first to attempt to do something about them in a systematic manner. Hinshelwood was truly a pioneer in learning disabilities.

A number of other individuals played important roles in the development of educational approaches that eventually came to focus under the general umbrella term *learning disabilities.* A more detailed description of the efforts of each of these individuals will be provided in Chapters 4 through 7; therefore, at this point only names and an extremely brief statement about their work will be provided. Among the most important of these individuals are the following:

Grace Fernald

In a clinic school at the University of California in Los Angeles, Fernald initiated a multisensory approach that is still in use (in various forms) today. Although initiated to serve students with a wide variety of problems, the program quickly evolved into one that accepted primarily those who had normal or above normal intelligence, but who were experiencing significant learning problems. This may have been the first actual learning disability program in the United States (or perhaps the world); however, the term learning disabilities was not in use at that time. Other earlier programs had served some students who would have been called learning disabled today, but this program was directed primarily at this population; thus it was unique for its time. A more detailed description of Fernald's work, which began in 1921, is in Chapter 6.

Samuel Orton

Dr. Samuel Orton was a professor of psychiatry at the medical school of the University of Iowa and in 1925 was involved in organizing an experimental mobile mental hygiene clinic to serve outlying communities. In the first of these clinics he encountered an unusual 16-year-old boy he called M. P. This boy had never learned to read, despite adequate intelligence, and through good fortune it was possible to arrange for a lengthy study by Dr. Orton and the staff at the university. In addition to M. P., Orton found a significant number of other students with similar disabilities. It was discovered that a number of these students had difficulty with reversals (for example, reading *saw* for *was*), confusion of *b* and *d*, and other such trouble with visual symbols. Orton became interested in this problem and, after further study, established hypotheses relating to both reading methodology and what was actually taking place neurologically.

Because Orton completed earlier work that correlated clinical symptoms with anatomical findings in adults who had suffered language impairment before death (a postmortem human brain study), he had both the interest and the background to pursue the question of possible neurological causation in reading disability. Orton presented his field findings and theories to the American Neurological Association meeting in 1925. As a result of enthusiastic acceptance and interest in his report, he received a Rockefeller Foundation Grant to carry on his work. He assembled an excellent clinical team and completed a number of studies of interest. Orton coined the word "strephosymbolia" (twisted symbols) to describe the memory-for-word pattern and letter orientation problems of the subjects with whom he worked. Further effects of his efforts are discussed in Chapter 6.

Anna Gillingham
Bessie Stillman
Marion Monroe

Gillingham, Stillman, and Monroe have one important point in common—their association with Samuel Orton. Monroe worked with Orton in the mobile mental health effort at the Iowa State Psychopathic Hospital, and Gillingham worked with him in New York, after Orton started his work there. Stillman became involved in joint efforts with Gillingham later. These three individuals made significant contributions through the remedial teaching methods they developed, with Monroe's efforts moving somewhat away from the initial Orton emphasis, but nevertheless retaining some of his influence. All three contributed to the developing bank of knowledge relating to how to teach word blind students, with particular emphasis on reading. In addition, all seemed to be somewhat influenced by the earlier work of Fernald. Their influence began in the 1930s and continues to some extent until today. More information about the remedial approach suggested by Gillingham and Stillman is in Chapter 6.

Heinz Werner
Alfred Strauss
Laura Lehtinen Rogan

Heinz Werner and Alfred Strauss came to the United States following Hitler's rise to power in Nazi Germany. Both had considerable background relating to the effects of brain injury, and through collaborative efforts in the United States, developed a number of concepts that were most important to the field that was soon to be called learning disabilities. Their research indicated that many of the confirmed characteristics of brain-injured adults were similar to those of certain mentally retarded students they called exogenous (condition caused by *external,* rather than hereditary factors). Their work with these students, whose characteristics included perceptual problems, figure-ground difficulties, and hyperactivity, was the foundation of a methods book by Strauss and Laura Lehtinen Rogan, which is recognized as a classic in the field of learning disabilities. Werner and Strauss completed much of their pioneering work in the 1930s; the Strauss and Lehtinen text was published in 1947. More information about their work is in Chapter 5.

Helmer Myklebust

Helmer Myklebust entered the learning disabilities arena via the education of the deaf. By the mid-1950s he had noted that a large number of children seen in his Child Study Center "had auditory disorders due to emotional disturbance, aphasia, or mental deficiency, but . . . had essentially normal hearing acuity when special diagnostic methods were applied" (Myklebust, 1954, p. 8). This interest in problems with language development and aphasia eventually led him squarely into the field of learning disabilities. He coauthored, with Doris Johnson, *Learning Disabilities: Educational Principles and Practices,* a 1967 text that remains in use as a significant methods resource in learning disabilities. Myklebust's long involvement with aphasia and related learning problems and his authorship of other significant works leads to his recognition as a major contributor to the field of learning disabilities. Some of Johnson and Myklebust's more significant recommendations (from their 1967 text) are presented in Chapter 7.

Newell Kephart
Gerald Getman
Ray Barsch

Kephart, Getman, and Barsch are all associated with perceptual-motor-oriented approaches. Kephart worked closely with Alfred Strauss, while Getman and Barsch were obviously interested in the manner in which motor development relates to perceptual abilities, and higher level intellectual abilities. All were interested in developmental psychology and the work of developmental theorists such as Gesell and Piaget.

Marianne Frostig

Marianne Frostig is perhaps best known for her work in visual perception and, like Getman, seems to focus major interest on the development of visually related skills. All developed educational methods and procedures to assist the learning disabled students to learn more effectively. The efforts of each of these individuals is further explored in Chapter 4.

William Cruickshank

Cruickshank may be viewed as either a perceptual-motor advocate or related to the brain-injury strand of the field of learning disabilities. He knew and worked with Werner and Strauss in the early days of his professional career and has in more recent years been Director of the Institute for the Study of Mental Retardation and Related Disabilities at the University of Michigan. His 1961 text,

A Teaching Method for Brain-Injured and Hyperactive Children, plus other related texts, have been of great interest and value in this developing field. His influence in the field began to be felt in the 1950s and has remained strong to this day. Further information regarding some of his ideas for teaching the brain injured is in Chapter 5.

Samuel Kirk

Samuel Kirk's work with students who today might be called learning disabled began in the early 1930s while he was a graduate student at the University of Chicago (Kirk, 1970). In some of his work there, in a school for delinquent, retarded boys, he used methods and ideas derived from the writings of Fernald, Monroe, and Hinshelwood (all mentioned earlier in this historical review) and achieved notable success. Kirk later studied with Monroe, and eventually became interested in young "mentally retarded" children (whom he suspected might not be actually mentally retarded). He developed a strong and lasting interest in the role of language development (as opposed to theoretical concern with brain function) and eventually became recognized as one of the leading special educators in the nation. We will continue our consideration of Kirk's contributions to the field of learning disabilities in the following section.

In closing this first section of our historical review, we should note several things. First, it should be recognized that some of the people mentioned in this review became even more active in the time period that followed. In fact, a number of these individuals remain active in the field as we enter the 1980s. Second, it should be noted that although the year 1963 has been chosen to call the beginning of the time in which learning disabilities became a recognized entity, the move to general recognition was not actually all that definite. However, there was a specific date when the term *learning disabilities* was used in a national meeting in such a manner that it encouraged parents to use it as a convenient point of focus for their advocacy efforts. April 6, 1963, is often recognized as the beginning of learning disabilities efforts as we know them today, and our historical review will be concluded by summarizing efforts from this date to the present.

LEARNING DISABILITIES: THE BIRTH OF A NAME (1963 TO THE PRESENT)

Students with learning disabilities were sometimes provided educational programs prior to 1963, but this was accomplished in a variety of settings. They were at times called: (1) hyperactive students, (2) brain-injured students, (3) Strauss syndrome students, (4) dyslexic students, (5) students with perceptual disorders, (6) students with perceptual-motor disorders, (7) minimal-brain-dysfunction (MBD) students, (8) dysgraphic students, (9) aphasic students, or (10) neurologically impaired students. In a few states there were viable programs for certain of these students as part of the public schools, but in many areas of the nation they could attend school only if parents could band together and provide private schooling. Some parents had been a part of the National Association for Retarded Children (NARC), but as that group helped force the public schools to provide classes for their retarded children, it was discovered that some children could not be permitted in classes for the retarded because their intelligence quotients were too high (according to state guidelines). In addition, such programs for the retarded were not really appropriate for these children. But the 1960s was a time of increasing advocacy on behalf of many causes, and these parents vowed that their children were not to be denied an appropriate education.

One such parent group, the Fund for Perceptually Handicapped Children, was determined to find better means to assist their children, and held its first annual meeting on April 6, 1963. Efforts of various professionals were known, and in recognition of his interest, Samuel Kirk was asked to be one of the major speakers. Dr. Kirk, in attempting to summarize existing problems and provide parents with insight regarding the futility of various labeling schemes, said:

> I have felt for some time that labels we give children are satisfying to us, but of little help to the child himself. We seem to be satisfied if we can give a technical name to a condition. This gives us the satisfaction of closure. We think we know the answer if we can give the child a name or a label—brain-injured, schizophrenic, autistic, mentally retarded, aphasic, etc. As indicated before, the term "brain injured" has little meaning to me from a management of training point of view. It does not tell me whether the child is smart or dull, hyperactive or underactive. It does not give me any clues to management or training. The terms cerebral palsy, brain injured, mentally retarded, aphasic, etc., are actually classification terms. In a sense they are not diagnostic, if by diagnostic we mean an assessment of the child in such a way that leads to some form of treatment, management, or remediation. In addition, it is not a basic cause, since the designation of a child as brain injured does not really tell us why the child is brain injured or how he got that way (Kirk, 1963, pp. 2-3).

Kirk then noted that he had been recently using the term *learning disabilities* to describe children "who have disorders in development in language, speech, reading, and associated communication skills needed for social interaction" (pp. 2-3). He further noted that he did *not* include as learning disabled those children whose primary handicap was generalized mental retardation or sensory impairment (blindness or deafness). It is ironic that, in a speech suggesting that both educators and parents have become overinvolved with labels that provide limited educational guidance, Kirk suggested a new label—learning disabilities—which soon became the fastest growing subarea of special education. Parents were so impressed with the potential of this new term that they voted, in this same convention, to organize the Association for Children with Learning Disabilities (ACLD). Thus learning disabilities was "born" and became a very rapidly growing "baby." The ACLD became a powerhouse as an advocacy organization almost overnight, with significant influence on national legislation.

A learning disabilities definition

At its "birth" in 1963, the name *learning disabilities* was given to this "infant," which was to go grow so rapidly; but, unlike a human child, it was difficult to simply point to a learning disability and say, "This is a learning disability." Learning disabilities came into being as a conglomerate of conditions or disabilities, included under one "umbrella" term for administrative convenience, providing a focal point for advocacy efforts on the behalf of parents and other interested persons. It was recognized from the beginning that this would require a multifaceted definition, and application of this definition seemed likely to lead to various types of difficulties. This likelihood became a reality in the years that followed.

One of the first nationally recognized definitions of learning disabilities came as a result of the establishment of a National Advisory Committee on Handicapped Children, a group whose origin was tied to the establishment of the Bureau of Education for the Handicapped. This first National Advisory Committee on Handicapped Children was headed by none other than Samuel Kirk, and it presented its first annual report on January 31, 1968. The committee made 10 major recommendations, including one which indicated that learning disabilities should be given high-priority consideration for federal attention, including funding. The committee provided the following statement regarding learning disabilities, including a definition.

Confusion now exists with relationship to the category of special learning disabilities. Unfortunately it has resulted in the development of overlapping and competing programs under such headings as "minimal brain dysfunction," "dyslexia," "perceptual handicaps," etc.

A Federal study, sponsored jointly by the National Institute of Neurological Diseases and Blindness, the National Society for Crippled Children, and the U.S. Office of Education, is now in progress to attempt to define more clearly the nature and extent of these problems, and to provide a basis for the planning of more effective programs of research and service. Prior to the completion of this study, it is necessary for the Office of Education to formulate a definition. To serve as a guideline for its present program the committee suggests the following definition.

Children with special learning disabilities exhibit a disorder in one or more of the basic psychological processes involved in understanding or in using spoken or written languages. These may be manifested in disorders of listening, thinking, talking, reading, writing, spelling, or arithmetic. They include conditions which have been referred to as perceptual handicaps, brain injury, minimal brain dysfunction, dyslexia, developmental phasia, etc. They do not include learning problems which are due primarily to visual, hearing, or motor handicaps, to mental retardation, emotional disturbance, or to environmental disadvantage.

From an educational standpoint, special learning disabilities must be identified through psychological and educational diagnosis.*

In response to this call for support for learning disabilities, certain very limited programs at the local level were provided through the use of existing legislation, but in April, 1970, a law that included specific provisions for learning disabilities research, training, and model centers was passed. This was Public Law 91-230, and learning disabilities provisions were included in Part G of Title VI of this law. From this point on, there was little question as to the recognition of learning disabilities as a major subarea of special education. But the definition controversy was far from settled, as we will see from the information that follows.

More controversy

The learning disability definition as proposed by Kirk and the National Advisory Committee on Handicapped Children included what is often called an "exclusion clause" at the conclusion of the definition. This clause read, "They do not include learning problems which are due primarily to visual, hearing, or motor handicaps, to mental retardation, emotional disturbance, or to environmental disadvantage." We should carefully note the word "primarily," for the sentence has sometimes been interpreted to indicate that mental retardation, hearing handicap, visual handicap, and other conditions listed in the definition can never exist concurrently with learning disability. This is not what was intended, and to understand the definition, we should consider the reasons why it was worded this way. These reasons were:

1. When this definition was first proposed, there were programs for the mentally retarded, hearing handicapped, visually handicapped, and so forth. Throughout the United States the definition was necessary to provide an administrative and funding vehicle whereby special state

*From Special education for handicapped children. First Annual Report of the National Advisory Committee on Handicapped Children, Washington, D.C., 1968, Office of Education, Department of Health, Education, and Welfare.

level reimbursement could be provided to encourage the development of special programs for children who did not have these other handicaps and therefore could not be served through existing programs. Ideally, local school districts should provide for the needs of all children, whether or not special state funds are forthcoming. In practice, we know that this is seldom the case and that special incentive monies are the best present solution to this problem.

2. It was agreed that a number of conditions led to unique learning difficulties but, taken singly, provided insufficient numbers of children for economical special programming. These conditions had (or were assumed to have) a variety of types of causation, but in fact all led to serious educational problems—to the existence of significant discrepancies between apparent ability to learn and actual learning. The concept of learning disabilities provided a convenient umbrella under which most of these conditions could fit without having to specify causation.
3. Special education leadership at the federal level was interested in providing demonstration centers, research funds, and other similar efforts. To establish such programs they needed a general term that would fit a number of conditions; *learning disabilities* seemed to serve this function satisfactorily.
4. Though some members of the specialty professions that banded together to form the initial learning disability cadre disagreed with the use of this general term, there was even more disagreement as to precisely what caused these problems and what to do about remediation. Even if it had been decided, for example, to use a series of terms more consistent with the model suggested by *blind, deaf,* or *mentally retarded,* there could have been no agreement as to causation and thus to acceptable terminology. "Learning disabilities" provided a middle ground on which these specialists could meet.

Problems related to the obvious vagueness of the learning disabilities definition came to a head as the United States Congress held hearings relating to Public Law 94-142, the Education for All Handicapped Children Act of 1975. In this comprehensive law, funding for programs for the learning disabled was to be included along with funding for other handicapping conditions for the first time.

As the House Subcommittee conducted hearings on Public Law 94-142, they called in many national authorities on learning disabilities. They soon found that these authorities could not agree on how to define (or redefine) learning disabilities. It soon became a matter of deep concern that if careful safeguards were not established, more and more children with other handicaps would not receive the share of funding intended by Congress. Data available at that time indicated that this might become a very real problem almost immediately in certain states.

The problem was resolved in this way: Public Law 94-142 provided that the states could serve (with federal funds) up to 12% of the children in the state as handicapped, but no more than one sixth of those served as handicapped may be those served as learning disabled. (If only 6% of the children in the state were served as handicapped, only one sixth—that is, 1%—could be served as learning disabled.) This would then protect services to other handicapping conditions from overapplication of the concept of learning disabilities.

Public Law 94-142 became law with the

limitations of percentage of handicapped that might be served as learning disabled and also with specific instructions to the Commissioner of Education to:

a. Establish criteria for determining which children are learning disabled
b. Establish diagnostic procedures which must be used to determine whether the child meets the criteria established in (a)
c. Establish regulations whereby state, local, and intermediate educational agencies can be monitored for compliance with (a) and (b)

The Bureau of Education for the Handicapped was, in effect, told to straighten this matter out—to come to grips with this dilemma and settle the question once and for all. In response to this directive, hearings were held throughout the United States and thousands of pages of testimony were taken. More specific identification criteria were proposed, submitted to national review, and in each case were rejected by parents and professionals in the field. After many months of essentially fruitless effort, the following definition and criteria for determining the existence of a learning disability were promulgated in the *Federal Register* (Vol. 42, No. 250, Dec. 29, 1977, p. 65083).

"Specific learning disability" means a disorder in one or more of the basic psychological processes involved in understanding or in using language, spoken or written, which may manifest itself in an imperfect ability to listen, think, speak, read, write, spell, or to do mathematical calculations. The term includes such conditions as perceptual handicaps, brain injury, minimal brain disfunction, dyslexia, and developmental aphasia. The term does not include children who have learning problems which are primarily the result of visual, hearing, or motor handicaps, of mental retardation, of emotional disturbance, or of environmental, cultural, or economic disadvantage.

Criteria for determining the existence of a specific learning disability

(a) A team may determine that a child has a specific learning disability if:
  (1) The child does not achieve commensurate with his or her age and ability levels in one or more of the areas listed in paragraph (a) (2) of this section, when provided with learning experiences appropriate for the child's age and ability levels; and
  (2) The team finds that a child has a severe discrepancy between achievement and intellectual ability in one or more of the following areas:
    (i) Oral expression;
    (ii) Listening comprehension;
    (iii) Written expression;
    (iv) Basic reading skill;
    (v) Reading comprehension;
    (vi) Mathematics calculation; or
    (vii) Mathematics reasoning.
(b) The team may not identify a child as having a specific learning disability if the severe discrepancy between ability and achievement is primarily the result of:
  (1) A visual, hearing, or motor handicap;
  (2) Mental retardation;
  (3) Emotional disturbance; or
  (4) Environmental, cultural, or economic disadvantage.

As a result of this involved chain of events, we have a national (federal) definition of learning disabilities, but state level definitions vary. In effect, learning disabilities in any given state are what the state definition indicates they are; there are variations, and at times these variations lead to problems.

In spite of variations, it is possible to analyze the various state definitions, and such an analysis leads to the following conclusions:

1. Most definitions indicate that there must be a significant discrepancy between the actual level of functioning of the child (in reading, mathematics, language development, and so on) and the level of functioning that might be expected when we

consider intellectual potential, sensory capability, and educational experiences (opportunity to have learned).

2. Many definitions exclude the mentally retarded, the visually impaired, and the hearing impaired. Many exclude the emotionally disturbed, *if* the emotional disturbance is primary, that is, if it preceded rather than resulted from the learning problem. This definitional facet (the principle of exclusion) is being modified in a number of states. The wording of the federal definition indicates that the term learning disabilities is not intended to include those whose *primary* problem is mental retardation, hearing impairment, and so forth. It is not intended to be totally exclusive, but in practice (in many states) it has become so.
3. Many definitions exclude the culturally *disadvantaged* and in some cases this includes the culturally *different* (different from the white, middle class).
4. Many definitions imply that there is a central nervous system dysfunction but do not typically require "proof" of such dysfunction.

Certain problems that result from the vagueness of the learning disabilities definition should be considered by those attempting to understand the field of learning disabilities. The discussion that follows (numbered for convenience) relates to these problems. This discussion will not provide answers, but perhaps will at least amplify and clarify the questions.

1. The definition does not specify *degree* of disability and thus might be used to include an inappropriately high percentage of children in any given school. "Significant discrepancy" is commonly agreed to be an important principle but is very difficult to define with preciseness. For example, is a 2-year discrepancy significant? If it is at the fourth-grade level, then how great a discrepancy must exist to be significant at the eighth-grade level? At the first-grade level?
2. The concept of significant discrepancy or of discrepancy depends on the determination of a child's ability to learn. Recent research and the results of widely publicized litigation lead to the conclusion that, at least for many minority and culturally different children, even the most highly respected tests of individual intelligence may be inappropriate. How then are we to determine intellectual potential? If we cannot determine intellectual potential, how can we determine degree of discrepancy?
3. Exclusion of the culturally different or culturally disadvantaged was believed necessary to keep the issues of education for these groups and the learning disabled distinct and separate. It was included so that schools, for example, would not attempt to use learning disability programs to substitute for badly needed bilingual programs. It was not intended to keep culturally different or culturally disadvantaged children *who were in fact learning disabled* out of learning disability programs. Unfortunately, some educators under pressure for having had too many minority children in special programs in the past may tend to use this provision to avoid serving such children, thus avoiding possible conflict.
4. The learning disabilities definition makes no attempt to differentiate between temporary, symptomatic problems and more specific long-term problems.

One solution would be to develop a precise, highly restrictive definition that would leave few interpretive questions. The problem with this solution is that any such definition would likely lead to a large percentage of the students presently served in learning disability programs being left without service because of ineligibility under the new definition. *It seems fairly obvious that parents who have played such a major role in establishing the need for present programs are not likely to accept a restrictive definition that leaves many of their children without special services.*

Therefore, the best plan may be to keep the general umbrella definition, but limit the funding of special programs in the public schools to some reasonable percentage of children who may be served under such a definition. We must continue investigative efforts directed toward a better solution, but in the meantime should continue programming under present general guidelines. Definitional preciseness is important, but programs for children should receive first priority.

Before leaving the topic of definitions, we should note that the vagueness of existing definitions has led to problems in estimating prevalence. Some have suggested that 20% to 30% of all schoolchildren may be learning disabled. Certain individuals have publicized such information to attempt to sell their services or materials. We should recognize that such suggestions can be handled through dissemination of more accurate information, and we can and should educate the public to the fact that "special" services through special education funding cannot go to such a large percentage of the school-age population. A figure of 2%, 3%, or 4% to serve at any one time might be left up to the local school district, within guidelines established by each state. Such variables as existence of other special programs, nature of the pupil population, and how long learning disabilities programming has been available will affect the "which children shall we serve right now" decision. Because learning disabilities are remediable in many young children, if 2% of the children of a given school district are served at all times, as many as 8% or 10% of the total school-age population may be served over the years. Learning disabilities is a relatively new area of effort and hasty moves at this point will likely lead to a new set of labels and problems and denial of programming to children who need special help, regardless of what we call it. Caution would seem to be the only wise and prudent watchword for the present. If caution is combined with continued investigation, careful observation, and objective analysis of programs that are of significant benefit to students who need assistance, we are probably on the right track.

CHARACTERISTICS OF STUDENTS WITH LEARNING DISABILITIES

Great variations may exist in some of the characteristics of learning disabled students, but one characteristic is found in all such students. *This is a severe discrepancy between achievement and intellectual ability in some area such as oral expression, written expression, listening comprehension, reading comprehension, reading, or mathematics.* This basic discrepancy in learning is the basis for the individual being considered learning disabled.

In addition to this one basic characteristic, certain others appear to be found in learning disabled students much more frequently than in the population as a whole. Some of these appear to be contradictory, but this is because of the umbrella nature of the definition. These characteristics include:

hyperactivity Learning disabled children may be hyperactive. This is particularly true among those with actual brain insult. These children have been described as restless, fidgety, unable to sit still, and so forth. It is not always that any one action is so much a problem, but rather that the child is moving in triple time and is a problem to others. Because he is doing so much, he is certain to cause trouble sooner or later. Also, with so much movement, it is difficult for him to attend to anything long enough to achieve much academically.

hypoactivity This is just the opposite of hyperactivity. Although not found as often among the learning disabled as hyperactivity, it is found often enough to be worthy of mention.

inattention This may or may not be related to the hyperactivity. It can simply be a matter of actual inability to focus on any particular activity for any length of time.

overattention With this disorder, which might also be called attention fixation, the child will focus on one particular object and seem unable to break the focus. This also can relate to figure-ground problems, or the inability to see the significant element or elements in a total setting while focusing instead on the background.

lack of coordination Although highly coordinated children may have learning problems, lack of coordination is often observed in children with learning disabilities. The younger schoolchild with learning disabilities is often slower to develop the ability to throw or catch a ball, to skip, or to run. He is also likely to have difficulty in writing and other fine motor-skills. He may be just generally clumsy; he may stumble or fall frequently. Some coordination problems are actually related to a kinesthetic perceptual problem, an inability to properly assess position in space, balance, or both.

perceptual disorders These might include disorders of visual, auditory, tactual, or kinesthetic perception. Less likely are disorders of olfactory or gustatory perception; however, these result in lesser academic problems. The child with visual-perceptual problems may not be able to copy letters correctly, or to perceive the difference between a hexagon and an octagon. He may reverse letters or produce mirror writing. The child with auditory perception problems may not perceive the difference between various consonant blends or be able to differentiate between the front doorbell and the first ring of the telephone. All these perceptual problems may at first make the child seem to be lacking in sensory acuity (that is, seem to have a visual loss or be hard of hearing), but when acuity checks out as normal, the possibility of perceptual disorder must be considered.

perseveration A child may perseverate, or repeat persistently, in almost any behavioral area, but this is more often seen in writing or copying. A child may copy a word over and over again involuntarily. He may also perseverate in oral response.

memory disorders This may include either auditory or visual memory. Memory is a complex process and is not fully understood, although various individuals have established theories that seem to explain the various observable facets of memory. In case study reports we hear of individuals who cannot remember where the window is or on which side of the room their bed is placed, even though it has been there for months. In others we hear of children who cannot repeat a simple sequence of three words immediately after hearing them. This kind of auditory memory deficit seriously affects the learning process.

The presence of any one of the preceding characteristics may mean absolutely nothing in terms of any relationship to learning disabilities. The presence of several of these characteristics, by their very nature, may likely lead to learning problems. Some combinations of these characteristics are more likely to cause difficulties in abstract, symbolic learning (such as reading or mathematics) and thus be a part of the syndrome we have come to call learning disabilities. When such characteristics have obviously resulted from a known instance in which there was brain damage, we may speak with at least reasonable assurance about causation. In many (if not most) instances we do not really know the "cause" of learning disabilities. What we see and what we can verify is the existence of a significant discrepancy between apparent ability to learn and actual learning. In many cases we also see some of the other characteristics, but these cannot necessarily be called causes. They are simply part of the total picture.

In Chapter 2 we will review certain screening and assessment practices and consider possible educational programs into which the learning disabled student may be placed for assistance. Then, in Section Two (Chapters 4 through 9) we will review some of the teaching approaches that are sometimes used with learning disabled students.

SUMMARY

The historical roots of the present field of learning disabilities go back at least to the early 1800s. At that time, we find a record of interest in brain function and dysfunction and in visual-perceptual problems. Since then interest has expanded in all directions (like the ripples that result from a rock thrown in the water), and a variety of remedial efforts have been initiated with students who have apparently normal learning potential but cannot learn in a normal manner. These students have been called word blind, strephosymbolic, dyslexic, dysgraphic, brain injured, hyperactive, perceptually disordered, and various other terms that indicate how they act or the academic or skill area in which they experience their major difficulties. Early approaches tended to focus on one, or perhaps two, of these major areas of difficulty; thus there were a number of specialized subareas of interest. But this situation changed in the early 1960s.

In 1963, Samuel Kirk suggested the term "learning disabilities," a term that was embraced by parents as a potential point of focus for advocacy efforts on behalf of their children, many of whom had been denied a free, effective public education. Since 1963, the field of learning disabilities has grown in a very rapid, though sometimes disorderly, manner, and today it is one of the largest of the recognized subareas of special education. A number of definitions have been proposed for this fledgling field, but the definition proposed by Kirk in conjunction with a 1968 call from the National Advisory Committee on Handicapped Children for better services for the learning disabled has persisted, with only minor changes, to this day. This definition, which is often described as an umbrella, includes all of the previously mentioned types of disability in a manner that emphasizes the academic difficulties of such students. The definition does not specify causation, but does indicate that an individual should *not* be considered learning disabled if the *primary* cause is mental retardation, visual impairment, hearing impairment, emotional disturbance, or lack of opportunity to learn.

This learning disabilities definition remains a source of continuing controversy. On the other hand, when attempts were made (in the mid-1970s) to develop a more satisfactory definition, all those proposed and discussed in any detail were even less well received. It is probably safe to say that many who do not particularly like the present definition are willing to accept it for now, given the fact that they cannot have *their* preferred definition accepted by the field as a whole.

In the remainder of this text we will attempt to establish some degree of understanding and order in this somewhat chaotic educational arena through a discussion of assessment and program placement practices and a consideration of various approaches that are sometimes used to teach learning disabled students. We will consider both theoretical rationale and actual educational practices, and will take a brief look at normal learning, so as to better understand those who are not learning normally. In total, we hope that the reader may become convinced that, despite controversy and confusion, many learning disabled students are being helped by existing programs, and at least some learning disabilities specialists "have their act together." We also hope to encourage the reader to attempt to learn more about this challenging field and perhaps to consider joining the effort (through further education, training, and direct involvement) to more effectively assist those individuals we presently call learning disabled.

REFERENCES AND SUGGESTED READINGS

Cruickshank, W. *The brain-injured child in home, school and community.* Syracuse, N.Y.: Syracuse University Press, 1967.

Cruickshank, W. (Ed.) *The teacher of brain-injured children.* Syracuse, N.Y.: Syracuse University Press, 1966.

Cruickshank, W., and others. *A teaching method for brain-injured and hyperactive children.* Syracuse, N.Y.: Syracuse University Press, 1961.

Dember, W. *Visual perception: the nineteenth century.* New York: John Wiley & Sons, Inc., 1964.

Fernald, G. *Remedial techniques in basic school subjects.* New York: McGraw-Hill Book Co., 1943.

Frierson, E., and Barbe, W. (Eds.) *Educating children with learning disabilities.* New York: Appleton-Century-Crofts, 1967.

Gearheart, B. *Teaching the learning disabled: a combined task-process approach.* St. Louis: The C. V. Mosby Co., 1976.

Gillespie, P., Miller, T., and Fielder, V. Legislative definitions of learning disabilities: roadblock to effective service, *Journal of Learning Disabilities,* 1975, *8*(10), 659-666.

Gillingham, A., and Stillman, B. *Remedial training for children with specific disability in reading, spelling, and penmanship* (ed. 7). Cambridge, Mass.: Educators Publishing Service, Inc., 1965.

Goins, J. *Visual-perceptual abilities and early school progress.* Chicago: The University of Chicago Press, 1958.

Hallahan, D., and Cruickshank, W. *Psychoeducational foundations of learning disabilities.* Englewood Cliffs, N.J.: Prentice-Hall, Inc., 1973.

Head, H. *Aphasia and kindred disorders of speech.* London: Cambridge University Press, 1926.

Hinshelwood, J. *Congenital word blindness.* London: H. K. Lewis & Co., 1917.

Hobbs, N. *The futures of children: categories, labels and their consequences.* San Francisco: Jossey-Bass, 1975.

Hoffman, M. A learning disability is a symptom, not a disease, *Academic Therapy,* 1975, *10*(3), 261-275.

Itard, J. *The wild boy of Aveyron.* New York: The Century Co., 1932.

Johnson, D., and Myklebust, H. *Learning disabilities: educational principles and practices.* New York: Grune & Stratton, Inc., 1967.

Kirk, S. Final Report of Advanced Institute for Leadership Personnel in Learning Disabilities, University of Arizona, 1970.

Kirk, S. Proceedings of the Annual Meeting of the Conference on Exploration into the Problems of the Perceptually Handicapped Child (vol. 1). Chicago, 1963.

Kirk, S., and Kirk, W. *Psycholinguistic learning disabilities: diagnosis and remediation.* Urbana, Ill.: University of Illinois Press, 1971.

Myklebust, H. *Auditory disorders in children.* New York: Grune & Stratton, Inc., 1954.

Myklebust, H. (Ed.) *Progress in learning disabilities.* New York: Grune & Stratton, Inc., 1968.

Orton Society. *Dyslexia in special education* (vol. 1). Pomfret, Conn.: The Society, 1964.

Orton Society. *Specific language disabilities* (vol. 13). Pomfret, Conn.: The Society, 1963.

Scranton, T., and Downs, M. Elementary and secondary learning disabilities programs in the U.S.: a survey, *Journal of Learning Disabilities,* 1975, *8*(6), 394-399.

Seguin, E. *Idiocy and its treatment by the physiological method.* New York: Teachers College Press, Columbia University, 1907 (reprinted).

Special Education for Handicapped Children. First Annual Report of the National Advisory Committee on Handicapped Children, Washington, D.C.: Office of Education, U.S. Department of Health, Education and Welfare, 1968.

Strauss, A., and Lehtinen, L. *Psychopathology and education of the brain-injured child.* New York: Grune & Stratton, Inc., 1947.

Wiederholt, L. Historical perspectives on the education of the learning disabled. In Mann, L., and Sabatino, D. (Eds.) *The second review of special education.* Philadelphia: JSE Press, 1974.

Leaders
Transportation
Income

chapter 2

Identification, evaluation, and program planning

It is extremely important that we properly identify and carefully evaluate any student who is under consideration for special education programs or services. It is equally important that we exercise great care in making initial program placement and in conducting regular, follow-up evaluation to determine whether the program is appropriate on a continuing basis. These are important considerations if we are truly concerned with providing the best possible learning environment for the student, and they are also important for at least two other specific reasons. First, we have learned through a variety of litigation (most of it relating to inappropriate testing and placement of minority children in special classes for the educable mentally retarded) that if we do not conduct meaningful evaluation and make appropriate placement, we will be quickly called to task for our actions. Second, the guidelines for assessment and placement contained in Public Law 94-142 and the various state plans that have been developed pursuant to this law make our responsibilities absolutely clear. Therefore the only question that remains is, "How do we go about this most important responsibility?" This chapter attempts to answer this question as it relates to the area of learning disabilities.

REFERRAL OR SCREENING: HOW WE FOCUS ON STUDENTS WHO MAY NEED SPECIAL ASSISTANCE

Nearly all children are eventually enrolled in school, but how do we find those who need additional special services so as to permit their maximum educational progress? In very obvious cases, the child is quickly referred for additional help; in fact, this referral may be made before the child actually enters school. In other cases, the classroom teacher refers a student after he or she cannot achieve in the regular school setting. Referral may also be made by parents, outside community agencies, or physicians. *Referral* means that we have our attention directed to the possibility of unusual educational needs and implies that we should conduct further investigation. Most school districts provide guidelines to assist the teacher in determining whether such referral should be made. This may consist of lists of descriptive characteristics of, for example, hearing impaired, mentally handicapped, and learning disabled children. Also included in such guidelines will be a description of the referral process and referral forms. These forms usually include a format that encourages teachers to objectify their observations to assist those who will further consider the referral. Usually teacher referrals are processed through the building principal, and at times they will also require information from appropriate special educators who are assigned to that particular building.

Referrals are certainly one good source of information regarding the possible need of certain children for specialized educational assistance, but many special educators in the area of learning disabilities have concluded that one of the most effective procedures is to screen total classrooms in kindergarten, first grade, and second grade. This leads to discovery of children with developing problems who can be helped before they fall too far behind and before they develop a deep-seated emotional attitude about school and lack of school success. Additional referrals should be taken from teachers at all grade levels, for with high population mobility even the best of early remediation programs will not eliminate the need for programs at older age levels. The manner in which referrals fit into the total pattern of events that lead to the determination of potential need for special programming is illustrated in Fig. 1. We will now turn our attention to the other major method whereby we first begin to consider the possibility of special educational needs of any given student.

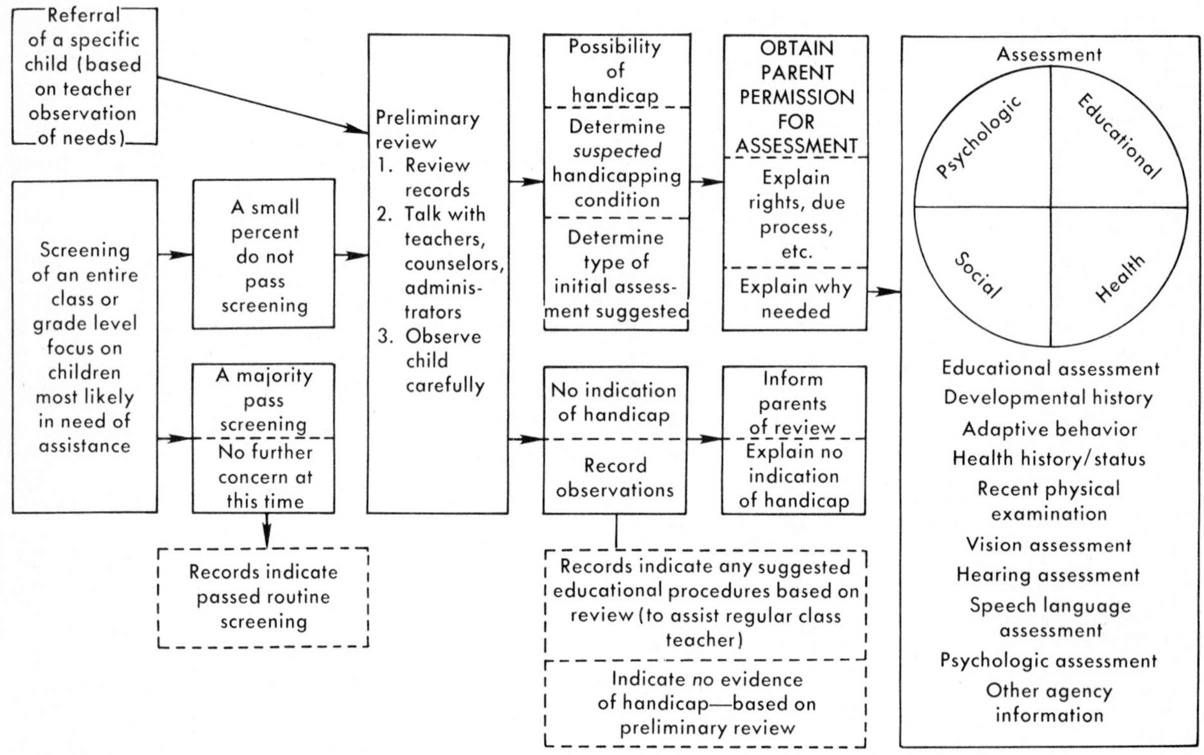

FIG. 1. Assessment. (From Gearheart, B. R. *Special education for the '80s.* St. Louis: The C. V. Mosby Co., 1980.)

Various school districts follow specific patterns of *screening,* designed to serve specific purposes within each district. Some districts have adopted plans in which kindergarten children are evaluated by their teachers near the close of the year, and on the basis of that evaluation and follow-up diagnostic work, small "developmental" first-grade classes are established for the following fall. These classes are often limited to 10 to 15 children and are taught by a teacher who has prepared especially for the task. If placement in these classes is viewed as highly flexible, with a well-defined provision for movement to and from regular classes, this can be an excellent program.

Kindergarten screening procedures vary, but the following might be considered as "typical." Step one is to explain the special first-grade program to the kindergarten teachers and to provide in-service training on learning disabilities. A second step may be rating by one of the behavior scales in which the teacher assesses each individual child's ability to copy forms, perform certain motor skills, such as skipping and hopping, and complete other perceptual competency skills. Only those who are viewed as likely candi-

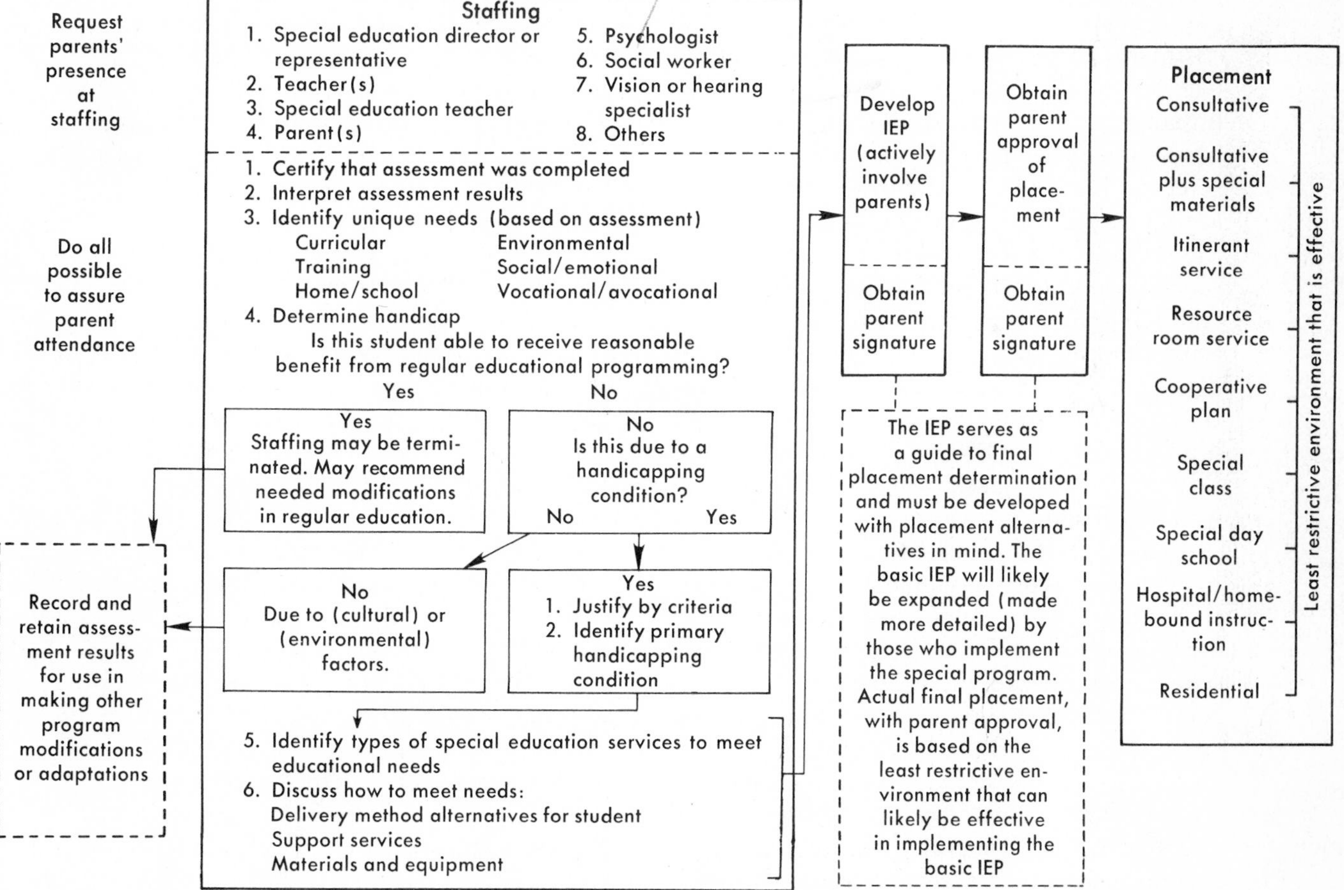

dates on total class screening are considered for further evaluation.

At the kindergarten level, eventual identification of a child as learning disabled, or at risk of becoming learning disabled, may lead to assignment of the child to the small, developmental first-grade classes mentioned previously, or perhaps to assistance in a resource room setting while attending a regular first-grade class. Beyond first grade, such developmental classes are not particularly common; therefore, the choices are more likely to be between the various types of programs outlined on pp. 27 to 32. In any case, *the results of screening do not indicate the presence of a learning disability or any other type of handicapping condition.* A learning disabilities screening instrument may "screen out" some students who are eventually determined to be hearing impaired or mildly mentally retarded, or to have some other difficulty or handicap. Such screening simply directs further attention of appropriate school personnel to the fact that the child in question *might* need additional, specialized educational assistance. (Two specific screening devices that have been used to attempt to discover students who are learning disabled, and thus in need of special educational assistance, may be found in Appendices A and B. They are the Pupil Behavior Rating Scale and the Alaska Learning Disabilities Ranking Scale.)

After it is determined, as a result of screening procedures or individual referral, that further consideration should be given to the educational needs of a particular student, most school districts will follow an established procedure for such an investigation. Specific procedures will vary from district to district, but certain steps are required by the guidelines and regulations of the various states, all of which are in general compliance with federal regulations. Therefore certain commonality of practices and procedures exist, with respect to the process that includes assessment, staffing, program planning, and program placement. The reader will note that the diagrammatic representation of this total process (Fig. 1) indicates a step between referral or screening and the assessment process. This step, *preliminary review,* is not utilized by all districts, but may be of considerable worth, given the nature of the total process. We might therefore consider the following discussion of the purpose of preliminary review.

Preliminary review is a procedure that may or may not be used between referral or screening and further formal assessment. It appears to be growing in acceptance as a means of further considering either teacher referrals or the results of screening that indicate assessment procedures may be necessary. It is not a substitute for assessment but may prevent further unnecessary efforts. It may also prevent unduly alarming the parents in cases where the screening or referral process has been based on incomplete or inaccurate information. After searching out and reviewing additional records, conferring with other school personnel, or observing the child in the learning setting, the evaluator may decide that no further assessment is required. This review process must be approached carefully, for we must *not* negate the purpose and value of screening and referral. On the other hand, additional information may lead to the obvious conclusion that no more investigative efforts are needed. In such cases, the procedure should be terminated through the filing of a short report indicating that, although some difficulties were suspected, there is, in fact, no evidence of handicap. The reasons for this conclusion, stated succinctly, plus any appropriate recommendations should be made a matter of record. If the procedure has gone this far, parents should be informed that there was a question as to whether or not the student needed specialized educational assistance, but that preliminary review indicated no handicap existed. Parents must know when concerns have been expressed and should know how it was determined that there was no real likelihood that a handicapping condition (as defined by the local educational agency) existed.

THE ASSESSMENT PROCESS

If the preliminary review indicates that there is a fair likelihood that further investigation is warranted, *then parents must be notified that the school would like to initiate a variety of individual testing.* In many cases the parents will have been well aware of the procedure up to this point, and in fact may have initiated the referral. *But in all cases the parents must give written permission for the individual assessment that must take place before further meaningful decisions can be made.* If the parents refuse permission, at least three different alternatives may be followed:

1. School officials may ask for another conference at a future date to consider the matter further. This means that the school will try to reevaluate the data that it already has on hand, perhaps bring other school personnel to the conference, and so forth. In following this first alternative, school officials are saying, "O.K., we may have been mistaken, but let's reconsider at this future date."
2. School officials may accept the parents' "No." In this case they may try to get the parents to sign a statement saying that they refused to give permission, or, at the very least, they will make an official record of the refusal.
3. School officials may bring the matter to an official hearing, with a state-appointed hearing officer.

Determination of which path to follow may depend on such things as the apparent urgency of the student's need for special services, the vehemence of the parents' refusal, the parents' local prominence or political clout, or the intestinal fortitude of the school administration. At any rate, for now, let us assume that parental permission is given and examine what happens next.

As indicated in Fig. 1, assessment has a variety of components. The overlying concern is to gather as much pertinent data as possible, so as to make the best decision as to (1) whether or not the student in question has a learning disability and (2) the nature of the disability, and thus some clues as to the type of remediation that might be required. It is also important to gather all possible indications of the degree of seriousness of the difficulty to determine which type of program placement might be best. Although there are variations in procedure, dependent in part on the type of information already in hand, but also on the assessment personnel available in any given school district, the following discussion illustrates what might take place.

A first step in nearly all school districts is to see that the child in question does not have a loss in visual or auditory acuity. As generally interpreted, *loss* means a loss for which compensation or correction is not possible. This is the case particularly with respect to vision and, for purposes of learning disability assessment, if glasses result in correction, then visual acuity is considered satisfactory. If, even with glasses, a serious loss remains in visual acuity, the child is often not eligible for a learning disabilities class (see the learning disabilities definition in Chapter 1). A similar situation exists with reference to auditory loss. The child will be given a comprehensive hearing evaluation and an audiogram will be plotted. (This is a graph indicating the child's

Assessment and the identification process may involve a variety of indirect, informal procedures. (From Gearheart, B. R. *Teaching the learning disabled: a combined task-process approach.* St. Louis: The C. V. Mosby Co., 1976.)

threshold of hearing at different frequency levels.) If he has a loss of any real significance, he may not be eligible for the learning disability class and instead should be immediately referred for an examination by a medical doctor who is a hearing specialist. He should also be considered for whatever type of special educational services are available for the hard of hearing. If his visual and auditory acuity are within normal limits, the evaluation for possible inclusion in a special program for learning disabled children will continue.

If the child is experiencing educational difficulty sufficient to warrant referral for consideration for a learning disability program, more information is needed. Therefore during the period when the visual and auditory testing is being completed (there might be a waiting period of several days), a medical examination and medical history are obtained, and a social history, completed by a qualified school social worker, is desirable. Together, these may provide valuable data that will assist in a final placement decision. An educational history, including a school attendance record, is also essential. For some children this is readily available. For others, whose parents are transient, this may require some effort to obtain. This record should also indicate what standardized tests the child has taken, along with any other pertinent data.

At this point the individual or individuals responsible will decide whether or not to continue the evaluation for the purpose of learning disability program consideration. Even if not continued for this specific purpose, the evaluation might be continued with other special education programming in mind.

The next step would probably be the administration of certain psychological tests. Because state regulations tend to require that the individual placed in a learning disability program *not* be mentally handicapped, that is, below the normal range of intelligence, one of the Wechsler Intelligence scales, the Stanford-Binet, or some other test of intelligence is generally administered. These tests, which will be briefly described in a later section of this chapter, must be individually administered by a qualified psychologist or psychometrist, who may also administer a brief achievement test to verify earlier achievement test results.

If testing indicates average or above-average intelligence, if the tests of visual and auditory acuity indicate no serious, uncorrectable losses, and if the educational history indicates no educational deficit as a result of inattendance at school or a cultural disadvantage, then the child is a likely candidate for some kind of learning disability programming.

THE INDIVIDUALIZED EDUCATIONAL PROGRAM (I.E.P.)

If it is determined that the student in question is eligible to be served as a handicapped student (in this case, a learning disabled student), federal regulations require that an individualized educational program be established. This requirement was established for several purposes, including the fact that in the past many students were assigned to special programs without specific, individualized planning and were provided with some type of "standard/special" program that was often no better than would have been provided in the regular classroom. According to federal regulations the individualized educational program (I.E.P.) must include the following:

(a) A statement of the child's present levels of educational performance;
(b) A statement of annual goals, including short-term instructional objectives;
(c) A statement of the specific special education and related services to be provided to the child, and the extent to which the child will be able to participate in regular educational programs;
(d) The projected dates for initiation of services and the anticipated duration of the services; and
(e) Appropriate objective criteria and evaluation procedures and schedules for determining, on at least an annual basis, whether the short-term instructional objectives are being achieved.*

The format and specific content and complexity of I.E.P.s vary throughout the nation, with a few states having specific forms that are followed throughout the state, while others allow for more diversity between the local educational agencies within the state. However, all must meet the content requirements just outlined. For illustrative purposes, an example of what may typically be included in an I.E.P. is indicated on p. 26. The actual I.E.P. may vary from a few pages to a dozen or more, and some school districts have a more general document that they call the I.E.P., which must then be supplemented by

*Federal Register, Vol. 42, No. 163, Aug. 23, 1977, p. 42491.

CONTENT OF THE INDIVIDUALIZED EDUCATIONAL PROGRAM (I.E.P.)*

I. Identification and background information

Student's name, parents' names, address, telephone number, birth date, sex, age, date of referral, primary language, and other similar information

II. Participants in I.E.P. conference

Names and titles and/or identification of all participants

III. Assessment information

Summaries of all assessment information used in any manner in staffing and development of the I.E.P.; definitive statement of the student's present level of academic functioning plus functioning in any nonacademic area that may be pertinent to and/or a target of program efforts

IV. Other information

Medical, sociocultural, or other pertinent information

V. Statement of annual goals

A description of educational performance to be achieved by the close of the school year, including evaluative criteria

VI. Statement of short-term objectives

More specific objectives (than annual goals), indicated on a monthly or quarterly basis; statements include (1) who will provide specific services, (2) where service will be provided, (3) materials or media required, and (4) such information as effective reinforcers and behavioral strengths

VII. Specific educational services provided

For example, study carrel and speech pathology services

VIII. Placement recommendations

Specific type of placement, time to be spent in various settings, and rationale for placement

IX. Significant time frame

Dates such as (1) initiation of service, (2) duration of service, (3) approximate dates for evaluation, additional conferences

X. Signatures

All conference participants plus specific parent signature indicating program approval

*A composite of the essential content of many different forms.

the later development of an I.I.P. (individualized implementation plan.) In all cases, the objective is that a specific, individual plan be developed for each student whose educational needs are so different that special educational services are required. In spite of considerable grumbling and complaining about the amount of time that this planning requires, it appears that for the most part the desired objective is being accomplished. It also appears that, as teachers and diagnosticians have more practice and develop more competence in this procedure, it becomes less onerous and more meaningful.

If the I.E.P. is properly developed, it provides essential guidelines for program implementation and a means for determining the extent to which educational goals are being met. In addition, it provides direction for the placement decision, a consideration that will be discussed in the following section.

THE PLACEMENT DECISION: A QUESTION OF ALTERNATIVES

Public Law 94-142 requires that "to the maximum extent appropriate, handicapped children . . . are educated with children who are not handicapped and that special classes, separate schooling, or other removal of handicapped children from the regular educational environment occurs only when the nature or severity of the handicap is such that education in regular classes with the use of supplementary aids and services cannot be achieved satisfactorily" (Federal Register, Vol. 42, No. 163, Aug. 23, 1977, p. 42497). However, the following sections of these same regulations note that a full continuum of alternative placements must be available, and specifically mention special classes, special schools, home instruction, and instruction in hospitals and institutions. In other words, we should attempt to keep a learning disabled child in the regular classroom, but if more extensive, segregated service is required, it must be provided. In the following sections we will briefly review the various types of settings that may be provided, starting with the most restrictive (which is also the least likely to be needed).

A residential setting or a separate special school

It is unlikely that any great number of learning disabled students will require a residential setting or separate special school setting, but the existence of a number of well-attended private schools for the learning disabled (many of them residential schools) indicates that there is at least some need of this sort. It appears that a number of the students enrolled in such schools may have other handicaps also (Marsh, Gearheart, and Gearheart, 1978), but their very existence and the fact that some operate on a contract basis with the public schools indicate this type of need.

In general, students who require such segregated settings are either those who have some additional handicapping conditions or they are learning disabled students who fit the hyperactive syndrome often associated with known brain injury. Some very large public school systems may have a separate special school for learning disabled students, but many schools having students who need this type of programming seem to be utilizing some of the existing private programs (on a contract/tuition basis).

Special (self-contained) classes

Self-contained classes for the learning disabled, usually limited to six to twelve children per class, are found at various grade levels. These self-contained programs are usually limited to hyperactive children with severe learning problems. Self-contained programs are among the less common methods of providing services to learning disabled children and should be used only when it seems absolutely *certain* that any less restrictive setting (resource, itinerant, and so forth) will not achieve the desired results. When students are placed in such classes, regular review procedures must be used to make certain that they are moved to less restrictive settings (appropriate to their educational needs) as soon as possible.

Resource rooms

Resource rooms are the most commonly used vehicle for providing services to learning disabled children. Because of this fact, we will consider them in some detail. As the various approaches and techniques are reviewed in Chapters 4 through 12, it should be considered that most of these could be applied in a resource room setting. A resource room may be staffed by only one resource room teacher, but a trend in the direction of some type of team effort, either two teachers or a teacher and an aide, seems to be under way.

The role of the resource room teacher is to provide assistance to children who have been identified as learning disabled but do not require the more intensive assistance provided in a self-contained program. Usually this means more than just temporary, minor difficulties with some new process in arithmetic or a new word attack skill in reading. In most school systems, a staffing or program planning committee will have reviewed a variety of information about any child referred for possible assistance in the resource room, and programming will be initiated only as this committee has indicated its feasibility. In all cases the parents should have been involved in such staffing/planning committee deliberations and will have given express permission for resource room program educational intervention.

It should be noted that the resource room teacher, if well accepted by the local school staff, will provide a great deal of valuable assistance to various teachers, sometimes in terms of general instructional ideas, but often in relation to a specific child. This is one of the more effective functions of the resource room teacher. Ideas and suggestions received in the halls or the coffee room continue to be of value in many settings, and materials provided—even if the child who will use them has not been approved for the learning disability program—may be major plus factors derived from a resource room program which are seldom publicized.

The resource room teacher should have the time, the materials, and the training to find more effective ways to teach children with special needs. Her function then becomes dual: (1) to initiate remediation and help the child find success in the resource room, and (2) to provide suggestions to the regular classroom teacher that may increase the odds that the child will find success in the regular classroom so that momentum toward remediation begun in the resource room is not lost.

Sometimes it is assumed that one of the best classroom teachers (in a given school) will make a very good resource room teacher. This *may* be so, but it is not a good assumption. Too often a teacher who is quite successful in the regular classroom tends to rely heavily on "the" method that she finds successful and in which she has invested much time and effort. Or sometimes a teacher who is quite effective when left to teach "her own" children with little or no outside observation and interference has real difficulty when she must spend much of her time dealing with other teachers—serving as their helper, having to consider their feelings and ego needs first, and needing to deal carefully and diplomatically with them, including some who are not doing a very good job of teaching. But to be successful in the resource room setting and to attain the desired educational goals for children who spend most of their school day in another teacher's classroom, such sensitivity, diplomacy, and ability to place one's own ego needs second are essential. Efforts within the resource room may be successful, but without a change in approaches used by the regular classroom teacher, the overall mission of the resource room may be a failure.

The following general guidelines and characteristics of a resource room may serve to best describe it.*

A. Resource rooms should be established in all buildings, and teachers should be assigned to only one building. If this ideal cannot be established, the next best choice (and it is definitely a second choice) is to have the teachers assigned to two buildings, with a specific room assigned in each, and with that room not used for other purposes during the time when the teacher is not at the building. Though this may seem like ineffective space utilization, in practice it is extremely difficult to maintain control of room materials, records, and so forth if the space is used by others.

B. Time should be set aside each week for interaction between the resource room teacher and teachers who send children to the resource room. Though this is sometimes opposed by those who want the resource room teacher to be "tutoring" children during all available time, if this is to be a resource room, not an office for a tutor, then the time must be set aside. One-half day per week for the teacher who is in one building all week should be sufficient.

C. A total pupil load of 15 to 20 should be the specific maximum. The variation (between 15 and 20 children) may relate to age of children, severity of problems, and other such factors but should be carefully spelled out.

D. No more than three, or in unusual situations four, children should be in the resource room at one time with one teacher. If an aide is available on a full-time basis this number may be increased to as many as six, *after* the aide is trained.

E. Ninety minutes to 2 hours per day of resource room assistance should be the usual expectation. If a child requires less than 1 hour per day, it is likely that he could remain in the regular classroom with consultive and materials assistance. If he requires much more than 2 to 3 hours, he should perhaps be in a self-contained program. There are exceptions to these generalizations, but too many exceptions mean that the program should be reconceptualized and replanned.

F. The resource room teacher will normally be asked to participate in staffing and placement. Although placement is an administrative function and responsibility, the resource room teacher may be indispensable in providing a variety of related input, such as information as to how a particular child may be helped and with which other children (already in the program) he can be effectively grouped.

---

*Adapted from Gearheart, B. *Teaching the learning disabled: a combined task-process approach.* St. Louis: The C. V. Mosby Co., 1976.

G. Parental understanding and cooperation with program efforts are important for all children, but particularly for those who are having educational difficulties. The role of the resource room teacher in parent conferences and in initiating parent-teacher cooperative efforts as special problems arise during the year must be carefully delineated. The regular classroom teacher has the primary responsibility for the child's program and should coordinate parental contacts for purposes of special conferences. As a general rule, the regular classroom teacher should be present at all such conferences and, if not, should have every opportunity to be involved. In other words, the regular classroom teacher should be the primary initiator of conferences; such conferences scheduled at a time when both the regular classroom teacher and the resource room teacher can attend. Then if last-minute conflicts arise and the regular classroom teacher asks the resource room teacher to "go ahead," there is little question about conflict of interest.

H. The parent-teacher conference relationship between the resource room teacher and other teachers with whom she shares responsibility for children is just one part of a larger consideration. That is the question of professional relationships with and responsibilities to all personnel in the building, central office consultants, and supervisors. This relationship must be carefully defined so that children are not shortchanged because of conflicts or misunderstandings. This would include other school district specialists (speech clinicians, remedial reading teachers, counselors, psychologists, and curriculum supervisors), building administrators (principal, vice-principal, and others, as they may have such responsibility), and all other teachers, both those who have children in the resource room and those who do not. Such considerations as the types of diagnostic and evaluative services that the resource room teacher can provide and how these must be obtained, the types of materials and equipment available and how these must be accounted for, and other such specifics must be carefully spelled out. The building principal is in charge of the building and thus responsible for the resource room, but he may need guidance on these matters, guidance that should come from the local director of special education. If the resource room teacher must provide services to two buildings (not the best practice, but it does happen), then these duties too must be specified. When the services of the resource room teacher are provided through some sort of larger, cooperative service district, the lines of authority and responsibility become even more complex; thus there is even more to be carefully delineated.

I. The resource room should normally be the same size as any other classroom. Because of the need to store a variety of materials and to provide for the possibility of use of an aide, a room of about two thirds the size of a normal classroom must be considered the absolute minimum size in which a meaningful program may be provided. Although many programs will not require space for motor activities, if such space is required, a full-size classroom is essential. A teacher desk, chair, and four-drawer file (plus another desk and chair if an aide is employed), student desks of various sizes, and at least two small work tables with chairs of various heights are required.

In the second of a two-part series of articles about the value of resource rooms, Harvey Leviton (1978b) outlines the reasons why he believes that resource rooms are generally preferable to the special class. The reasons include: (1) better results with respect to academic achievement, (2) better results with respect to social behavior, (3) less stigma effect, (4) elimination of problem of reintegration into the regular classroom, and (5) administration conducive to individualization. Leviton bases his conclusions on a rather extensive review of both opinions and research, and although all may not agree with his conclusions, he does make a persuasive case for the resource room. Careful reading of Leviton's discussion (see references) is recommended for those who wish to further explore this question.

Itinerant teacher program

In the itinerant teacher program direct service is provided by a traveling teacher on a regularly scheduled basis, usually 3, 4, or 5 days per week. A minimum period of direct service to each child of 1 hour per day is the least service that is likely to be of significant value. This is a *minimum;* many children served by an itinerant teacher should be seen for longer periods of time, depending on the type and severity of the problem.

The itinerant teacher will likely do many of the same things that a resource room teacher will do but is limited by time constraints and the difficulties involved in moving equipment, materials, and so on. This is not to say that the itinerant teacher program cannot be effective, but rather to indicate that if direct service to children is the major thrust of the program, the resource room program is usually more effective than the itinerant program because of the physical limitations of the latter. One other disadvantage must be cited—limited contact with the faculty of the various schools served by itinerant teachers. This factor, with the added consideration of personnel time lost in travel, has led to the itinerant program being second in preference when either itinerant or resource programs may be chosen for a given setting.

Certain conditions lead to adoption of the itinerant program, and in some of these situations it appears to be the best method of service delivery. In sparsely populated areas of the country, where schools tend to be quite small in total pupil enrollment, it is difficult to justify busing children into a specific school. Therefore, in such areas the itinerant program may be the most effective under the given conditions. In larger population centers, a combination of resource room and itinerant programs may be used, with the itinerant service providing assistance in the very mild cases. A third possibility is the use of part-time itinerant service, in combination with consultive and materials assistance. In this pattern, one learning disabilities teacher may work part of the day providing direct service to children through the itinerant program model, and during the same day, perhaps even in the same school, she may serve a consultive role. The adoption of this combination service model may relate to a variety of needs or to space variables.

Consultive or special materials program

A *consultive program* or a *special materials program* may be used to provide service to the regular classroom teacher and to the learning disabled child. Consultive and materials program services are usually called "indirect," in that specialized personnel limit their activities primarily to contact with the teacher. In contrast, in the resource and itinerant programs there is direct contact with children. Though it would be theoretically possible to have either the consultive or special materials program alone, in practice there are usually components of each in any program that carries either name.

When the emphasis is on special instructional materials housed in some central facility there must be a procedure to account for such materials. This could be a purely clerical/record-keeping task, but often a well-qualified specialist is employed to check out materials and to consult with teachers who come looking for ideas or help. This then becomes a combination special materials/consultive operation. When the consultive facet is the major emphasis, as the specialist goes from school to school (usually on a request basis), almost invariably teachers ask for assistance with materials, and the function becomes a consultive/special materials function. In essence, we have learned that consultive assistance without help with materials is relatively ineffective, and a supply of materials without assistance in how to use them is equally ineffective.

Any of these service delivery alternatives can be organized and implemented in such a way that children other than learning disabled are served, a very common practice with the special materials/consultive program.

Special materials and consultive assistance are probably most useful in dealing with the mild learning problems, or as a support service for the teacher who has considerable experience with children with unique learning problems but because of time limitations must have extra help. They may be sufficient for many children with moderate learning disabilities, and seldom are for severe learning disability cases.

The actual placement decision

The placement decision must be made after consideration of the types of existing programs, the age of the child, his level of intelligence, the types of disabilities he may have, the severity of his disabilities, and the prognosis for remediation. In most communities every school will not have a full complement of services, so details such as transportation problems and possible modification of existing program patterns must come under consideration. *In all cases, placement should be considered as tentative; that is, if it does not work out, reevaluation and additional consideration must be ensured.*

The purpose of learning disabilities programming is to assist the child toward more successful academic achievement, personal adjustment, and eventual retention in the regular classroom. A placement should be made that will maximize this possibility.

A SUMMARY OF ASSESSMENT AND PROGRAM PLANNING CONSIDERATIONS THAT HAVE BEEN GREATLY INFLUENCED BY PUBLIC LAW 94-142

The assessment that must precede formal consideration of provision of special educational services has changed greatly in the past 10 to 15 years. Public Law 94-142 provides guidelines that have tended to lead to more extensive, comprehensive procedures throughout the nation. These guidelines have also tended to make practices more similar between the various states, although certain variation continues to exist. Among the major concerns are the following:

1. Making certain that the tests used are given in the child's native language or in some mode of communication that permits meaningful response.
2. Using tests that were developed and validated for the purposes for which they are being used.
3. Making certain that tests are given by a trained administrator and that test instructions are carefully followed.
4. Ensuring that when a test is given to a student with impaired sensory, manual, or speaking skills, it reflects what it was designed to measure, not the impaired abilties.
5. Making certain that a student is *never* placed in a special program nor a remedial program planned on the basis of a single test. In other words, using various measures to verify important facets of assessment or program planning.
6. Ensuring that placement and program planning are accomplished by a team of professionals, not by a single individual.

In addition to the preceding concerns, which relate to the assessment and program planning, Public Law 94-142 regulations require specific parental involvement as follows:

a. Must have parent permission before initiating assessment.
b. Must invite parent(s) to staffing and attempt to arrange time, place, etc., so they can participate.
c. Must invite and try to make parents a part of the development of the Individualized Education Program (I.E.P.).
d. Must have parent permission for actual program placement.

In composite, these changes, along with the requirement of the I.E.P., have led to greatly improved programs for learning disabled students.

TESTS USED IN THE IDENTIFICATION OF LEARNING DISABLED STUDENTS AND IN PLANNING EDUCATIONAL REMEDIATION AND INTERVENTION

Three major types of assessment tools are in common use for purposes of identification of learning disabled students and the subsequent planning for remediation. These are: (1) measures or indicators of level of intellectual functioning, (2) measures or indicators of level of academic functioning, and (3) measures in such areas as visual or auditory perception, memory, sensory integration, or motor abilities. Other assessment tools might include neurological screening tests or tests that are believed to infer the possibility of minimal brain dysfunction.

Because of the definition of learning disabilities, it is essential that an estimate of intelligence be obtained for a student to be identified as learning disabled. It is also required that a discrepancy in academic functioning (between projected level of ability in subject or skill areas, based on the estimate of intelligence, and the actual level of academic functioning) be demonstrated; thus achievement-type tests are required. The third category of tests indicated in the preceding paragraph may be used either prior to completion of staffing and identification or after actual identification. In many cases, some will be used to verify the concern of those completing the evaluation, but others may be utilized at a later date. In some states, trial program placements may be used, in which additional formal evaluation is used, along with informal, teacher-diagnostic efforts in the actual teaching/learning situation. At any rate, a wide variety of tests may be used. In the following discussion certain of these tests will be reviewed, in the order previously indicated.

Measures of intelligence

Although there is considerable concern about the ability to meaningfully measure the level of intelligence of students who are experiencing learning problems, with even more concern indicated if those students are members of minority racial or ethnic groups, this must be attempted. Two tests, the *Stanford-Binet* and the *Wechsler* tests (WPPSI, WISC-R, and WAIS) are by far the most often used instruments to make a first assessment (or estimate) of intelligence.

The *Stanford-Binet* grew out of the work of a French psychologist, Alfred Binet. Binet, in 1904, was asked by Paris educational authorities to find a way to separate the educable from the uneducable. The major interest was to discover a way to identify children on whom society should not waste educational effort. Binet took an approach that was new at the time and related ability to learn to the ability to successfully perform a varied series of tasks that logically appeared to require mental ability. He attempted to find familiar tasks to which all children were likely to have been exposed and then to arrange them in order of ascending difficulty. Binet searched for tasks that could be categorized in terms of averages of performance at successive age levels. After much effort, the elimination of many of the original tasks and the addition of others, he was able to establish a series that could be arranged by patterns of performance at successive age levels.

In 1916, Dr. Lewis Terman at Stanford University published a modification of Binet's test, standardized on a set of tasks that were more appropriate for American children and youth. This test was called the Stanford-Binet.

American psychologists and educators quickly recognized the superiority of this test over any previously developed measures of intelligence, and it gained acceptance in the United States. The Stanford-Binet has been revised in the intervening years and its use is widespread, however, a second test of intelligence has now become more popular nationwide as a measure of individual performance based on a global concept of intelligence. This test, actually a series of three for different age groups, is the Wechsler.

David Wechsler is the author of the three Wechsler tests, or scales—the *Wechsler Preschool and Primary Scale of Intelligence* (WPPSI), the *Wechsler Intelligence Scale for Children, Revised* (WISC-R), and the *Wechsler Adult Intelligence Scale* (WAIS). These tests, like the Stanford-Binet, are individually administered, require a specially trained test administrator, and are based on the assumption that there is such a thing as global intelligence. Scores from these tests, like the Stanford-Binet result in an IQ (intelligence quotient), a score originally based on the idea of a relationship between actual, or chronological, age (CA) and mental age (MA). For example, if the child is actually 10 years of age and performs about like the "normal" 9-year-old child, his IQ is $\frac{\text{MA (9)}}{\text{CA (10)}} \times 100$. His IQ is the product of his mental age, divided by his chronological age, times 100. In this case it would be 90. Thus an IQ of 100 means essentially normal, above 100 is above normal, and below 100 is below normal.

The Wechsler scales have at least one definite advantage over the Stanford-Binet, which has led to their rapid acceptance. They provide not only an IQ (called, in the case of the Wechsler, a full-scale IQ) but also a "performance IQ" and a "verbal IQ." These are help-

The reader should note that although we continue to use the term *IQ* because of familiarity with it, IQ scores on various tests of intelligence today are actually *deviation IQs*. The deviation IQ is a standard score with a mean of 100, and a standard deviation which is usually established to approximate that of the original Stanford-Binet IQ distribution. Therefore, if the various IQ tests have approximately the same distribution of scores as the original Stanford-Binet, IQ scores can be more meaningfully compared from test to test. This also permits common understanding regarding expectations of an individual with, for example, an IQ of 50. In addition, deviation IQs are necessary to permit similar interpretation of the meaning of IQ between various age levels on any given test.

ful in making certain types of predictions in the evaluation of minority cultural groups, particularly bilingual children, and of those who have been culturally or educationally deprived.

IQ tests, including the Stanford-Binet and the Wechsler scales, have been under considerable attack recently, particularly when used with the culturally disadvantaged or with black or Mexican-American children. Much of this criticism is justified, but these tests remain the best single indicator of likely ability to achieve academically, and, within limitations, they are good indicators of intelligence.*

*A major question is, "What is intelligence?" but this is far beyond the scope of this text. In presently accepted definitions of learning disabilities, there may be an express requirement to indicate a child's level of intelligence. The Stanford-Binet and Wechsler scales remain the best available tools to attempt to determine intelligence. Efforts such as the use of the Spanish version of the Wechsler, administered by a Spanish-speaking psychologist, are highly recommended.

Other tests of intelligence might be used in certain instances. One such test, *The Columbia Mental Maturity Scale,* has been widely used. It requires approximately 20 minutes, much less time than the Stanford-Binet or one of the Wechsler tests requires, and may be used with children of ages 3½ years through 9 years and 11 months. It is a nonverbal "response to drawings" test that requires only a pointing response.

In contrast, the *Slosson Intelligence Test for Children and Adults,* a highly verbal test, has also grown in popularity in recent years. It has been used in some learning disability programs for identification purposes, but its verbal nature makes its use with culturally different subjects unacceptable. These tests are unacceptable if results are used to indicate mental retardation. However, if they indicate normal ability, and all that is required is establishment of "average" or "normal or above" intelligence for further consideration for learning disabilities placement, they may be considered acceptable in some areas of the nation. IQ tests administered on a group basis should not be considered of value for purposes of identification and, in general, the best rule is to use the Stanford-Binet or the Wechsler tests.

Before leaving the topic of establishment of level of intelligence, it should be noted that if the question of possible mild mental retardation should arise (for example, a Stanford-Binet IQ of 65), other measures *must* be initiated before concluding that the overall level of intellectual functioning is really that low. There are various *adaptive behavior measures* designed to indicate the ability of an individual suspected of being mentally retarded to cope with the natural and social demands of his or her environment. The American Association of Mental Deficiency (AAMD) defined mental retardation in such a manner that to be called mentally retarded the individual must have both subaverage general intellectual functioning *and* deficits in adaptive behavior. Adaptive behavior, as defined by the AAMD, is "effectiveness or degree with which an individual meets the standards of personal independence and social responsibility expected for age and cultural group" (Grossman, 1977, p. 11). There will be no further comment on the topic of mental retardation, except to note that in cases where a too low IQ appears to be a reason for ineligibility for learning disabilities programs, IQ should be verified by measures other than the results of a single test of intelligence.

Measures of academic functioning

Measurement of academic level is necessary to satisfy the requirement (in the definition of learning disabilities) of an existing discrepancy between potential to learn and actual level of learning. This requirement is clearly stated in the "Criteria for determining the existence of a specific learning disability" of federal regulations (see p. 12) and is stated in some form in the regulations of the various states.

North Carolina states the discrepancy in terms of its size for various grade levels and with respect to levels of severity of the learning disability. Table 1 adequately illustrates this approach. In the North Carolina standards a great deal more detail is provided relative to identification; this is only one aspect of the standards. It is of some interest to note that these severity levels are related to recommendations for placement. These recommendations are not rigid and must be related to all other variables for a given student, but, in general, students with moderate learning disabilities would be served in a resource room setting. Students with severe learning disabilities would be served in a self-contained program. Programs in the regular classroom with consultant help would provide for students with lesser educational retardation (mild learning disabilities).

TABLE 1. Discrepancy requirement in months

Grade level	Moderate learning disability	Severe learning disability
Kindergarten	6-10 mo	10 or more mo
Grade 1	8-15 mo	15 or more mo
Grades 2-3	10-20 mo	20 or more mo
Grades 4-6	20-30 mo	30 or more mo
Grades 7-12	30-40 mo	40 or more mo

From *Specific Learning Disability Programs: Rules and Regulations,* Division for Exceptional Children, North Carolina, Department of Public Instruction, 1979.

Other states have various versions of guidelines for this facet of the definition. Regulations may state a number of years of educational retardation, use percentages (that is, 50% behind expected grade level), or leave a great deal of discretion to the assessment team. It is of some significance that the federal guidelines do *not* specify the amount or degree of discrepancy. *However, in all states some statement about discrepancy or degree of educational lag or retardation must be made or implied. Thus, there must be some measurement of academic functioning.*

Unlike the area of intellectual ability reviewed in the previous section, some variability exists regarding how the level of academic functioning may be measured, and there is no particularly great debate about which test or tests should be used. In practice, it appears that the tests in the following discussion are used in various states.

The *Wide Range Achievement Test (WRAT)* is used by many psychologists to provide a quick indication of approximate academic level. The WRAT is mentioned in some state guidelines and provides scores in reading, spelling, and arithmetic. These scores may be indicated in terms of grade equivalent, a standard score, or a percentile. WRAT scores provide limited diagnostic value and are considered by some as providing only very rough estimates of achievement level; however, the WRAT is convenient to give and apparently provides sufficient information for identification purposes in a number of states.

Another frequently used measure, the *Peabody Individual Achievement Test (PIAT)*, includes five subtests: mathematics, spelling, general information, and two tests of reading, recognition, and comprehension. The PIAT provides grade equivalent (or age equivalent) scores, a percentile rank, and a standard score. It requires more time to administer than the WRAT but provides more information, including some that may be of value in later program planning.

A newer series of measures, the *Brigance Diagnostic Inventories* (three different tasks), appears to be in use in a number of learning disabilities programs, though it may be used as often for diagnostic purposes as for identification purposes. The Brigance tests are deliberately constructed to be consistent with teacher needs as they relate to development of I.E.P.s through criterion-referenced results but can also be used (in many states) to satisfy the educational discrepancy requirement of the definition of learning disabilities.

In addition to the aforementioned measures, in some schools the results of group achievement tests that are administered to all students may be used to indicate degree of academic lag of a given student as part of the identification as learning disabled. Some would question this practice in that the large group administration (and lack of opportunity for individual observation during the testing situation) may lead to test results that reflect something other than what the test scores supposedly indicate (for example, low arithmetic scores that, in fact, reflect low reading ability). In cases where the test used for identification has little or no diagnostic capability, such diagnosis must be planned later in the assessment continuum.

Other tests used for identification and program planning

Tests mentioned in this section are included to provide a broad sample, not a comprehensive listing, of the various ones used for (a) identification purposes, through indication of characteristics that are often associated with learning disabilities, (b) diagnostic purposes, so as to provide a basis for meaningful educational planning and programming, or (c) both (a) and (b). The tests are listed in alphabetical order and described very briefly. Those who complete a training program to become learning disabilities teachers often complete a two- or three-course assessment sequence in which skills in evaluation are developed. The major purpose of this listing is to provide the reader with a general picture of the variety of testing that may be initiated and the focus of these tests. For more details as to validity, reliability, appropriate age ranges, or authors of these tests the interested reader is directed to the *Eighth Mental Measurements Yearbook*, Oscar Buros, Ed., Highland Park, N.J., Gryphon Press, 1978. As noted in the brief descriptions, certain of these tests are described in more detail in later chapters of this text.

Assessment of Children's Language Comprehension (ACLC). This test provides guidelines for remediation of language disorders. The ACLC uses a core vocabulary of 50 common words arranged into two-, three-, and four-element phrases that may be used to diagnose difficulties in receptive language. Subjects point to what they believe to be the ap-

Interpretation of visual materials may provide valuable clues in program planning for learning disabled children. (From Gearheart, B. R. *Teaching the learning disabled: a combined task-process approach*. St. Louis: The C. V. Mosby Co., 1976.)

propriate picture in response to a word or phrase from the examiner.

Auditory Discrimination Test. This test, more often called the Wepman (after its developer, Joseph Wepman), is designed to evaluate the subject's ability to discriminate between 30 word pairs, different in a single phoneme, which children with auditory discrimination difficulties might not hear as different. Examples are the pairs *tug* and *tub*, *thread* and *shred*, and *coast* and *toast*. The subject cannot look at the examiner, so that discrimination is on an auditory basis alone. Ten word pairs that do not differ are interspersed with the 30 different word pairs as false choices.

Basic Concepts Inventory (BCI). The BCI evaluates a series of basic concepts that appear to be those least likely to be taught by the classroom teacher. It helps to determine whether the child can (a) follow basic instructions, understand the words ordinarily used in giving instructions, (b) repeat statements and provide answers usually implied by such statements (the words used are those most commonly assumed to be known and understood by young children), (c) understand the patterning base for similarities, follow a sequence. Unlike many other tests for young children, the BCI does not determine knowledge of colors, number recognition, ability to count, and so forth.

Bender Visual-Motor Gestalt Test. The "Bender," as it is often called, is composed of a group of nine designs, or figures, which the subject is asked to copy. The Bender has been used for a variety of purposes, but educators are more often concerned with the visual-motor gestalt function. Gestalt, in this case, simply means the ability to respond to the designs as a total, or whole. Children of normal intelligence and without neurological dysfunction tend to copy these designs in a stable, predictable way, with variations relating to chronological age. Rotation of designs, perseveration, omission of parts, and similar irregularities have significance to the trained diagnostician.

Boehm Test of Basic Concepts (BTBC). The BTBC, another concepts test, is based on response to pictures rather than spoken language. It includes 50 basic concepts and can be given in small groups, but it is more often given individually. Though grade norms are provided, the BTBC is most commonly used as a diagnostic tool.

Colored Progressive Matrices. In this test (often called the *Raven,* for the author, J. C. Raven) the subject is shown a design with one part (one-fourth) missing. He must then select from a group of six pictures—on the same page—the part that will correctly complete the design. The designs become progressively more difficult, and the author suggests that this test may be used *along with other measures* to estimate intelligence.

Developmental Test of Visual-Motor Integration (VMI). The VMI is designed to assess the degree to which visual perception and motor ability are integrated. This test includes a series of 24 geometric forms, which subjects are asked to copy without erasing or working over their original copy. Scoring criteria provide a VMI age equivalent. Also included in the VMI package is a procedure for assessment and remediation, which is not directly related to the VMI age equivalent. This procedure moves through five levels of visual-motor skills, from visual-motor integration (the highest level) through visual perception, tracing, and tactual-kinesthetic sense to simple motor proficiency.

Developmental Test of Visual Perception (DTVP). The DTVP is more often called the Frostig, after its developer, Marianne Frostig. This test measures five perceptual skills: eye-motor coordination, figure-ground perception, constancy of shape, position in space, and spatial relationships. It can be administered by the classroom teacher with a minimum of special instruction and is used in a large number of learning disability programs as a standard testing instrument. A number of worksheets, which go with specific deficits as measured by the test, are available commercially. The Frostig test and program will be further discussed in Chapter 4.

Goldman-Fristoe Test of Articulation. This test provides an assessment of articulatory skills of children, with distractible or mentally handicapped children considered an appropriate, special target group. It includes three subtests—"sounds-in-words," "sounds-in-sentences," and "stimulability."

Goldman-Fristoe-Woodcock Test of Auditory Discrimination (GFW). The GFW is designed to measure auditory discrimination under quiet conditions and those in which background noise is present. A prerecorded tape provides a standardized presentation of speech sounds, and the use of a pointing response ensures applicability to a wide range of subjects.

Harris Tests of Lateral Dominance. In this test, hand, eye, and foot dominance are assessed. Manual dominance is assessed by using such tests as hand preference, left-right knowledge, tapping, and dealing cards. Ocular dominance is established through monocular, binocular, and stereoscopic tests. A kicking exercise is used to determine foot dominance. The test does not yield an overall score; the purpose is to provide a clinical impression.

Illinois Test of Psycholinguistic Abilities (ITPA). The ITPA was developed to provide a point of reference for planning appropriate teaching materials and strategies. It is composed of 12 parts (10 subtests and 2 supplementary tests) that measure performance in three dimensions of cognitive abilities. The test provides a number of scores, but one of its most important uses is as a diagnostic tool, inferring intrachild differences from the profile that can be constructed from these 12 scores. The ITPA evaluates abilities in the visual-motor and the auditory-vocal channels of communication and in relation to receptive, organizing, and expressive psycholinguistic process. For a more complete description of the ITPA and its classroom utilization, see Chapter 7.

Meeting Street School Screening Test (MSSST). Specifically designed for use as a learning disabilities screening test, the MSSST requires no reading by subjects. It includes measures of motor patterning, visual-perception motor ability, and language development.

Memory-for-Designs Test (MFD). This test is used as one of several possible measures to assist in the medical assessment of possible brain damage. It requires the subject to reproduce 15 straight-line designs from memory after seeing each for only 5 seconds.

Motor-Free Test of Visual Perception. This test was developed in an attempt to measure visual perception without involving motor ability. Rather than drawing or tracing (as in most tests of visual-perceptual abilities), this one requires only a pointing response. The subject must respond to the 36 items by pointing to the correct one of four alternatives for each item.

Picture Story Language Test (PSLT). In the PSLT the subject is given a picture about which he is to write a story. Though possible to give in small groups, the PSLT is more often given individually. A total of five scores is possible: total words, total sentences, number of words per sentence, syntax, and an abstract-concrete score. Motivation is essential to this test, which may be given to children who have achieved sufficient *written* language facility to address themselves to it.

Purdue Perceptual-Motor Survey. In this survey the evaluator observes behavior within a structure that permits scoring and the plotting of a profile. Survey results are recorded in terms of five general areas: balance and posture, body image and differentiation, perceptual-motor match, ocular control, and form perception. An explanation of the meaning of these terms and a further discussion of the Purdue Perceptual-Motor Survey will be found in Chapter 4 in the discussion of the educational approach of Dr. Kephart.

Southern California Sensory Integration Tests (SCSIT). This battery of 17 tests includes: space visualization, figure-ground perception, position in space, design copying, motor accuracy, kinesthesia, manual form perception, finger identification, graphesthesia, localization of tactile stimuli, double tactile stimuli perception, imitation of postures, crossing the midline of the body, bilateral motor coordination, right-left discrimination, standing balance, eyes open, and standing balance, eyes closed. The SCSIT can be used as a total battery (to measure this broad range of perceptual-motor/sensory-integrative skills), or subtests may be used as required.

Standardized Road Map Test of Direction Sense. In this test, the examiner traces a maze (the road map) and the subject must follow the tracing visually. At each of 33 turns the subject must indicate whether the turn is to the right or the left.

Templin-Darley Tests of Articulation (TDTA). The TDTA, a revision of the much used, older Templin-Darley test, utilizes 141 items, grouped into 13 phoneme categories, to accomplish what has been called a "phoneme inventory."

OTHER ASSESSMENT PROCEDURES

Although a great deal of the information on which day-to-day educational planning is based may come from tests such as those just reviewed, a number of less formal methods and techniques are also of considerable value. Some techniques are relatively simple, while others require a high degree of training. Most require practice to develop and maintain at the optimum level. One such procedure is planned behavioral observations.

Planned behavioral observations are becoming increasingly important in the total assessment process. Such observations may be made in the classroom or in the testing situation. These observations are most important when considered *in total,* and some of them may be almost totally insignificant when observed as single entities. For example, clues to problems in auditory discrimination, if taken as isolated bits of information, may add up to little or nothing. If taken in composite they may be very important as clues to further evaluative needs.

Each child's unique approach to problem solving (how he approaches a new learning task) may provide important hints as to what may be the most effective teaching approach. How he starts, speed of response, sequence of responses, what provides added motivation, and what causes him to stop trying—all may have great importance in learning disability planning. The child's motor abilities in use of the pencil or crayon, how he holds the paper, whether he loses his place regularly, how he responds to outside noises, and a variety of such observational data should be carefully observed and recorded. Teachers must be trained in *what to look for, how to look for it, and how to analyze it.* This kind of assessment has only recently received widespread systematic attention, and much remains to be accomplished in this interesting assessment arena.

Although most teachers appear to want to be considered as teachers, not "clinicians," the kind of insight into a child's learning difficulties, which is more often called clinical impression (or judgment), is something that learning disabilities teachers need to develop to a greater degree. This does *not* mean the abandonment of utilization of valuable standardized measures or departure from objectivity. It does mean a sharpening of observational skills and broadening of the ability to infer meaning and potential teaching procedures from such observation.

SUMMARY

The matter of identification of learning disabled students and accomplishment of comprehensive evaluation that will lead to appropriate program planning and placement is of critical importance. This procedure is complicated by the varied nature of those conditions we call learning disabilities and by the fact that, even though there is a national (federal) definition, there is less acceptance of the details of this definition than is the case with many other handicapping conditions. Nevertheless, it appears that there is more agreement in criteria for identification and the steps through which this identification should take place than was the case 5 to 10 years ago.

We have reviewed the steps that will normally be taken from the time that a student is first under consideration for further assessment (usually as a result of referral or screening) through the assessment process, staffing, development of the I.E.P., and finally, placement. We have noted that there are times in this sequence when parental permission *must* be obtained or the process must halt. There are other times when parents (and their advocates or representatives, if they so desire) must be invited and encouraged to participate, but if they decline, the process can continue.

After it is determined that special programming is required, the placement procedure must be approached with great care. We must be certain that the least restrictive educational setting that will provide an appropriate educational program is utilized. This might include a separate school setting, a special, self-contained class in a regular school, a resource room, an intinerant teacher program, or a consultive/special materials program, which permits the student to stay in his regular class full time. The resource room setting is the most used alternative on a nationwide basis today; therefore considerably more details were provided regarding how such programs may be organized.

The last half of this chapter included a discussion of the various tests that may be used to identify learning disabled students and consequently plan their individual programs. These tests were considered in three major categories: (1) measures or indicators of level of intelligence, (2) measures or indicators of level of academic functioning, and (3) other tests that may be used to indicate types of learning problems. These "other tests" may be used prior to identification, after identification and prior to development of the I.E.P., or after the original program is initiated.

Learning disabilities programs are evolving and maturing and appear to be increasing in effectiveness. The identification and assessment process must now be in compliance with a number of federal directives, and the generalized result of this compliance has undoubtedly been good. However, as programs continue to develop and mature, we might hope that maturity will lead to wisdom and insight. We must recognize that the procedures and processes outlined in this chapter may need to change. The information provided here must therefore be viewed as a status report that may soon be out of date. Let us hope that future changes may strengthen programs for boys and girls and that those programs may accomplish the goals for which the first learning disabilities programs were established in the early 1960s. We must never forget that these programs were *not* initiated for the benefit of teachers or diagnosticians nor to permit us to construct complex flowcharts of the assessment process. They were established for learning disabled students, who must remain the central focus of all our efforts.

REFERENCES AND SUGGESTED READINGS

Badian, N. A., and Serwer, B. L. The identification of high-risk children: a retrospective look at selection criteria, *Journal of Learning Disabilities*, 1975, *8*, 283-287.

Beatty, J. R. The analysis of an instrument for screening learning disabilities, *Journal of Learning Disabilities*, 1975, *8*, 180-186.

Beery, K. *Developmental test of visual-motor integration: administration and scoring manual.* Chicago: Follett Publishing Co., 1967.

Bender, L. *The Bender visual-motor gestalt test for children.* Los Angeles: Western Psychological Services, 1962.

Bender, L. *A visual motor gestalt test and its clinical use.* New York: The American Orthopsychiatric Association, 1938.

Burgemeister, B., Blum, L., and Logge, I. *Columbia Men-*

tal Maturity Scale (revised). Tarryton-on-Hudson, N.Y.: World Publishing Co., 1959.

Buros, O. (Ed.) *Eighth mental measurements yearbook.* Highland Park, N.J.: Gryphon Press, 1978.

Bush, W., and Giles, M. *Aids to psycholinguistic teaching.* Columbus, Ohio: Charles E. Merrill Publishing Co., 1969.

Coy, Michael N. The Bender visual-motor gestalt test as a predictor of academic achievement, *Journal of Learning Disabilities,* 1974, *7,* 317-319.

DeGenaro, J. Informal diagnostic procedures: what can I do before the psychometrist arrives? *Journal of Learning Disabilities,* 1975, *8,* 557-563.

Dunn, L. *Peabody picture vocabulary test.* Minneapolis: American Guidance Service, 1959.

Eaves, L., Kendal, D., and Crichton, J. The early identification of learning disabilities: a follow-up study, *Journal of Learning Disabilities,* 1974, *7,* 632-638.

Feshbach, S., Adelman, H., and Fuller, W. Early identification of children with high risk of reading failure, *Journal of Learning Disabilities,* 1974, *7,* 639-644.

Frostig, M. *Frostig developmental test of visual perception.* Palo Alto, Calif.: Consulting Psychologists Press, 1963.

Frostig, M., and Horne, D. *The Frostig program for the development of visual perception: teacher's guide.* Chicago: Follett Publishing Co., 1964.

Frostig, M., Lefever, D., and Whattlesey, J. *The Marianne Frostig developmental test of visual perception.* Palo Alto, Calif.: Consulting Psychologists Press, 1964.

Gearheart, B. *Special education for the '80s.* St. Louis: The C. V. Mosby Co., 1980.

Gearheart, B. *Teaching the learning disabled: a combined task-process approach.* St. Louis: The C. V. Mosby Co., 1976.

Gearheart, B., and Willenberg, E. *Application of pupil assessment information* (ed. 3). Denver: Love Publishing Company, 1980.

Goins, J. *Visual-perceptual abilities and early school progress.* Chicago: University of Chicago Press, 1958.

Grossman, H. *Manual on terminology and classification in mental retardation.* Washington, D.C.: American Association on Mental Deficiency, 1977.

Hartstein, J. *Current concepts in dyslexia.* St. Louis: The C. V. Mosby Co., 1971.

Hellmuth, J. (Ed.) *Learning disorders* (vols. 1-4). Seattle: Special Child Publications, 1965-1971.

Keele, D., and others. Role of special pediatric evaluation in the evaluation of a child with learning disabilities, *Journal of Learning Disabilities,* 1975, *8,* 40-45.

Keogh, B., and Becker, L. The Bender-gestalt for educational diagnosis, *Academic Therapy,* 1975, *11,* 79-82.

Kirk, S., and Elkins, J. Identifying development discrepancies at the preschool level, *Journal of Learning Disabilities,* 1975, *8,* 417-419.

Kirk, S., and Kirk, W. *Psycholinguistic learning disabilities: diagnosis and remediation.* Urbana, Ill.: University of Illinois Press, 1971.

Kirk, S., McCarthy, J., and Kirk, W. *Illinois test of psycholinguistic abilities: revised edition, examiner's manual.* Urbana, Ill.: University of Illinois Press, 1968.

Koppitz, E. *The Bender gestalt test for young children.* New York: Grune & Stratton, Inc., 1963.

Lee, L., and Canter, S. Developmental sentence scoring, *Journal of Speech and Hearing Disorders,* 1971, *36,* 315-340.

Leviton, H. The resource room: an alternative (1), *Academic Therapy,* 1978a, *13*(4), 405-413.

Leviton, H. The resource room: an alternative (2), *Academic Therapy,* 1978b, *13*(5), 589-599.

Marsh, G., Gearheart, C., and Gearheart, B. *The Learning Disabled Adolescent.* St. Louis: The C. V. Mosby Co., 1978.

Public Law 94-142, The Education for All Handicapped Children Act of 1975.

Roach, E., and Kephart, N. *The Purdue perceptual-motor survey.* Columbus, Ohio: Charles E Merrill Publishing Co., 1966.

Rules and Regulations for the Education of the Handicapped Act, *Federal Register,* Aug. 23, 1977, *42,* 42474-42518.

Saunders, B. T. Similarities in system analysis and assessment theory, *Academic Therapy,* 1975, *10,* 413-418.

Specific learning disability programs: rules and regulations (mimeographed material), Division for Exceptional Children, North Carolina Department of Public Instruction, 1979.

Terman, E., and Merrill, M. *Stanford-Binet intelligence scale, manual for third revision.* Boston: Houghton-Mifflin Co., 1961.

Valett, R. *The remediation of learning disabilities.* Palo Alto, Calif.: Fearon Publishers, 1967.

Wechsler, D. *Wechsler adult intelligence scale: manual.* New York: The Psychological Corp., 1955.

Wechsler, D. *Wechsler intelligence scale for children, Revised.* New York: The Psychological Corp., 1974.

Wechsler, D. *Wechsler preschool and primary scale of intelligence: manual.* New York: The Psychological Corp., 1967.

Wepman, J. *Auditory discrimination test.* Chicago: Language Research Associates, 1958.

Wilson, J., and Spangler, P. The Peabody individual achievement test as a clinical tool, *Journal of Learning Disabilities,* 1974, *7,* 384-387.

chapter 3

The development of normal learning abilities

As we have established in the preceding two chapters, the term learning disabilities indicates that in some manner or to some significant degree the individual is not learning normally. Given this agreement regarding "other-than-normal" learning, it seems only logical that those who are engaged in the study of learning disabilities, and especially teachers who plan to work with learning disabled students, should have a solid, basic understanding of how learning takes place in students who are learning "normally." Unfortunately, despite a great deal of effort by researchers from various disciplines, uncertainties remain regarding many aspects of the learning process. On the other hand, a number of widely recognized hypotheses have been formulated, and for the present these provide the best framework within which to analyze learning. We will consider certain of these hypotheses (theories) in this chapter before proceeding to a review of various recognized approaches to the education of learning disabled students. Then, in reviewing various approaches in Chapters 4 through 12 it will be noted that certain aspects of theories presented here are basic to the theoretical formulations of those who developed specific approaches for use with learning disabled students.

Some of the variation between approaches relates to differences in how those authorities view the learning process, while other differences relate to the type of learning disabilities on which they have tended to focus or to the age levels in which they tend to be most interested. Whatever the reasons for variation among the authorities, it seems obvious that *a teacher of the learning disabled cannot function with maximum effectiveness without having some solid theoretical concept of how normal learning takes place, as a basis for the educational assessment and planning for the student with learning disabilities.* The most effective teachers of learning disabled students are those who have learned to be highly skilled "learning detectives," with all that the classic definition of "detective" implies. It is a matter of gathering a great deal of pertinent data and relating the implications of this data to the learning process in a manner that can provide guidance as to how to proceed with a given student. Knowledge of the learning process and of the normal steps through which most individuals pass on their way to competence as successful learners may be the integrative catalyst that provides meaning and logic to various types of information that otherwise might be meaningless.

THE NATURE OF LEARNING

Various learning theorists have offered definitions of learning, but most have hastened to say that their definition is provisional, partial, or tentative. General purpose dictionary definitions tend to be quite simplistic; for example, a definition offered by *Webster's New Universal Dictionary of the English Language* (1976) is "the act of gaining knowledge or skill." A number of authors of books designed to assist the teacher to promote learning (educational progress in some or all academic areas) do not define learning at all but apparently assume that the various readers of their work will have a common understanding of what is meant by learning. Others have defined learning as a process of change in behavior as illustrated by the following:

1. "Making sense has been characterized as relating events in the world around us to cognitive structure; and learning is the process of elaborating and modifying cognitive structure when it fails to make sense of the world" (Smith, 1975, p. 118).
2. "Learning, then, is the process by which an organism, in satisfying its motivations, adapts or adjusts in behavior in order to reach a goal" (Garry and Kingsley, 1970, p. 8).
3. "Learning is a change in human disposition or capability, which persists over a period of time, and which is not simply ascribable to processes of growth" (Gagné, 1977, p. 3).

These three examples are representative of the manner in which learning may be defined.

Although educators may likely be most interested in learning as it relates to organized educational programs, we must remember that a great deal of learning is *incidental* to some other purpose. We should, in addition, note that although most dictionary definitions emphasize the idea of learning knowledge and skills, individuals also learn (develop in interaction with their surroundings) attitudes. Most would agree that attitudes are highly important regarding such things as lawfulness, racial and ethnic biases, and responsible citizenship. It should also be recognized that attitudes are very important in learning knowledge and skills and that in the area of learning disabilities at times we may pay too little attention to them.

For purposes of our consideration of learning disabilities, the following definition of learning is proposed:

Learning is the process through which an individual develops or acquires knowledge, skills, or attitudes. It is influenced by the interaction of many individual and environmental variables, is highly related to language development, and its development or acquisition may be originated or modified through planned educational intervention.

This does not explain how learning takes place but may serve as a starting point from which to consider this important question.

Although the term learning theory may not convey any high degree of excitement to prospective teachers, most adults already have a fairly definite (if limited) concept of how people learn. Every time we study in preparation for college exams, review the driver's license requirements before reapplying for a license, or read the owner's manual for our new electronic, digital clock-radio, we demonstrate how we think *we* learn. When we try to teach a young child to ride a bike or read a book or an older one to drive a car or understand geometry, we indicate how we believe *they* learn. Yes, we all have a theory of learning, but it may be somewhat hazy and fragmented. This is perhaps no great reason for concern for some, but, if we are to become effective as educators, it is important that we understand as much as possible about the individual and environmental variables that can influence learning (promote desired learning and behavior and reduce undesirable behavior). The major task of the learning disabilities teacher or specialist may be viewed as that of influencing learning in the desired direction. It is to this end that the descriptions of the following learning theories are presented.

MAJOR LEARNING THEORIES AND THEORISTS

The ideas of certain learning theorists have unusual importance and application as we consider the area of learning disabilities. B. F. Skinner is among the more prominent of these theorists; his efforts and the methods of other behaviorists who have followed his lead will be more fully explored in Chapter 9. Another individual, Helmer Myklebust, provided a simple theory of how children develop language, which is highly pertinent to learning disability programming. Although not a learning theorist in the usual sense of the word, his concept of language learning can be of great value in understanding learning disabilities and is presented in Chapter 7.

The theoretical constructs of certain perceptual-motor theorists will be described in Chapter 4 and it will be seen that the ideas of many of these theorists are somewhat parallel to the thinking of a much better known authority, Jean Piaget. Piaget is not a learning disabilities theorist, and in fact he indicated that he did not really think of himself as a learning theorist. Nevertheless, his theory of cognitive development has great relevance to learning disabilities; thus it will be reviewed in this chapter.

Most educators of today are still strongly influenced by the learning theories that were developed during the first half of the present century. The list of learning theorists of this period includes (but is not necessarily limited to) such individuals as John Watson, Edward Thorndike, Edwin Guthrie, Clark Hull, B. F. Skinner, Max Wetheimer, and Edward Tolman. Beginning at about mid-century, other theorists began to have an increasingly significant effect, including D. O. Hebb, Charles Osgood, and Jerome Bruner. Also included in this period of influence was Jean Piaget, whose work began more than two decades earlier but whose major influence in the field of learning theory was not felt until about mid-century.*

Although there may be some small degree of danger in attempting to condense and generalize regarding the work of these major theorists, we will take that risk in the interest of expediency and in the belief that some readers of this text may have forgotten what they earlier learned regarding learning theories. We will consider the major categories of learning theory into which these learning theorists may be placed and certain implications of these general orientations. Because most practicing educators are not "purists," that is, they do not necessarily espouse one given approach to the exclusion of all others, readers may discover that they believe in a number of aspects of various major theoretical frameworks. The purpose of this review is to call attention to the potential importance of learning theories and to encourage further thought and study about how children learn. It should become

*Unlike the others mentioned, Piaget is not always viewed as a learning theorist. He considered himself an epistemologist (one who studies how knowledge is acquired). Most who write about him and his work related to learning theory speak of him as a cognitive psychologist.

TABLE 2. Major divisions in learning theory

Key words and concepts	Representative theorists
Behaviorism or association theories	
Classical conditioning	Watson
Stimulus-response	Thorndike
S-R bond	Guthrie
Parts built into whole	Skinner
Law of effect	
Trial and error	
Stamping in, stamping out	
Operant	
Respondent	
Shaping	
Contiguity	
Neobehaviorism*	
(Many of the same as behaviorism)	Hull
Intervening processes (between S and R)	Spence
Habit strength	Osgood
Drive	Hebb
Decoding, encoding	
Integration	
Cell assembly	
Neurophysiology	
Cognitive theories†	
Perception	Lewin
Wholes	Tolman
Field	Bruner
Life space	Piaget
Structure	
Coding systems	
Categories	
Assimilation	
Stages	
Equilibration	
Insight	

Note: The order (top to bottom) in this table represents the approximate order in which these theories attained general recognition and acceptance.

*Some authorities would recognize only two major divisions: behaviorism and cognitive theories.

†Earlier called field theories; includes gestalt theories.

quite clear before the reading of this text is completed that how we view learning—that is, how learning normally takes place—will have a great effect on how we teach students who have learning disabilities.

Table 2 indicates a type of grouping of theories of learning that may be of value in considering the efforts of major learning theorists. In addition to indicating major divisions of learning theory, it reflects certain differences in terminology that may be used by various authorities who attempt to anlayze and categorize learning theories. For example, in an earlier, more traditional classification system, theories were usually classified as *association* theories or *field* theories. More recently, the term *behaviorism* has replaced *association*, and *cognitive* has replaced *field* for the most part. Also, as reflected in Table 2, behaviorism may be subdivided into *behaviorism* and *neobehaviorism*. These possible variations in terminology are presented here so that those who have other books to which they may turn for reference purposes (perhaps a general psychology text) can make any needed translations. The following discussion characterizes the major differences between behavioral theorists and cognitive theorists and considers the reason for the "neo," in neobehaviorism. In so doing, some specific contributions of certain of the leading theorists are very briefly mentioned.

Next, in somewhat more detail, the contributions of Jean Piaget are considered. Finally, this chapter closes with a review of the work of Robert Gagné, who may be viewed as having an "integrated position" among the theorists (Lefrancois, 1972).

Behaviorism

The general underlying principle of those theorists who have come to be called behaviorists is that the behavior of humans is made up of a variety of responses that may be observed and related to other observable events. The earliest use of this terminology is often attributed to J. B. Watson, who authored an article in *Psychological Review* entitled "Psychology as the Behaviorist Views

It" (1913). Behaviorists are concerned with establishing verifiable relationships between stimuli, responses (behavior), and consequent conditions. These consequent conditions are most often thought of in terms of reward or punishment but may also include essentially neutral conditions.

In its simplest form, behaviorism may be thought of as stimulus-response psychology in which there is the *activity* or *situation,* which affects the individual, a *response,* which the individual makes to the situation, and a *connection* between the two. This connection was (historically) called the S-R bond, and those who espoused this theory were someties called "connectionists." When accepted as the explanation of all behavior, this means that all of learning is a process of building S-R bonds and organizing "wholes" by putting together or compounding parts (smaller S-R units). Thorndike had more direct effect on education than most, if not all, of the early behaviorists because he proposed a set of major principles or "laws" of learning. His *Law of Effect* has influenced teachers for decades. In essence it states that when an S-R connection is accompanied by a pleasant or satisfying state of affairs, the connection is strengthened. His *Law of Exercise,* which states that bonds are strengthened if exercised regularly, has also greatly influenced the way that teachers have taught. Thorndike addressed himself to certain specific subject areas, arithmetic and Latin, for example, and because of his pedagogical orientation received more attention from educators than did other behavioral theorists, until the time of B. F. Skinner.

B. F. Skinner expanded the efforts of earlier behaviorists by postulating that two general classes of responses must be recognized: (1) responses elicited by a known stimulus (which he named *respondents*) and (2) responses (actions) that are spontaneous (which he named *operants*). In the first class, the organism *reacts to* the environment, while in the second, the organism *acts upon* the environment. Respondent behavior (Skinner named this *Type S* conditioning) could be explained by the theorization of earlier behaviorists, but Skinner became famous for his work and writings related to *operant* or *Type R* conditioning. Through the work of Skinner and many others who adoped his theory, *operant conditioning* became a dominant force in schools throughout the United States and Canada and has remained of great importance to this day. Some of the results of Skinner's efforts, with greater expansion and discussion than is appropriate in this chapter, are presented in Chapter 9.

In summary, the work of behaviorists remains very much alive, although the earlier concepts of S-R bonds and what Skinner would call Type S conditioning are now agreed to have application in only limited situations. Skinner's operant conditioning and the work of many others who have researched and written about their interpretation of Skinner remain of great influence.

Neobehaviorism

Neobehaviorism is a term sometimes applied to the work of individuals such as Clark Hull, Kenneth Spence, and, to some extent, to D. O. Hebb and Charles Osgood. Hull and Spence were behaviorists, but they added a strong concern for events or variables that take place between the S and the R. Their total systems (as they enunciated them) are quite complex and more characterized by symbols and mathematical terms than are the works of earlier behaviorists. Hull and his follower, Kenneth Spence, were concerned with intervening variables (events or influences between S and R) such as drive, habit strength, incentive motivation, reaction potential, and aggregate inhibitory potential. They placed such variables within a formula, which they used to attempt to explain learning. Lefrancois (1972, p. 134) describes the systems of both Hull and Spence as "hypothetic-deductive," and most authors who comment on their work indicate that, although their theories may not explain all types of learning, they are applicable in many situations, and their rigorously scientific approach helped provide the groundwork for the work of others.

D. O. Hebb, who at times describes his own system as pseudobehavioral, developed a learning theory based on neurological functioning. Hebb may be called a neobehaviorist in that his theory is highly concerned with what takes place between the S and the R. His work is relatively complex and requires knowledge about the nervous system, which may not be common to many readers; thus it is not practical to attempt to explain it in any detail here. Simply stated, he provides a theory that accounts for higher level learning in terms of connections that are formed between neural cell assemblies (formed as the result of sensory input) and more complex phase sequences (combinations of cell assemblies that are associated neurologically). His theoretical formulations seem to account for a great deal of learning—as we understand it—but like other theories, they do not appear to be applicable in all settings.

Charles Osgood developed a model of behavior, designed primarily to explain higher level learning, that is in some ways similar to Hebb's. Osgood postulates that there are two stages of behavior, *decoding* and *encoding*. Decoding is "the total process whereby physical energies in the environment are interpreted by the organism," while encoding is "the total process whereby intentions of an organism are expressed" (Osgood, 1957). Thus decoding is the S side of the S-R model; encoding is the R side. Each of these stages (encoding and decoding) have three levels of organization—the projection level, the integration level, and the representation level.

Osgood's theory (his model), like Hebb's, is somewhat complex and must be studied in depth to be understood. It is based on his concept of neurological functioning, a concept that may not be totally proved or disproved for many years. His work led to the development of the semantic differential, a tool that has been of considerable value in better defining affective meanings and thus in various types of counseling. In addition, his model was used by Samuel Kirk in developing the Illinois Test of Psycholinguistic Abilities (ITPA), a diagnostic tool that has been of considerable value in the field of learning disabilities. The ITPA will be further discussed in Chapter 7.

Cognitive theorists

Garry and Kingsley indicate that cognitive theories "stress changes in cognition and the learner's perception as crucial to learning" (1970, p. 76). Lefrancois indicates that "cognitivism is . . . characterized by a relative lack of concern with stimuli and responses" and that cognitive theorists are preoccupied with "such subjects as perception, problem solving through insight, decision making, information processing, and understanding" (1972, p. 186). Most knowledgeable reviewers of the present field of cognitive psychology recognize that it had its origins in the work of the Gestaltists, who were highly concerned with the "wholeness" of learning as opposed to the part-to-whole orientation of the behaviorists. Cognitive theories differ from association (behaviorist) theories in that they are concerned with acquisition of cognitive structures rather than of habits, and problem solving rather than trial and error. Whereas behaviorists emphasize the effect of prior learning and experience and view the whole as being the sum of the parts, cognitive theorists believe that the whole is greater than the sum of the parts and that it precedes the parts. Perhaps one of the more commonly mentioned concepts of cognitive theorists is that of *insight.* Through insight, animals (the subjects used for much of the research of learning theorists) are sometimes able to "size up" a situation and proceed to a solution without going through the many steps that might be expected if we accept only the possibility of trial and error learning. Humans are even more likely to demonstrate such ability, many times solving situations with which they have had no actual experience or even any obviously parallel experience.

Jerome Bruner has had a great deal of influence throughout the English-speaking nations. Bruner uses a number of concepts that are similar to those of other theorists (notably Hebb and Osgood) but proceeds in a somewhat different direction, coming to different conclusions regarding the nature of learning. His work in concept formation has been of particular interest to educators. Learning, as viewed by Bruner, occurs primarily in relation to the ability to recognize similarities and differences. This may relate to either objects or events and results in the development of categories. The ability to manipulate and relate these categories meaningfully is the essence of information processing, and humans make decisions in relation to how they process information (available data).

Bruner has developed a relatively complex system, which he believes explains the manner in which we learn; this system has had considerable influence on the thinking of curriculum developers in the schools for the past several decades. One of the major conclusions reached by Bruner is that the use of discovery approaches in the schools should be promoted, a position that has ardent supporters and equally ardent critics.*

The work of several other cognitive theorists could be briefly reviewed, but we will consider (in somewhat more detail than we have with other theorists mentioned in this chapter) the work of Jean Piaget, because of his popularity and the potential value of his point of view as it relates to learning disabilities.

THE DEVELOPMENT OF COGNITIVE STRUCTURES AS VIEWED BY JEAN PIAGET

For the last two decades, the work of Jean Piaget has had considerable impact on education in America. His writings have influenced various leading psychologists throughout the world for the past 50 years, but for a variety of reasons, including the fact that all of his original works were written in French, and even when skillfully translated are laborious to read, they did not have an immediate impact on education in America. Piaget was a precocious youth, receiving his undergraduate degree at age 18 and his doctorate (in the natural sciences) at age 21. He moved into the field of psychology soon after receiving his doctorate and in 1924 published his first two books in psychology. Piaget remained unusually active throughout a long and illustrious career, and according to some authorities, "Whether Piaget's efforts and basic assumptions prove to be correct or incorrect in total or in part, his works have generated more interest and research than those of any other person in psychology in the last fifty years" (Wadsworth, 1971, p. 5). Much of Piaget's

*Critics of the use of discovery approaches more often are concerned with what they believe to be overuse of this concept to the near exclusion of all others. Most agree that discovery approaches are of value, if appropriately utilized.

work, particularly his earlier efforts, was not well received by other psychologists because of his style of research. Piaget developed a clinical-descriptive technique that involved working with and observing in depth individual children. In addition, many of his conclusions are greatly influenced by "intuition" or "insight." This contrasted sharply with the work of experimental psychologists during the first half of the century, who were attempting to rigorously control experimental variables, use acceptable sampling procedures, and so forth. It is indeed interesting that his early work in psychology did not conform to the "scientific method," when by training he was a biological scientist.

However, despite criticism of his methods, his results have been widely recognized. Piaget's description of the development of cognitive structures is perhaps his most widely referenced work in English-edition texts on education; however, his writings on children's reasoning, moral judgment, conception of number, the world, play, dreams, imitation, and many others are widely circulated in English in both hardbound and paperback editions. Piaget's theory of cognitive development has the most direct relationship to our consideration of learning disabilities and is closely related to the work of the perceptual-motor theorists, whose efforts in learning disabilities are described in Chapter 4. The general description that follows and the summary presented in Table 3 are taken from a number of his writings and reflect the organization of his theory as expressed in *The Child and Reality* in a chapter entitled "The Stages of Intellectual Development in the Child and Adolescent" (1973). In this chapter, Piaget speaks of *three* major periods in this development. In some of his earlier writings he spoke of *four* major stages but later apparently preferred to group two stages or subperiods together (the stages of preoperatory representations and concrete operations) to form one more comprehensive period. This fact is mentioned because some students have commented that they "have seen so many different versions of Piaget that they don't know what to accept." In this instance, it is merely a matter of whether one wants to emphasize three major periods or four, and here attempts will be made to be consistent with his more recent writings. As far as the impact or meaning of his writing with regard to cognitive (or intellectual) development, it matters little whether one speaks of three or four periods. Reference to his particular difference is provided in an attempt to reassure the reader that, although slight differences in format may exist, many such differences are of about the same consequence as the fact that some people call a bottled soft drink "soda" and others call it "pop."

The sensorimotor period

Piaget places a great deal of emphasis on the *sensorimotor period* of life. The importance of this period (0 to aproximately 24 months of age) is at times not fully appreciated because the child has little language with which to express himself, and thus adults do not understand all that is taking place. Piaget believes that this period is the basis of the later evolution of intelligence as it is normally inferred to exist in school-age children and youth. He believes that the young child must progress through a series of stages, which leads from the purely reflex activity present at birth to a stage (stage 6 in Table 3) where he is able to think through motor problems, arriving at solutions without an excessive amount of trial and error. The child can infer that certain movements have taken place (movements hidden from his visual field) and deal with new locations of objects or people without confusion. He knows that even though, for example, a bottle is cov-

TABLE 3. Piaget's periods of cognitive development

Period	General characteristics	Summary
Sensorimotor (0-2 yr)		
Stage 1 (0-1 mo)	Reflex activity; sucking; grasping; crying	The child moves from pure reflex activity to the ability to see cause and effect relationships, to use trial and error experimentation, and to think through actions required to gain desired ends. He moves from complete egocentricity to the realization that he is an object among others in space and that he can deliberately and intentionally act on other objects. He is now ready to learn to operate in a symbolic and representational rather than a purely sensorimotor arena. (Note that this does *not* mean that sensorimotor development stops.)
Stage 2 (1-4¼ mo)	First habits; eyes follow moving objects; behavior lacks "intention" but is to some extent coordinated	
Stage 3 (4¼–8 or 9 mo)	Hand-eye coordination; manipulates all he can reach; reproduces some events	
Stage 4 (8 or 9–11 or 12 mo)	Searches for lost objects; anticipates events; uses known means to achieve objective	
Stage 5 (11 or 12–18 mo)	Experiments; uses trial and error; repeats operations to verify results	
Stage 6 (18-24 mo)	Uses internal representation; thinks through solutions without "groping"; develops cause-effect understanding	
Concrete operations, categories, relations, and numbers (2-11 yr)		
Subperiod A: Preoperational representations (2-7 yr)	Symbolic functions appear, i.e., language, symbolic play; focuses on elements in a sequence, rather than on successive states or steps; cannot exercise reversability in thought or solve problems involving conservation concepts; unable to decenter perceptual exploration	Symbolic thought becomes possible; the child can think beyond immediate motor and perceptual events. Language develops rapidly, providing additional means to manipulate thought. Throughout this period, the child relies more on perceptual input (how something looks, feels, etc.) than on what his thinking processes tell him to be true. Overall, this is a repetition of the sensorimotor period except that it relates to symbolic rather than motor functions.
Subperiod B: Concrete operations (7-11 yr)	Develops logical operations (thought processes) that he can apply to concrete problems; tends to choose logical conclusion when forced to choose between perceptual input and what is logically true; can accomplish transformations, use conservation concepts, exercise reversability, and decenter perceptual exploration; attains seriation and classification abilities	The child accomplishes a number of logical operations, which form the base for formal operations. These include transformations, reversibility, conservation concepts, seriation, and classification. He can use logical thought to solve problems relating to concrete objects and events and is becoming an increasingly social, communicative being.
Formal operations (11–14 or 15 yr)		
	Range of application of thought expanded—now includes hypothesis testing and scientific reasoning; cognitive structures modified through assimilation and accommodation	The individual reaches full cognitive potential. He is able to reason through areas of concern with which he has basic familiarity. (Note that this does not indicate that he *uses* logical thought in all activities but that the *potential* to do so is present.) The ability to formulate and test hypotheses is present, and all that remains is the accomplishment of a broadened base of information, more practice in using cognitive abilities, and an appreciation of realism (how the world actually works as opposed to what logically should be true).

ered by the lid of a box the bottle is still there. He can anticipate constant movements of objects and act accordingly. He has evolved from interpreting the position of all objects only in relation to himself to a basic understanding of the relationship between objects in space.

During this sensorimotor period, the child has developed from a totally egocentric being with only basic reflex actions to one who can interpret what he sees, hears, and feels. He has also learned to interrelate these interpretations. He can motorically manipulate objects, find lost or hidden objects, and think through the physical manipulation necessary to accomplish his goals with regard to physical objects. He has learned to experiment, has begun to understand cause and effect, and is ready to move into language (representational and symbolic) activity. All of this has been accomplished by movement through the series of stages included in the sensorimotor period, as shown in Table 3. This may be accomplished by the age of 21 months or not until the age of 27 or 28 months, but 24 months is about average, as observed by Piaget. Note also that movement through these stages is accomplished through a relatively smooth evolution and that each stage involves an incorporation of the learning of previous stages—an improvement on what was previously mastered. The same is true for the movement from the sensorimotor period to the more conceptual-symbolic activities of the following period. Sensorimotor evolution does not stop but rather continues throughout childhood; however, at about 24 months of age a new type of development begins to take place.

The period of preparation and organization of concrete operations, categories, relations, and numbers

As outlined in *The Child and Reality: Problems of Genetic Psychology* (1973), Piaget has combined two periods, which he earlier seemed to recognize as separate, into the *period of preparation and organization of concrete operations, categories, relations, and numbers* (2 to 11 or 12 years of age). The two subperiods are *preoperational representations* and *concrete operations.* Subperiod A, often called the time of *preoperational thought* (ages 2 to 7), includes the time in which the child experiences a rapid development of language, with vocabulary growing by leaps and bounds. Piaget views this as a period of development of conceptual-symbolic activities, which roughly parallels the development of sensorimotor abilities in the sensorimotor period. He notes that, despite the rapid development in language, logical thought remains severely restricted in many areas. For example, in the matter of *conservation,* the preoperational child is clearly deficient. When shown a row of six blocks and asked to construct a row "just like this one," the four-year-old will typically construct a row that is just as long as the model row, but it may have the same, more, or less blocks. A five- or six-year-old may construct a row with one-to-one correspondence, but if one row is lengthened by moving the blocks further apart, the child may indicate that the number of blocks in the two rows are no longer equivalent. He does not "conserve" number. In the example more often cited, that of conservation of volume, the situation starts with two containers of equal size and shape, filled with equal volumes of liquid. The child is first asked to verify the equal amounts of liquid in the two containers. Then liquid from one is carefully poured into a taller, thinner container. He will then usually indicate that the taller, thinner container has more liquid in it, even though he witnessed the whole event. The preoperational child is literally unable to understand all aspects of the *transformation* that has taken place. He can see the beginning and the end and reacts to how he interprets what he sees at the end of the process. *Experience* is the key to understanding that when one dimension changes (in these two cases, the length of the row of blocks and the height of the liquid in the second container), the other dimension (number of blocks and volume of liquid) does not change.

Subperiod B, the time of *concrete operations* (7 to 11 years of age), is the final part of this period of concerete operations, categories, relations, and numbers. The subperiod of concrete operations is a time of transition between the beginnings of conceptual-symbolic thought (the preoperational subperiod) and the final formal operations period. In this subperiod, thought is no longer a slave to perceptions. In the social realm, the child can understand the viewpoints of others and can operate and converse in such terms. Although he may be highly competitive, he can cooperate successfully.

At the concrete level, the child can easily understand the process of pouring water from one container to a narrower, taller one and understands through a process of mental logic that, although final visual input may give the impression of a larger amount of water, the amount is actually the same. He has witnessed the whole procedure (the transformation), and he comprehends and trusts what he has witnessed. A number of other higher level mental processes are developed during this period. These include an understanding of reversibility and seriation, the development of classification skills, and a meaningful concept of time, speed, and velocity. The term *concrete* is used, with respect to this period, to indicate that these developing cognitive (thought) processes relate primarily to concrete objects and events. At the concrete operational level, the child remains unable to successfully solve most problems that are totally verbal or hypothetical. This highest level of cognitive development comes with the next major period.

The period of formal operations

The final, highest level of cognitive development is called the *period of formal operations* (11 to 14 or 15 years of age). This is the culmination of development of the structure with which we think. At the completion of this period, the individual has the capability to attack a broad range of learning tasks and is limited mainly by motivation, scope of basic information, and the opportunity to learn. Attainment of this level does not mean that the individual will use logical thinking processes but rather that he has the cognitive structure that makes such thinking possible. It means that, unlike earlier levels, he can apply logical thinking to all classes of problems.

After having attained the abilities assumed to be included in this period, the individual can successfully attack hypothetical problems that might have been most difficult at the concrete level. For example, if a problem were presented to a child at the concrete operational level, prefixed by "suppose that you had wings and could fly," he might well indicate that he did not have wings and thus could not solve the problem. The child at the formal operations level could separate the hypothetical statement from the rest of the question and would proceed to solve it hypothetically.

A number of such higher level problems become solvable to the individual at the formal operations level. Some students will develop some of these formal operational skills much earlier than others, but it is the development of the total range of skills that Piaget views as completion of this highest level of cognitive development. When the adolescent com-

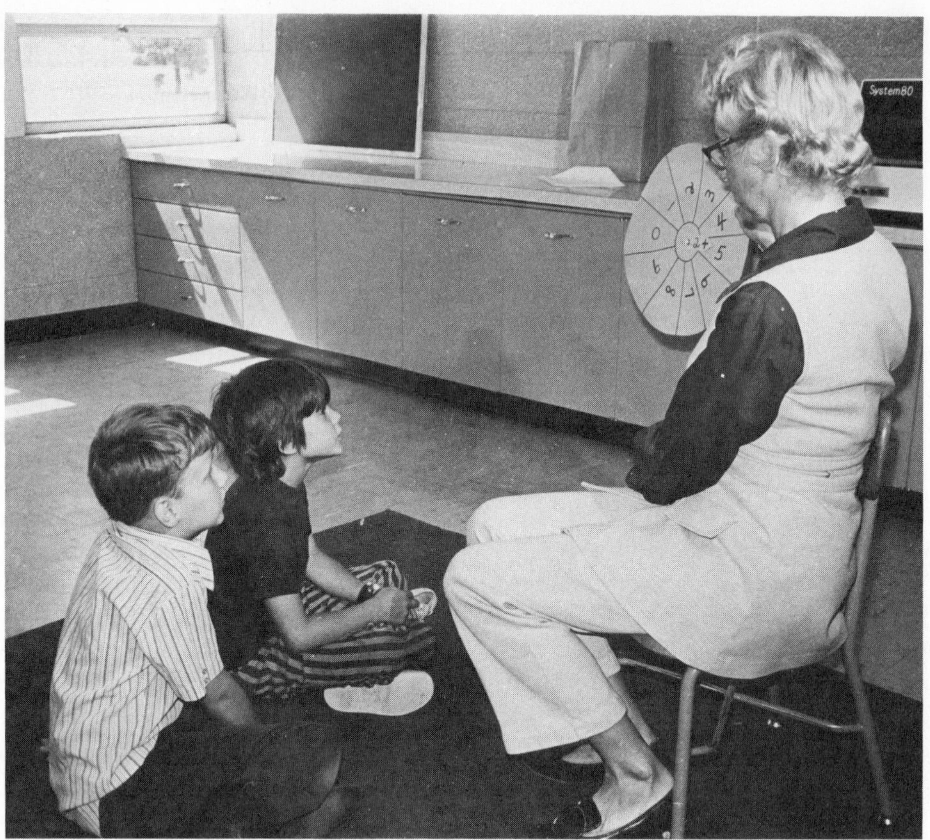

Learning disabled students may require any of a wide variety of additional assistance in order to master facts that other students learn with little difficulty.

pletes this development, he is ready for adult thinking. What is still required is opportunity, experience, and motivation. These are what should come in the remainder of secondary school, in college or other advanced educational programs, and in adult learning, which should take place throughout the rest of life.

THE CONDITIONS OF LEARNING—AN INTEGRATED VIEW

Gagné, as a learning theorist, does not fit "comfortably" within any of the groupings that have previously been described. As noted earlier in this chapter, some have referred to his work as presenting an integrated view of learning. In the second edition of his text, *The Conditions of Learning* (1970), Gagné presented a discussion of eight basic *types* of learning: (1) signal learning, (2) stimulus-response learning, (3) chaining, (4) verbal association, (5) discrimination learning, (6) concept learning, (7) rule learning, and (8) problem solving. In the third edition of this same text (1977) he reviews essentially the same eight types of learning, but places more emphasis on varieties of learning capabilities

TABLE 4. Major categories of learned capabilities and examples of performance made possible by each type of learning

Type of learning	Example of performance
Motor skills	Ability to hit the head of a nail with a hammer or write a given letter or number
Intellectual skills*	
Discrimination	Ability to tell the difference between *h* and *b*
Concrete concept	Ability to correctly apply the concepts *above* or *preceding*
Defined concept	Ability to understand the concept *aunt*—understanding that an individual's father's sister is that individual's aunt
Rule	Ability to divide various combinations of fractions (in new mathematical problems) through application of the appropriate mathematical rule
Higher-order rule	Developing a procedure or rule for deciding when to switch to the outside lane on a given stretch of interstate highway, based on the density of traffic at another specific point of reference
Cognitive strategy	Developing a procedure for relating names and faces so as to permit efficient recall of names
Verbal information	Ability to state the rule for computing the standard deviation of a set of scores
Attitude	Compliance with orders of a police officer

Patterned after Gagné's summary of the five major categories of learning outcomes (Gagné, 1977, p. 47).
* Subordinate categories are listed in order of increasing complexity.

and outcomes. These include: (1) motor skills, (2) intellectual skills, (3) cognitive strategies, (4) verbal information, and (5) attitudes. The general approach to understanding learning, as advocated by Gagné, is to first "identify the general types of human capabilities that are learned" and then to understand the "conditions that govern the occurrence of learning and remembering" (1977, p. 18). In his 1977 text (*The Conditions of Learning*, ed. 3), Gagné provides both meaningful theory and practical suggestions for classroom instruction. However, the following account will relate primarily to two aspects of his theory, the five major categories of learned capability and the eight basic types of learning.

Five major categories of learned capability

Motor skills represent a very basic type of learned capability. This area of development starts when the child is very, very young and is expanded to include (for example) those skills required to write successfully, to play games, and to manipulate tools. Motor skills are particularly subject to improvement with continued practice; that is, although we may learn to do something—for example, throw a ball—it takes years of practice to be skilled enough to be paid a million dollars a year as a big-league pitcher.

The types of learning outcome with which educators are more often concerned are what Gagné calls *intellectual skills.* This category is subdivided by Gagné into five subareas: discrimination, concrete concepts, defined concepts, rules, and higher-order rules. Examples of the performance made possible through the use of these types of capability are indicated in Table 4. All of these skills involve the use of symbols, and this hierarchy of skills is learned in a process that proceeds from simple to complex, often involving the combining or integrating of simple skills to produce the more complex skills. The interdependence of intellectual skills is indicated by the schematic representation on the top of p. 58.*

*Adapted from Gagné, 1977, p. 35.

Higher-order Rules
depend on the development of
Rules
which depend on the development of
Concepts
which depend on the development of
Discriminations
which depend on the development of
Basic Forms of Learning
(S-R learning, signal learning, and so forth)

Whether or not the development of intellectual skills deserve the near worship accorded by some is debatable, but, as noted by Gagné, these types of capabilities are "the essence of what is meant by 'being educated'" (1977, p. 29).

A third type of capability listed by Gagné is *cognitive strategies.* Cognitive strategies are described as those skills "by means of which learners regulate their own internal process of attending, learning, remembering, and thinking" (1977, p. 35). These may be called by various names by different learning theorists, but most would agree that they are skills that must be organized internally and that much is left to be learned about how they are developed. The learner must learn to organize his own attending skills, abilities of recall, and the like so as to be able to tap the information necessary and relevant to whatever task is being undertaken at a given time. As an internal organization of thought, these skills remain somewhat of a mystery; however, it does appear that opportunity for practice is essential to refinement and improvement. Table 4 provides a specific example of the type of performance made possible through cognitive strategies.

A fourth type of learned capability indicated by Gagné is *verbal information.* He notes that we all need certain basic verbal information, which may be called "common knowledge." This would include knowledge about such things as common colors, shapes (square, circle, rectangle, etc.), days of the week, or rules for crossing the street at a traffic signal. This common knowledge is necessary for the accomplishment of everday tasks and as the basis for higher levels of verbal information.

Gagné indicates that there are various levels of complexity within the general category of verbal information. The simplest is a *label* or *name* (for example, "dog"). The next level may be called a *fact* (for example, "my dog likes to play with me" or "my neighbor's dog will bite me if I go into his yard"). The highest level (following the preceding examples) might be a large set of facts about dogs relating to their size, color, how they act, and so on. This *body of knowledge* about dogs requires a great deal of other common knowledge regarding color, size, and so forth, and when an individual learns more facts about a given area of interest than anyone else and has them properly interrelated, this body of knowledge makes him an "expert."

The fifth type of learned capability is *attitudes.* Gagné defines attitude as "an internal state that influences (moderates) the choices of personal action made by the individual" (1977, p. 44). Many of the most important actions we take in our lives are obviously the result of attitudes. Attitudes may be learned through imitation of the behavior of others, through a series of experiences, or at times through a single experience. Although there is general agreement about the desirability of many attitudes (for example, respect for the law), there is less agreement about such attitudes as cooperation as contrasted with competition. There is also some question as to whether we (educators, parents) fully understand how to change attitudes. Nevertheless, there is agreement that the development of attitudes is highly important and often overlooked.

These five major categories of learning outcomes, as presented here and in Table 4, should *not* be considered to be in order of importance nor in the order in which they normally develop. Their order is arbitrary; they are different skills, and our purpose here is to recognize them as different. They interrelate (as may be seen when we think through what is required to accomplish any one of the examples provided in Table 4) and they cut across traditional subject areas of the curriculum. In his theoretical presentation, Gagné discusses each area in terms of the *internal conditions* and *external conditions* that will promote their development. He also reviews the educational implications with respect to each type of learning outcome. But for consideration here, the following discussion reviews the eight different *types* of learning, as conceptualized by Gagné. These are quite different from the *learning outcomes* just discussed; any one learning outcome might require the use of several types of learning.

Eight basic types of learning

The following discussion of eight basic types of learning has the potential to resolve some of the conflicts that develop when we read the explanations of learning provided by various respected learning theorists. Each of these theorists has something of value to say about learning, and most readers will remember a time in their own lives when a particular theory seemed to explain how *they* learned or how they assisted another to learn. Gagné's discussion of eight basic types of learning recognizes the possibility (I believe it to be a *fact*) that there is no single explanation for learning that fits all circumstances. Our knowledge of the brain, incomplete though it may be, indicates that to some extent different parts of the brain may provide the major control functions for different types of learned capability. For example, simple motor learning is apparently controlled, at least in part, by an area of the brain that has little to do with other types of learning. In still another example, it seems logical that the type of simple learning exemplified by the baby learning to find the end of the bottle that produces milk may be significantly different from the learning/thinking process that may take place when that baby matures and discovers a cure for the common cold.

If our purpose in this text is to begin to understand how students normally learn so that we might better understand learning that is not proceeding normally, then we need a functional theory of learning, simple enough to understand and apply but complete enough to fit the variety of learning situations that confront students in our schools. The following description of eight basic types of learning is not a complete theory of learning but may assist the reader to better think through what he or she believes about learning and how it takes place. Eight types of learning will be identified (hypothesized) and certain educational implications will be noted. If this discussion "makes sense" to the reader, I strongly suggest a further investigation of the writings of Robert Gagné.

Signal learning. Signal learning, as described by Gagné, would be called a conditioned response by many learning theorists. This type of learning requires simultaneous or nearly simultaneous presentation of two forms of stimulation. For example, if a child reaches for the electrical outlet and his mother simultaneously says "no" sharply, he may stop reaching for almost any object. There may be other factors in the situation (for example, the desirability of the object for which the child is reaching), but in pure signal learning the reaction becomes nearly automatic. Fear responses are often in this category, as may be pleasure responses.

Gagné points out that some signal learning may occur rapidly, while in other instances it may require many pairings of the proper stimuli. He also notes that people who tend to be anxious develop signal-response connections more rapidly than less anxious people and that ability to learn through signal-response connections is not highly related to intelligence or ability to learn in the academic arena. Signal learning is probably less important to teachers than the other more complex types of learning that follow.

Stimulus-response learning. Stimulus-response learning, as described by Gagné, would be called operant learning by Skinner. Also a response to a signal, it differs from signal learning in that it requires more precise actions in response to specific stimuli or combinations of stimuli. In stimulus-response learning, the learner responds *in relation to satisfying some motive.* Gagné uses the example of a dog learning to shake hands. The response is a much more precise skeletal-muscular act than the generalized response in signal learning.

Stimulus-response learning is usually characterized by gradual learning—that is, the learner becomes better able to make the desired response through practice. It is somewhat similar to the "shaping" process in behavior modification. Still another point in stimulus-response learning is that reward or reinforcement is associated with correct responses.

A final and important difference between stimulus-response and signal learning is that in stimulus-response learning a component of the *stimulus itself* is generated by muscular movements as the process is developed. In the case of the dog the external stimulus is "shake hands," and a related proprioceptive stimulation is caused by the muscles that raise the paw.

This appears to be the form of learning involved when a child learns to vocalize a new word. In such vocalization, the "feel" of the word as it is said is part of or becomes part of the stimulus. Gagné believes that "simple learned motor acts . . . perhaps come as close as any human behavior does to being pure cases of stimulus-response learning" (1977, p. 89).

Chaining. Chaining is the connecting in sequence of two or more previously learned stimulus-response patterns. The building of such "chains" is the means whereby children are taught many of their early habits and is the reason that some habits or other early learning may seem to take place almost overnight. What often happens is that two stimulus-response patterns are learned over a relatively long period of time. If these have the potential of being easily connected, it can be accomplished in such fashion that the final end result (chaining) appears to have taken place very quickly.

Chaining has many applications in various types of learning that take place in the school. Printing and writing, the fundamental athletic skills, learning to manipulate any of a wide variety of science equipment, the basics of art, and the playing of musical instruments are examples of chaining, a term which Gagné applies only in the motor area of learning.

Verbal association. Verbal association is a term that Gagné applies to chaining that involves language rather than motor activities alone. At the simplest level, this may mean nothing more than *naming.* When a child learns that a given object is called a "basketball" and is able to recognize it and call it a basketball when he next sees it, the process may be considered to be composed of two steps: (1) observing the round shape of the ball, its size, and its unique characteristics, and (2) providing the inner stimulation to say "basketball." Thus, these might be considered two S-R events, linked together to permit the final verbal response. In another example, we might consider learning a word in a foreign language, a task that is accomplished by building a chain between the native language and the foreign language word. Compound words and verbal sequences such as "utterly exhausted" are further examples of verbal association. The "Pledge of Allegiance," the "National Anthem," or the colors of the spectrum (learned in sequence) are examples of verbal association. As noted by Gagné, the development of effective original speech "requires the ready recall of a large fund of verbal sequences that can be woven into novel passages of spoken English in a countless variety of patterns" (1977, p. 102). This is perhaps the most important application of verbal association in the lives of most adults.

For verbal association to occur, what Gagné calls a coding connection must be available (previously learned). Highly verbal persons should have more coding connections readily available than those with little verbal ability; therefore, if all factors are equal, the highly verbal person should learn more effectively through verbal association. This type of learning is limited to humans because it requires a previously learned repertoire of language.

Discrimination learning. Learning to discriminate between various parts of the environment is an important part of learning in childhood. Shapes, sizes, textures, colors, and the like are all learned through discrimina-ion. Discriminations are often developed through the ability to recognize *distinctive features* of various stimulus objects. A great deal of discrimination learning takes place before entrance to school, and skills developed in such early learning appear to be much of the basis for later discrimination between symbols. This is supported by the observations of Piaget and by most of the perceptual-motor theorists whose efforts are outlined in Chapter 4.

Discrimination may be thought of as a type of learning that ordinarily requires some type of instruction. For example, to learn to differentiate between the letters in his name, Sammy may be taught to recognize S by many repetitions in which he is shown the S and told that this is an "ess." He learns to say "ess" when he sees the S and learns to not respond "ess" to other symbols. It is often a matter of practice, and authorities are not really certain what takes place in the brain that permits Sammy to recognize the S. A similar procedure takes place for the rest of the letters in his name, and eventually he can recognize them and differentiate them from other letters.

Discrimination obviously is likely to be more difficult when the stimuli are more similar. This may be true with respect to an *m* and an *n*, or a *d* and a *b*. A similar situation exists with respect to spoken symbols. In each case it is a matter of recognition of distinctive features that permits discrimination, and unfortunately all individuals do not respond to the same distinctive features. One child may be able to relate letters to visual images, such as relating an *h* to a chair. Other children may find this approach essentially useless.

One difficulty experienced by many adults who attempt to teach young children discrimination-related tasks is that to the adult the difference between, for example, red and pink may be very obvious. This discrimination, learned early in life, has been practiced over and over and it is difficult to realize that the child, learning it for the first time, requires practice. This same principle applies

Active involvement in learning activities may increase the speed of learning for certain students. (From Gearheart, B. R. *Teaching the learning disabled: a combined task-process approach*. St. Louis: The C. V. Mosby Co., 1976.)

for all discrimination learning. Once learned, discrimination tasks seem extremely simple, but original learning may require the development of chains that are quite long and complex.

Multiple discrimination, a term sometimes applied to recognizing the differences between two or more very similar stimuli, often requires exaggerating existing differences. This makes the distinctive characteristics easier to see (or hear or feel) and remember, and thus differentiation is easier. Adults who cannot understand the difficulty some children have with "simple" discrimination tasks should be reminded of the wine tasters who can with ease and certainty differentiate between wines that most of us cannot possibly detect as being different. It is a matter of experience and practice; with learning disabled students, it may be a matter of finding a significantly different way than that used in the ordinary classroom setting.

Concept learning. Gagné notes that "the acquisition of concepts is what makes instruction possible (1977, p. 122). When the young child arrives at school, he has already acquired many concepts, and much of the process of education is a matter of acquiring additional ones. A great deal of our early educational programming is based on the assumption that the child already understands a wide variety of concepts, such as the place concepts *below, above,* and *middle* and the environmental concepts *street, sidewalk,* and *street corner.* Progress through the early grades is dependent on the rapid learning of concepts such as *plus, minus, same, different,* and *opposite.* It appears that older students can learn concepts much more rapidly than younger ones because of experience and a broader vocabulary, much of which involves previous learning of other concepts. Although some of the higher animals may be able to accomplish something similar to concept learning on a very limited basis, in humans this is accomplished through the representative capability of language. Humans not only are quite capable of concept learning, but their voluminous written and spoken efforts indicate that they enjoy or are stimulated by such representative manipulation.

In learning concepts we learn to identify specific objects with other objects that may be said to belong to the same class or category. This obviously requires internal representative manipulation and the establishment of multiple chains and interconnections. Although the objects may be concrete, the class or category is representative and abstract.

Gagné points out that, although much concept learning relates to concrete objects (chairs, desks, and tables are furniture), another important type of concept learning relates to defined classifications that must be initially learned on a purely verbal basis because they are not concrete. His example is entities such as mothers, fathers, uncles, and aunts. An uncle is an uncle *by definition.*

The difference between *concrete* and *defined* concepts is quite important. It is altogether possible that a learning problem in conceptualization might affect defined concepts more than concrete ones or vice versa. In the realm of conceptualization it becomes apparent why we must develop accurate, wide ability to use language. Without adequate language a child cannot conceptualize effectively.

In summarizing the importance of concept learning, Gagné notes that concepts make it possible to "free thought and expression from the domination of the physical environment" (1977, p. 124). He views the mastery of concepts as a major prerequisite to "learn(ing) an amount of knowledge that is virtually without limit" (1977, p. 124).

Rule learning. Rule learning might be defined by some other theorists as conceptualization. It may be thought of as developing a chain of two or more concepts. In their simplest form, rules may be illustrated or represented by the statement "If A, then B," where both A and B are concepts. If A and B are merely words or phrases and "If A, then B" is just a verbal sequence, then the learning involved is verbal association.

It is quite important (especially for those who plan to work with learning disabled students) to differentiate between ability to *state* a rule (meaning that a particular sequence of words has been memorized) and *understanding the meaning* of the rule. For example, with the coming of the Metric Age in the United States, young students may be asked to learn "One inch equals 2.54 centimeters." Ability to state this rule does *not* mean that they understand the rule, but it is an important step toward such understanding. To understand it, they must have an accurate understanding (concept) of *inch, centimeter, equals,* and the *decimal concept* involved in "2.54."

Gagné notes that although the two-concept structure ("If A, then B") for rules is the most basic possibility, the three-concept rule is probably more typical. He cites the example:

"A pint, doubled, is a quart." This rule involves the concepts of *pint* and *quart*, plus the concept of *doubled*. In this, and many three-concept rules, one concept is relational (doubled); the other two concepts are concrete, "thing-concepts." Rule learning may involve six, eight, or a dozen or more concepts; learning such complex rules will usually require subdividing the rule into parts for initial learning or understanding and then putting the parts together into the total rule. Rules are important to higher level learning, and just as concepts are related to make up rules, groups of rules may be related to make up *learning hierarchies*.

Problem solving. Problem solving, like rule learning, might be included as a specific type of conceptualization by some other learning theorists. Gagné sees problem solving as one of the major practical uses of rule learning but cautions that we should not confuse this type of problem solving with purely arithmetic problem solving. At the simplest level, problem solving might be viewed as the combining of two rules to produce a new capability, an answer to a question or a problem. For this type of learning to take place efficiently, the learner must know something about the type of response that might be the solution *before* he arrives at the solution. This procedure involves many lengthy chains; many would use the more general term *thinking*.

Problem solving may be, in some instances, simply a matter of applying rules to accomplish some specific goal. However, problem-solving activities may have a considerably greater outcome, and in education we must be constantly aware of this additional outcome and promote it whenever possible. As individuals solve problems, a higher level of learning may take place. This is because we can often generalize from one experience to another, so that a series of three or four situations in which a given approach leads to successful problem solving may lead to much greater facility in solving similar problems in the future. This may be considered *new knowledge*.

Gagné notes that "problem solving as a method of learning requires that the learners *discover* the higher-order rule without specific help" (1977, p. 163). In effect, learners construct their *own* rule (as opposed to learning a rule provided by others). The kind of learning, which may be called "insightful" or "creative," is one variety of what Gagné calls "problem solving." It is important to remember that such insight is not a flash of light with no identifiable base but rather the cumulative effect of a great deal of knowledge about the underlying "rules." Problem solving may seem rather ordinary to nearly all adults, but it must be learned by children. People who are characterized as logical usually tend to be individuals who accomplish this level of learning consistently and with apparent ease.

Summary of Gagné's contributions

Gagné has provided the educator with an integrated view of learning that includes his conceptualization of the five major categories of learned capability and eight basic types of learning. In his 1977 text, he includes a discussion of the educational implications of each of these types of learning as applied to the five categories of learned capability, including simple examples in each area. In addition, he provides a procedure that may be used to analyze any given student's requirements for learning, including an important discussion of required *entering behavior*. Throughout his work, he emphasizes the importance of considering both *internal* and *external* conditions that promote learning. In his 1970 text (second edition), Gagné emphasized three major preconditions for learning. These were: (1) attention, (2) motivation, and (3) developmental readiness. These remain important considerations even though not discussed in the same manner in his third edition.

Gagné's writings indicate and explain, perhaps more than the work of any other learning theorists, the existence of many different types of learning. There is no indication that these are not related; in fact, their relationship is clearly delineated. On the other hand, the fact that they may (at times) be considered independently for purposes of learning analysis makes his view of learning practical for the learning disabilities specialist. This practicality and the fact that his writing is more easily read than that of most other learning theorists dictate that it should be placed high on the list of important reading for educators, particularly those who work with students with learning problems.

SUMMARY

This chapter has been about how normal individuals learn. Several points of view have been presented, for, in fact, there is no general agreement on the precise process whereby a one-day-old infant develops into an adult with a broad range of motor abilities and the abilities to read and write, converse effectively with others, and approach and solve new problems. In considering how normal individuals learn, we cannot find total agreement on how to define learning, but, in composite, definitions tend to include some mention of the following: (1) the acquisition of knowledge, skills, and attitudes and (2) a process of adapting, adjusting, or modifying behavior (separate from simple growth processes) in order to accomplish various goals. Since the turn of the twentieth century, vast strides have been made in the investigation of how learning takes place, and various authorities and schools of thought are now generally recognized. Some of the more recognized theorists were mentioned in this chapter, and three major divisions of learning theory, representing three schools of thought, were discussed. These divisions were: behaviorism, neobehaviorism, and cognitive theories.

In addition to the discussion of general beliefs prevalent within the three divisions of learning theory, the writings of Jean Piaget and Robert Gagné were reviewed in more detail. More information on the thinking of other theorists (for example, B. F. Skinner) will be provided in later chapters. The basic rationale for this chapter is that learning disabilities teachers must develop a working theory regarding how normal learning takes place to be maximally effective in dealing with students who are not learning normally. Such students need assistance because the basic school program—presumably based on how most students learn—is not effective for them. Simply providing "more of the same" is not logical and has been found to be unworkable in most instances. Knowledge of the variety of ways in which learning may take place and thus how it may be facilitated is essential to the learning disabilities teacher. The contents of this chapter have been presented in the hope that the teacher (or teacher-in-training) may be stimulated to further study. In the chapters that follow, a number of methods will be presented. Each is based on some concept of learning, and each may have some value, if used at the proper time in the appropriate manner with the right students. When attempting to understand these various methods and approaches, the reader is encouraged to consider the concept of learning espoused by those who use this method, as well as its inherent strengths and limitations. If such thought and consideration take place, this chapter will have been worthwhile.

REFERENCES AND SUGGESTED READINGS

Bruner, J. S. *The process of education.* Cambridge, Mass.: Harvard University Press, 1961.

Bruner, J. S. *Toward a theory of instruction.* Cambridge, Mass.: Harvard University Press, 1966.

Campbell, S. (Ed.) *Piaget sampler.* New York: Jason Aronson, Inc., 1977.

Di Vesta, F. *Language, learning, and cognitive processes.* Monterey, Calif.: Brooks/Cole Publishing Co., 1974.

Gagne, R. M. *The conditions of learning* (eds. 2 and 3). New York: Holt, Rinehart & Winston, 1970, 1977.

Garry, R., and Kingsley, H. *The nature and conditions of learning* (ed. 3). Englewood Cliffs, N.J.: Prentice-Hall, Inc., 1970.

Hebb, D. O. *A textbook of psychology* (ed. 2). Philadelphia: W. B. Saunders Co., 1966.

Hilgard, E., and Bower, G. *Theories of learning* (ed. 4). Englewood Cliffs, N.J.: Prentice-Hall, Inc., 1975.

Jackson, N., Robinson, H., and Dale, P. *Cognitive development in young children.* Washington, D.C.: The National Institute of Education, U.S. Department of Health, Education, and Welfare, 1976.

Lefrancois, G. R. *Psychological theories and human learning: Kongor's report.* Monterey, Calif.: Brooks/Cole Publishing Co., 1972.

Osgood, C. E. A behavioristic analysis of perception and language as cognitive phenomena. In Bruner, J. S. (Ed.) *Contemporary approaches to cognition.* Cambridge, Mass.: Harvard University Press, 1957.

Piaget, J. *The child and reality; problems of genetic psychology.* New York: The Viking Press, 1973.

Piaget, J. *Psychology and epistemology: towards a theory of knowledge.* New York: The Viking Press, 1971.

Skinner, B. F. *Science and human behavior.* New York: Macmillan Publishing Co., Inc., 1953.

Smith, F. *Comprehension and learning.* New York: Holt, Rinehart & Winston, 1975.

Wadsworth, B. J. *Piaget's theory of cognitive development.* New York: David McKay Co., Inc., 1971.

Watson, J. B. Psychology as the behaviorist views it, *Psychological Review,* 1913, *20,* 157-158.

SECTION TWO

Major approaches and techniques for teaching the learning disabled

Section Two is the major section of this text. Chapters 4 through 9 discuss perceptual-motor approaches, approaches related to control of hyperactivity, multisensory approaches, language-development approaches, medically related approaches, and the techniques of behaviorists, often called behavior modification approaches. Some of these approaches (for example, the medically related) cannot be implemented by the teacher, but he or she must sometimes play an assistive role and certainly should know something about them. Some (behavior modification) are not really approaches but are actually techniques, which may be used along with other approaches. Certain approaches are believed to be quite discrete entities and properly applicable only if they are used in the "pure" form. At least that is what some of their advocates seem to believe. This issue will not be debated, and Chapters 4 through 9 will treat these approaches in as separate a manner as possible, so as to feature the unique aspects of each. Even so, by the very nature of various approaches and the manner in which they are named and characterized for this discussion, some very obvious overlapping will be evident.

Before studying the perceptual-motor approaches (in Chapter 4), it may be helpful to consider the true story of Ricky S., a learning disabled student who enrolled in our university's summer program for the learning disabled a few years ago. His story will help to demonstrate the need to understand a variety of approaches and the difficulty in determining which approach is the best for any given student.

RICKY S.—A LEARNING DISABLED NINE-YEAR-OLD BOY

Ricky S. had moved through the first four grades, experiencing increasing academic difficulty each year. He had not repeated a grade as yet, but that had been discussed a number of times. In some of the activities of the school, his efforts were within the normal range of expectations, but in reading and arithmetic he was near the bottom of the class. His performance was also very poor in various physical-education-related activities. It appeared that when information was presented through audiovisual means he could learn in a nearly normal manner, but even then he was in trouble if he had to indicate what he had learned in a written form. In most ways he did not appear to fit the pattern of educable mental retardation, for (as the teacher put it) he seemed "bright" in some types of activities. Finally, when he was referred for an educational evaluation, it was discovered that his I.Q. was 101, but his academic level was low second-grade level in arithmetic, reading, and spelling. Ricky came from a very normal, stable, middle class home, his medical history was remarkably normal, and in total there were few clues to the source of his difficulties. When his mother enrolled him in the concentrated, 6-week summer school program for students with learning problems (an absolute diagnosis of learning disabilities was not required; if students were having academic problems, they were accepted) about all that was known was what has just been outlined. Except for the academic difficulties, poor motor skills, and normal intelligence, very little else could be said with much certainty about Ricky.

After two weeks of the summer program, Ricky's mother called the program supervisor. The essence of the call was, "I don't know what you are doing to Ricky, but he is eager to go to school each day, and I believe he is reading better. He is wanting to go 20 to 30 minutes early each day; I've never seen anything like it. Whatever it is you are doing, just keep it up." Pleased with the call and curious about the source of such improvement, the supervisor made a special visit to Ricky's classroom the next day and asked several questions about any special program efforts being provided for Ricky. The teacher, a male, seemed reluctant at first to say much about the matter, but when he fully understood that the parent was completely happy, he explained as follows:

"Well, I'm just doing some of the normal remedial activities in the classroom, but I did find out one interesting thing when we had our first outside free time. Ricky wanted to learn to play baseball better, and since I played baseball in college, I started talking and playing catch with him. I had noticed that he was a bit clumsy, and he threw and caught a ball about like a second grader. But he was eager to learn and we get along real well outside. He wanted to stay after class and play ball, and pretty soon we made a deal. The deal was that he could earn additional before or after school 'baseball time' with me in return for satisfactory completion of his classwork. He started asking many more questions about his arithmetic, was really attentive, and his work is looking better. And I have been coming early to play ball with him if he earns the time the day before. He is really working to get that extra time to play ball, and his ball playing is getting better too."

The happy end to this story is that by the end of the 6-week summer program, Ricky had made about 1½ years of improvement in reading and arithmetic. Ricky's attitude regarding school, and especially reading, had greatly improved. His mother had contacted the supervisor and the teacher several more times just to express her great satisfaction with the results. Toward the end of the session, the teacher had wisely introduced a new factor into the remedial setting—football. Ricky's father was included in a conference in which it was recommended that the father allocate some time to both baseball and football. It was suggested that the father *not* relate the baseball/football time to school work but rather make it a father-son fun activity.

Summary comments—Ricky S.

A number of points should be made about the case of Ricky S. *First,* he had few of the traditional "characteristics" of learning disabled students—only the academic discrepancies and the poor motor skills. Some school districts might not have considered him to be learning disabled. *Second,* because of the nature of our summer program, specifically the very limited time period, we do not spend the time that would be required to gather all of the data to develop a good individualized educational program (I.E.P.). In many cases, we have more information from the school the student has attended, but in Ricky's case the school had not really determined what to do with him. Maybe that is fortunate in this case; they might have missed the strong motivational factor that the baseball reward program provided. We must admit that the teacher's success with Ricky was partly because of good luck. *Third,* the major reason for outlining the Ricky case is to emphasize the need to understand several approaches to teaching the learning disabled. There are more obvious reasons for several approaches when we consider a number of different students with widely divergent characteristics and verified deficits. In this case, with only one student, there was still good reason to know several approaches and techniques. If we were to ask a panel of experts to analyze this case and to indicate what approach was the *major* approach, we might receive the following analysis.

1. A behaviorist might focus on the manner in which the teacher used a reward system to encourage Ricky to complete his assignments. This might be referred to in terms of contracting arrangement or might simply be called the use of rewards.
2. A multisensory approach advocate might look further into the kinds of activities that actually took place in the classroom. If this were done, it would be discovered that a number of multisensory-type teaching/learning tasks were involved. The multisensory advocate might then conclude that it was the multisensory nature of the learning tasks that made the difference.
3. Perceptual-motor enthusiasts might well consider the manner in which the motor tasks were used and believe that the underdeveloped motor skills, with related underdeveloped perceptual skills, were the basic cause of Ricky's academic difficulties. If more general, Kephart-related theory were applied, it might be considered that the additional perceptual-motor abilities facilitated more understanding of the academic tasks. If a Cratty-related theory were applied, these perceptual-motor abilities would be viewed as important, but the added ego-strength and self-confidence, which can be generated through improvement of motor skills, especially as these factors related to increased athletic prowess, might be viewed as important.

The preceding consideration of what *might* be concluded is, of course, hypothetical. Most well-informed authorities would undoubtedly recognize the likelihood that it was an interaction of these many factors that led to the unusually rapid improvement in learning ability. There is also the considerable possibility that some other outside motivational factor was involved. However, the story of Ricky may illustrate why it is of value to understand and to be able to implement a number of approaches. *In some instances, it may be very obvious which approach will be the best, and only one basic approach may be required. In others, as in the case of Ricky, a combination of approach components may be the key to improved academic functioning.* With this in mind, we will proceed with a review of several, recognized approaches.

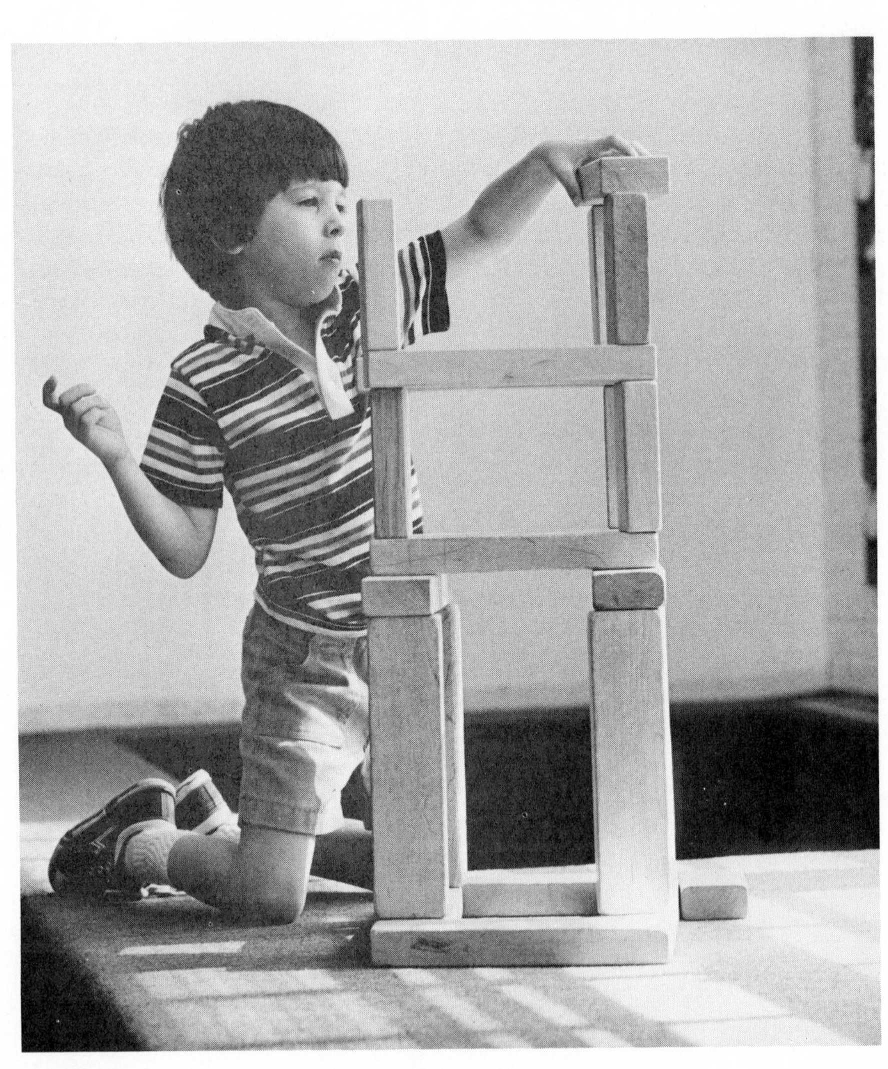

chapter 4

Perceptual-motor approaches

The work of perceptual-motor theorists includes some of the more interesting efforts, and also some of the more controversial, to assist the learning disabled. Hallahan and Cruickshank stated in 1973 that "problems of a perceptual-motor nature have come to achieve first priority among workers within the domain of learning disabilities" (p. 159). They further noted, however, that the concern of most perceptual-motor authorities is not with the perceptual-motor disability per se, but that "what individuals such as Kephart, Getman, Barsch, Ayres, and Frostig are most attentive to are the deleterious effects of such impairment upon children's learning and academic achievement" (1973, p. 159).

Although related to the efforts of highly regarded developmental psychologists (for example, Jean Piaget) and containing a great deal in its theoretical foundations, which is generally accepted with relation to child development, there is continuing controversy as to the extent to which remedial efforts directed primarily at perceptual-motor development will directly affect academic functioning. In other words, even if early perceptual-motor development is an important part of the base for the future learning ability and academic functioning of the preschool child, some question whether perceptual-motor efforts with a 10-year-old student will improve academic functioning. The statement by Hallahan and Cruickshank (cited above) about "first-priority" recognition of problems of perceptual-motor nature among workers in learning disabilities may no longer be true, but many of the perceptual-motor theorists' ideas and methods are still in use, even by those who do not profess to believe in perceptual-motor theory. The question of a cause-effect relationship between perceptual-motor abilities and academic achievement may never be settled with certainty, but it is generally accepted that many students called learning disabled have much lower than average perceptual-motor abilities. Investigators have not been able to conduct the kind of research that might prove beyond a shadow of a doubt that early perceptual-motor dysfunction causes later academic difficulties. Some research seems to suggest a definite relationship, but how this applies to higher level cognitive processes remains uncertain. However, interest remains high among certain authorities with particular interest in application to younger children.

An indication of the degree to which underdeveloped motor and perceptual-motor skills are felt to be related to a prediction of possible learning disabilities may be seen in a recent publication of the U.S. Department of Health, Education, and Welfare publication, entitled *Mainstreaming Preschoolers: Children with Learning Disabilities* (Hayden and others, 1978). This guidebook for Project Head Start introduces a discussion of characteristics of children with learning disabilities by suggesting six skill areas in which we may observe behaviors that may indicate learning disabilities. One of these six areas is motor skills, which is subdivided and discussed in the following section.

GROSS MOTOR SKILLS*

Gross motor skills involve movement of the large muscles in the arms, legs, torso, and feet. Children with learning disabilities may show problems in the following areas.

Developmental milestones. They may exhibit delays in developmental milestones such as crawling, sitting up, and walking.

Body control. They may lack body control and rhythm in activities such as jumping, hopping, skipping, throwing, kicking, and lifting things. Lack of body control results in jerky and uncoordinated movements.

Bilateral movement. Some children may have difficulty moving both arms and hands at the same time (bilateral movement), and in tasks such as lifting or throwing.

Crossing the midline. Some children may have difficulty crossing the midline of the body. For example, a child might have trouble using her right hand to pick up a toy placed to the left of her body.

Cross-lateral movement. Cross-lateral movement (using opposite arms and legs at the same time) may be hard for some children. For example, a very young child may have trouble using his left leg and right arm to crawl.

Balance. General clumsiness may result if a child is not able to control his or her balance while moving: the child may frequently trip, bump into things, or drop things.

Spatial orientation. Some learning disabled children have poor spatial orientation skills—that is, they do not understand their position in space and the relationship between themselves and the objects around them. You may notice that such a child cannot recognize objects (or shapes) when they are placed in different positions. For example, a child may be able to recognize a teddy bear when it is in the upright position but not when it is upside down or sideways. Or a child who can recognize three-dimensional objects may not recognize the same object in pictures.

Spatial relations. Some children may also have trouble with spatial relations. These children cannot judge the relationship of objects to each other and to themselves in a reliable and predictable way. They may have difficulty stepping over or walking under objects, such as a rope held at various heights. Some may not recognize the need to crouch or crawl in order to move through narrow tunnels or low spaces. Others may consistently try to fit big objects into small boxes. Difficulty putting on clothes, going up and down stairs, and fitting lids on boxes or keys in locks may also indicate a problem with spatial relations.

Problems in spatial relations may also result in fear of heights, hesitation of movement, and difficulty in understanding the direction or extent of a movement necessary to accomplish a task. For example, you may have a five-year-old in your program who cannot coordinate his or her arm movements so that he or she throws a ball in the right direction. You may also notice that the child has difficulty running or riding a tricycle.

FINE MOTOR SKILLS

Fine motor skills include movement of the small muscles used to move the fingers, wrist, lips, and tongue. Learning disabled children may have problems in the following areas.

Finger and wrist movements. Children who have problems with fine motor skills frequently are clumsy in handling small objects. These youngsters cannot button and unbutton, snap and unsnap, tie and untie, use a pair of scissors correctly, or hold a crayon securely. They may have difficulty gripping things between the thumb and index finger (pincer grip). You may notice poor pincer grip when children are picking up very small items such as beads or buttons. They may also have difficulty copying vertical or horizontal lines and circles, a

---

* From Hayden, A., and others. *Mainstreaming preschoolers: children with learning disabilities,* Washington, D.C., 1978, U.S. Department of Health, Education, and Welfare.

skill that is usually mastered by age five. Some children may also have poor control of wrist and finger movement, so that they have difficulty with such tasks as grasping a pencil, using scissors, handling rhythm instruments, and stringing beads.

Lip and tongue movements. Some children may also have difficulty with fine motor coordination of the lips and tongue. Since the ability to make rapid movements of the lips and tongue is a fine motor skill necessary for clear speech, these children may not speak clearly or may be reluctant to talk.

The second of the six areas mentioned in the Project Head Start guidebook is visual skills. The five subskill areas are: (1) visual perception, (2) visual discrimination, (3) visual tracking, (4) visual memory, and (5) visual-motor integration. Thus motor and perceptual-motor abilities are strongly emphasized in this guidebook developed by individuals who are not primarily perceptual-motor advocates but who believe that these are important points of emphasis and focus when dealing with preschool children who are learning disabled or at risk of becoming learning disabled.*

Thus far we have reviewed comments and evidence that perceptual-motor abilities are considered to be closely related to learning disabilities, by at least some authorities. Two questions remain: (1) Just what do perceptual-motor authorities believe? and (2) What is a perceptual-motor approach? The answers to these questions will be provided in this chapter. The theories of authorities in this area are somewhat complex if considered in detail; therefore these questions will only be pursued in sufficient depth to provide very basic levels of information. The first question is "What do the various perceptual-motor authorities have in common?" and then a consideration of the basic conceptualizations of several specific authorities follows.

*A simplified chart of normal development in the areas of motor and language abilities through age fifteen is provided in Appendix C. This may be of value in better understanding expected levels of development.

THE BASIC BELIEFS OF PERCEPTUAL-MOTOR AUTHORITIES

Perhaps the only belief that nearly all perceptual-motor authorities would support is that, for the most part, higher-level mental processes develop out of and after adequate, integrated development of the motor system and the perceptual system—that is, they believe that perceptual abilities provide the base for later conceptual abilities. Some might verbalize this belief in a somewhat different manner than others, but this appears to be the essence of their basic rationale.

We will consider the work of Ayres, Barsch, Cratty, Delacato, Frostig, Getman, and Kephart, noting some of the contributions of each to what is generally recognized as perceptual-motor theory and practice. Kephart may fit the central perceptual-motor framework more fully than the rest, Delacato is undoubtedly the most controversial, and Frostig is not always considered a perceptual-motor theorist, since her efforts have involved many other approach components. All of these individuals have achieved some recognition in this field and each has made his or her own unique contribution. We will start with Newell Kephart, since his work might be considered more "middle-of-the-road" among the theorists, thus more representative of the field as a whole.

The overview that follows should be of assistance in the acquisition of sufficient information for determining if further research into the work of these recognized authorities is desired. To develop any depth of understanding in the perceptual-motor approach to teaching the child with learning disabilities, much more reading and research into the writing of these individuals, as opposed to writings *about* them, must be undertaken.

NEWELL C. KEPHART

Newell Kephart would probably receive very prominent mention if we asked a broad group of experienced special educators from coast to coast whom they think of first when perceptual-motor education is mentioned. There would be regional preferences, but Kephart might well receive the most national recognition. Kephart devoted most of his life to developing and refining his concept of perceptual-motor training, beginning in the 1930s when he worked with Alfred Strauss. His coauthorship, with E. G. Roach, of the Purdue Perceptual-Motor Survey (described later in this chapter) and his continued dedication to the cause of brain-injured and other learning disabled students have left a significant mark on the field of learning disabilities. Kephart believed that "the development of the child [may be] seen as a series of stages, each stage representing the emergence of a more complex method of processing data" (1971, p. 38). He further believed that "it is logical to assume that all behavior is basically motor, that the prerequisites of any kind of behavior are muscular and motor responses" (1971, p. 79). In relation to these beliefs, Kephart developed a theoretical construct that led to a system of training activities designed to remediate diagnosed deficiencies. The description that follows is intended to present some of his basic ideas as they apply to learning disabilities.

As most who have observed very young children know, the young child begins life with certain innate, primarily reflexive, capabilities. In normal children these very quickly evolve in the direction of more meaningful activities and movements. One of the earlier levels of concern, in Kephart's frame of reference, is that of acquisition of perceptual-motor match.

Perceptual-motor match

Perceptual-motor match is the establishment of relationships between purely perceptual elements (which lead to the development of a body of perceptual information) and motor information. As long as the two types of information are not correlated, speed and accuracy of learning are greatly retarded. Kephart uses the development of eye-hand coordination as an example of perceptual-motor match. This may be described as follows:

> When a child first moves his hand, it is done randomly and with limited direction or meaning. Soon, however, the exploring hand touches something, and the eye, watching the hand, correlates the visual information with the tactual. The eye learns to see what the hand feels. This is the first step in eye-hand coordination.
>
> As the child becomes more and more experienced and the perceptual and motor information input more closely correlated, the child is able and likely to automatically substitute one for the other without hesitation. The child may occasionally use the hand simply for assurance or in new situations, but motor and perceptual data are so closely matched they merge as one for most practical purposes.

This is what Kephart called perceptual-motor match. Kephart believed that many connections between perceptual and motor data must be made by the young child and that many young children in the lower grades have not sufficiently completed this process so as to be able to relate effectively to typical classroom presentations. He believed that perception must be matched to motor, not the reverse. His insistence in this directionality was one point with which some disagree.

A second major step in the learning path relates to development of the ability to establish figure-ground relationships. This, of course, depends on the earlier development of adequate perceptual-motor match. The ability to separate *figure* from *ground* simply means the ability to concentrate, or focus, on items of present major importance while relegating other aspects of the environment to the backgound. This does not mean losing all awareness of the presence of background but rather giving it much lower precedence in the field of consciousness. Kephart made specific suggestions regarding two types of children, hyperkinetic and hypokinetic, who tend to have the most difficulty in figure-ground relationships.

In Kephart's continuing description of the course of development of the child, movement control, systematic exploration, perception, intersensory integration, and concept formation follow in that order. Kephart viewed the development of the child as being accomplished in a series of stages, each involving the development of a more complex system, or method, of processing data. The preceding steps are his labels for these stages. According to his theory this development can go in only one direction—toward greater complexity. Development cannot back up or remain stationary. To undo such development would mean to erase neurological alterations that are permanent in nature. This therefore cannot happen. New stages, resulting in new data-processing methods, are viewed as compulsive—the child *must* use them in preference to simpler ones.

According to Kephart, a major reason why teaching the child whose development has been interrupted is so difficult is that the child has been forced into stages that he cannot handle adequately. However, he makes some kind of adaptation, and even though attempts are made to go back to redo the earlier stage, techniques usually applicable and appropriate at the earlier stage—and at an earlier age—are not likely to apply.

Kephart's ideas about the motor basis of achievement will be briefly discussed to assist in better understanding of his total frame of reference and his recommended training activities.

The earliest behavioral responses of the human organism are the early motor, or muscular, responses. Through early motor explorations, the child learns about his surrounding environment. As explained in the example of eye-hand coordination, the child develops perceptual-motor match. Kephart believed that the "efficiency of the higher thought processes can be no better than the basic motor abilities on which they are based" (1971, p. 81). He defined and described these motor bases as follows.

Motor bases of learning

Posture is the basic movement pattern from which all other movement patterns must develop. There are two major reasons why posture is so significant. The first is that through the maintenance of posture we have a constant point of reference in our universe. Where we go, what we do, directionality, and all spatial orientation are dependent on our ability to maintain a consistent zero position. The second reason relates to safety. To be able to move quickly, efficiently, and consistently away from danger (for example, automobiles on the street, dangerous moving objects of all kinds, and burning material), we must have a zero point from which to establish movement. For man, this zero point is the upright posture, controlled and maintained by a series of muscle groups. Young children have to learn this first basic pattern. This is not just the one specific pattern that allows the organism to maintain an upright posture while standing still but must include flexible posturing that permits successful walking, running, leaning over (as in picking up objects), and all the various situations in which th organism maintains its control over its relationship to gravity. Recent investigation indicates the extreme complexity of the learning patterns that result in smooth, controlled movements of the human body. For the organism to be able to explore and thus learn effectively, posture must be well developed.

Laterality is the second in the sequence of motor bases of learning as recognized by Kephart. It should be noted that the directions we recognize and use in everyday activities are all in relation to the individual organism and are meaningful mainly with respect to that organism. Up, down, right, left, before, and behind are all relative. The first of these to develop, or to have potential for development, is recognition of laterality, or recognition that there is a right and left side.

This does not mean that the young child learns to *say* right or left but rather that the human organism develops an ability to detect the difference between the two sides. Kephart noted that neurologically the nerve pathways that control and direct the two sides of the body are primarily separate. This, of course, makes it much easier to develop laterality, but *it must be learned.* The child must learn when to activate muscles first on one side and then on the other to maintain balance. From this beginning the child should learn such things as when to use his right hand (for example, to reach for something to his right) and vice versa. Otherwise his movements are very inefficient, and he may develop the use of one hand for all hand usage actions or may almost always reach out with both hands. Kephart believed that, in relation to reading, laterality is what permits the child to recognize the difference between symbols such as a *b* and a *d.*

Directionality is described as the ability to translate the right-left discrimination within the organism (laterality) into right-left discrimination among objects in space. That is, first the child learns to recognize that two balls, a green one and a blue one, are to *his* right. Then he learns to see that the blue one is to the right of the green one. It is at this point that eye control becomes extremely important. To be able to sense that one ball is to the right of the other, the child must know that, when his eyes are turned in a certain direction and he sees the ball, the ball actually is in that direction. He must have passed through the stage at which he has learned to match eye and hand movements, and he must have confidence in his visual perceptions in this regard. Only than can he efficiently use his eyes to project directionality in space.

Body image is the next motor base of achievement in Kephart's scheme of things. As was pointed out earlier, each individual's body is the point of reference around which relative impressions of the universe and objects within it are organized. The child must learn to maintain his own body posture, and laterality and directionality are with reference to his body and its position in space. Body image is learned by observation of the movements of the various body parts, as well as the relationship of these parts to each other and to other objects in space. If the child does not have a proper concept of the amount of space it takes to pull a wagon through a doorway, the wagon gets stuck. A similar happening in the home in the vicinity of ceramic breakables can be disastrous. The opposite extreme is feeling a need for much more space than is really required. Inability to move one part of the body independently of other parts is also usually interpreted as poor body image. Poor body image will generally have an adverse effect on interpretation of outside relationships, since these all relate to the body as the zero point.

After the child has developed posture, laterality, directionality, and body image, he is ready to move about the environment with some efficiency. To learn in an effective manner, he should be exploring for the purpose of involvement and contact with new and unknown environmental elements. To permit this meaningful exploration, four basic movement generalizations are required.

Basic movement generalizations

Balance and posture are the most obvious first requisite movement generalization. The child must be able to move about in a balanced, controlled, purposeful manner, or he cannot systematically explore.

Locomotion (ability to move about) is mentioned above in relation to balance and posture. Included in the definition of locomotion are walking, running, jumping, and skipping. The less efficient his locomotion and the more attention he must pay to locomotion, the less successful will be his spatial exploration. Kephart noted that many slow-learning children may have a collection of motor skills but no really effective motor generalization as regards locomotion. They may walk, but they do so awkwardly, stiffly, or inflexibly. This, of course, slows their learning through exploration.

Contact is a third necessary generalization of movement. In man this includes primarily hand skills—the capability to reach, grasp, and release. Without this capability it is difficult to explore the many objects of the environment.

Receipt and propulsion are the fourth of the required motor generalizations. Receipt refers to activities through which the child interreacts with objects moving toward him. Catching is the most common receipt activity. Propulsion includes throwing, pushing, batting, or any activity through which movement is given to an object, or body.

Through these four basic motor generalizations, the child can and usually will explore his environment and form an effective base for further learning. Children who do not develop the four motor generalizations in a normal manner will likely become retarded in later perceptual learning and the higher mental processes will develop more slowly.

Purdue Perceptual-Motor Survey

Kephart's ideas about perceptual-motor development, including his suggestions for training students with possible perceptual-motor deficits, can be viewed from the vantage point of an assessment tool that he developed in conjunction with Eugene Roach, the *Purdue Perceptual-Motor Survey.* As indicated by its name, this is a survey instrument, not a test. It was one of several major tools used by Kephart in diagnostic work in his clinic, and it is certainly not the only basis for his prescribed educational and remedial activities. The following description outlines the scope and content of the Purdue Perceptual-Motor Survey and also further reflects Kephart's thinking, with respect to the nature of critical areas of perceptual-motor development.

The Purdue Perceptual-Motor Survey presents specific administration and scoring instructions, just as any test might do. The instructions are complete and concise and involve testing, or observation, in the five main areas of prime consideration to Kephart. The scope of this instrument with limited comments follows:

1. *Balance and posture.* Four scores, or ratings, are taken—three on the walking board and one in jumping ability. The walking board scores are in walking

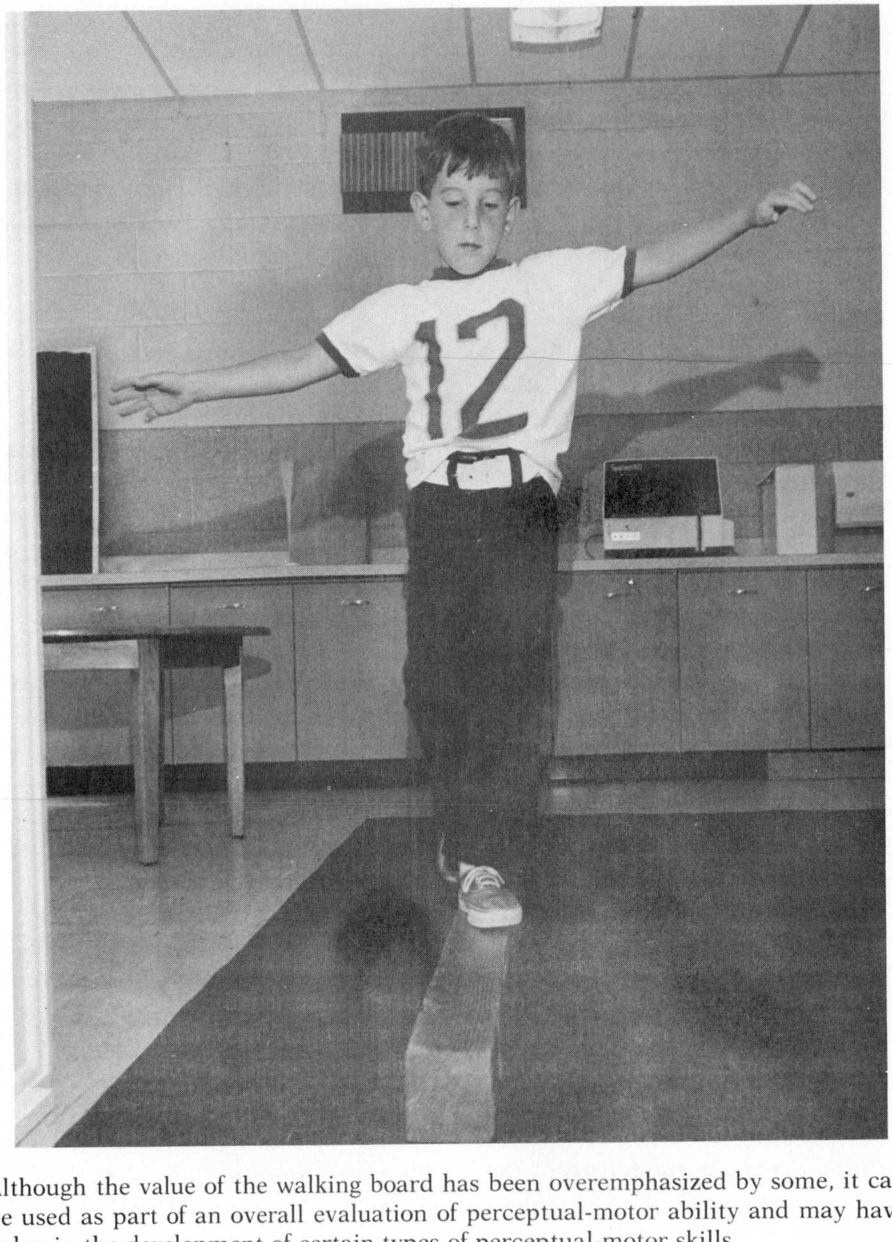

Although the value of the walking board has been overemphasized by some, it can be used as part of an overall evaluation of perceptual-motor ability and may have value in the development of certain types of perceptual-motor skills.

forward, backward, and sideways. The jumping score reflects a series of jumping and hopping tasks. Together they reflect balance and posture.

2. *Body image and differentiation.* Five scores, or ratings, are taken—one each under the subtitles of "Identification of Body Parts," "Imitation of Movement," "Obstacle Course," "Kraus-Weber," and "Angels-in-the-Snow." Identification of body parts and imitation of movements consist of the child following instructions and imitating a series of positions of the arms. The obstacle course is a simple obstacle course; Kraus-Weber is composed of two tasks from a physical fitness test of that same name. Angels-in-the-snow is taken from a game in which the child lies down in the snow and moves his arms and legs, making angel patterns in the snow. In this task there are specific movement patterns to observe and score.
3. *Perceptual-motor match.* Seven scores, or ratings, are taken—four under the "Chalkboard" subtitle and three under "Rhythmic Writing." The chalkboard ratings involve drawing a circle, drawing double circles (one with each hand, simultaneously), drawing lateral lines, and drawing vertical lines. The rhythmic writing scores emphasize rhythm, smooth movement, and directional change.
4. *Ocular control.* Four scores, or ratings, are taken relating to ocular pursuit. The child watches movement of a light, first with both eyes, then with the right eye alone, then the left eye alone. Finally, with both eyes, he watches the light as it moves from far to near.
5. *Form perception.* Two scores, or ratings, are taken. Seven visual achievement forms (provided with the survey manual) are provided for the child to copy. Children over 5 but under 6 years of age are given forms 1 through 4, those 6 but less than 7 years of age are given forms 1 through 5, and those 7 years of age or older are given all 7 forms. The children copy these forms with a pencil on plain paper, and their copying is scored for form and organization.

These five parts of the Purdue Perceptual-Motor Survey are recorded on the first page of the survey record form. The following pages of the form are the records kept as the child completes each part of the survey. In total, the record form should indicate the more crucial areas of faulty performance, if such exist. Normative data, standardization statistics, and so on are presented in the survey manual.

Conclusion

As a result of information gathered through the Purdue Perceptual-Motor Survey, other recognized tests of perceptual development, various academic achievement measures, and his own clinical experience and judgment, Kephart provided specific training suggestions for individuals diagnosed in his clinic. Those who have followed his lead have generally attempted to emulate his procedures and general recommendations and may have fallen short primarily in the matter of overinterpreting the results of the Purdue Perceptual-Motor Survey and other standardized instruments and in some cases promising too much immediate academic improvement as a direct result of motor or perceptual-motor training. Many, if not most, have been unable to match Kephart's depth of clinical judgment, which was undoubtedly one of his stronger points and a major source of information in individual student planning.

Kephart's training suggestions included but were not limited to:

A. Perceptual-motor training, including use of (1) the walking board, (2) the balance board, (3) the trampoline, (4) angels-in-the-snow, (5) a variety of stunts and games, and (6) certain rhythmic activities.

B. Training for perceptual-motor match, including training in (1) gross motor activities, (2) fine motor activities, (3) visualization, and (4) auditory-motor match.

C. Training for ocular control, including suggestions for evaluation of ocular control and training activities in (1) visual fixation and (2) ocular pursuit.

D. Training in form perception, including training for (1) differentiation of elements, (2) matching, (3) symbol recognition, (4) identification of missing parts, (5) manipulation of items and subforms, (6) figure-ground relationships, (7) basic position concepts, (8) cutting and pasting activities, and (9) various scanning activities.

Kephart did not not promise some of the near "miracles" that some perceptual-motor advocates seem to promise, although some who claim to follow his ideas at times may overdo their claims. Perhaps the best understanding of his basic thinking may be obtained by reading his 1971 text, *The Slow Learner in the Classroom* (ed. 2) or *Steps to Achievement for the Slow Learner* (Ebersole, Kephart, and Ebersole, 1968).

GERALD N. GETMAN

Gerald Getman, along with Kephart, was a major shaping force in the field of perceptual-motor training as applied to individuals with learning problems. Getman worked with Kephart, with Gesell, at the then world-famous Gesell Child Development Clinic at Yale University, and with Sheldon Rappoport, founder of the Pathway School for brain-injured and learning disabled children. According to Hallahan and Cruickshank, "It is inconceivable to speak of Kephart and his contributions . . . without also considering the optometrist, Gerald Getman" (1973, p. 76). In full agreement with Hallahan and Cruickshank, we will therefore consider Getman's contributions and particularly his *visuomotor model,* a graphic representation of the manner in which he believes an individual's higher level cognitive abilities develop, based on motor abilities. This model is of interest because it generally reflects the basic ideas of many perceptual-motor authorities. It is quite consistent with the beliefs of developmental psychologists and undoubtedly shows the influence of Getman's work at the Gesell clinic.

The Getman visuomotor model

The Getman visuomotor model illustrates the manner in which Getman believes higher level intellectual abilities develop from lower level motor systems. This model (Fig. 2) may be further described as follows.

I. *Innate responses* are those that normal children have at birth. These include: the *tonic neck reflex* (TNR on the model), the starting point for infant movement; the *startle reflex* (SR), the reaction to a sudden flash of light or sudden loud noise; the *light reflex* (LR), eyelid tightening (in response to light) and later reduction in pupil size; the *grasp reflex* (GR), grasping of objects; the *reciprocal reflex* (RR), the facility of thrust and counterthrust of movements of the body; the *statokinetic reflex* (SKR), relaxed attentiveness; and the *myotatic reflex* (MR), a stretch reflex system with a built-in feedback system. These various innate response systems, according to Getman, become the base for all further learning. To the extent that these are not intact and fully and normally operational at birth, the child will be at a disadvantage in developing intellectually.

II. *General motor development* includes those

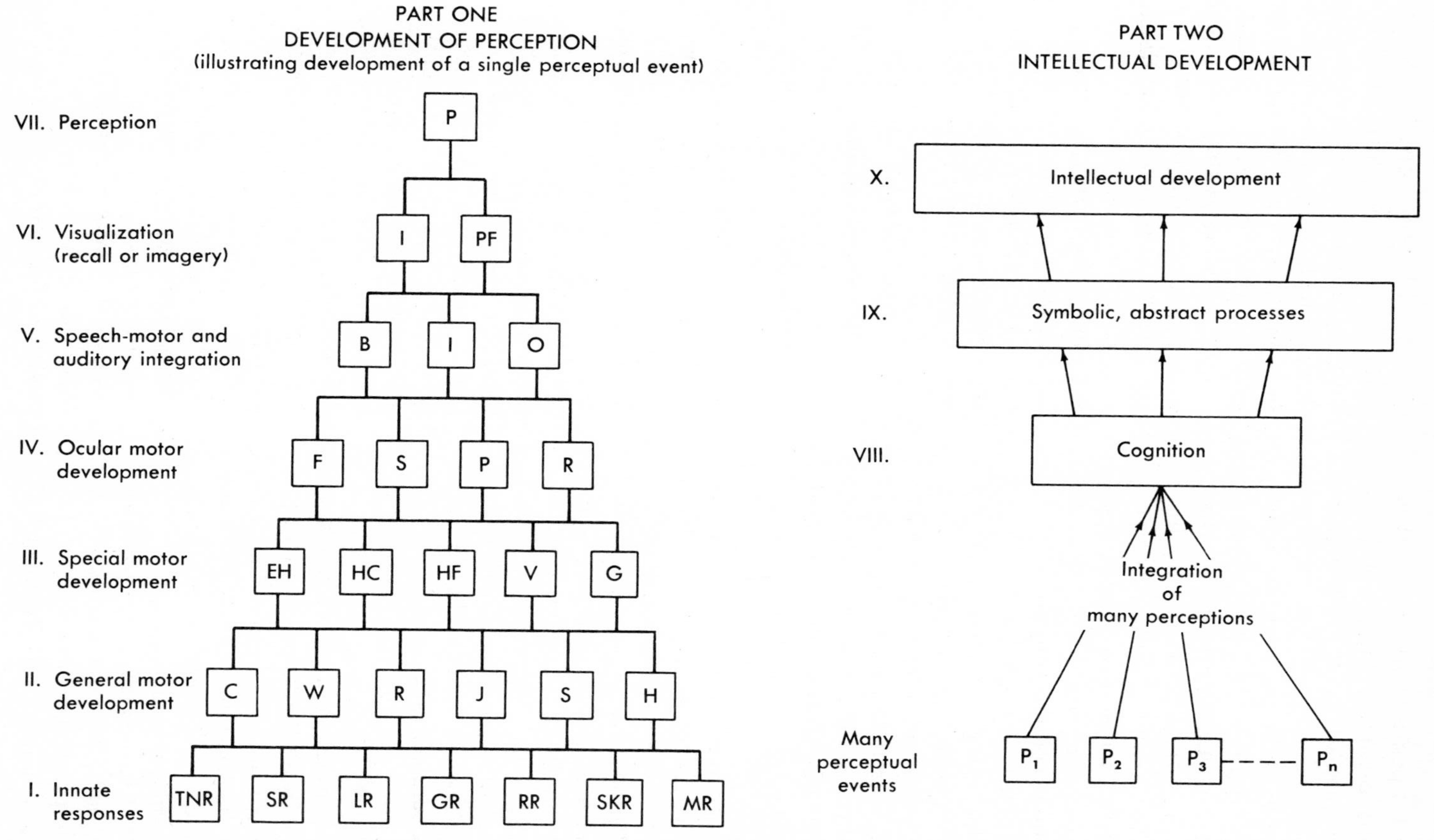

FIG. 2. The visuomotor model. (Adapted from Getman, G.: The visuomotor complex in the acquisition of learning skills. In J. Hellmuth [ed.]. Learning disorders, Vol. 1, Seattle, Wash.: Special Child Publications, 1965, p. 60.)

abilities usually associated with locomotion or mobility. Development of these abilities tends to receive priority attention from all perceptual-motor theorists. These include: *creeping* (C), *walking* (W), *running* (R), *jumping* (J), *skipping* (S), and *hopping* (H). Through this series of skills, the child utilizes and builds on the information obtained at the lower, innate response system. These skills provide the base for higher, more complex skills that are necessary for continued, effective learning. General coordination, which should develop at this level, is required to permit adequate development of more specific and specialized coordination at higher levels. Full development at this level requires a wide variety of physical activities. Children who, for any reason, do not develop these more general motor skills must have planned opportunities to do so or suffer the consequences later.

III. *Special motor development* includes a variety of special motor systems that develop out of the first two levels. These abilities, like those in level II, are given high priority by all perceptual-motor theorists. These include: *eye-hand relationships* (EH), *two hands working in combination* (HC), *hand-foot relationships* (HF), *voice systems* (V), and skill in *gestures* (G). Getman believes that children are often asked to perform at this level before they have developed solid skills at levels I and II.

IV. *Ocular motor development* includes the ability to control the movement of the eyes, a system that is much more complex than realized by many in that it involves two separate systems—one for each eye—that must be matched and balanced constantly. Getman may well be the best informed of all perceptual-motor theorists in relation to this complex system, and he believes many children are less than maximally effective as learners because of problems that appear at this level. Of particular concern is that many educators attempt to teach children at levels above this one without being certain that skills at this level are well developed. Though children have 20/20 vision, they may have serious problems in bilateral relationships—problems that tend to be devastating when doing close work such as reading. Too often we check only midpoint vision and ignore near-point vision, which is of the greatest importance in reading.

Ocular skills, which appear on the model (Fig. 2), are: *fixation* (F), the ability to fixate upon or visually locate an object; *saccadics* (S), the visual movement from one target (object) to another; *pursuit* (P), the ability to successfully follow a moving target with both eyes; and *rotation* (R), the ability to rotate or move the eyes freely in any direction.

V. *The speech-motor and auditory integration system* includes: *babbling* (B), *imitative speech* (I), and *original speech* (O). Getman believes that skill in the speech-motor and auditory integration system is interrelated with vision. For most children, he would insist that these language processes are dependent on effective visual and ocular systems.

VI. *Visualization (or recall or imagery)*, in the Getman model, means the ability to recall what has been seen, heard, or sensed tactually. It means the ability to revisualize what is not now present. (Myklebust would call this *imagery*.) Getman recognizes two types of visualization, *immediate* (I) and *past-future* (PF). An example of immediate visualization is feeling a key in a pocket or purse and "seeing" it simultaneously. Revisualizing a near-accident in an automobile 2 days ago is past-visualization. Contemplating how to get through that same dangeorus corner tomorrow is future-visualization.

VII. *Perception*, often simply called vision by Getman, is the ability to differentiate between similar but different sensory stimuli. It is obvious, following this model, that unless an individual can visualize (level VI) accurately, at times there will be problems in perception. According to Getman's model, unless each level below the level of perception has been fully developed, perceptual difficulties can occur.

VIII, IX, and X. *Intellectual development* (X), representing the best and highest (in learning) in the human species, is the result of a variety of abstract mental processes, such as ability to generalize, to conceptualize, to elaborate, and to transform thoughts and ideas. These occur as the result of interrelating and integrating a variety of perceptions. Because Getman's major emphasis is on those events leading up to accurate perception, not too much is made of the levels above the perceptual.

Conclusion

Getman's visuomotor model represents a pyramid of skills, each dependent on the skills at the preceding (next lower) level. This model provides a simple, graphic illustration of how children learn; however, Getman would be among the first to indicate that learning is much more complex than indicated in this representation. The model may be interpreted as implying that without vision and the development of visual abilities children will not learn effectively, but evidence provided by the many children who have been blind from birth clearly indicates that this implication is not correct. Getman is well aware of this but intends the visuomotor model to represent the path of learning that is followed by the majority of children in the highly visually oriented schools of our nation.

Getman provided activities and exercises that are designed to promote the development of each of the stages outlined in his visuomotor model. These are primarily *readiness to learn* activities and are more applicable with younger children; among the more widely recognized of these programs is the *Developing Learning Readiness* program (Getman and others, 1968). Many of the activities outlined in this and other Getman programs are quite similar to those of Kephart and other perceptual-motor authorities.

RAYMOND H. BARSCH

Ray Barsch is regularly, and properly, mentioned in most historical accounts of the development of perceptual-motor approaches. He developed many of his ideas regarding perceptual-motor training, space, and movement and their interrelated implications for education while serving as Director of the Teacher Preparation Program for Teachers of the Physically Handicapped and Neurologically Impaired at the University of Wisconsin. During this same period he was supervising development of a special experimental curriculum for learning disabled children in the Madison Public Schools. To this university position he brought experience gained in some 15 years as the director of an Easter Seal Child Development Center.

Movigenics (a combination of two Latin words, *movere*, meaning to move, and *genesis*, meaning origin and development) is the name that Barsch has given to his theory of movement and its relation to learning. Barsch believes that movigenics "is, above all, a theory for education" (1967). Without question, his is a perceptual-motor theory, and his credits to Getman tell at least part of the story of the origin of his theoretical framework. The *movigenic theory* is based on ten constructs, which go a long way in explaining the theory. These theoretical constructs lead to certain practical instructional guidelines, which may be implemented (in most cases) in the regular classroom if the teacher understands the basic movigenic concept.

Ten curriculum guidelines

1. The teacher should record each child's movement patterns in terms of efficient/inefficient. Orientation must be to efficiency/inefficiency rather than to successful/failing. Efficient foundations are essential as a base for more efficient performance in more complicated behavior.

2. The teacher must judge the degree to which the child is becoming a more complex organism as a result of his learning. This judgment must not be limited to only reading, spelling, and so forth.

3. Educational activities must provide ample opportunity to explore muscular relationships, balance, and body relationships and to relate these to both space and time.

4. All six perceptual modes must be exercised within the school framework. Teachers should beware of assuming that the learner is efficient in all areas of modal processing.

5. Opportunities to explore and process information from sources in near, mid, and far space should be deliberately and systematically provided.

6. After a task apparently has been "learned," the learner should be provided with opportunities to perform this task in a variety of settings and contexts. He should learn to do it more slowly, more rapidly, forward and backward, and so on to make certain he has really learned it.

7. Each learner must discover and develop the limitations of his own movement efficiency. The teacher must establish conditions in which this is possible.

8. Movement must be cognitively directed. The learner must develop the ability to plan movement to achieve his goals.

9. All performance can be considered as spatially oriented and can and should be spatially defined.

10. The space-oriented approach can be integrated with most existing practices and activities. It is a matter of achieving spatial emphasis within the existing framework.

Conclusion

Raymond Barsch developed a conceptualization, which he calls movigenics, of how he believes students most effectively learn (and thus how they should be taught). His theoretical model is somewhat different from Kephart's and Getman's but is much more similar than different. He too believes that the visual mode is highly important, and his basic concern is that excellent perceptual-motor abilities be developed, but his vehicle for arriving at this goal is movigenics, a space-oriented theory of learning.

The purpose of his theory is to develop better capability in the total motor-movement area of life, something he describes as "movement efficiency." Barsch's guidelines for teachers make good common sense. They sound somewhat different from those of Kephart and Getman, but in the last analysis the outcome in terms of actual classroom activities is not much different from that of other perceptual-motor authors.

BRYANT J. CRATTY

Bryant Cratty became involved in the area of perceptual-motor learning in a somewhat different way than Kephart, Getman, and Barsch and brings a different point of view to educational efforts in this area. He is well known in two fields, physical education and sensory motor learning. Cratty is a professor of kinesiology and director of the Perceptual Motor Learning Laboratory at the University of California at Los Angeles. He is an unusually prolific writer (more so than the previously mentioned authorities), with some 50 books to his credit.

Cratty believes that "movement games may help the child with learning problems, may aid the active normal child to learn better, and may improve the academic progress of the culturally deprived and retarded child" (1971). In his writing and speaking, he notes that inability to play games well (including unsuccessful athletic participation of older children) may lead to lowered social acceptance by peers, lowered self-concept, and thus reduced academic performance. This may be particularly true with boys. Cratty also notes that hand-eye coordination is essential to writing and that general coordination appears to be important in a number of academic tasks.

Many of the physical activities suggested by Cratty are similar to those supported by other perceptual-motor authorities, and his theoretical bases are similar, but his educational suggestions that are most likely to be used by a classroom teacher are those that involve games or game-related activities that may improve learning. Cratty has conducted and directed a wide variety of research in the perceptual motor area, and the following are some of the conclusions that may be derived from his efforts:

1. There are optimum levels of alertness or arousal for efficient performance of a given task. Simple tasks appear to require higher levels of arousal; more complex tasks require less tension or arousal.
2. Excessive tension, which may inhibit good performance, may be reduced through physical activities. There is some indication that moderate exercise is usually best to reduce tension and promote optimum potential for mental activities.
3. A wide variety of games or game-related activities may be used to directly stimulate learning in the areas of reading and language.
4. Success in athletic activities or endeavors may often contribute to success in cognitive areas through enhancement of ego and a type of "success syndrome."
5. Concentration on motor tasks (which may be more interesting and thus receive more motivated effort from the student) may help develop an attitude or ability to concentrate in students who are easily distracted. This attitude or ability may then be carried over into academic areas.
6. Gross movement may be used as a learning modality. The following examples may illustrate this principle.

Examples of gross movement as a learning modality*

Playground markings have been (used) . . . to enhance serial memory ability, pattern recognition, spelling, and number manipulations. For example, grids six feet by six feet have been painted, containing squares one foot by one foot. Within the squares in some of these grids have been placed letters, while others contain numbers. Thus a child, by jumping or hopping from square to square, can not only improve the components of agility contained in the activity itself but also through gross movement can improve his spelling and numerical abilities.

Other markings involve a series of lines, squares, and zigzags which not only present the children the opportunity to practice the perceptual-motor attributes necessary to negotiate the lines, squares, etc., but are intended to improve their ability to order a series of events correctly. The extent to which the child can accomplish remembering one, two, or more things in a series is also made quite apparent to the observing teacher. For if a child cannot remember a series of two or three movements chained together, how can he be expected to spell a three-letter word in which letters must be remembered and placed in correct order?

Pattern-recognition practice on the part of immature and atypical children has been encouraged through the use of triangles, rectangles, and half-circles placed on playgrounds in addition to the

*From Cratty, B. *Perceptual-motor behavior and educational processes.* Springfield, Ill.: Charles C Thomas, Publisher, 1969.

traditional squares and circles usually found there. Teachers working with children on shape recognition, using tactile and visual modalities within the classroom, then take them to the playground where the children attempt to discover similar shapes, name them, play on them, in them, and around them in various ways. This type of transfer must be taught, rather than being expected to occur incidentally. In any case it appears that this is another important way in which gross motor activities can contribute to basic concepts helpful in the formation of basic perceptions underlying letter recognition, word recognition, and reading.

Conclusion

Cratty has been and continues to be an important, positive force in the perceptual-motor arena. He may have somewhat greater personal recognition in the field of physical education, and his contributions to efforts on behalf of the learning disabled come from the interrelated nature of physical/motor activities and cognitive learning. Cratty has often noted that we may expect too much from perceptual-motor exercises and activities and has suggested that, although motor activities can be of concrete value in the schools, we must "carefully examine research findings rather than simply paying blind devotion to one of the popular 'movement messiahs'" (1969). Cratty's apparent objectivity regarding the potential value of perceptual-motor activities has led to genuine credibility, and his suggested learning activities have been used with apparent success by many classroom teachers.

A. JEAN AYRES

Jean Ayres, like Bryant Cratty, represents a significantly different background and orientation from Kephart, Getman, and Barsch. Ayres became involved with learning disabilities through efforts in the area of sensory integration related to her basic professional field of occupational therapy. Occupational therapists remain among her strongest advocates, but she has provided insights that are of value to educators of the learning disabled, and she definitely fits into the perceptual-motor framework. Ayres' text, *Sensory Integration and Learning Disorders* (1972), provides a description of her model of sensory integrative processes and is necessary for those who use her tests. Ayres developed over a number of years a series of tests, which are now called the *Southern California Sensory Integration Tests* (SCSIT). She suggests the use of this battery of 17 tests to provide a starting point for clinical evaluation of sensory integrative skills and abilities. A description of the SCSIT follows.

The Southern California Sensory Integration Tests (SCSIT)

Space visualization: utilizes form boards to determine visual perception of form and space and ability to mentally manipulate objects in space

Figure-ground perception: involves use of stimulus figures, superimposed and imbedded so as to determine ability to distinguish foreground from background

Position in space: utilizes various simple geometric forms to determine ability to recognize such forms in different positions and orientations

Design copying: the child must duplicate a design on a dot grid

Motor accuracy: involves drawing a line over an existing (printed) line; the motor coordination component is the major concern in this task

Kinesthesia: the child must place his finger on a point at which his finger previously had been placed (by the examiner) with vision occluded

Manual form perception: requires matching the visual counterpart of a geometric form held in the hand

Finger identification: involves ability to identify (point to) the finger on his hand that was touched by the examiner while the child was not watching

Graphesthesia: the child must draw a design on the back of his hand, copying a design drawn on the back of his hand by the examiner

Localization of tactile stimuli: the child must touch, with his finger, a spot on his hand or arm that was previously touched by the examiner

Double tactile stimuli perception: the child is touched simultaneously on either (or both) the cheek and the hand; he must identify where he was touched

Imitation of postures: the child imitates positions or postures assumed by the examiner

Crossing the midline of the body: the child imitates the examiner in pointing to one of the examiner's eyes or ears

Bilateral motor coordination: involves use of and interaction between both upper extremities

Right-left discrimination: the child must discriminate right from left: (1) on himself, (2) on the examiner, and (3) relative to an object (This test is the only part of the SCSIT that requires verbal responses.)

Standing balance, eyes open: indicates ability to balance on one foot with eyes open

Standing balance, eyes closed: indicates ability to balance on one foot with eyes closed

In addition to the above standardized measures, Ayres recommends structured observations to assess the possibility of poor sensory integration.

Poorly integrated tonic neck and tonic labyrinthine reflexes are considered to be of prime importance. These two, abbreviated TNR and TLR, may be observed in a variety of settings. The purpose of such observation and evaluation is to determine the degree to which these reflexes have been integrated into the nervous system. Ayres provides extensive remedial/developmental suggestions for use with children in whom TNR or TLR are poorly developed for age and general developmental level.

Other indications of sensory integrative dysfunction may be obtained from structured observations of: (1) capacity to simultaneously contract antagonistic muscles, (2) general muscle tone, (3) control of extraocular muscles, (4) integration of functions of the two sides of the body, and so forth. Although the SCSIT includes standardized measures that provide information pertinent to several of these functions or abilities, structured observation provides more complete information.

In the preface to Ayres' 1972 text, she notes that she is presenting a neurobehavioral theory and that this theory should be considered a guide for action, *not* established fact. She further notes that continued brain research will undoubtedly lead to required change in her hypotheses and thus may require modifications in her recommended therapy. Her frame of reference may perhaps be best explained in her own words:

> A sensory integrative approach to treating learning disorders differs from many other procedures in that it does not teach specific skills such as matching visual stimuli, learning to remember a sequence of sounds, differentiating one sound from another, drawing lines from one point to another, or even the basic academic material. Rather, the objective is to enhance the brain's ability to learn how to do these things. If the brain develops the *capacity* to perceive, remember, and motor plan, the ability can then be applied toward mastery of all academic and other tasks, regardless of the specific content. The objective is modification of the neurological dysfunction interfering with learning rather than attacking the symptoms of that dysfunction.
>
> This type of therapy—therapy being defined as any intervention with an intent to remediate given by educator, psychologist, speech pathologist, physical or occupational therapist, or other professional person—does not necessarily eliminate the

need for the more symptomatic approach. Therapy is considered a supplement, not a substitute, to formal classroom instruction or tutoring. It reduces the severity of the difficulty and allows specifics, such as the sum of two and two or reading the word 'cat,' to be learned more rapidly.

It is not claimed that sensory integrative therapy eliminates the underlying causes of inadequate neural organization and resultant learning disorder. Rather this therapy is seen as mitigating some of the conditions, usually arising from unknown causes, that directly interfere with learning. It is supposed that normalizing these conditions through therapy comes closer to altering the underlying neurological dysfunction (regardless of cause) than do typical academic procedures. Only some and not all of the different types of neurological dysfunction are thought to be influenced by this therapeutic approach.*

Ayres' recommendations for remediation (she calls it intervention) include suggestions in areas that are generally similar to those included by Kephart and Getman but, in addition, note an area that is not emphasized by some of the other perceptual-motor authorities. This area has implications outside of the usually prescribed limits of learning disabilities, in that it may be exhibited by a student who is learning relatively well. This area is *tactile defensiveness* and may be misinterpreted by teachers and other students as lack of acceptance, thus leading to a degree of social isolation.

Ayres believes that the child who exhibits tactile defensiveness actually experiences stimuli in a different manner than the child with normal neurological integration. This may lead to unusual reactions when faced with any testing situation (such as in Ayres' SCSIT) that involves localization of tactile stimuli. Ayres suggests particular care when testing children with behavior problems or those with unusual levels of general hyperactivity. Such children may interpret many tactile signals as signs of danger and react as anyone might be expected to react to danger signals. It may be even more important for the classroom teacher to carefully consider this type of reaction when dealing with such children. Whereas many children respond positively to a friendly touch on the arm or shoulder as a part of a total attempt to encourage or congratulate for work accomplished, the tactilely defensive child may have the opposite reaction. Ayres provides some suggestions for remediation of this problem but notes that the evidence is not conclusive as to when, how, and with whom to apply such remediation. Tactile defensiveness is just one of several syndromes outlined by Ayres that are of potentially great importance to teachers, especially to teachers of the learning disabled.

Conclusion

Ayres represents a different background and orientation than most other perceptual-motor authorities and has provided a number of thought-provoking hypotheses about sensory integration and its relationship to learning disorders. She usually refers to "therapy," which may tend to make some teachers wonder if her recommendations are appropriate for them. Ayres' major target (the presumed audience for much of her writing) has been the therapist, not the teacher, but many of her ideas have considerable potential value for the learning disabilities teacher. In more clinical settings, Ayres is often the most highly recognized of the perceptual-motor authorities, and her efforts and ideas should be carefully considered by all who teach learning disabled students.

---

*From Ayres, J. *Sensory integration and learning disorders* (p. 2). Reprinted by Permission © 1972, 1973. Western Psychological Services.

MARIANNE FROSTIG

It is somewhat difficult to categorize Marianne Frostig in an overview of learning disabilities; however, Hallahan and Cruickshank (1973) considered her contributions along with the perceptual-motor theorists in their text, which addressed the historical foundations of learning disabilities. We will accept their judgment on the matter and consider her here.

Dr. Frostig founded, and is presently Executive Director Emeritus of, the Marianne Frostig Center of Educational Therapy in Los Angeles, California. She has written a number of books, tests, and various training materials and has long been recognized for her efforts on behalf of children with learning problems. She entered the field that was to become learning disabilities through early contact with brain-damaged children in a hospital setting at the University of Vienna. Frostig identified with the children with whom she was working (she was only 18 at the time) and decided then and there that her task in life would be to assist such children (Frostig, 1978).

Frostig had a recognized test of visual perceptual abilities developed and in use *before* the field of learning disabilities began to really take shape in the early 1960s. This test, the Developmental Test of Visual Perception (DTVP), is so totally associated with Dr. Frostig that it is seldom called anything other than "the Frostig." Partly because this test was one of the few available at that time, it was overused and used to the exclusion of other measures and observational techniques. As a result it was maligned by some, without properly considering that it may have been the people using (or misusing) the test, not the test, that was at fault. The DTVP is of value if properly used and should be considered as one measure (among many) that may provide information of significant value. The following section includes a discussion of the DTVP and a further look into other contributions of Marianne Frostig.

Developmental Test of Visual Perception and related remediation

The Frostig DTVP was originally published in 1961 and has been revised twice. It may be administered to groups by a classroom teacher after minimal instruction and takes less than an hour to give. Five subtests measure visual perceptual skills in five areas, all of which are recognized by a number of authorities in the field. Frostig indicates that she included these particular skills, or abilities, because: (1) they are necessary to success in academics, (2) they are more general in their applicability to the total organism than many other functions (such as color vision), (3) they are, or should be, developed early in life, (4) they are frequent problems in children who are neurologically impaired, (5) they are skills that may be assessed in the group setting, and (6) they are a practical target area—that is, training in these particular visual perceptual skills is often successful.

These five areas, which are the five subtests of the DTVP, are: (1) eye-motor coordination, (2) figure-ground, (3) form constancy, (4) position in space, and (5) spatial relations.

The type of skill, as measured by the DTVP, and the importance of that skill, as viewed by Frostig, may be summarized as follows.

Eye-motor coordination is the ability to integrate body movements and visual skill. In this test the child must draw lines between boundaries that become increasingly narrow. This includes drawing lines between pairs of parallel straight lines, then between pairs of parallel curved lines. The ability to draw a line from one dot to another is also included. This skill is believed to be an important prerequisite to reading, and the child without this ability cannot write.

Figure-ground is the ability to distinguish the figure (the center of attention) from the ground (the other, less important background stimuli). In this subtest the child must select and outline with a colored pencil a specific figure that is intersected by a number of other figures. Also included are tasks involving the discovery of hidden figures. Several investigators have demonstrated the generally accepted belief that this figure-ground capability is important to reading ability.

Form constancy is the ability to recognize any figure, regardless of its size, position, or texture, such as always recognizing a square as a square. In this test the child must outline squares and circles, regardless of their size and textural quality, on a page that contains a variety of geometric forms. It is important that he recognize all the squares and that he not interpret nonsquares as squares. Word recognition out of familiar context (in different size print or in a different setting) is essential to reading success.

Position in space is the ability to recognize a particular form in any position. This test requires the child to differentiate (mark as the same or different) a series of reversed or rotated figures from some that are similar but different. Position in space a particularly important in recognition of language symbols that differ only in that they are the reverse of one another. Examples are the letters *b* and *d*.

Spatial relations is the ability to recognize the position of objects in relation to one another and to the observer. In this test the child must duplicate patterns by connecting a group of dots to match a given figure. This test has three levels of complexity, the last being reserved for administration to children in or beyond the first grade. Spatial relation adequacy is necessary if a child is to recognize the sequence of letters in a word or of words in a sentence.

The DTVP has been outlined here because it is, in a number of ways, similar to other tests that purport to measure certain basic perceptual skills. Because of Frostig's interest in visual perceptual problems, there is considerable emphasis at the Frostig Center on research efforts in this arena, but children served at the center include those with no visual perceptual problems and thus no emphasis on DTVP-related remediation. The Center is a complete diagnostic facility with psychiatric, psychotherapeutic, and counseling functions. It also has individuals who are engaged in behavioristic efforts, obviously the opposite of many psychiatric emphases. It is a total program, emphasizing the needs of the child, not a particular philosophical bias.

Frostig has written a number of texts that deserve mention. In one, a brief paperback entitled *Selection and Adaptation of Reading Methods* (see References and Suggested Readings at the end of this chapter), Frostig lists apparent reading difficulties, possible underlying deficits, evaluative methods, and suggested remedial methods. This information, presented in chart form, may be of concrete assistance to the teacher. In the second section of this paperback, Frostig provides a description of 18 methods or techniques necessary to understand the material on the chart in the first part. This is not intended to provide a teacher or prospective teacher with all they must know to remediate learning difficulties in reading, but it may be a valuable guide for many.

A second, more comprehensive text, *Learning Problems in the Classroom: Prevention and Remediation* (1973), was coauthored with Phyllis Maslow. This text, like Frostig's other efforts, has a practical orientation but does include a discussion of the implications of behaviorism, humanism, the cognitive-developmental point of view and psychoanalytical theory, as applied to education. Chapters relating to child development, evaluative approaches, auditory perception, and language development lend themselves to classroom application and effectively demonstrate that Frostig is not totally visual-perceptual in orientation. This text also includes chapters on topics more often associated with Frostig—movement education and visual-perceptual abilities, plus a valuable chapter on problems in beginning mathematics.

Conclusion

Dr. Frostig is an important pioneer in the field of learning disabilities who has contributed through a wide variety of activities that have taken place over the years at the Marianne Frostig Center of Educational Therapy. She has also contributed through various books and written programs that provide educational guidance for teachers of students with learning disabilities. For young children whose difficulties relate to the visual-perceptual areas tapped by the DTVP the test and the training program that accompanies it may be of real value. Other children have benefitted, as suggestions provided by Frostig have assisted teachers to help children in areas other than visual perception. Though more often associated with visual-perceptual efforts, Frostig believes in diagnosis in all areas of potential disability and the use of methods that fit the identified needs of the student.

CARL DELACATO

Delacato, along with Glen Doman, developed an approach for use with neurologically handicapped children, which has been regularly in and out of popular news reports for years. At the Institutes for the Development of Human Potential in Philadelphia, and to a more limited extent through "satellite" centers in other parts of the nation, they have used perceptual-motor related procedures to attempt to improve the performance of mentally retarded and learning disabled students.

Delacato views his system as a neuropsychological approach to the development of language; his basic concept is called the neurological organization concept. Delacato's original treatment of this topic was in a statement made in *The Treatment and Prevention of Reading Problems* (1959). In this statement, Delacato defined neurological organization as "that physiologically optimum condition which exists uniquely and most completely in man and is the result of a total and uninterrupted ontogenetic neural development. This development recapitulates the phylogenetic neural development of man, begins during the first trimester of gestation and ends at about 6½ years of age in normal humans" (1959 p. 19). This statement further indicates Delacato's position as to how the neurological system develops, how either the left or right cortical hemisphere must become dominant, and how, if a higher level of development is nonfunctional or incomplete, lower levels become operative and dominant.

An important aspect of his theory is that a basic difference between man and lower animals exists because "man has achieved cortical dominance wherein one side of the cortex controls the skills in which man outdistances lower forms of animals" (Delacato, 1959 p. 21). If there is some obstruction to this development, communication and language problems result.

Based on this neurological organization theory, Delacato believes that, if an individual does not develop normally (as outlined in this theory), a communication or mobility problem will result. This individual should then be evaluated in a search for missing or incomplete areas of organization. Then, by passively imposing this organization on the nervous system of those with mobility problems and by teaching it to those with speech or reading problems, the problems may be overcome.

Delacato believes that we have tended to treat *symptoms* rather than *causes* of problems. He believes that he can treat causes by directly treating the brain. Delacato started by treating mainly those with brain injuries and has supported the value of his methods for preventive purposes in regular classes.

Ontogeny recapitulates phylogeny

Delacato's theoretical position is based on the belief that ontogeny recapitulates phylogeny—that the individual organism repeats the pattern of development of the species. This is a concept based to a considerable extent on the work of Dr. Temple Fay, a well-known neurologist with whom Delacato worked. Delacato also mentions men such as Orton, Gesell, and Getman in reviewing the background for this theory.

To understand Delacato, we must understand how he views and applies this "ontogeny recapitulates phylogeny" concept. He believes that, phylogenetically, neurological organization has developed in the following manner.

Up to the level of the first vertebrate, there is limited specialization of neurological function. Vertebrates of the lowest form live in water and move by undulating the spine or by vertically moving the fins. These movements are controlled through the spinal cord, and the medulla oblongata is the functional neural area.

Amphibians are in the next highest level, or class, of vertebrates. They spend part of their lives on land and part in water. To achieve this transition from water to land-and-water existence, amphibians underwent many changes from the lower vertebrate form, all of which required a more specialized neurological system. At this level the pons and the midbrain both developed into functioning organs. Amphibians, when moving in the water, move in a homolateral pattern, that is, they push with the foreleg and hindleg on one side of the body, then with the foreleg and hindleg on the other side. This homolateral movement is dictated by the pons. But when they move on the land, they raise their bodies from the ground and move with cross-pattern movements. They move the right foreleg and left hindleg simultaneously, then move the left foreleg and right hindleg simultaneously. These alternating, cross-pattern movements are dictated and controlled by the level of the neurological system above the pons, the midbrain. (Surgical removal of these parts of the amphibian brain appears to confirm this.)

The next major level of evolutionary development includes reptiles. These are the first true land animals, and they have a relatively large midbrain. They always move in a cross pattern.

Mammals are next on the developmental ladder. They have a larger brain cortex, their walk is cross pattern, and the highest form is the primates. Cortical development in the lower primates is greater than in lower mammals, but several basic factors that differentiate the highest primate, man, are missing. The mammals, even the higher primates, do not develop single-handedness or language until the human level.

The preceding is an oversimplification of the concept of phylogenetic development of the brain but will suffice for purposes of this discussion. The suggestion is that man, in his embryonic and fetal development, goes through these evolutionary stages, following the phylogenetic pattern of the species. The newborn infant already has developed to a point where the medulla is in control, having developed above the spinal cord stage before birth. From that point on the normal child develops so that at 4 to 5 months of age, he is at the pons level of development (the amphibian level—homolateral crawling). By 10 months of age, the midbrain has developed sufficiently to permit cross-pattern creeping (as in the reptile). By approximately 1 year of age, crude walking will take place (as in the lower primate). Delacato believes that, if neurological development is normal, by 7 to 8 years of age the child has completed the major steps of neurological development and has cross-pattern walk and a dominant eye, foot, and hand. He can read and write or at least has the capability to read and write.

Delacato also postulates that as man evolved, starting approximately 1 million years ago, he began to develop handedness. Next (250,000 years ago) came development of sidedness sufficient to organize his brain into a dominant (language) and a nondominant hemisphere. As a result, he developed speech. Then 25,000 years ago man began to use tools and began to develop cortical hemispheric dominance. The right or left eye gained dominance for distance vision. As man began to draw, he began to use his near-point vision, which resulted in a dominant eye for near points.

Therefore the establishment of handedness, which started development toward cortical hemispheric dominance, led to eyedness, which reinforced dominance and promoted organization.

At this stage, man developed music. Delacato notes here that speech is controlled in the dominant cortical hemisphere, tonal qualities in the subdominant. This tonal quality development was one more step toward the potential ability to read through differentiation. The hemispheric organization into dominant and subdominant was aided by this differentiation into separate speech and tonal hemispheres.

Then, in the next 20,000 years, sufficient drawing, singing, and evolving speech developed enough cortical hemispheric dominance to lead to written language.

Delacato believes this long, slow process was the only way to reach neurological readiness to read. If any step had been missed, we would not be reading at the present time. The point is that cortical hemispheric dominance could not be developed until there was sufficient lower-level neurological organization on which it could be based. Throughout his discussion the focus is on functional, not anatomical, levels of the central nervous system.

If ontogeny recapitulates phylogeny, then the development of the neurological system in each human being is a recapitulation of the phylogenetic development just reviewed. This means that the final stage—cortical hemispheric dominance—in any individual cannot be established until each of the preceding stages has been completed. In brief, this means that the "process of development of readiness to read begins at birth at the level of spinal cord and medulla. It goes on to the level of pons, which functions in an alternating one-sidedness, to the level of midbrain, which provides two-sidedness, and to the level of cortex and the development of complete cortical hemispheric dominance. This continuum forms the basis of human perceptual abilities" (Delacato, 1966, p. 17). The implications are obvious. Children must achieve full development at each level, and no level can be skipped. Neurological organization is a continuum, with cortical hemispheric dominance being the end result, dependent on proper completion of all steps at a lower level. Language problems, including those in reading, are the result of incompleteness or otherwise inadequate neurological organization. Diagnosis of a reading problem therefore becomes diagnosis of a problem in neurological organization.

Diagnosis, for Delacato, involves the question "What is the child's present level of neurological organization?" In the diagnostic procedure one ordinarily begins at the cortical hemispheric dominance level and moves successively lower to the lower cortex, the midbrain, and then to the pons. Delacato has very specific procedures for completing this diagnosis, although, as indicated in a statement by various parent and professional organizations, noted later in this description, there are serious misgivings as to whether his diagnostic methods really accomplish what he says they do.

Treatment in the Delacato model assumes that experience affects the brain and that specific types of experience will affect specific levels of the brain. Therefore this is a *treatment of the brain,* not a *treatment of the symptoms,* program. Delacato also stresses that "treatment procedures are synonymous with prevention procedures" (1963, p. 102), so that the treatment he prescribes can also be considered as effective for preventive purposes.

Concerns about the Delacato approach

Delacato and the Doman-Delacato prescribed methods have likely stirred more heated controversy among parent and professional groups than all of the other perceptual-motor advocates mentioned in this chapter. Whereas most of the others discussed here have received a variety of honors and commendations from one or more of these groups, none has received the kind of attention that Doman and Delacato received in 1968.

After years of debate within various organizations, in 1968 a group of prestigious professional groups, joined by equally well-known parent groups, adopted a jointly supported official statement about "the Doman-Delacato Treatment of Neurologically Handicapped Children."* The statement indicated specific concern about: (1) promotional methods, (2) effect on other family members, (3) restrictions on age-appropriate activities, (4) lack of validity of diagnostic methods, (5) undocumented claims for cures, and (6) undocumented indictments of various accepted child-rearing practices.

Conclusion

Delacato, along with Doman, developed a method that is designed to treat disabled children through directly treating the brain. Although Delacato and Doman continue to have strong supporters, they have received more nationally documented negative comment than any other perceptual-motor advocates and, for that matter, any other learning disabilities authorities. It seems that any method that is subject to such severe criticism should be carefully examined to attempt to discover any genuine strengths that may be more fully utilized and any weaknesses that must be avoided. Unfortunately, after years of efforts to achieve an outside appraisal of the Doman-Delacato theoretical construct and its related practices and procedures, the Institutes for the Development of Human Potential withdrew at the last moment from a well-designed, comprehensive study, supported by federal and private agencies (Hallahan and Cruickshank, 1973). This withdrawal led to additional questions from those who desired truly objective information about this controversial approach.

*Endorsing this official statement were the American Academy for Cerebral Palsy, American Academy of Physical Medicine and Rehabilitation, American Congress of Rehabilitation Medicine, Canadian Association for Children with Learning Disabilities, Canadian Association for Retarded Children, Canadian Rehabilitation Council for the Disabled, and National Association for Retarded Children. Other groups, such as the American Academy of Neurology and the American Academy of Pediatrics, had issued earlier, cautionary statements (Hallahan and Cruickshank, 1973).

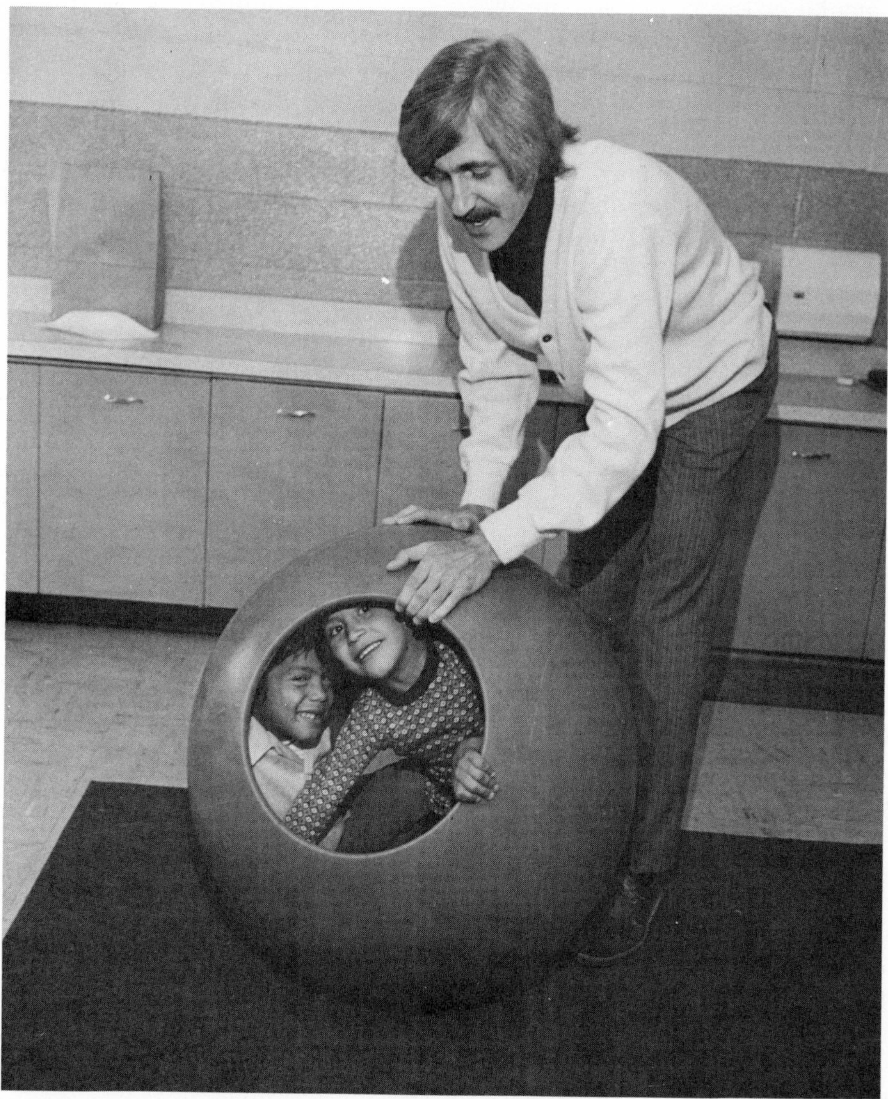

The degree to which gross motor abilities may be improved through this type of activity depends on the individual student and the degree of motor underdevelopment. However, one thing seems certain—the interpersonal relationship between these boys and the teacher will be considerably enhanced, and, as a result, greater learning may take place.

SUMMARY

Perceptual-motor approaches are those that are based on the belief that, for the most part, higher level mental processes develop out of, and after, adequate, integrated development of the motor system and the perceptual system. For most perceptual-motor authorities, this means that poorly developed perceptual-motor abilities may be part of the cause for learning disabilities and that training programs should relate to such poorly developed abilities.

Pioneers in the development of perceptual-motor programs began their work with brain-injured individuals, and other, later proponents have based much of their efforts on the work of these early authorities. One criticism of perceptual-motor approaches relates to the fact that many learning disabled students are not brain-injured (or are not known to be), and methods developed for the brain-injured are not necessarily appropriate for many other learning disabled students. Another major criticism is that there is little research indicating a direct relationship between perceptual-motor training and improvement in academic performance. On the other hand, the developmental conceptualizations of the perceptual-motor authorities are very similar to those of leading developmental psychologists, and there seems to be face validity to the idea that, for example, ability to differentiate between various visual symbols and to move the eyes across the page from left to right are important prerequisites to reading.

This chapter has included some of the basic ideas of Kephart, Getman, Barsch, Cratty, Ayres, Frostig, and Delacato, noting the similarity between certain of these individuals' efforts and also some significant differences. Perceptual-motor approaches were considered first in this section on methods or approaches, for they were among the first to be associated with the concept of learning disabilities. On the other hand, as noted above, the early perceptual-motor authorities were also "brain injury" authorities—that is, the children with whom they worked were often recognized as brain injured. With this in mind, we shall proceed to Chapter 5, which reviews approaches to use with hyperactive or hyperkinetic students, including those who are considered to be brain injured.

REFERENCES AND SUGGESTED READINGS

Ayres, J. Characteristics of types of sensory integrative dysfunction, *The American Journal of Occupational Therapy*, 1971, *25*, 329-334.

Ayres, J. Improving academic scores through sensory integration, *Journal of Learning Disabilities*, 1972, *5*, 338-343.

Ayres, J. *Sensory integration and learning disorders.* Los Angeles: Western Psychological Services, 1972.

Barsch, R. *Achieving perceptual-motor efficiency.* Seattle: Special Child Publications, 1967.

Barsch, R. *A Movigenic curriculum: bulletin no. 25.* Madison, Wis.: State Department of Public Instruction, 1965.

Barsch, R. Teacher needs—motor training. In Cruickshank, W. (Ed.) *The teacher of brain-injured children.* Syracuse, N.Y.: Syracuse University Press, 1966.

Bush, W., and Giles, M. *Aids to psycholinguistic teaching.* Columbus, Ohio: Charles E. Merrill Publishing Co., 1969.

Chaney, C., and Kephart, N. *Motoric aids to perceptual training.* Columbus, Ohio: Charles E. Merrill Publishing Co., 1968.

Cratty, B. *Active learning: games to enhance academic abilities.* Englewood Cliffs, N.J.: Prentice-Hall, Inc., 1971.

Cratty, B. *Developmental sequences of perceptual-motor tasks.* Freeport, N.Y.: Educational Activities, 1967.

Cratty, B. *Movement behavior and motor learning.* Philadelphia: Lea & Febiger, 1967.

Cratty, B. *Perceptual-motor behavior and educational processes.* Springfield, Ill.: Charles C Thomas, Publisher, 1969.

Cratty, B. *Psychology and physical activity.* Englewood Cliffs, N.J.: Prentice-Hall, Inc., 1968.

Cratty, B. *Social dimensions of physical activity.* Englewood Cliffs, N.J.: Prentice-Hall, Inc., 1968.

Cratty, B., and others. *Movement activities, motor ability, and the education of children.* Springfield, Ill.: Charles C Thomas, Publisher, 1970.

Delacato, C. *The diagnosis and treatment of speech and*

reading problems. Springfield, Ill.: Charles C Thomas, Publisher, 1963.

Delacato, C. *Neurological organization and reading.* Springfield, Ill.: Charles C Thomas, Publisher, 1966.

Delacato, C. *Treatment and prevention of reading problems.* Springfield, Ill.: Charles C Thomas, Publisher, 1959.

Ebersole, M., Kephart, M., and Ebersole, J. *Steps to achievement for the slow learner.* Columbus, Ohio: Charles E. Merrill Publishing Co., 1968.

Frostig, M. Five questions regarding my past and future and the past, present, and future of learning disabilities, *Journal of Learning Disabilities,* 1978, *2*(9), 536-539.

Frostig, M. *Frostig Developmental Test of Visual Perception.* Palo Alto, Calif.: Consulting Psychologists Press, 1963.

Frostig, M. *Movement education: theory and practice.* Chicago: Follett Publishing Co., 1970.

Frostig, M. *Selection and adaptation of reading methods.* San Rafael, Calif.: Academic Therapy Publications, 1973.

Frostig, M., and Horne, D. *The Frostig program for the development of visual perception: teacher's guide.* Chicago: Follett Publishing Co., 1964.

Frostig, M., and Horne, D. Marianne Frostig Center of Education Therapy. In Jones, M. (Ed.) *Special education programs: within the United States.* Springfield, Ill.: Charles C Thomas, Publisher, 1968.

Frostig, M., Lefever, D., and Whattlesey, J. *The Marianne Frostig Developmental Test of Visual Perception.* Palo Alto, Calif.: Consulting Psychologists Press, 1964.

Frostig, M., and Maslow, P. *Learning problems in the classroom: prevention and remediation.* New York: Grune and Stratton, Inc., 1973.

Getman, G. *Instructor's guide: pathway school program.* Boston: Teaching Resources Corp., 1968.

Getman, G. The visuomotor complex in the acquisition of learning skills. In Hellmuth, J. (Ed.) *Learning disorders* (vol. 1), Seattle: Special Child Publications, 1965.

Getman, G., and others. *Developing learning readiness* (teacher's manual). St. Louis: Webster Division, McGraw-Hill Book Co., 1968.

Getman, G., and Hendrickson, H. The needs of teachers for specialized information on the development of visuomotor skills in relation to academic performance. In Cruickshank, W. (Ed.) *The teacher of brain-injured children.* Syracuse, N.Y.: Syracuse University Press, 1966.

Getman, G., and Kane, E. *The physiology of readiness.* Minneapolis: Programs to Accelerate School Success, 1964.

Hallahan, D., and Cruickshank, W. *Psycho-educational foundations of learning disabilities.* Englewood Cliffs, N.J.: Prentice-Hall, Inc., 1973.

Hatton, D., Pizzat, F., and Pelkowski, J. *Erie Program for perceptual-motor exercises.* Boston: Teaching Resources Corp., 1969.

Hayden, A., and others. *Mainstreaming preschoolers: children with learning disabilities,* Washington, D.C., 1978, U.S. Department of Health, Education, and Welfare.

Hebb, D. *The organization of behavior.* New York: John Wiley & Sons, Inc., 1949.

Kephart, N. *The brain-injured child.* Chicago: National Society for Crippled Children and Adults, 1963.

Kephart, N. *The slow learner in the classroom* (rev. ed.). Columbus, Ohio: Charles E. Merrill Publishing Co., 1971.

Lerner, J. *Children with learning disabilities.* New York: Houghton-Mifflin, 1976.

Roach, E., and Kephart, N. *The Purdue perceptual-motor survey.* Columbus, Ohio: Charles E. Merrill Publishing Co., 1966.

Strauss, A., and Kephart, N. *Psychopathology and education of the brain-injured child. Volume 2, Progress in theory and clinic.* New York: Grune & Stratton, Inc., 1955.

Valett, R. *Developing cognitive abilities: teaching children to think.* St. Louis: The C. V. Mosby Co., 1978.

SLU

chapter 5

Approaches used with hyperactive students

Difficulties in the classroom with the hyperactive or hyperkinetic student are the topic of considerable discussion in both the popular press and professional journals. Some accounts in newspapers and popular news magazines are confusing because of lack of objectivity or actual misinformation. Articles in professional journals vary considerably with respect to the professional specialization or bias of the author.

For example, in a comprehensive article on hyperkinesis by Jan Loney (the written version of a presentation made at the 1979 meeting of the American Orthopsychiatric Association) it is inferred that the first heuristic description of the hyperkinetic impulse disorder of childhood was presented in the mid-1950s (1980). In fact, the references cited by Loney (Lauter, 1956, 1957) were preceded by entire texts about brain-injured children by Strauss and Lehtinen (1947) and by Strauss and Kephart (1955) that systematically described the hyperactive/hyperkinetic syndrome. Other journal articles on the topic date back several decades. Perhaps the reason for this confusion or lack of recognition of obvious references is that members of various disciplines do not always recognize the work of those in other disciplines. This lack of recognition, which may also mean lack of cooperation and retardation of maximum progress, is not the province of any one profession or discipline but afflicts all. In this chapter I will attempt to be aware of this tendency and relate to contributions of disciplines other than education, but the emphasis is on educational difficulties and potential remedial or management techniques that may be implemented by educators. Further information about medical approaches relevant to hyperactivity will be provided in Chapter 8.

DEFINITIONS AND CHARACTERISTICS

Before proceeding further, we will consider definitions of hyperactivity and hyperkinesis. *Hyper* is prefix indicating "more than usual" or "excessive"; *activity* deals with "motion" or "movement"; *kinesis* relates to movement and is used in medicine in relation to muscular action. In other words, hyperactivity is a more general, nonmedical word; hyperkinesis is the term that physicians tend to use in describing children that educators would call hyperactive. In discussions of differences, the point is made by some that hyperkinesis refers to "more purely muscular action" than does hyperactivity. Since any "activity" requires muscular movement, this differentiation seems to be pointless. In an interesting listing of features of the "*hyperkinetic* impulse disorder of childhood," Loney lists *hyperactivity* first (1980). In another interesting usage of these two terms, Rapp, a medical doctor, authored an article entitled "Food Allergy Treatment for *Hyperkinesis*" (1979). She begins by speaking of the relationship between food allergy and *hyperactivity* and refers to hyperactivity throughout the article.

In fact, a diagnosis of hyperactivity *or* hyperkinesis is a matter of clinical judgment. Although there are scales to determine whether hyperactivity actually exists (for example, by Connors, 1969), we have little agreement on which, if any, scales to use. We may only conclude that a diagnosis of hyperactivity or hyperkinesis is subjective and judgmental.

Characteristics of the hyperactive student (as listed by both medical and educational authorities) usually include the following:

Short attention span
Perseveration
Impulsivity
Low frustration tolerance
Visual-motor difficulties (figure-ground reversal, rotation of symbols, and others)
Incoordination
Irritability
Academic difficulties

Both hyperactivity and hyperkinesis are *general* terms, neither of which is precise or specific, and most efforts, educational and medical, have been concerned with the *symptoms*. Most definitions and descriptions have emphasized the extent and type of motor activity or the behavioral, psychological, and social characteristics that are associated with individuals called hyperactive. For educators, the emphasis is on the reduction of socially unacceptable, acting out behavior and improvement in academic learning.

One of the more complete reviews of hyperactivity, provided by an educator, was that by Barbara Keogh in 1971. Although there have been advances in certain types of medical control of hyperactivity since that time and special educators have had more experience with behavior management techniques, her summary discussion remains highly relevant. The comments that follow are based on her review.*

Although quantitative activity level differences between normal and hyperactive children are not as clearly documented as one might expect, it appears that hyperactive children are less able than normal children to modify activity levels and behavior in response to compelling environmental influences. It may be concluded that the *character*, and not just the *amount*, of activity determines which children are called hyperactive. The normal child can respond much more readily to expectations or requirements of the social situation, whereas the hyperactive child tends to continue to exhibit hyperactivity even when it is obviously inappropriate socially and is leading to serious conflict with peers or authority figures. (Keogh notes that some *high*-achieving children may also have high activity levels, but these children are more likely to be called "enthusiastic," "vigorous," or "hard-working.")

It is common to read that hyperactivity is a characteristic of children who are diagnosed as having cerebral dysfunctions, but perceptual problems and other commonly given characteristics such as distractibility and disorganization are not necessarily correlates of hyperactivity. *It can be safely said that all brain-damaged children are not hyperactive and that all hyperactive children are not brain damaged. However, hyperactivity is much more likely in a brain-damaged individual than in the population as a whole.*

*Keogh's summary, entitled "Hyperactivity and Learning Disorders: Review and Speculation" (in the October, 1971, *Exceptional Children*), is extensively documented regarding the statements that will be made here; her list of 80 references will not be repeated.

Both clinical and educational observers report consistently that hyperactive children are unusually variable in learning performance. This includes both day-to-day and task-to-task variability. Some research has indicated that educational deficits of hyperactive children cut across all subject areas; others report difficulty in reading and language areas but little difficulty in arithmetic and attainment of number concepts. We may conclude that hyperactive children tend to have many more educational problems than normal children, but it is difficult to generalize further than this.

HYPERACTIVITY—CAUSAL HYPOTHESES

Pediatricians, neurologists, psychiatrists, psychologists, and educators have had varying degrees of interest in hyperactivity for the past 30 to 40 years, but interest has accelerated considerably since about 1970. This interest may be seen in increased attention in the news media and in articles relating to hyperactivity in professional journals. This increased interest has been sparked by a number of factors, including new information about the possible negative effects of food dyes, various foods and beverages, simple sugar, or inhalant allergies, as well as controversies about the use of various stimulant or tranquilizing drugs. Charges that physicians and educators (in some sort of diabolical partnership) are drugging many of the children in the United States have achieved headline status in newspapers and popular magazines. Last, but not least, growing interest in educational programming for learning disabled children and youth and national changes of attitude brought about by federal legislation requiring the public schools to provide for all handicapped children have led to increased awareness by educators, school board members, legislators, and medical professionals.

Management (by educators) or treatment (by physicians) of hyperactive children is based, at least in part, on causal hypotheses. Keogh, in her previously mentioned summary of research efforts relating to hyperactivity, established certain hypotheses that may explain the learning problems experienced by hyperactive children. She notes that these hypotheses are "in no sense exhaustive nor mutually exclusive, but do have different theoretical and remedial implications" (1971, p. 103). She further indicates that they are only speculative. A description of these hypotheses, derived from her analysis, follows.

One hypothesis proposed by Keogh is the *neurological impairment hypothesis. This is a medically oriented explanation and assumes that there is specific organic etiology.* Proponents of this hypothesis disagree as to the specific mechanisms involved, but there is often a tendency to use medication to treat hyperactivity when this hypothesis is the basis for treatment. More recently, much more attention has been devoted to dietary measures. (This is discussed later in this chapter and in Chapter 8.)

Keogh notes that, even if the neurological impairment model is accepted, *the effect of medication on learning is unclear.* If medication changes the level of motor activity and thus makes the child more socially acceptable or if it increases attending behavior, then perhaps more learning can take place. Keogh believes that the neurological hypothesis may be used to explain the *behavior* of many hyperactive children but does not believe it to be a satisfactory explanation for their *learning problems.*

A second hypothesis is the *information acquisition hypothesis. This hypothesis presumes that the child is neurally intact but that the nature and extent of his motor activity interfere with the accurate acquisition of information.* Hyperactivity interferes with attending to the learning task; thus a learning problem results. This might occur, for example, if there is disruption in the early stages of problem-solving situations where problem solving is dependent on accurate information. This point of view seems to be supported by research that indicates that some hyperactive children can be as successful as normal (comparison group) children if conditions of reinforcement are established that lead to significant increases in their attending behavior during information acquisition stages. This would seem to indicate that their learning problems were not caused by actual neurological impairment. Keogh suggests that certain research may be interpreted to indicate that "if the hyperactive child can get the information into the system, he can learn successfully" (1971, p. 105). Excessive movement, particularly movement of the head and eyes, appears to be associated with learning difficulties. Some research indicates that either medication or behavior management approaches can increase the probability of successful learning if they reduce such motor activity. This hypothesis, then, suggests an emphasis on control of motor activity, particularly at the information acquisition stage of the learning process.

A third hypothesis is the *decision process hypothesis. This hypothesis pinpoints the decision-making process rather than the information acquisition stage as critical for the hyperactive youngster.* In essence, this hypothesis indicates that hyperactive children make decisions too rapidly. If hyperactive children make decisions much more rapidly than other (normal) children, this means that too little information is acquired; and, presumably, if decisions are made based on this information, the hyperactive child assumes the information is adequate and accurate. Using this too-fast, impulsivity model, we may explain the learning difficulties of the hyperactive child in terms of lack of thoughtfulness, inability to consider and think things through, and inability to delay responses. Studies have indicated that increased response time usually affects performance in a positive manner and that impulsive children make more errors in reading than do reflective children. These studies seem to support the decision process hypothesis.

If hyperactive children tend to have inconsistent perceptual functioning, they will be confronted with considerable ambiguity in environmental interactions. If impulsivity is increased in situations of uncertainty, then the perceptual inconsistency leads to impulsivity, which disrupts the development of more consistent, stable percepts and concepts. This leads to even higher levels of motor activity, which in turn increases disruption of stable percepts and concepts, and on and on and on.

A recent decision by the American Psychiatric Association will lead to the replacement of the diagnostic category of Hyperkinetic Reaction of Childhood (DSM-II) with the category Attention Deficit Disorder (DSM-III). This change reflects a refocusing of psychiatrists on the attention deficit factors in the syndrome rather than the hyperkinesis. It also includes the specification of types and numbers of symptoms required for psychiatric diagnosis but may or may not eventually serve to establish this disorder (whatever it is called) as a medical syndrome with specific etiology. Loney notes that "although sophisticated theories about brain metabolism and arousal have been proposed and tested, many have abandoned the search for organic determinants" (1980, p. 32). In a similar manner (according to Loney), lack of success with research related to minimal brain dysfunction has led to abandonment of this concept by other researchers. Fortunately, it appears that success can often be found, even in the absence of positive knowledge of etiology.

In the next section we will review three approaches that seem to hold promise. Two of these approaches are discussed in more detail in later chapters; thus they are mentioned only briefly in this chapter. The third approach, an educational approach used primarily, if not exclusively, with the hyperactive student, is examined in more detail.

MAJOR APPROACHES FOR REDUCING HYPERACTIVITY

Three major approaches have been used to attempt to reduce hyperactivity in school-age children. They may often be used in combination, but, for purposes of discussion, they are listed separately. They are:

1. Medical treatment
2. Behavior management
3. Environmental control programs

Medical treatments require prescription or guidance from a medical doctor. Wunderlich, in commenting on types of medical treatment that can sometimes effectively manage the hyperactive child, lists the use of stimulants, tranquilizers, megavitamins, corticosteroids, antihistamines, anticonvulsants, food elimination, air filtration, and allergic desensitization (1973). It appears that many physicians have not yet accepted some of these forms of treatment, but continued apparent successes seem destined to change this state of affairs. Overuse of stimulants, tranquilizers, and anticonvulsants has led to various forms of public outcry, and this reaction may slow the acceptance of other forms of treatment listed

Great care must be taken with respect to the overuse of the term *hyperactive*. This boy is very active but in fact is in no way hyperactive.

before. Comments by a pediatrician, Dr. William Crook, regarding the allergic tension-fatigue syndrome, its relationship to hyperactivity in children, and its diagnosis might well summarize the problems connected with the medical treatment approach. Dr. Crook states, "The allergic tension-fatigue syndrome has been described by numerous physicians during the last 50 years. Yet it continues to be overlooked or ignored by many physicians" (1974, p. 4). He states that the disorder is usually caused by allergy (or intolerance) to common foods. Food coloring, various additives, dusts, chemical fumes, or pollens may also cause this syndrome. Crook notes that "Diagnosis of this syndrome [first] requires that the physician be aware of the disorder" (1974, p. 4). Considerable further discussion of a variety of medically related approaches will be found in Chapter 8. One of the more significant problems in medical treatment for hyperactivity is the variability in acceptance of certain medical treatments by physicians as a whole.

Behavior management or behavior modification is a second major type of approach. According to Simpson and Nelson, drug therapy (that is, medical approaches) and behavior modification are the two most frequently employed approaches to treatment of hyperactive children (1974, p. 275). Various studies have been conducted to attempt to compare varieties of medical approaches with behavior modification approaches, but results are inconclusive. For example, a study by Gittleman-Klein and others (1976) suggests that stimulant drug treatment may be more effective than behavior management in many respects, while a study by Loney and others (1979) seems to indicate that the two are of about equal value but that the behavior modification may have some very desirable spin-off effects. Because there are a variety of types of both behavioral and medical treatments, it is difficult to generalize from the results of the various studies.

Behavior management, considered to be any of a number of specific approaches used with hyperactive students and others who simply may be poorly motivated, is outlined in some detail in Chapter 9. Behavior management, unlike medical treatment, can be "prescribed" and implemented by educators. It might be noted, however, that the two approaches may often be used together to very good effect.

A third general approach, environmental control, is considered next in some detail, because it is not included elsewhere in this text.

THE ENVIRONMENTAL CONTROL APPROACH

Of the three approaches for dealing with the hyperactive child in the school, environmental control is the oldest and the one that has been the scene of the least attention and activity in the past decade. Medically related approaches have been the topic of much debate and have received a significant amount of research effort. A wide variety of behavior management techniques have been used with children with learning disabilities and other handicapping conditions, notably the mentally retarded and the emotionally disturbed. The procedures characterized here as part of the environmental control approach have not made educational headlines. One can only speculate as to the reasons for this lack of recognition, but it may be that a number of elements of this approach have become so much a part of eclectic teaching systems that they are not recognized as part of the environmental control frame of reference. Whatever the reasons, the environmental control approach has value, either alone or in conjunction with other measures (such as, along with behavior modification). To be consistent with the review of other approaches, the major advocates of this approach—Alfred Strauss, Laura Lehtinen, and William Cruickshank—are considered next.

Alfred Strauss and Laura Lehtinen*

Alfred Strauss, along with several others, organized the Cove Schools for Brain-injured Children in the late 1940s. Strauss was the school's first president. At about the same time (1947) the text *Psychopathology and Education of the Brain-injured Child* by Strauss and Lehtinen (educational director of Cove Schools) was published. Thus Strauss and Lehtinen were responsible for some of the first meaningful educational programming for brain-injured children who were, among other things, extremely hyperactive. Most of these children had been denied the right to attend public schools because of their hyperactivity, the negative effect their behavior had on other students, and their inability to profit from available school programs.

Strauss, assisted by Lehtinen and others, developed procedures for educational programming based on his own theories of cortical functioning. Strauss and Lehtinen's methods were designed to take into account these students' brain dysfunctions and reduce erroneous perceptual interpretations and resulting conceptual disturbances. By reducing these inaccurate and often conflicting interpretations of sensory input, it was hoped that unacceptable behavioral manifestations (including hyperactivity) would be reduced. It was also hypothesized that much more effective cognitive learning could take place.

The students toward whom Strauss and Lehtinen's educational methods were directed were viewed as children who had normal (potential) ability at birth but for some reason or combination of reasons had received actual brain damage. This damage was believed to have had two effects—a reduction in the original potential of the brain and modification in the manner in which present potential might be reached.

The brain damage or disturbance under consideration by Strauss and Lehtinen was that occurring above the midbrain level. In addition to the different types of outward manifestations of this damage, there are significant similarities, resulting from the fact that most children damaged above the midbrain level tend to be abnormally responsive to environmental stimuli and to react randomly, without logical predictability. The major general effect in the classroom is one of interference with the orderly process of the class because of inattentiveness to teacher-directed tasks and overreaction to small noises, movements, and various minor stimuli that have little effect on the remainder of the class. With this inattentiveness (which is actually attentiveness to almost everything—one second at a time), the brain-injured child does not learn efficiently, if at all, and also interferes with the learning of others. Most of the problem is organic in nature, but this does not change the situation. One major question, then, is how can the brain-injured child be assisted to control his attention and his motor activity?

Strauss and Lehtinen assumed that the actual damage could not be treated; therefore they attempted to control the environment—the factors that tend to stimulate the child to actions that inhibit normal academic learning. They further assumed that, in most cases, after the environment is manipulated so as to reduce distractions and stimulation of hyperactive behavior, children will be able to slowly develop and exercise additional inner

* Laura Lehtinen is now known as Laura Lehtinen Rogan.

control. This capability is partly because of the ability of undamaged portions of the brain to substitute and compensate for damaged areas, taking over many of their functions. Research with brain-injured adults and with the cerebral palsied is cited as support for this theory and expectation. This is the basic underlying rationale for what Strauss and Lehtinen refer to as the therapeutic educational environment.

The controlled, therapeutic educational environment is planned to counteract, that is, to reduce, by not stimulating, the behavioral manifestations of brain injury. A maximum of 12 children is prescribed; they should be housed in a room large enough to provide considerable space between them. An absence of pictures, bulletin boards, and decorations, usually thought to make a room pleasant and attractive, is a second guideline for a classroom for the brain injured. A room above the first floor, so that the windows do not look out on outside activity, and an opaque covering on the lower quarter of the windows are also recommended.

The teacher's dress may also be overstimulating; that is, earrings, bracelets, and bright ornaments may be distracting to many of the children. The teacher should investigate this factor and then dress as required by her particular class.

All children are somewhat stimulated by the presence of other children, and brain-injured children are affected to an even greater extent. Even with all possible measures to provide a neutral learning environment, the presence, particularly the visual awareness, of other children and their movement may cause serious problems for many brain-injured children. Therefore seating the child so that he faces a blank wall may be necessary. This action should be explained to the child so that he will not interpret it as punitive. He knows he has trouble attending to tasks, and he should be told that the seating is to help him attend and to keep others from bothering him. One further step is using screens to completely cut off visual contact with others while the child is attempting to do seatwork.

Strauss and Lehtinen note that many children, on being moved to such an environment from a large, regular class, indicate that they are certainly glad to be out of the other situation and that they can "get more work done here." Strauss and Lehtinen also note that they have found no tendency for such procedures to promote withdrawal or autism.

Another type of learning problem may be distractions caused by the multiplicity of detail in textbooks. Strauss suggests actually cutting away borders, pictures, or any unnecessary visual stimuli. Another technique is using a cover page with a minimum amount of cutout area so that only a small part of the printed page is exposed at one time.

The tendency of the brain-injured child to focus on movement can be used to educational advantage. If lessons are planned to maximize the use of manipulative material, attention to the learning task will increase, and this particular tendency will then be directed *toward,* rather than away from, learning. All of these adjustments fall within the central thesis of environmental control or adjustment to the special needs of the child.

As these adjustments are effective, the child tends to gain in knowledge and skill, and there is a reciprocal gain in his *inner* ability to control his actions and general behavior. *The control from within is the final goal of the program* and will be achieved comparatively quickly by some children. It will take a good deal longer for others.

Just as most other, nonhandicapped children tend to be able to concentrate and attend to learning tasks for longer periods of time as they grow older, so can the brain-injured child progress in these areas, with the controlled environment assisting toward this goal.

However, specific educational goals cannot necessarily be accomplished in their normal sequence, even within the controlled environment, without additional help. Because the brain injury may lead to severe perceptual, figure-ground, visual, and auditory channel problems of various types, as well as to integrative disabilities, special instructional materials must be provided.

Strauss and Lehtinen suggest a number of materials that may help—counting boards which force a slowdown of the counting process, the abacus for mathematical processes, number wheels, and other aids that help to make these processes more concrete. The final goal is to develop the ability to learn without these devices, but, while initial learning is getting underway, they may be essential.

Strauss and Lehtinen were most careful to emphasize that the restricted, therapeutic environment is only an interim environment. It should not and cannot take the place of the wider experiences of the regular classroom. In this respect, they were 25 years ahead of more recent advocates of "mainstreaming." The special class is viewed as a means whereby the brain-injured child can overcome some of his reactions to the regular class environment and can begin to feel accomplishment and success. It also has another important advantage. With a smaller class and a specially trained teacher, the teacher can devote more time to observation of the child's learning habits—what works and what is ineffective—and can then make the required adjustments. In a class of 30 or 40 this can be a most difficult task.

Other unique characteristics of the brain-injured child, as observed by Strauss, should be considered. On the plus side is the fact that brain-injured children may have excellent verbal memory. However, because of this good verbal memory a child may sometimes repeat verbally what he was told earlier, although he may have little actual understanding of its meaning. The teacher should be alert to this possibility. For the child with this excellent verbal memory, drill may be undesirable because it may lead to an ability to verbalize without understanding and without the ability to generalize and apply what has been memorized.

Other characteristics include both extremes—meticulousness and careless, illegible work. Still another characteristic of the brain-injured child is perseveration, the inability to shift (without great difficulty) from one activity or point of attention to another. Among the most trying characteristics (to the teacher) is the extreme day-to-day variability of general performance, both academic and behavioral. On the "off" days, the only workable solution is to ask as little as possible and then not expect to get even that.

Strauss and Lehtinen were among the first to systematically analyze the differences between teaching reading to the brain-injured and to the normal child. Their discussion of the validity of mental age as a criterion for readiness for reading has been of value to educators of those with brain injuries. They point out that most children develop readiness to learn to read during the 6- to 8-year-old age range. This maturity, or mental readiness, may be seen in many ways, such as in heightened interest in stories, attention to symbols that have meaning, ability to recognize alphabetical symbols, accurate recall of material read to them, and eagerness to start to read. They further note that a mentally retarded child may be ready to learn to read when his mental age reaches the 6- to 8-year-old range, but, because mental age is a composite of many factors, the 6- to 8-year-old mental age may have limited meaning for the child in whom these factors are developing unevenly. Each child must be considered separately and his education individually programmed. No matter how well other abilities may be developed, if the child cannot attend to learning tasks, he cannot exercise or utilize these competencies that might permit him to learn to read with relative ease.

Strauss and Lehtinen, assisted by others who felt that brain-injured students (or hyperactive students who acted like those who were brain-injured) deserved an educational opportunity, made important contributions to a developing field. Many of their ideas, which could be called careful application of good common sense, are still in use today. Although their original efforts were with children who represent only a small percentage of those we would now call learning disabled, the problems of inattention, inaccurate interpretation of incoming sensory signals, and conceptual deficits based on faulty perceptual abilities are considered part of the problem with many nonhyperactive learning disabled students. There have been a number of critical evaluations of Strauss' efforts, particularly with respect to a lack of statisical controls in his research and brain-injury diagnoses that were often questionable. On the other hand, some of the educational procedures that he supported appear to be of value, and many good practitioners would say, "If it works and has no negative side effects, use it."

William Cruickshank

William Cruickshank has made a series of important contributions in special education, with concentrated efforts in the areas of mental retardation, cerebral palsy, and later, learning disabilities. He was influenced by contacts with Heinz Werner and Alfred Strauss, and some of his major contributions were in the area of teaching techniques used with hyperactive/brain-injured children. One major contribution was *A Teaching Method for Brain-injured and Hyperactive Children* (Cruickshank and others, 1961). This report of a study of brain-injured, hyperactive children contained a number of specific, detailed teaching techniques that appeared to be effective with the group under consideration. In describing the rationale for his educational program, Cruickshank noted that "four elements comprise the essentials in a good teaching environment for brain-injured children with hyperactivity and for hyperactive children whose disturbance may result solely from emotional maladjustment" (1961, p. 14).* These elements, as hypothesized by Cruickshank and applied in his study, were:

1. Reduction in environmental stimuli.
2. Reduced space.
3. A structured school program and life plan.
4. Increased stimulus value of teaching materials (organized stimulation to call attention to specific teaching/learning materials).

Cruickshank's educational recommendations are for the most part expansions or refinements of the Strauss-Lehtinen ideas. A brief summary of his basic ideas follows.

With respect to *reduction in environmental stimuli* (element No. 1), Cruickshank's recommendations are very similar to those of Strauss. Cruickshank believes that "if the learning environment can be stripped of unessential stimuli, . . . the hyperactive child has an increased opportunity to attend for necessary periods of time to those stimuli which are essential to his learning and achievement" (1961, p. 16). In another book, Cruickshank states that "usually the best classroom in

*Note that Cruickshank expanded the Strauss idea of "brain-injured" to include other hyperactive children. Although he uses the term "emotional maladjustment," his writing indicates that he refers to those who are very hyperactive (like the brain-injured) without respect to causation.

your community for normal children is the worst classroom for brain-injured children" (1967, p. 103). These two statements seem to express his beliefs quite clearly.

This "inappropriate" classroom vs. "appropriate" classroom is further explained in the following paragraphs.

In the "inappropriate" (for hyperactive students) classroom you would find an attractive science corner, children's artwork on the walls, perhaps an aquarium, a pet hamster, bright curtains, and stimulating, colorful charts and educational aids. The teacher and 30 children are dressed in a variety of interesting, colorful clothing. When children pass the windows to go to the pencil sharpener or an activity table, they can look out at the playground, trees, cars, and adjacent homes. This is just the kind of classroom environment all children should have—all, that is, except the brain injured. Even the out-of-class areas such as the library, cafeteria, and gymnasium are not appropriate for this child until he gains additional control.

An "appropriate" class setting for the brain-injured child would have the following details and characteristics. Teaching/learning materials, many of which are colorful and interesting to look at, are stored on shelves enclosed by plain wooden doors. No bulletin boards, chalkboards, calendars, or posters are to be seen. No science corners, reading tables full of interesting books, or any of the ordinary classroom items of this nature are included. The teacher has no desk in the classroom. She will have one elsewhere in the building, and she may keep a minimum of materials on the enclosed shelves in the special classroom. The child has a chair and a desk and has out on that desk only the material with which he is presently working.

Like Strauss, Cruickshank recommends sufficient, but limited, space and also recommends a learning cubicle for each child, just large enough for his desk, which faces a blank wall. The cubicle should have permanently constructed walls, extending far enough so that the child at his desk cannot see children on either side. These walls should be made of some hard surface (perhaps a plain, Formica-like material) so that there is no point of focus (as there would be with natural wood grain) to cause distraction and no writing or carving surface.

The preceding description illustrates Cruickshank's elements No. 1 and also No. 2, *reduced space*. Cruickshank believes that the *space in which learning activities take place* must be held to a minimum. Although he has stated that "a room smaller than the typical standard classroom would probably be most appropriate for the hyperactive child" (1961, p. 17), the overall size of the *room* is not the most important factor, but rather it is the learning space, that area in which the student's desk and chair is placed. The area should be small and unstimulating, with the learning materials being the point of focus.

The *structured school progam and life plan* (element No. 3) might include a number of components. For example, a specific procedure may be established for each day—coming into the room, going directly to the coat hanging area, hanging the coat and hat on one designated hook, and placing the lunchbox in one specific place reserved for that purpose. The procedure, in this case, is designed to be simple, with no real choices to be made. The objective is to learn to perform the required tasks without confusion and thus to develop some concept of order and to experience social approval and the inner satisfaction of having completed a required task.

The entire school day and the total school experience must be structured to reduce anxiety, confusion, and failure. *Order* and *structure* are the key words. A feeling of accomplishment and success is the desired goal. After it appears that the student has many of the distracting factors in his life under control, then very limited, carefully monitored opportunities to make choices should be offered. Cruickshank notes that the major thrust regarding the matter of structure is to "keep all activities, including the total social organization of the classroom, within the limits of tolerance or within the level of success of the children, both as individuals and as a group" (1961, p. 19).

The fourth and final element suggested by Cruickshank is *increased stimulus value of teaching materials.* This may be accomplished in a variety of ways—for example, in teaching the word "play," the four letters may be written in four different bright colors. Other examples are using different colors for different words in a sentence or using a bright red background to "frame" a word to be learned. Such stimuli may be too much for some students, but, more often, if this is the only stimulating feature in the immediate school environment, it will cause the student to focus attention on the task at hand.

The application of these four elements in a coordinated manner is the approach recommended by Cruickshank. The procedure is not simple and will require trial-and-error efforts with each child, but the basic principle remains the same. However, one other important set of factors must be considered—the specific types of behavior characteristics exhibited by any one student and the adjustments in class setting or materials that must be made in recognition of these unique, individual needs. There are a number of major predictable characteristics (listed earlier in this chapter), but individual students will exhibit these characteristics to differing degrees. Planning individual programming requires adjusting educational practices by taking these characteristics into consideration.

With regard to the various school settings, the following suggestions are made. Many brain-injured children, those who actually fit into the hyperactive category, should eat lunch in the classroom rather than in the cafeteria. A similar attitude should be taken with regard to special assemblies and auditorium activities. After, through careful, limited tryout, it is determined that the child can handle this type of activity and setting, he should by all means participate. The final goal is the maximum possible reintegration into the classroom, but this may require a long time for some hyperactive, brain-injured children.

Cruickshank believes that unstructured art activities are usually too threatening for the brain-injured child until he has made considerable progress toward self-control of hyperactivity. The same principle applies to unstructured music and free-play periods.

It would be difficult to overemphasize that structure is the common element to be desired in programming for the brain-injured child. The brain-injured child is threatened when he has to make choices. Freedom (lack of structure) involves choices, and this is what he cannot handle. This does not imply that the teacher or the educational program should not reflect warmth and love, but the warmth and love must be within boundaries that will give the child confidence rather than lead to confusion.

In all the educational planning for this population, Cruickshank recommends an attitude of habilitation, not rehabilitation. Although many learning disability programs can properly be viewed as remedial in nature, Cruickshank views the one for brain-injured children as a building program—one in which the teaching emphasis is directed toward the disability.

Many of the educational suggestions provided by Cruickshank are the same as those made by such individuals as Kephart, Getman, and Fernald (discussed in the following chapter). One major modification is that materials emphasized are those which simplify the visual presentation so as to not overstimulate. Also, whereas other children might be involved in more self-selection of materials, the teacher of those with brain injuries would more likely present materials in a carefully planned, structured sequence.

Two specific books are suggested for those who want to learn more about Cruickshank's recommendations or his basic theoretical rationale. They are *A Teaching Method for Brain-injured and Hyperactive Children* (1961) and *The Brain-injured Child in Home, School, and Community* (1967).

Perhaps the most important single element of either Cruickshank's or Strauss and Lehtinen's ideas is the need (of some children) for a great deal of order and structure throughout the total environment. A teacher who has a real grasp of this concept and has relatively good teaching skills can make the proper environmental adjustments for many students with more minor problems of hyperactivity or distractibility, right within the regular classroom. This ability will be of great benefit to many teachers who seldom, if ever, see severely hyperactive students. It will also be of great value to the students they are assigned to teach.

THE USE OF BIOFEEDBACK TO REDUCE HYPERACTIVITY

Biofeedback is a technique developed by experimental psychologists in which certain physiological processes are made directly monitorable by the subject. In some manner, usually through hearing a tone at varying frequencies or watching a light or the movement of a needle on a graduated scale, the subject can be made aware of and thus can attempt to control what is happening internally. In the studies cited here electronic equipment was used to indicate electromyographic activity (muscle tension) in the frontalis (forehead) muscles. The frontalis muscles are used because other investigations have indicated that they provide a good index of both physical and mental activity. This type of equipment and the related biofeedback training is in fairly common use to help adults gain better control over activities such as blood pressure and heart rate.

In a study of a 6½-year-old boy described as "extremely hyperactive" electromyographic (EMG) biofeedback training was provided twice per week for 3 weeks, then once per week for the following 5 weeks (Braud, Lupin, and Braud, 1975). The subject could hear a specific tone if his activity rose above an established level. He directed his efforts toward "keeping the tone off." Both parents and the teacher were asked to encourage use of the relaxation procedure at home and school as needed. The results of this training were most encouraging. Ability to reduce EMG-monitored muscle tension over the 11 biofeedback training sessions was quite good. A twelfth session, which came 7 months later, indicated that the subject had retained the ability to control his tension and level of muscle activity.

Flemings conducted a similar study to determine the effectiveness of biofeedback as a practical tool for use within the public schools (Flemings, 1978). Biofeedback procedures were used with 10 hyperactive children enrolled in grades three through six. Average EMG readings for the group as a whole were significantly reduced after 10 sessions, but this improvement resulted from the efforts of seven subjects; three did not improve significantly. Efforts to find significant relationships between reduction in tension and other variables were fruitless; male and female subjects experienced similar success, regular class enrollees were no different from special class enrollees, and those on medication did no better, or worse, than those not on medication. The general results of the study were a success, but, as in other biofeedback studies, attempts to pinpoint factors or variables that might *predict* success were to no avail.

A review of research relating to muscle relaxation therapy in hyperkinesis as reported by Bhatara, Arnold, Lorance, and Gupta (1979) indicates a need for caution. Included in this review were eight studies of muscle relaxation treatments that utilized either EMG biofeedback or progressive muscle relaxation. Conclusions reached by these reviewers include the following:

1. Results of these studies were inconclusive; some reviewers reported improvement, others reported no change, and one reported worsening of classroom behavior.
2. Very different subject selection criteria were used.
3. Measures taken in the various studies were very different; some reviewers included measures of cognitive changes, and others did not attempt to measure anything but noncognitive behavioral outcomes.

The results of this review of research and of most individual research studies on the effectiveness of biofeedback training suggest some potential value of such procedures for some children, but researchers must initiate more carefully constructed and controlled studies and adopt a "wait and see" attitude. This is a new and possibly rewarding area of training, but it requires much more careful investigation before any definitive statements regarding efficacy may be made with assurance.

When biofeedback works, it has certain potential advantages that cannot be duplicated by approaches that depend on medication. The self-control required to find success in biofeedback efforts is almost certain to be of value in improving the self-confidence of learning disabled students, especially those who are recognized as tending to have a low self-concept. In addition, the problems of negative side effects do not occur as with medical treatment. The future value of biofeedback efforts is uncertain, but it does seem that more research in this area will be done in the very near future. Hopefully it will become another effective tool that may be used to reduce the problems of hyperactive students.

SUMMARY

The effects of brain injury have concerned researchers for over 100 years, but the focus on educational programs for hyperactive, brain-injured children did not receive serious attention until the 1930s and 1940s. One of the first well-organized educational efforts was directed by Strauss and Lehtinen in programs provided through the Cove Schools for Brain-injured Children, initiated in the late 1940s. Out of the work of Strauss and Lehtinen and the later efforts of Cruickshank, procedures have developed that have been characterized in this chapter as environmental control approaches. In this type of approach, structure is maximized and extraneous stimuli are minimized; the class setting would undoubtedly be called "sterile" for the normal child. For severe cases, a self-contained class is recommended with the children participating to whatever extent is possible in other areas of the school plant. Careful consultation and planning with the family is highly recommended, and reintegration into the regular classroom may be slower than for learning disabled children without the brain injury characteristics. In addition to environmental control approaches, which were given major attention in this chapter, two other major types of approaches, medical treatment and behavior modification, were noted. These topics, discussed more extensively in subsequent chapters, were reviewed only briefly here.

One last, newer technique, the use of electromyographic biofeedback to assist the individual to learn to control his own hyperactivity, was also discussed. This technique has been used to only a very limited extent but appears promising.

Taken as a whole, efforts to reduce hyperactivity may be viewed as in a state of continuing progress with more effort presently being expended on medically related and behavioristic approaches than on those that might be called strictly environmental control approaches. However, there also appears to be more tendency to combine various approaches, a trend that has yet to be fully explored. It is difficult to predict the probability of success in some of the newer efforts to assist the hyperactive child, but research activity levels of the last decade indicate continuing concern of professionals in a growing number of disciplines. A more carefully integrated, broadened, interprofessional effort may help to find answers to a number of very important questions in this field.

REFERENCES AND SUGGESTED READINGS

Bhatara, V., and others. Muscle relaxation therapy in hyperkinesis: is it effective? *Journal of Learning Disabilities,* 1979, *12*(3), 182-186.

Braud, L., Lupin, M., and Braud, W. The use of electromyographic biofeedback in the control of hyperactivity, *Journal of Learning Disabilities,* 1975, *8,* 420-425.

Conners, C. A teacher rating scale for use in drug studies with children, *American Journal of Psychiatry,* 1969, *126,* 152-156.

Crook, W. The allergic tension-fatigue syndrome, *Pediatric Annals* Reprint. New York: Insight Books, 1974.

Cruickshank, W. *The brain-injured child in home, school, and community.* Syracuse, N.Y.: Syracuse University Press, 1967.

Cruickshank, W. (Ed.) *The teacher of brain-injured children.* Syracuse, N.Y.: Syracuse University Press, 1966.

Cruickshank, W., and others. *A teaching method for brain-injured and hyperactive children.* Syracuse, N.Y.: Syracuse University Press, 1961.

Flemings, D. A study of electromyograph biofeedback as a method to teach hyperactive children how to relax within a public school setting. Published doctoral dissertation, University of Northern Colorado, 1978.

Freidus, E. *New approaches in special education of the brain-injured child.* New York: New York Association for Brain-injured Children, 1957.

Frierson, E., and Barbe, W. (Eds.) *Educating children with learning disabilities.* New York: Appleton-Century-Crofts, 1967.

Gittleman-Klein, R., and others. Relative efficacy of methylphenidate and behavior modification in hyperkinetic children: an interim report, *Journal of Abnormal Child Psychology,* 1976, *4,* 361-374.

Keogh, B. Hyperactivity and learning disorders: review and speculation, *Exceptional Children,* 1971, *38,* 101-109.

Kephart, N. *The brain-injured child.* Chicago: National Society for Crippled Children and Adults, 1963.

Loney, J. Hyperkinesis comes of age: what do we know and where should we go? *American Journal of Orthopsychiatry,* 1980, *50,* 28-42.

Loney, J., and others. Comparing psychological and pharmacological treatments for hyperkinetic boys and their classmates, *Journal of Abnormal Child Psychology,* 1979, *7,* 133-143.

Rapp, D. Food allergy treatment for hyperkinesis, *Journal of Learning Disabilities,* 1979, *12,* 608-615.

Ross, D., and Ross, S. *Hyperactivity: research, theory and action.* New York: John Wiley & Sons, Inc., 1976.

Shapiro, D., and others. (Eds.) *Biofeedback and self-control.* Chicago: Aldine Publishing Co., 1973.

Siegel, E. *Helping the brain-injured child.* New York: New York Association for Brain-injured Children, 1962.

Simpson, D., and Nelson, A. Attention training through breathing control to modify hyperactivity, *Journal of Learning Disabilities,* 1974, *7,* 274-283.

Speer, F. (Ed.) *Allergy of the nervous system.* Springfield, Ill.: Charles C Thomas, Publisher, 1970.

Strauss, A., and Kephart, N. *Psychopathology and education of the brain-injured child* (vol. 2). *Progress in theory and clinic.* New York: Grune & Stratton, Inc., 1955.

Wasserman, E., Asch, H., and Snyder, E. A. A neglected aspect of learning disabilities: energy level output, *Journal of Learning Disabilities,* 1972, *5,* 130-135.

Weithorn, C. Hyperactivity and CNS: an etiological and diagnostic dilemma, *Journal of Learning Disabilities,* 1973, *6,* 41-45.

Wunderlich, R. Treatment of the hyperactive child, *Academic Therapy,* 1973, *8*(4), 375-390.

I GO TO
HE GOES TO
THEY GO TO

chapter **6**

Multisensory systems

The prefix *multi* can be used to indicate *more than one, more than two,* or *many.* The reason for using the senses in the teaching/learning process is obvious, for we receive new information *only* through the senses. Therefore multisensory learning could mean learning through the use of two or more of the senses; however, in practice the term more often describes learning in which three or more of the senses are used. *For purposes of discussion of the multisensory systems used with learning disabled students, multisensory will mean the deliberate use of three or more of the sensory channels in the teaching/learning process.* More often, in this discussion, reference will be made to the use of four sensory modalities: visual, auditory, kinesthetic, and tactile.

Many teachers have heard about or experienced so many multisensory approaches, systems, or methods that they tend to regard the term *multisensory* as too nebulous. Others relate it to one specific approach with which they have had notable (either good or bad) results. The fact that the term multisensory may be applied to any approach that utilizes more than one sensory modality—and of course nearly all meet this criterion—does little to simplify the issue. This chapter relates to certain specific multisensory methods or multisensory techniques that can be used with various methods and concentrates on those that have demonstrated effectiveness with students with learning problems.

The idea of sense training goes back to the ancient Greeks. The practice of sense training has been an integral part of the educational procedure in a number of primary reading approaches used in the last half of the nineteenth century and early twentieth century in the United States. For example, an interesting book entitled *Games, Seat Work, and Sense Training Exercises,* written by Martha Holton and Eugenia Kimball and published in 1905, had many of the same procedures used today in efforts with young learning disabled students. In this text Francis W. Parker states, "If the child's knowledge reaches to a solid foundation of sense training, the floods of time will beat in vain upon that knowledge. Other things may pass away, but that will remain" (Holton and Kimball, 1905, p. 56).

Holton and Kimball recommend extensive work in "visualization" in "eye training," "recognition of objects," "recognition of form and color," "sense of touch," and a variety of observation and visual memory skills. In fact, many of their recommendations (with slight modernization of writing style) could have come from the suggestions of the perceptual-motor theorists reviewed in Chapter

4, or could be related to the ideas presented in this chapter. The existence in 1905 of this practical, how-to-do-it book clearly indicates that it has long been known that educators must carefully attend to the manner in which children receive sensory signals and must maximize accurate sensory input so as to maximize learning.

Multisensory methods are specifically recommended by Cruickshank, Bentzen, Ratzeburg, and Tannhauser (1961); Johnson and Myklebust (1967); Kephart (1971); Hammill and Bartel (1975); Lerner (1976); Valett (1978); and a host of others. However, these recommendations are not without cautions. Several authorities, in writing on the special difficulties of the hyperactive, brain-injured student, note that educators may "overload" the neural circuitry, thus leading to catastrophic reactions. It appears, however, that many such predictions of possible overloading were based mainly on clinical observation of extremely hyperactive students whose total difficulties were go great that they required separate, special class settings. A study by Erwin Koepsel (1974) reported that students who were rated as hyperactive were observed to be exhibiting *reduced* hyperactivity following the use of the Fernald multisensory approach in the teaching of reading. In this study there were no indications of overloading, as might have been predicted by some authorities. The students involved were not extremely hyperactive but appeared to be the moderately hyperactive type often found in learning disabilities programs provided through the resource room setting. In summary, multisensory methods are widely recommended by many authorities in the field of learning disabilities. Some cautions are voiced with respect to the possibility of overloading, but these may have more validity when extreme hyperactivity and known brain injury are part of the total diagnostic picture.

KINESTHETIC AND TACTILE LEARNING

The majority of traditional, academic learning is through the visual and auditory channels. This appears to be the most effective procedure for most children (excluding, of course, the deaf and the blind), and the most significant questions relate to how to balance the use of visual and auditory learning, how to determine readiness, or in what sequence the various component steps in the process should come. A majority of educators would likely agree that children must be able to discriminate between visual symbols (letters) to be able to learn to read and that adequate auditory abilities are equally essential, but the role of tactile and kinesthetic abilities are often almost ignored.

Educators of the blind have demonstrated that we can learn to read without sight, but for children with adequate vision the ability to learn in this manner has limited value. It is interesting, however, that in isolated cases braille has been used with unusual success with the learning disabled. (For a case study of a severe dyslexic who achieved unusual success in learning to read with braille, see McCoy, L. Braille: a language for severe dyslexics, *Journal of Learning Disabilities,* 1975, *8,* 288-292. This story, told by the girl's mother, Lois McCoy, describes how a girl with normal visual acuity who had been unable to learn to read or write by age 15, progressed through 3 years of reading—in braille—in 1 year. She also improved dramatically in pronunciation, grammar, and other language and academic areas.) It is not my intent to recommend braille for any great number of learning disabled children but rather to emphasize that the kinesthetic and tactile are effective learning channels and are too often overlooked even though children have indicated significant difficulties in learning in the normal (visual/auditory) manner. The olfactory and gustatory channels may have limited value in some instances (see The Apples, Bananas, and Candy Approach on pp. 138 and 139), but the emphasis here is on the proven value of the tactile and kinesthetic channels.

Perceptual-motor authorities, such as those reviewed in Chapter 4, are very obviously interested in tactile and kinesthetic learning modalities and believe that they provide the base for higher levels of learning. For the student who is *not* learning normally, the tactile and kinesthetic modalities may be the source of considerable support. It is not primarily a matter of *developing* them further (although this may be required also) but of *using* them to support the visual and auditory modalities. In most of the better-known multisensory methods, the assumption is that they are used, along with the auditory, to support or strengthen the visual channel. However, this cannot necessarily be proved to be what is taking place.

A number of activities may effectively serve this supportive function. One example may be playing with alphabet blocks or large plastic letters or numbers. In other activities the young child may learn to differentiate between two similar but different solid objects without looking at them. Such experiences appear to assist in the development of better visual discrimination. Many other possibilities are outlined in a wide range of learning activity books (see References and Suggested Readings). Simple examples include the use of solid objects in a cloth bag and the use of a blindfold so that objects placed in front of the child cannot be seen. Sandpaper letters or geometric configurations provide another variation of this same principle. With 5- and 6-year-olds these activities can be accomplished in a game format.

In each of these examples the major purpose is to provide tactile or kinesthetic support for the visual modality, either to assist in developing skills that have been slow evolving or in an attempt to "straighten out" previously scrambled reception and interpretation of visual signals. In some cases it may be well to have children feel a letter or word as they look at it, thus providing simultaneous reception through the visual and tactile senses. In other cases it may prove to be more effective to cut off the visual signal and to be certain that the student is 100% accurate in tactile sensing alone before adding the visual. In all of these examples *it is important to understand the principle of utilizing additional sensory modalities to assist in the development of normal perception in other modalities.* The most common application of this principle is in the use of the tactile and/or kinesthetic modality to support or assist the visual.

A somewhat different application of this same principle involves the teacher or a helping student tracing letters, or sometimes words, on the arm or back of the student who needs help. This is significantly different in that the student receives no kinesthetic input, only tactile. He may be looking at letter cards on his desk, attempting to find one that matches the letter he feels traced out on his back, or he may have his eyes closed, concentrating on feeling the letter or word accurately. In any event, a whole variety of games or activities can be developed with this type of assistance when the evidence indicates that this may be one of the child's needs. It is often not possible to "prove" diagnostically that this is what is required, but there may be clinical (observational) indications, and it is certainly worth a try.

THE MAJOR MULTISENSORY APPROACHES

The preceding discussion has considered the potential value of the tactile and kinesthetic modalities in the learning process and certain simple ways to use them in the teach-

Multisensory approaches are recommended by a majority of the various learning disability authorities. In addition to the more formal, systematized approaches, activities such as these will also be of benefit in most instances. (From Gearheart, B. R. *Teaching the learning disabled: a combined task-process approach.* St. Louis: The C. V. Mosby Co., 1976.)

ing/learning process. The remainder of this chapter is concerned with two major multisensory systems or approaches that are generally recognized with respect to the field of learning disabilities. Also discussed are certain variations on these major approaches and one very unique report of a multisensory effort that involved the olfactory and gustatory modalities. The two major approaches, those of Fernald and one often called the Orton-Gillingham approach, are discussed first. These originated with research and remedial efforts of the 1920s and have been used to varying degrees ever since that time.

The Fernald simultaneous multisensory (VAKT) approach

In the foreword to Fernald's 1943 text, *Remedial Techniques in Basic School Subjects,* Lewis Terman (whose international reputation in relation to research with the gifted and his development of the Stanford-Binet placed him among the leading scholars in education) stated, "It is my considered judgment that Dr. Fernald's conquest of word-blindness is an achievement comparable to that of Miss Sullivan." (He had referred in the previous paragraph to Anne Sullivan's efforts in the training of Helen Keller, who was deaf and blind from early childhood.) Terman summarized his earlier comments by noting that Fernald's research suggests that if educational methods are properly understood and applied, all children may find academic success. His concluding sentence was, "It is largely for this reason that I believe this book is one of the most significant contributions ever made to experimental pedagogy" (Fernald, 1943).*

Certain other educational approaches in use with learning disabled students may be called multisensory, but Fernald's is the "original" and represents a more total, comprehensive multisensory approach than almost any other. In her system a balanced use of the *v*isual, *a*uditory, *k*inesthetic, and *t*actile is featured, and thus it has been sometimes called a VAKT approach. Her method has also been called the "kinesthetic" or the "tracing" method, but this is because she so specifically adds tracing to the auditory and visual components.

The Fernald VAKT approach was developed through experience in the clinic school at the University of California, Los Angeles. This school, established in 1921 to replace an earlier program there, evolved from a general purpose facility serving children with a variety of educational problems to one serving primarily those of normal or above-normal intelligence with specific, severe educational problems—usually those closely allied to reading and spelling disabilities.

Although Fernald worked with the local public schools and with other universities, the clinic school at UCLA was the site of her major efforts, and the following description will relate mainly to her work there. At the time Fernald published the account of her methodology (1943), the clinic school was a full-day, 8-month school where all subjects were taught to approximately 20 students in small groups. A summer program attended by 60 to 80 students was also a part of the clinic school operation, but it required a modified approach. University personnel and graduate students under Fernald's supervision staffed the program.

Prior to actually starting a remedial program, the Fernald procedure requires "positive reconditioning." This is based on the assumption that almost all children who have experienced school failure have developed a low self-concept, particularly in relation to anything connected with school or formal education. Four conditions are to be carefully avoided in initiating and carrying through the remedial program:

1. *Avoid calling attention to emotionally loaded situations.* Attempts, either by teachers or parents, to urge the child to do better generally have negative effects. Reminding the child of the future importance of academic success or telling him how important it is to his family should be avoided. If the child is already a failure and knows it, these urgings are at best useless and sometimes result in a nearly complete emotional block.

2. *Avoid using methods that previous experience suggests are likely to be ineffective.* This is important both during remediation and during the time of reentry to the regular class. If the child is experiencing success in a temporary, out-of-class remedial setting (after school or for a set time period each day) and then must return to class and to methods

*In preparing the third edition of this text, I found that my copy of Fernald's text had mysteriously escaped from my personal library; thus it was necessary to try to purchase another copy. This turned out to be a very small problem. Fernald's 1943 text was still in print and available from the publisher in 1979, an obvious testimonial to its continued value. In fact, except for certain terminology, which is obviously 40 years out of date, the text is remarkably current today.

by which he was earlier unable to learn, the remedial program may be negated. Or, if, after a period in which he has been out of class on a full-day basis and has found success in a new method, he must make an immediate return to the former methods with no planned transition, he may return to his old inability to learn.

3. *Avoid conditions that may cause embarrassment.* Sometimes a new method used in the new setting is effective and satisfactory, whereas in the old setting, unless some special provisions are made, it may seem childish or silly. For example, the tracing involved in the Fernald approach may seem so unusual as to be absurd back in the regular classroom. The reward, that is, the learning, may not be worth the feelings of conspicuousness and embarrassment.

4. *Avoid directing attention to what the child cannot do.* This is just a special kind of problem that might be included as a part of condition 1.

Regardless of later requirements, attempting to bring about positive reconditioning and avoiding emotional reversal after the reconditioning has taken place are of great importance.

The first step in the classroom or clinic procedure with the child is to explain that there is a new way of learning words that really works. The child is told that others have had the same problem he is having and have learned easily through this new method.

The second step is to ask the child to select any word he wants to learn, regardless of length, and then to teach him to write and recognize (read) it, using the method that will now be explained in some detail.

1. The word chosen by the child is written for him, usually with a crayon in plain, blackboard-size cursive writing. In most cases, regardless of age, cursive writing is used rather than manuscript. This is because the child will then tend to see and "feel" the word as a single entity, rather than as a group of separate letters.

2. The child traces the word with his fingers in contact with the paper, saying the word as he traces it. This is repeated as many times as necessary until he can write the word without looking at the copy.

3. He writes the word on scrap paper, demonstrating to himself that it is now "his" word. Several words are taught in this manner, and as much time as necessary is taken to completely master them.

4. When the child has internalized the fact that he can write and recognize words, he is encouraged to start writing stories. His stories are whatever he wishes them to be at first, and the instructor gives him any words (in addition to those he has mastered) he needs to complete the story.

5. After the story is written, it is typed for him, and he is to read it in typed form while it is still fresh in his mind. It is important that this be done immediately.

6. After the story is completed and the new word has been used in a meaningful way, the new word is written by the child on a card that he files alphabetically in his own individual word file. This word file is used as a meaningful way to teach the alphabet without undue emphasis on rote memory.

This procedure is often called the Fernald tracing method because the tracing is an added feature in contrast to the usual methods of teaching reading or word recognition. However, it should be noted that the child is simultaneously *feeling, seeing, saying,* and *hearing* the word. Thus this is truly a multisensory approach.

Several points should be carefully observed and followed for maximum success:

1. *The word should be selected by the student.*

If it is, motivation is maximized, and the likelihood of interest in using the word in a story is greater than with a teacher-selected word. In Fernald's case studies and in cases that I have known personally, children are able to master long, complicated words and in fact may be able to do so with more ease than with short ones in some instances.

2. *Finger contact is essential, using either one or two fingers.*

3. *The child should write the word, after tracing it several times, without looking at the copy.* Looking back and forth tends to break the word into small and sometimes meaningless units. He must learn to see, think, and feel the word as a total unit.

4. *In case of error or interruption in writing, the word should be crossed out and a new start made.* If necessary, the child should go back to the tracing stage, but correcting the word through erasures is not permitted, because the word must be seen as a unit.

5. *Words should be used in context.* If the word the child wants to use is unfamiliar, a different one should be encouraged, or at least he should learn the meaning of the word before going through this procedure. He must learn that the group of alphabetic symbols called a word really means something.

6. *The child must always say the word aloud or to himself as he traces it and as he writes it.*

Although many additional details could be given, the preceding ones outline the essence of the Fernald approach. Addition of the tactile and kinesthetic avenues, or channels, to the visual and auditory ones deserves the major credit for any success this method has over more traditional approaches. After a period of tracing, stage 1, which may vary in time from a few weeks to a few months, the child will be able to enter what Fernald calls stage 2. In stage 2, tracing is no longer required. The child simply looks at the new word in cursive writing, says it to himself as he looks at it, and then writes it without looking at the copy. He proceeds in the same manner as in stage 1, except that he does not trace. In theory, the child is now "tracing" the word mentally.

If, during stage 2, the child encounters difficulty with any particular word, he should go back to actual tracing until he masters that word. As soon as tracing is no longer necessary, the large box used as a word file for the large, cursive words is exchanged for a smaller one for typed words.

At stage 3 the child is able to substitute the printed (typed) word for the cursive version for original learning of a new word. From this point on the Fernald remedial procedure is little different from other reading approaches.

The Fernald method is precise and has been carefully spelled out. It is essentially the same for all children with reading difficulties, although Fernald did recognize various possible causes for reading disability. However, in reviewing these possible causes, Fernald concluded that "most cases of reading disability are due to blocking of the learning process by the use of limited, uniform methods of teaching. These methods, although they have been used successfully with the majority of children, make it impossible for certain children to learn because they interfere with the functioning of certain abilities that these children possess" (1943, pp. 175-176).

Fernald noted that one of the main blocks to reading skill may be the use of an extremely visual method in the schools, with suppression or omission of kinesthetic factors. She also noted that perhaps a number of conditions that are often seen as *causes* of learning difficulties are in reality *results* of learning difficulties. Listed are: (1) emotional instability, (2) visual and auditory perception problems, (3) poor eye coordination, (4) inability to distinguish between similar stimuli (*was* and *saw* and *d* and *b* are given as examples), and (5) inversions, reversals, and other symbol confusion.

Many present authorities would probably disagree with the idea that problems such as poor auditory or visual perception, reversals, inversions, and mirror writing are caused *by* poor learning rather than being possible causes *of* poor learning, but Fernald's reasoning and the basis for it are most interesting. She indicates that all children make errors such as inversions and reversals when learning to read. Sometimes they write in mirror style, they transpose letters, and they confuse short words with other short words. But "learning to read is, in part, a process of eliminating these errors. The child who fails to learn continues to do the things all children do before they have learned. In all our cases, inversions, reversals, and confusion of symbols were part of the picture but disappeared as learning progressed" (1943, p. 178).

An example of one of Fernald's practical teaching suggestions is related to mirror writing, a topic that still causes concern today. Fernald noted that "all our reading disability cases make numerous reversals" (1943, p. 89). She then described the method used in the clinic to deal with mirror writing. The method is as follows:

> If the child is right handed, he is told that he is to always start at the edge of the page *opposite* the hand with which he writes. This is demonstrated, and he has to start at the left hand side of the page, thus the only direction in which he can write is from left to right (unless he writes on the desk). If he is left handed, he is told to always start at the edge of the page on the *same* side as the hand with which he writes. This, too, is demonstrated. Fernald tells an interesting story about an 11-year-old boy who was a complete mirror writer and had been for years. Public school personnel had apparently been unable to implement successful remediation. This boy started at the clinic on Monday, but it was explained that he would have to miss the following Monday, since he was to be part of a demonstration of mirror writing (with his regular school supervisor) before a group of "important educators." The boy attended the Fernald clinic for five days, then was absent, to be a part of the demonstration. At the demonstration, in front of the large audience, he was asked to write on the chalkboard. There he moved to the extreme left of the chalkboard and wrote in a quite ordinary manner. After repeated admonitions to "try it again," it became clear that the mirror writing demonstration was an utter failure. Asked about the situation, the boy said, "Yes, I used to write differently, but I have been going to the University of California, and now I write this way." He further indicated that he liked his "new way" better because people could read it. Then he demonstrated to the assembled educators how he had learned to write the new way (Fernald, 1943, pp. 91-92).

Fernald noted that the same general results were achieved in other cases. The only "remedial" technique was establishing the initial position at the left-hand margin of the paper or chalkboard. She further stated, "These children seem to have as one of their common characteristics an ability to make motor adaptations and reversals. This motor flexibility is perhaps partly responsible for the original establishment of a wrong direction and is the means of its easy correction" (1943, p. 92). This example is repeated here to show the simplicity of some of Fernald's suggestions; it does not imply that *all* remediation is so quick or simple.

Fernald's remedial techniques are not limited to reading nor to those students whom we today call learning disabled. She provided equally specific procedures for teaching spelling and arithmetic to children of normal ability, as well as remedial techniques modified for use with the mentally retarded. However, the VAKT approach to teaching reading to children of normal or above-normal mental ability is the contribution for which she is best known. Several case studies of children with whom Fernald worked follow. In addition to being interesting, these studies indicate why the Fernald method has attracted advocates down through the years.

It must be recognized that the Fernald approach cannot always bring results similar to those outlined in the following case studies. Factors such as the careful selection of cases to present in her text and the exceptional clinical competence of Fernald must be considered in evaluating her almost miraculous results. Also, it must be taken into account that many of her students may have been faced with extremely rigid procedures. However, a number of current methodologies include certain of her basic remedial techniques, and her efforts have historical interest, as well as considerable value for present-day application. Perhaps the following case studies will lead to further interest in Fernald's methods. Then the only reasonable next step is to read *Remedial Techniques in Basic School Subjects.*

CASE 12 (B. L.)* □ TOTAL READING DISABILITY

MALE: Age, 10 years 7 months (May 25, 1929).
I.Q.: 106 (Stanford Revision Binet-Simon).
VISION: Left eye injured when a small child. Vision of right eye normal. *Monocular vision.*
HEARING, SPEECH: Normal.
HANDEDNESS: Right. EYE DOMINANCE: Right.
PHYSICAL CONDITION: Sturdy, no history of illness, very well built, fine looking.
SOCIAL STATUS: Popular with other boys, fond of games such as baseball and football.
FAMILY DATA: Father, head of the purchasing department of a large grocery concern, reports that he has always had difficulty in learning to read and spell. Mother graduate of eighth grade; no reading disability; seems reliable; keeps a good home. One older brother also a serious reading disability. Two older sisters, high school students, no reading disability.

Case history

There is a history of regular school attendance from kindergarten at the age of five until remedial work was begun at the age of 10 years 7 months. B. L. attended a good public school in a first-class neighborhood. When he was 9½ years old, his teachers became so concerned over his reading disability that they arranged a schedule so that he had individual instruction for the greater part of the day.

In spite of everything that had been done, B. L. was a total reading disability case at the age of 10 years 7 months. He could not read the simplest primer or score on any reading test. During all these years in school, he had succeeded in learning to read and write just one word. This word was *her* which he thought spelled *chicken.*

On May 25, 1929, B. L. wrote the following from dictation: *loiy* (boy) *licool* (school), *livui* (them). On May 28, he wrote the following sentences:

"Biuy . . . little loiy, . . . licool is . . . to"
(My good little boy, your school is out today)

---

*Case studies on pp. 125 to 130 from Fernald, G. *Remedial techniques in basic school subjects.* New York: McGraw-Hill Book Co., Inc., 1943.

NOTE: The only words that were written correctly in the above, *little* and *is*, had been learned by B. L. for use in stories he had written on May 26 to 28.

Remedial work

METHODS. B. L. learned to write his first words by tracing them. He drew diagrams, which he labeled, wrote stories, and learned words in connection with projects in geography and history. These were printed for him. After about three months of work, tracing dropped out and B. L. learned new words by the techniques described under stages 2 and 3. He read magazines and books as his ability to read developed.

RESULTS. On the first day of remedial work (May 25, 1929) B. L. drew a diagram of an airplane. He learned to write the following words: *propeller, wheel, tire, aviator, step, canvas, wire for tail, run rudder, biplane.* All these words were recognized by him in print the next day and at various times thereafter when he had occasion to read them.

On this same day, he learned to write the word *Deutsch* in *German script* after tracing it. He wrote the word correctly the next day without seeing the copy again, this in spite of the fact that he knew no German.

B. L. was so excited over his newfound ability to learn words that he insisted on climaxing his first day at the Clinic School by learning the word *hallucination* which he saw on the blackboard of one of the psychology lecture rooms. He went about the neighborhood that evening, asking other boys if they could write *hallucination* and read *Deutsch,* which he wrote for them in script. His mother came to school with him the next morning and said, "I don't know what language it is *B* is learning but could he learn English first?" As a matter of fact, the two words no one in his family or his neighborhood knew were more potent factors in his emotional reconditioning than any ordinary words could have been.

B. L. attended the Clinic School for ten months (May, 1929, to June, 1930) somewhat irregularly. He learned 503 words in 49 days (Sept. 30, 1929, to Jan. 1, 1930) and was able to read them in print. For over two months he continued to write *her* for *chicken* without the least idea that it was incorrect. In this case this was allowed for experimental purposes only. One day in connection with a demonstration, a sentence was dictated to him containing the word *chicken.* He hesitated and then said, "I can't write the word chicken." He was told, "You have been writing it ever since you have been here." He said, "I don't think that word I have been writing is 'chicken.' It doesn't begin right and it isn't long enough." As he said this he moved his hand as if he were making the letters *her.*

At the end of ten months, B. L. was able to read at about fifth-grade level. His spelling was about fourth grade. Against our advice, he was returned to the sixth grade of the public school. He never went through the final stages of reading for speed and comprehension. At the time of our last report from B. L. he was in the tenth grade at the age of 16. He was doing excellent work in science and mathematics. He still read slowly but well enough to get along in school or in some job but not easily enough to read for pleasure.

CASE 22 (M. L.) □ EXTREME READING DISABILITY

MALE: Age, 9 years 1 month (Oct. 3, 1933).
I.Q.: 126
VISION, HEARING, SPEECH: Normal.
HANDEDNESS: Right. EYE DOMINANCE: Right.
PHYSICAL CONDITION: Fine looking, sturdy, great physical dexterity, strong and healthy from infancy.
SPECIAL CHARACTERISTICS: Remarkable ability in art. Draws and paints constantly. Adjudged unusual by competent art critics.
FAMILY DATA: Father very intelligent, self-educated, great reader from early childhood. Did not having schooling above eighth grade. Artistic. Mother, very intelligent and well informed, two years college, majored in art, no reading disability. One brother, two sisters all in superior intelligence group by city school ratings. One sister, two years younger, had difficulty in reading until remedial work was done with results similar to those reported here.

Case history

Very happy, well-behaved child at home and school through kindergarten and during greater part of first grade. He failed to make any progress in first-grade reading. At end of first year he could not read or write the simplest monosyllabic word. As he began to realize he was not keeping up with the other children in his class, be became sullen and hard to manage. During his second year in the first grade, he became a serious discipline problem, both at home and at school. He said he did not want to go to school, did not care to learn to read, and so forth. When the case was brought to our attention, we were told that the difficulty with the boy was indifference—that he did not care to learn.

The boy was used to demonstrate the kinesthetic method at the Pasadena meetings of the A.A.A.S., May, 1931, when he was 7 years 8 months old. There he learned to write, "The horse ran into the barn." These were the first words he had ever learned. On the way home, when he was told he had done well, he said, "I did write the horse ran into the barn, didn't I?" Then he broke down and cried. His parents say that he never cries even when he is badly hurt.

He attended the university Clinic School for three weeks the next year. He found he could learn words by tracing and writing them and made three very nice books, illustrated with his own drawings. He was unable to continue at the university as the family lived at a distance from the school. He went back into the second grade in the public school, confident that he could learn by the new method. There his teacher noticed that he was attempting to trace words and at the same time moving his lips as he said the words. She insisted that he stop both practices and learn as the other children did. When asked the reason for not allowing a method by which the child learned so easily, the teacher said, "I know he can learn if he traces his words but it isn't in the county course of study, and besides we want him to be normal. Unless I watch him all the time, he even traces the words under his desk."

The result was that M. L. slipped back into his old reactions and emotional upset and became more of a behavior problem than ever.

Remedial work

In the fall of 1933, when M. L. was 9 years 1 month of age, he had three months of remedial work with a group of ten children in a special room in one of our city schools. The work was given for three hours every morning, from Oct. 3, 1933, to Jan. 21, 1934. All the children in the group were reading failures.

Results

M. L. learned rapidly. He made six beautiful books about various projects. These books were illustrated by original drawings. Tracing was unnecessary after three weeks. He began to read incessantly. He read "Tom Sawyer" and "Treasure Island," among other books. His parents reported that he wanted to read all the time and that it was often necessary to turn his light out to keep him from reading too long after he had gone to bed. By fall he was reading books in connection with his school projects, magazines, books by Mark Twain, Scott, and so forth.

After three months of remedial work, M. L. was promoted to the third grade. His teacher reported that he wanted to read all the time, that he disliked the "baby" stories the other children were reading. She obtained books that he asked for from the school library. One of these was Macaulay's "History of England," which he read with great interest. The teacher reported that he was easily the best reader in the room. When interviewed at this time with reference to his hobbies, he gave them as "reading, arithmetic, and art."

M. L. was promoted an extra half year in the fall and refused the offer of a second promotion in the spring because he wanted to finish a history project on the California missions with the fourth-grade class. His teacher asked to have him stay with the class until the project was finished as he had looked up the details of making adobe bricks and of the general construction of the missions in encyclopedias and other books and was managing the entire project.

At the age of 15 years 11 months, he entered the tenth grade. He was an incessant reader. Our last report of M. L. from the public school said that he was considered the most gifted child in the school.

CASE 49 (R) □ EXTREME READING DISABILITY

MALE: Age, 9 years 2 months (April 2, 1932).
I.Q.: 131.
PARENTS: Father, well-known playwright. Mother and father divorced. Father remarried. Boy lives with father. Home luxurious. Child well cared for.
SIBLINGS: One half brother, 2 years old.
VISION, HEARING, SPEECH: Normal.
HANDEDNESS: Right.
PHYSICAL CONDITION: Strong, healthy child, very fine looking.

Case history

No report of any behavior difficulty until school failure. Attended kindergarten. Entered first grade at age of 6. From the beginning of his schoolwork he was unable to learn to read. After two years of failure in the public school he was sent to a private school of good standing and was tutored outside of school. At the age of 9 years 2 months, after three years of school, R was unable to score on any reading test or to read the simplest primer. He had developed negative attitudes toward his teachers and toward other children. He was constantly fighting and refused to play with other children during recess periods. He was extremely sensitive concerning his inability to read.

Remedial work

METHOD. R learned his first words by tracing and wrote stories, which were printed for him. He was particularly interested in writing because he wanted to be an author like his father whom he adored. His first stories were quite elaborate tales of adventure. Several of them were plays, which the children acted out. The project method was used to cover the work of the first four grades. He was very much interested in the *National Geographic Magazine* and worked up special topics from copies of the magazine obtained at secondhand book stores. In arithmetic he did not know his number combinations and could not read problems, but was superior in his ability to solve problems if they were read to him.

RESULTS. R's progress in reading was very rapid; his recall for words used in his writing was practically 100 per cent. Tracing was no longer necessary at the end of two months. He still wanted to write about his school projects and about adventures of all sorts. After one year of remedial work he went into the fifth grade of the public school. He was reported as doing very good work in the fifth grade and was promoted to the sixth grade at the end of the year. In June, 1940, at the age of 17 years 2 months, he was graduated from high school. He was admitted to Princeton University in the fall of 1940 at the age of 17 years 5 months.

After the completion of the remedial work, there was no trace of the pervious emotional difficulties. At the end of his high-school course, R was a friendly, charming, well-adjusted individual.

CASE 5 (W. J.) □ TOTAL READING DISABILITY

MALE: Age, 8 years 9 months (June, 1924).
I.Q.: 92.
VISION, HEARING, SPEECH: Normal.
HANDEDNESS: Left.
FAMILY DATA: Incomplete. Reported as having a good home with respectable parents. Lived in a city in northern California. No siblings.

Case history

Difficulty in learning in first grade. Repeated first grade without learning anything. The third year in school he began to play truant, often running away after a day's absence from school and staying away overnight. He was sent to the Whittier State School on account of his continual truancy and his absence from home.

When he entered Whittier it was found that he could recognize only one word and that was Wm. He could not recognize his name "William" or "Willie" in script or print. It was then discovered that he would call any combination of a large and a small letter "William" provided a line was drawn under the small letter, as Dx.

The first day he was started in school at Whittier he attempted to run away but was caught and brought back. It was immediately after this episode that the case was brought to our attention to see what could be done about the reading disability. It was impossible to get a special teacher for him, so one of the older boys in the school who was a leading boy scout was shown how to teach Willie. The first "story" Willie wrote for the boy scout teacher was "I am going to school tomorrow."

A week later we found Willie working away filing words in his "word file." We were told that John, the teacher, was "printing" a story Willie had just written. We stepped out of sight as John rushed in, spread a typed page on the table in front of William, and said, "There, read that." Willie made a book with illustrations cut from magazines. The stories for the dates from Sept. 6 to Oct. 27 are given just as the boy wrote them.

At the end of seven weeks, tracing was no longer necessary and Willie was eager to read. He was especially anxious to take all the tests given at the school although he had refused to go into the room where a group test was being given the first day we attempted to test him.

At the end of three months he had made three grades progress in reading and spelling and was allowed to go into regular classes. There was no further difficulty either in his school progress or in attendance.

A year after he had been returned to his home the school report was satisfactory.

On Mar. 15, 1940, W. J. was holding a good job in a printing establishment where he had been for six years.

Stories written by W. J. with the help of J. M., a high-school boy scout

"I am going to school tomorrow." (Sept. 6)

The Cat (Sept. 10)

"We have a cat. His name is Kitty. He is a black cat. He is very tame. We feed him meat and milk. He likes for us to pet him. He sleeps in a basket. We like him very much. He is a good pet."

The Horse (Sept. 17)

"We have a horse. We call him Benito. We ride on his back. He can run fast. He can trot too. When he trots we bounce up and down. When he runs we do not bounce. I like to ride at a gallop. He is a Spark Plug. He will not kick or bite me."

The Brown Bear

"The Brown Bear lives in the woods. The Brown Bear likes meat. He likes to play in the woods. He can run and jump. He stands on his hind legs. The bear likes honey. There are no bears in Los Angeles that will bite little boys."

The White Lamb (Oct. 6)

"We have a little lamb he is white. When we feed him he goes baa baa. The little white lamb has a brother. He is a black lamb. They play all the time. They play and eat in the tall grass. We all like the little lambs. They are good pets. They like for little boys and girls to play with them. They have pink ribbons on their necks."

The Indians (Oct. 15)

"The Indians live in North America and South America. The Indians were fierce people. The Indians liked dogs. The Indians ride horses. They killed Buffalos. They killed deer and caught fish in the rivers. They ride in canoes on the rivers. They hunt ducks for their supper. They cook the ducks over the fire and eat them. They live in wigwams made out of Buffalo skins. They shoot bows and arrows."

The Sailor Boy (Oct. 20)

"The sailor rides in a boat. The boat sails over the waves. He is on a war ship. They fight other ships. They have airplanes on the ship. The airplanes drop bombs. The bombs sink the ship. The sailor gets into a life boat when the ship sinks. Then they row to land. Sometimes the sailor get drowned. When the life boat sinks they have to swim to land. They like to ride over the waves. When it is rough they get sick. I would like to be sailor."

Football (Oct. 27)

"I like to play football. You have to run fast. You get hurt lots. We have three foot ball teams. The C team. The B team and the A team. The C team won three games. I lost one game. The B team lost one game. The A team won two games."

CASE 26

This boy was diagnosed as "feeble-minded," with an I.Q. of 37, by group tests given in the schools of a large city when he was 12 years old. He was a total reading disability case at the age of 17 when he came to Los Angeles. He had heard of the reading work that was being done at the university and he saved money enough to buy a ticket to Los Angeles. On arrival he went to the Traveler's Aid office and asked to be directed to the place "where they could teach you to read." He had a copy of Alfred Wiggam's story in *The Reader's Digest*, which he could not read but had heard read. He was finally delivered at the laboratory in company with an energetic lady who had become sufficiently interested in what the boy had told her to make the trip to the university with him.

A carefully given individual intelligence test showed that his I.Q. was at least 108, even with the reading disability. He was unable to score on any reading or spelling test. He had attended school quite regularly as a child but had been unable to learn to read even the simplest material.

At first we said we could not take him in the Clinic School as it was full beyond capacity already. "But he said, "I came more than 2,000 miles to learn to read." We finally arranged to give him work for two hours in the afternoon. We suggested that he might be able to get a morning job. The next day we told him one of the teachers would try to help him get a job for the morning. He said, "Why you told me to get a job yesterday. So I did." This was during the worst period of the depression when jobs were supposed to be nonexistent. The job was in a garage washing cars. For this he was given a place to sleep, two meals a day, and money enough to pay car fare and buy lunch. Case 26 thought it was a "swell" job and held it till he had finished his remedial work.

In the first three months, working two hours for five days a week, he learned 787 words. He made five grades progress in ten months. He passed his examinations for a driver's license. He could read newspapers and pulp magazines. He found a full-time job managing a little moving-picture theater, so he discontinued school.

One day in the fall, he burst into my office and asked if I knew how to find his teacher of the year before. I inquired what he wanted of him in such a hurry. "Why," he said, "the poor fellow graduated last June and he hasn't been able to get a job. I am just giving up my job for a better one and I thought he would like my old job." We helped him locate his former teacher. A few days later we visited the theater and found our university graduate happily occupied with the job that had just been relinquished by his former pupil.

The use of number fact cards, reinforced by three-dimensional representations of the answers (which may be experienced tactually), is one variation of a multisensory technique.

The Orton-Gillingham structured multisensory approach

Anna Gillingham is the major author of an approach that at times is called the Orton-Gillingham approach, the Gillingham approach, or the Gillingham-Stillman approach. This structured, multisensory teaching method is outlined in the book *Remedial Training for Children with Specific Disability in Reading, Spelling, and Penmanship* by Anna Gillingham and Bessie Stillman. This book was first published in 1946, with a number of revisions since that time. Orton's name is usually included in speaking of this approach since, by Gillingham's own account, it was developed as a result of her contact with Orton and based on his theoretical ideas. Stillman became acquainted with Gillingham and with Orton's work, and thus became a partner in the development of this approach.

Because this widely recognized multisensory approach began with the work of Orton, this account should undoubtedly start with Orton's efforts with word blind students in Iowa. The national recognition of Orton's interest in what was later to be called dyslexia started when he presented a report on a 16-year-old nonreader to the American Neurological Association in 1925 (Orton Society, 1963).

Orton's report documented the case of M. P., a 16-year-old boy who had normal visual acuity and intelligence and no medically substantiable evidence of brain defect or damage but was unable to recognize whole word patterns and therefore was unable to learn to read. Orton coined the word *strephosymbolia* (meaning twisted symbols) to describe M. P.'s condition and was convinced that it could be overcome with proper training.

Orton attempted to understand and explain the problem of language disabilities in children without brain injury in relation to his work and research with adults who had sustained brain damage. He noted that brain-damaged adults often suffered a language facility loss similar to these children who had no apparent or known brain damage. His hypothesis was that specific language disabilities, often exhibited as severe reading problems, may be because the child had not developed hemispheric dominance in specific areas of the brain. He postulated that, when mixed dominance was evident in the motor areas of performance a similar mixing might occur in the language-controlling areas of the brain. Orton related dominance to the "quality" of the brain structure, meaning number of brain cells and abundance of blood supply to the brain. His explanation of mirror writing and reversals was that, when the records of the association between written words and their meanings are stored in the dominant hemisphere, a mirror copy of these words and their meanings perhaps is stored in the nondominant hemisphere. Then, with mixed dominance the child might select inconsistently, thus causing the reversals, mirror writing, and so forth.

Orton remained interested in the effect of actual brain injury or neurological dysfunction, whether demonstrable or not, throughout his life. By the 1930s he had developed a basis on which he described and prescribed educational remediation for a particular type of reading disability that can occur in the child with adequate intelligence and normal visual and auditory acuity. (Note how well this description fits our present definition of learning disabilities.)*

Gillingham met Orton while receiving special training in the Language Research Project, a reading clinic in New York City connected with the New York Neurological Institute and Columbia University. Based on ideas from Orton, she developed a remedial approach that quickly received wide recognition. Her first complete remedial guide was published during the Depression, at a time when a clamor was arising to do something about the seriously high numbers of poor or nonreaders. Her dedication to Orton and his beliefs and theories is indicated by words from the foreword of her text *Remedial Training for Children with Specific Disability in Reading, Spelling, and Penmanship.* She stated, "His charge to me to organize remedial techniques consistent with his working hypothesis has steadily enlarged in scope until it has become the consummation of my lifelong service to children." This is undoubtedly a major reason why her approach, though developed by her, is usually called the Orton-Gillingham approach.

Gillingham characterized her approach as phonetic; however, she also specifically stated that "our technique is based on the close association of visual, auditory, and kinesthetic elements" (1968, p. 40). In contrasting her technique to that in which sight words are

*Much of Orton's theoretical base is no longer accepted, but it was most important to the original development of the Orton-Gillingham method. It also provided the base for further investigation and thus was of considerable importance for this reason as well.

taught, then later broken down into letter sounds, she stated "our technique is to teach the sounds of the letters and then build these letter sounds into words, like bricks in a wall" (1968, p. 40). She further noted that this method *could not* be used as supplementary to that of learning a sight vocabulary. She believed that the two methods, and the concepts underlying them, were mutually exclusive.

In simple terms, Gillingham's method is based on the following rationale: *Children must be taught through the constant use of association of (1) how a letter or word looks, (2) how it sounds, and (3) how the speech organs and the hand feel when producing the word.*

As part of her program, Gillingham provides a narrative entitled "The Growth of Written Language." This story explains how people once communicated only through spoken language and then evolved to picture writing, pictographs, ideograms, and finally alphabetic writing. The teacher is provided with examples of early American Indian writing, Egyptian pictographs, Chinese writing (evolution from pictographs to ideograms), and the modern Roman alphabet. She is advised to adapt the story to the age and interest level of the child. The narrative ends by explaining that many other boys and girls have difficulty in reading and that many important and famous adults had such difficulty when they were children. The closing "clincher" is telling the children that they will be taught in an entirely different way. Gillingham's use of the idea that many others, including famous people, have had reading difficulties is quite similar to the reconditioning approach used by Fernald at the beginning of work with a new student.

Although a number of school districts in the nation presently use the Orton-Gillingham method in modified form, the techniques outlined by Gillingham are quite specific and the admonition to teachers is to use these techniques precisely. *Remedial Training for Children with Specific Disability in Reading, Spelling, and Penmanship* is a large book, 340 pages long, complete with examples of a wide variety of potential difficulties (and what to do about them), illustrations of children's work, and step-by-step instructions to the remedial teacher. It is initially phonic in approach but evolves into a truly multisensory approach. Examples of guidelines and techniques recommended for use in remedial reading are given in the following paragraphs, with priority given to those that are unique and tend to differentiate this approach from Fernald-type multisensory approaches.

Letters are always introduced by a key word. These key words must always be given by the pupil whenever the phonogram is shown. For example, when the *b* card is shown, the pupil is to respond *boy.*

The pupil must learn to recognize and explain the differences between vowel and consonant sounds. Gillingham consonant drill cards are printed on white, and vowel-sound cards are salmon-colored. The child must understand differences in the manner in which vowels and consonants are formed by the vocal cords and mouth.

Drill cards must be presented so as to utilize the "associative processes." Each new phonogram (drill card) is taught by the following associative processes:

1. Two-part association of the visual symbol with the name and sound of the letter. This is accomplished by exposing a card with the letter while the teacher says the *name* of the letter and the pupil repeats it. As soon as the child has learned the name, the *sound* is made by the teacher and repeated by the pupil. Association 1 then is visual-auditory (V-A) and auditory-kinesthetic (A-K).

(The K refers to vocalization muscle response.)

2. Association of the sound represented by a letter with the name of the letter. This is done by the teacher making the sound and asking the child what letter has that sound. The card is covered. Association 2 then is auditory-auditory (A-A).
3. Two-part association of the form of the letter with how it feels and looks. This is accomplished by the teacher carefully writing the letter and then explaining its form. The pupil then traces the letter, moving over the teacher's lines. After tracing the letter, the student copies it, writes it from memory, and then writes it while not looking at what he is writing. Association 3 then is visual-kinesthetic (V-K) and kinesthetic-visual (K-V). (Here the K refers to finger, hand, and arm kinesthetics.)

The first group of letters presented to the child must include only unequivocal sounds and nonreversible forms. Although there is no "magic" list, the Gillingham text is organized so that the following group of ten letters should be given first.

a	apple	**h**	hat	**k**	kite	**t**	top
b	boy	**i**	it	**m**	man		
f	fun	**j**	jam	**p**	pan		

Writing procedure must be applied in a specific way with all letters. This procedure includes the following:

1. The teacher writes the letter.
2. The pupil traces the letter.
3. The pupil copies the letter.
4. The pupil writes it without copy.
5. The pupil writes it with eyes averted.

Experience indicates the cursive writing is to be preferred to manuscript. Certain specific suggestions on writing procedures are also given, such as not to use the words *before* and *after* in giving instructions (as in the instructions about making the circular bottom part of the small *b* or *d*). This is because the child typically placed in such a remedial class will have trouble with this concept. Alternative strategies are suggested.

A specific spelling procedure is given. The child should learn to spell a few days after sound blending has been started. The teacher first says the word slowly, overemphasizing its phonetic parts. She makes certain the child hears all the letters in the word. Then, after the teacher pronounces the word once again, the child (1) repeats the word, (2) names the letters, (3) writes the word, naming each letter as he writes it, and (4) reads the word he has just written. This is called the Four-point Program. The naming of letters aloud as each one is written is featured as a point that Orton favored to establish visual-auditory-kinesthetic associations. It actually is simultaneous oral and written spelling, but because its unique feature is the oral spelling, it has been named by Gillingham *simultaneous oral spelling* and abbreviated S.O.S. It is used as a linkage between sound and letter form. S.O.S. is also used by Gillingham to teach nonphonetic words through impressing of letter sequences. S.O.S. is recommended throughout the remedial program.

After the pupil learns to read and write any three-letter, perfectly phonetic word, sentence and story writing is begun. Gillingham believes that, although these first stories are simple ones (limited by the three-letter words that have now been mastered), this is not inhibiting and does not cause dissatisfaction on the part of 11- or 12-year old children. As the pupil makes up a sentence, the teacher is to help if asked but only in sounding out the troublesome word.

Syllable concepts are specifically taught to remedial pupils of all ages. Gillingham teaches detached syllables such as *pel* and *vil* before teaching actual words separated into syllables. It is stressed that just as short words are built from letters, longer words are built from syllables. Specific spelling rules for building words with syllables are taught and systematic exercise is provided.

Nonphonetic words are taught by jingles, drill, and "tricks."

Writing to dictation is encouraged, and a specific procedure is outlined. Toward the end of the program of building reading ability by introduction and understanding of phonograms, some sight words are introduced. Although pupils may learn to exercise sight recognition of words already acquired through the phonetic approach, they should learn new words throughout their school careers by the alphabetic rather than the sight-word approach. Slowly the child is permitted to read other materials and can take part in reading with his regular class on a planned basis. Eventually he will be encouraged to read on his own as much as possible.

As noted at the beginning of this review, many teachers use parts of Gillingham's approach, with some school districts using a modified version developed by staff members of that district. It is regularly used with both learning disabled students and the mildly mentally retarded. It is attractive to those teachers who prefer the phonetic initial approach and who believe in the manner in which Gillingham views phonics instruction. In view of its persistence as a method used from the late 1930s until today, the Orton-Gillingham method likely may still be in use in some form in the 21st century.

MULTISENSORY APPROACHES—VARIATIONS AND ADAPTATIONS

The Fernald and Orton-Gillingham multisensory approaches are undoubtedly the most often cited in reviews of learning disability methods, but many variations and adaptations are of interest. We will review a method suggested by Harold and Harriet Blau, variations of the Fernald approach proposed by Jeanette Miccinati, and a motoric/linguistic method advocated by Helen Kaufman and Phyllis Biren. Also included is a review of an innovative modification of more standard multisensory approaches, the Apples, Bananas, and Candy Approach, suggested by Rita Brown. These authors are suggesting what they consider to be improvements or adaptations of the major multisensory approaches, or related techniques, that have grown out of their practical experience. Their suggestions and recommendations are representative of a wide variety of multisensory-related approaches in use with learning disabled students.

The AKT modality blocking approach

Harold and Harriet Blau have reported considerable success with a method that presumes that at times one of the modalities (visual, auditory, kinesthetic, or tactile) may be actively interfering with the ability to learn through the other modalities (Blau and Blau, 1969, pp. 404-408). They believe that this is most often the visual channel; therefore they recommend blocking visual input in initial remediation. They propose an initially nonvisual, AKT method, which may be described as follows:

1. The child closes his eyes or is blindfolded.
2. A word is traced on his back.
3. The word is then spelled aloud by the teacher, letter by letter, as it is traced.
4. In some cases the same letters in three-dimensional plastic or wood are placed before the child so that he may trace them with his fingertips as the teacher traces on his back. (This might, in certain cases, cause overloading and should be tried with care.)
5. Three-dimensional letters are placed in

front of the student in scrambled form, and he is to reproduce the sequence he has just felt traced on his back. He is still blindfolded.

6. When the child has the letters in the right order, he takes off the blindfold and experiences the letters (the word) visually.
7. He writes the word on a card for his word file.

Blau and Blau indicate that once a word has been mastered in this manner it seems to be recognizable in the purely visual form with little difficulty. This is similar to Fernald's observation in the VAKT method.

In many instances, a teacher's aide can effectively provide this training, thus reducing the cost factor. Blau and Blau observe that remediation is often rapid, and they believe that a number of children who have learned through the VAKT method may have learned in spite of inclusion of the visual modality rather than because of it. Their work suggests that visual input is the most likely offender in obstructing or short-circuiting the other modalities, and their reported success with individual cases provides adequate reason to consider the possibility of nonvisual AKT, along with VAKT.

Variations and motivational techniques for use with the Fernald approach

Of the many possible variations of the basic Fernald approach, Miccinati (1979) has provided one of the more interesting published overviews. Some of Miccinati's suggestions are as follows:

1. Place a piece of plain paper over a screen and write the word to be learned on the paper with a black crayon or grease pencil. After removing the screen, the raised effect that results provides greater kinesthetic and tactile feedback than simply tracing over a "smooth" word. Experimentation may be necessary to provide the maximum effect. (It may be noted that this type of sensory feedback is similar to what permits the blind to read braille.)
2. After tracing a word on paper, some students may receive valuable additional assistance in revisualizing the word if they are assisted in tracing it in the air. This addition of large muscle movements may be of greater value to some students with eyes open and to others with eyes closed. Individual experimentation is required to determine the best procedure.
3. Although Fernald indicated that subjects should pronounce the entire word while tracing it, some students seem to do better when they first say the word one letter at a time. Miccinati suggests that when students want to do this it should be permitted, but the student should be encouraged to pronounce the entire word, not the letters, as soon as possible.
4. Writing in sand in response to words pronounced from a word list, then matching this word to the same word (selecting from a set of word cards prepared in advance by the teacher) may prove of value to some students. Students with very poor visual imagery may not benefit from this method because of the lack of sharpness of the sand image of the word, but for some students it is quite effective.

In addition to these and other variations, Miccinati suggests a number of reinforcement techniques that may be of value when used with the basic Fernald approach. The inference is that the exposure provided by tracing simply may not be enough. Although Fernald indicates that students should trace words over and over until they can write them correctly without looking at them, motivation to continue such a repetitive task could become a problem. Miccinati's recommended reinforcement techniques are variations that, in addition to being multisensory in nature, should be more likely to sustain interest. A few activities suggested by Miccinati follow (1979, p. 141):

1. Have the students type the words that they previously traced.
2. Spell the traced word with plastic letters, scramble the letters, and then have the student place them back in the correct sequence.
3. Have the student write on this chalkboard with a paintbrush dipped in water. (The "water-writing" soon fades, but there is initial visual feedback along with the large muscle kinesthetic input.)
4. The teacher may write new stories, using the words the student has already mastered and added to his file. The student then proceeds as though he had just developed the story.
5. A story may be written in two colors, for example, blue and red. The blue words the student already knows, and the red are new words or words of which the student is uncertain. The story is then read by the teacher and student, with the teacher reading the red words and the student reading the blue. As words are learned, they become blue words. (This procedure is suggested for use with more severely disabled readers.)

Innovative teachers have developed many such variations and adaptations of the Fernald method. If the variation is logical in terms of the basic rationale, then it is worth trying. Using multisensory reinforcement techniques is certainly a good idea, because some students will tire of the tracing activity before they have mastered a new word. Much of the value of the various Fernald-related techniques seems to be in the motivation of doing something different and in the opportunities for the student to learn through some of the major learning modalities.

A motoric/linguistic method

Kaufman and Biren have developed a "structured, logical, and sequential method of teaching cursive writing" (1979, p. 209) that they use as a vehicle for teaching spelling and reading. Indicating that "since it is necessary to spell as you write, and then to read what you have written, it is natural and meaningful to teach writing, spelling, and reading together" (1979, p. 209). Their method, which is more like the Orton-Gillingham than the Fernald approach, is initially based on a number of assumptions about the value of cursive, as opposed to manuscript, writing. These include: (1) it is continuous and connected and thus represents a whole-word gestalt, (2) it provides for more consistent left-right orientation, (3) the links between letters encourage writing on a straight line, and (4) the various cursive letters (for example, *d* and *b*) are more clearly different than their manuscript counterparts and thus are not so likely to be confused. They observed that a number of students who had been having serious problems with manuscript writing were able to learn to write cursively with considerable ease and success.

Their teaching method follows. (This is a condensed description to provide understanding of some of the major steps.)

1. The *manuscript* letter is written on the chalkboard, and the teacher asks what sound the letter makes.
2. Emphasizing the *sound,* not the name of

the letter, class members suggest words that begin with that sound.

3. The *cursive* letter is then superimposed over the manuscript letter on the board, thus demonstrating the similarity and assisting the students to develop an association between the two. (The superimposition works for 19 of the letters; for the other 7, the cursive and manuscript are placed on the board side by side.)
4. The first cursive letter actually taught is *n*. How it is formed and written is stated in a very specific way. How each letter is to be written is always explained in the same way, using specified words in such explanations.
5. The first rule—stressed with respect to each of the letters—is "every letter begins on the line, ends on the line, and gets a short link" (Kaufman and Biren, 1979, p. 213). A "link" is the connection between two letters, and a graphic way for explaining this concept is provided. Later, after many of the letters have been taught, the students will learn that there are exceptions to this rule, but at the beginning it is taught as an absolute.
6. The first letter taught is *n,* the second is *i;* then the word *in* is taught. The next letter is *t;* then *tin* can be taught. Next is *e,* permitting the spelling of *ten,* followed by *m,* so that *men* can be taught. Then, in combination, the phrase *ten men* can be used. When the recommended sequence of letters is followed, each new letter permits the learning of a new, phonetic, three-letter word.
7. As the student begins to write words, the second rule is taught. This rule is: "You must keep your crayon on the paper until the whole word is finished" (Kaufman and Biren, 1979, p. 214).

This Kaufman and Biren variation of multisensory teaching has a number of interesting features and techniques. For example, students are provided with individual stimulus cards (pipe cleaner or sandpaper letters) that they finger-trace as they say the sound. Next they progress to finger-writing on their desks. They begin by writing on a piece of paper with just one horizontal line and a starting dot at the left so that they must write in the proper left-to-right manner.

Certain specific terminology must be used by the teacher; the student's familiarity with these basic terms leads to confidence and eliminates confusion. Various activities and worksheets are recommended, all related to the concept of consistent, cursive writing. This method relates the memory of kinesthetic patterns to phonemes and provides for the integration of writing, spelling and reading through the construction of stories.

Kaufman and Biren provide for selection from a variety of related activities and materials, but the basic, initial presentation of letters and three-letter words, including the manner in which letters are formed and linked together, should be followed closely. This interesting method is an excellent example of some of the more structured multisensory variations in use today in learning disabilities programs across the nation.

The apples, bananas, and candy approach

Although most multisensory approaches use some combination of visual, auditory, kinesthetic, and tactile modalities, with little attention to the gustatory and olfactory, Rita Brown reported on one in which these two modalities were used with good results (1975). She titled her report "Apples, Bananas, and Candy," in reference to the edibles that were provided as each new beginning sound or letter was introduced.

Children in Brown's study were first graders who had not progressed satisfactorily with the Fernald approach and who had serious difficulty with the names of letters and initial consonant sounds. They also had difficulty in correctly recalling words and in naming objects associated with everyday activities. By March of their first-grade year, standardized tests indicated that they were approximately 1 year behind the majority of their age and grade peers.

In Brown's approach, something edible was provided as each new sound or letter was introduced. Edibles used in the Apples, Bananas, and Candy Approach were:

Apples	Juice	Raisins
Bananas	Ketchup	Sandwiches
Candy	Lollypops	Tomatoes
Doughnuts	Marsh-mallows	Ugli-fruit
Eggs		Vinegar
Fritos	Nuts	Watermelon
Grapes	Oranges	Xmas candy
Honey	Peanuts	Yams
Icing	Quinces	Zero food

This approach included tracing, writing in a tray of salt, writing on the chalkboard with a wet brush, and tracing on the child's back as both child and teacher vocalized the letter or sound. Each letter was introduced with food, but before a child could proceed to a new letter (and new food) it was required that understanding of previous learning be successfully demonstrated. The food proved to be an effective memory device, for all of the children in the program were able to move on to more conventional approaches after they had mastered the alphabet through this extraordinary approach. As reported by Brown, the motivation provided through this approach was exceptional and, along with the other multisensory components, permitted the children to progress to writing and reading experience stories and to the use of the regular basal readers.

This approach may not be practical or desirable in all cases; however, if it is used, other foods might be more appropriate. In this case, it seemed to provide interest, high motivation, and a mnemonic bridge to more effective learning for this particular group of children. This and other similar approaches using food to introduce letters or sounds are the only ones that have used the senses of taste and smell as part of an overall multisensory approach. They provide an interesting contrast to the various combinations of VAKT approaches that have been reviewed in this chapter—an appropriate way to conclude this consideration of multisensory approaches.

SUMMARY

Many programs, techniques, and approaches have been called multisensory, but this chapter has focused on those utilizing the visual, auditory, kinesthetic, and tactile modalities in some coordinated, integrated manner. The emphasis has been on two major methods, the Fernald and the Orton-Gillingham; these two (or some adapted version of them) seem to be the most often used in programs for the learning disabled.

Fernald's program was developed first, with an approach initiated in the early 1920s in a remedially oriented school at the University of California at Los Angeles. The Orton-Gillingham approach was developed primarily by Gillingham but was based on the theoretical postulations of Orton. It became known nationally at a somewhat later date than the Fernald approach but appears to have become more widely used, perhaps because it is more structured and does not require as much teacher innovation.

The Gillingham and Fernald methods have many similarities: (1) both use positive reconditioning before commencing remediation; (2) both use visual, auditory, and kinesthetic channels for teaching reading; (3) both involve tracing; and, (4) both prefer cursive writing. However, certain *major* differences exist between these two methodologies as well. The first and most important difference is the insistence on the phonetic initial approach element of Gillingham. In contrast, Fernald is concerned with an initial VAKT approach—that is, stimulation through all channels at once. A second difference is the emphasis of Gillingham on one sound, one letter at a time. Fernald is equally concerned that children *not* learn one sound, one letter at a time. A not-so-major, but nevertheless specific, difference is the manner in which Fernald deliberately encourages the child to select long or complicated words of high-interest level for the first words to read, whereas Gillingham starts with three-letter words (after use of the phonogram drill cards). It is interesting that both methods have had considerable success in actual application. Certain variations and adaptations of these two basic multisensory approaches gain acceptance from time to time, and many teachers use multisensory components, perhaps without even realizing it. Some may use a part of one of these approaches (for example, Fernald's "tracing") thinking they are using the entire approach. At times when we hear that a given approach "did not work," it is later established that critical elements were left out and meaningful substitutes were not provided.

Like all other approaches, the multisensory types apparently do not work with some students, but they do work well with many others. In fact, as noted in this chapter, more of the various learning disabilities authorities may support at least some use of the multisensory techniques than they do any other approach. One of the common cautions—the suggestion that use of multisensory approaches may cause overloading with some students, especially those who are hyperactive—has not been supported in some studies with students who might be called mildly hyperactive. It seems, then, that this concern should be further investigated; it may not be valid with many students who are today called hyperactive.

Because multisensory approaches work (at least theoretically) through all of the major learning modalities, they have the potential to be of value even in those cases where it cannot satisfactorily be determined just where the teaching emphasis should be placed. They must not, however, be considered the final answer. The varied nature of the disabilities that have come under the learning disabilities umbrella definition dictates the continuing need for a wide range of teaching approaches based on accurate, comprehensive, ongoing assessment.

REFERENCES AND SUGGESTED READINGS

Blau, H., and Blau, H. A theory of learning to read by "modality blocking." In Arena, J. (Ed.) *Successful programming: many points of view.* Pittsburgh: Association for Children with Learning Disabilities, 1969.

Brown, R. Apples, bananas, and candy, *Elementary English,* 1975, *52,* 539-540.

Bush, W., and Giles, M. *Aids to psycholinguistic teaching.* Columbus, Ohio: Charles E. Merrill Publishing Co., 1969.

Carbo, M. A word imprinting technique for children with severe memory disorders, *Teaching Exceptional Children,* 1978, *11,* 3-5.

Cruickshank, W., and others. *A teaching method for brain-injured and hyperactive children.* Syracuse, N.Y.: Syracuse University Press, 1961.

Fernald, G. *Remedial techniques in basic school subjects.* New York: McGraw-Hill Book Co., 1943.

Frostig, M. *Selection and adaptation of reading methods.* San Rafael, Calif.: Academic Therapy Publications, 1973.

Gillingham, A. *Collected papers, Orton Society Monograph III.* Pomfret, Conn.: The Society, 1967.

Gillingham, A., and Stillman, B. *Remedial training for children with specific disability in reading, spelling, and penmanship* (ed. 7). Cambridge, Mass.: Educators Publishing Service, 1968.

Hammill, D., and Bartel, N. *Teaching children with learning and behavior problems.* Boston: Allyn and Bacon, Inc., 1975.

Holton, M., and Kimball, E. *Games, seat work, and sense training exercises.* Chicago: A. Flanagan Co., 1905.

Johnson, D., and Myklebust, H. *Learning disabilities, educational principles and practices.* New York: Grune & Stratton, Inc., 1967.

Kaluger, G., and Kolson, C. *Reading and learning disabilities.* Columbus, Ohio: Charles E. Merrill Publishing Co., 1969.

Kaufman, H., and Biren, P. Cursive writing: an aid to reading and spelling, *Academic Therapy,* 1979, *15,* 209-219.

Kephart, N. *The slow learner in the classroom.* Columbus, Ohio: Charles E. Merrill Publishing Co., 1971.

Koepsel, E. A comparison of teaching reading to educationally handicapped children using Fernald's VAKT method, Blaus' AKT method, and existing methods. Unpublished doctoral dissertation. Greeley, Colo.: University of Northern Colorado, 1974.

Lerner, J. *Children with learning disabilities* (ed. 2). Boston: Houghton Mifflin Co., 1976.

McCoy, L. Braille: a language for severe dyslexics, *Journal of Learning Disabilities,* 1975, *8,* 288-292.

Miccinati, J. The Fernald technique: modifications increase the probability of success, *Journal of Learning Disabilities,* 1979, *12,* 139-142.

Orton, S. *Reading, writing, and speech problems in children.* New York: W. W. Norton & Co., Inc., 1937.

Orton Society. *Specific language disabilities* (vol. 13). Pomfret, Conn.: The Society, 1963.

Thompson, L. *Reading disability.* Springfield, Ill.: Charles C Thomas, Publisher, 1969.

Valett, R. *Developing cognitive abilities.* St. Louis: The C. V. Mosby Co., 1978.

chapter 7

Language-development-related approaches

Why do children learn language? What motivates them to continue to learn, once the process starts? Just how does the language learning process take place? What are the essential steps? A number of hypotheses propose answers to these questions, but with no real consensus. Observing and recording what a child says as he develops language is possible, but authorities are not certain what has taken place to elicit each new word or communicative attempt. Some believe that language is an *innate*, rather than an *acquired*, human attribute (Smith, Goodman, and Meredith, 1976, p. 16). According to this theory, language learning is instinctive; the infant needs only to be exposed to natural language. Support for this idea stems partially from language developing so rapidly, and with little encouragement, in many cases. The child with normal intelligence and sensory ability simply learns, regardless of variations in culture and language.

In tracing the origins of the human species and the development of intelligence and language, Leakey notes what he believes to be "powerful demonstration of just how firmly language is rooted in the human brain" (1977, p. 180). He refers to evidence indicating that, when we talk to a very young baby, the sound of our voice elicits faint, coordinated muscular movements that occur in infants of all races and cultures. These reactions to the human voice indicate some sort of built-in recognition and muscular response that in most children soon results in a vocal response and the beginning of language learning. The young child appears to respond in this manner to any voice in any language; thus it may be interpreted as the innate reaction of one member to any other member of the species.

An insightful series of observations about language learning was made by Smith, Goodman, and Meredith with regard to why children learn language. They first noted that, in contrast to, for example, the growth of bones and muscles, "Language learning is not a natural organic part of growing up. Children who grow up isolated from society do not develop "language" (1976, p. 11). They further observed that the ability of children to think symbolically and to produce sounds makes it *possible* for them to develop meaningful language, but it is "the need to communicate that makes it *necessary* for children to learn language" (p. 11). Finally, they noted that "as language develops, it becomes a tool of the child's striving to derive meaning from his world. In turn, language is expanded by this striving. *There must be a purpose in learning, and communication is the immediate reason for language learning*" (p. 12). Other authors make similar statements about language, although not all so effectively and succinctly.

Although there are differing theories about many aspects of language, and lively debate continues about various language hypotheses, authorities generally agree on certain "facts." These include:

1. All human infants with normal intelligence have the ability to develop language.
2. To develop normal language, a child must have opportunities to *hear* language. This means that other humans must be around, auditory acuity must be adequate, and the central nervous system must be functioning normally.
3. The child's psychological adjustment must be sufficient to permit him to relate to and identify with other humans, or language learning may be significantly inhibited.
4. Even though language learning is initiated in a relatively normal manner, it may be retarded by negative environmental factors.
5. The development of adequate language provides a significant part of the basis for the child to think—that is, to efficiently derive meaning from the world.
6. The need to communicate provides continued motivation for the child to develop language.

Chalfant and Scheffelin (1969) have provided a summary of how children acquire auditory receptive language and expressive auditory language in the form of a task analysis (Tables 5 and 6). Although some might suggest a slightly different sequence, their efforts are probably representative of a general consensus in the field.

Regardless of debates concerning precisely how language is developed, authorities almost universally agree that the development of adequate language ability is the focal point of much of what is done in the existing system of formal education. The primary grades are concerned with developing basic skills in reading, arithmetic, spelling, and writing. In upper elementary grades the emphasis continues on basic skill development, and goals are expanded to include the development of understanding and concepts essential to functioning in society. Benjamin Bloom and others in *Taxonomy of Educational Objectives* recognize three major domains within which educational objectives may be classified: (1) the cognitive, (2) the affective, and (3) the psychomotor (1956). *The cognitive, which has*

TABLE 5. Acquiring auditory receptive language: a task analysis

I. Attention: Attend to vocally produced auditory sound units, i.e., noises, speech sounds, words, phrases, sentences.
II. Discrimination: Discriminate between auditory-vocal sound units.
III. Establishing correspondences: Establish reciprocal associations between the auditory-vocal sound units and objects or events:
   A. Store and identify auditory-vocal sound units as meaningful auditory-language signals. Substitute auditory-language signals for actual objects and/or events.
   B. Establish word order sequences and sentence patterns.
IV. Automatic auditory-vocal decoding:
   A. Improve interpretation by analyzing increasingly more complex auditory-language signals.
   B. Increase the speed and accuracy of the reception of auditory-language signals through variation, practice, and repetition to the point of automatic interpretation.
   C. Shift attention from the auditory-language signals to the total meaning that is carried by the signal sequence.
V. Terminal behavior: Respond appropriately to verbal commands, instructions, explanations, questions, and statements.

From Chalfant, J., and Scheffelin, M. *Central processing dysfunctions in children,* NINDS Monograph No. 9. Washington, D.C.: U.S. Department of Health, Education, and Welfare, 1969, p. 77.

TABLE 6. Acquiring expressive auditory language: a task analysis

I. Intention:
   A. Possess the need to communicate.
   B. Decide to send message vocally.
II. Formulate message by retrieving and sequencing the appropriate vocal-language signals.
III. Organize the vocal-motor sequence:
   A. Retrieve the vocal-motor sequence for producing the selected vocal-language signals.
   B. Execute the vocal-motor sequence for producing the vocal-language signal.
IV. Automatic vocal encoding:
   A. Combine simple vocal-language signals to form more complex vocal-language signal sequences.
   B. Increase the rate, accuracy, length, total number, and types of vocal-language signal sequences to the point of automatic production.
   C. Shift attention from the mechanics of producing vocal-language signal sequences to the contents of the message to be sent.
V. Terminal behavior: To produce appropriate verbal instructions, commands, explanations, descriptions, and questions.

From Chalfant, J., and Scheffelin, M. *Central processing dysfunctions in children,* NINDS Monograph No. 9. Washington, D.C.: U.S. Department of Health, Education, and Welfare, 1969, p. 77.

been the traditional major concern of the schools, includes a wide variety of knowledge and many different types of intellectual abilities and skills. The development of each of these areas within the cognitive domain is dependent on adequate language ability.

The second general domain, the affective, includes "changes in interest, attitudes, and values, and the development of appreciations and adjustment" (Bloom, 1956, p. 7). Some disagreement remains regarding how to classify and prioritize concern with the affective domain, but most agree that the schools and society must be concerned. *Whatever the goals and priorities, the ability to communicate clearly within a broad framework of meaning is essential to development in this domain. This, in turn, requires adequate language ability.*

Bloom's third general domain, the psychomotor, relates to manipulative skills and those that might be called motor skills or motor abilities. Adequate language ability is important in this domain but not so much as in the cognitive and affective. In many cases, well-developed language skills are necessary to carry out the teaching/learning process in the psychomotor domain; however, if such skills are absent, it is more nearly possible to develop adequate abilities in this third domain than in the cognitive and affective.

To summarize, language is one of the major characteristics that differentiates humans from the lower animals and the all-important means to transmit knowledge from generation to generation. With respect to the role and function of educators, the development of adequate language abilities is a major goal of education at lower grade levels, and the use of language skills is essential to carry out the goals of secondary school programs. Educators of the deaf and blind have long recognized the need for specific adaptations to maximize language development for students with sensory deficits. Educators of the learning disabled now generally recognize that most of their students require carefully planned efforts to assist them in developing adequate language. Educational approaches that relate directly to language abilities and disabilities are the concern of this chapter. One approach, developed by Doris Johnson and Helmer Myklebust, is discussed in some detail.

The educational recommendations of Johnson and Myklebust, if considered in their broadest sense, may be considered a total approach and are worthy of serious consideration by all learning disabilities specialists. A second language-related conceptualization, developed by Samuel Kirk, is not an approach but may assist in educational planning. Kirk's concept of psycholinguistic learning abilities, as reflected in the *Illinois Test of Psycholinguistic Abilities,* and his writing related to the ITPA should be of value in understanding the various types of language abilities and how they interrelate. In total, this chapter provides an understanding of the underlying philosophy of those who support language-development-related approaches and some of the educational practices recommended by advocates of such approaches. Actual classroom methods are not included in this chapter, unless they are essential to the explanation of the work of Myklebust or Kirk. For further consideration of language-development-related teaching methods, see Chapter 10 (a review of various reading methods) and Chapter 11 (methods related to written language disorders).

HELMER MYKLEBUST

Helmer Myklebust is the one individual most likely to come to mind when language development systems or approaches in relation to learning disabilities are mentioned. Myklebust's earlier efforts on behalf of the handicapped related to the deaf and aphasic and quite naturally evolved into research and writing regarding what he calls "psychoneurological learning disabilities." The theoretical base for his recommendations for teaching the learning disabled therefore is quite different from all others previously reviewed in this text. Myklebust did not work with the retarded, with the brain injured, nor in the broad field of remedial reading. His emphasis is not perceptual motor nor heavily related to sensory integration. Rather, he is concerned with how language develops in those individuals who are not developing language normally. His many years of work with deaf and aphasic children and adults led to a conceptualization of how language learning takes place and what to do when this language learning sequence is not progressing normally. Along with Doris Johnson, Myklebust formalized his ideas regarding teaching the learning disabled in their text *Learning Disabilities: Educational Principles and Practices* (1967). The theoretical base and most of the suggested educational procedures described in this text remain of value today; like the Fernald text described in the preceding chapter, it might be considered a "classic." Much of the following discussion is based on the ideas of Johnson and Myklebust, as expressed in their text.*

Myklebust's use of the term *psychoneurological learning disabilities* indicates that the *disability* is behavioral and the *cause* is neurological. He believes that it is most important to recognize what is taking place when children learn "normally." His remedial recommendations are based on his concept of how normal language learning takes place, which will be the subject of much of the consideration here.

Myklebust is convinced that children can learn normally only if certain basic factors (he calls them "integrities") are present and only if the child has had appropriate learning op-

---

*From this point on in this chapter, I will refer to the theories, concepts, and teaching suggestions provided in the text *Learning Disabilities: Educational Principles and Practices* as being the work of Myklebust, rather than Johnson and Myklebust. This is because, even though Doris Johnson was the senior author of this text, much of the theoretical basis was Myklebust's, and he is generally recognized as the central authority in this field. However, the reader should be aware that when the reference is directly to this particular text, we could properly say that it is the work of "Johnson and Myklebust" rather than just "Myklebust." A review of the References and Suggested Readings at the end of this chapter may provide better insight as to why Myklebust is usually recognized as the central figure in this area.

portunities. The culturally disadvantaged child is a good example of one who has not had the right learning opportunities, at least not to promote maximum academic learning. But, given this learning opportunity, other "integrities" must be present and functional to ensure learning. These are categorized into three types: *psychodynamic factors, peripheral nervous system functions,* and *central nervous system functions.*

Myklebust reviews the role of psychodynamic factors, such as those he has observed in the deaf, particularly in the congenitally deaf. He believes that infant babbling, the apparently essential prerequisite to development of spoken language, comes only after the child has *identified* with his parents, particularly his mother. Also, the child must receive adequate auditory feedback to babble and receive all the emotional significance of this interaction with the parent. Congenitally deaf children do not babble and neither do autistic children. (It may be more accurate to say that many of these children *start* to babble, but, because of lack of interaction or inability to interact, they do not *continue* to babble.)

Other studies indicate that *imitation* and then *internalization* are are also necessary for normal language development. Identification, imitation, and internalization are necessary for the child to be able to begin to assimilate the world and make it his. This sequence is necessary for the young child to be motivated to continue those simple vocalizations that lead quickly into communication and relatively complex language skills. In composite, these three factors may be called emotional-psychic, or psychodynamic, and they must occur for the child to learn normally. If a child has psychodynamic problems (with respect to learning and language development), then Myklebust would *not* consider him learning disabled within the framework of his definition.

The second of Myklebust's three required integrities (those required for normal learning to take place) is normal peripheral nervous system functions. This simply means the sensory system—the ability to see, hear, taste, feel, and so on. Although deficits in these sensory abilities will lead to difficulties (especially if the problem is with the auditory or visual systems), these peripheral nervous system deficits are *not* included in Myklebust's concept and definition of learning disabilities.

This leaves just one of the three major types of integrities that is necessary for normal learning—the central nervous system. Even if psychodynamic factors are normal and peripheral nervous system functions are adequate, some children do not learn normally. Myklebust would conclude that this was then likely to be a central nervous system difficulty. He would say that the child has a psychoneurological learning disability.

Given the assumption that learning disabilities are those behavioral manifestations that relate to central nervous system dysfunction, it is then important to briefly consider how the central nervous system functions in the learning process. The following discussion includes some of the more important features of Myklebust's conceptualization of brain functioning, and, though perhaps oversimplified, it provides at least a limited basis for developing a better understanding of some of Myklebust's other views.

Myklebust accepts the semiautonomous-systems concept of brain functioning and applies it in his learning disability theoretical construct. This concept presumes that the brain is composed of systems that at times function semi-independently, at times in a supplementary manner, and at times in a totally related manner. If this is accepted, it is then necessary to view each psychoneurosensory system as it functions in these three ways. As applied to learning disabilities, this means, for example, that the visual system may function semi-independently from the auditory or the tactile systems, it may function in a coordinated manner with either of them, or all may function as a total system. Myklebust gives little attention to the olfactory, gustatory, or proprioceptive systems, because he believes that they are less associated with learning disabilities than the visual, auditory, and tactile. His lack of emphasis on the proprioceptive (for example, body position) as compared to strong emphasis of perceptual-motor theorists illustrates how major authorities differ in their views of learning disabilities. Myklebust divides learning processes into three general categories—*intraneurosensory* (learning that involves primarily one brain system), *interneurosensory* (learning that involves more than one brain system), and *integrative* (learning that involves all systems functioning simultaneously).

Although it may be difficult to totally isolate intraneurosensory learning, some functions are *primarily* related to only one sensory system. An example is the spoken word. Both reception and expression of the spoken word are primarily auditory, and, even though the motor system is involved in producing the speech, the *learning* involved is mainly through auditory channels. The point here is not to debate the possible existence of single-system learning but rather to note that in practice some children appear to exhibit problems of auditory discrimination or memory without any similar involvements of visual or tactile processes. The same situation can apply to certain visual problems, and it is in this manner that we speak of intraneurosensory learning dysfunctions.

Interneurosensory learning appears to be a common occurrence. Others have used the terms intersensory perception and cross-modal learning, with the same or similar meaning. The condition, or disability, sometimes called expressive aphasia may be used to exemplify an interneurosensory disability. With this disability the individual apparently can understand spoken language, can integrate and recall it, but is unable to *say* the word he wishes to say. It has been hypothesized that he cannot speak because he cannot transduce these auditory signals into the motor-kinesthetic equivalent necessary for vocal expression.

Myklebust also views dyslexia as an interneurosensory learning disability. In auditory dyslexia, he explains, the child knows (learns) the spoken word and knows what the symbols (letters) look like but is unable to associate the visual images with the way the letters sound. In visual dyslexia the child learns what letters sound like but is unable to make an accurate association between this auditory image and the way the letters look.

The various types of agnosia are another example of interneurosensory learning disabilities. In agnosia the individual receives information through the sensory channels but is unable to interpret what he sees, hears, or feels. This dysfunction of reception and expression is a common type of learning disability.

Integrative learning is the most complex type, and difficulties with it may be hard to remediate. Further mention of integrative learning is made in the description of Myklebust's five levels of learning, and some of the complexities of learning are discussed at the symbolic and conceptual levels. However, before proceeding to the description of these five levels, it is important to remember that these "types of learning" are not provable in the normal sense but are explanations of observable events that appear to provide a practical theoretical base for remedial work with students whose behavior obviously indicates some malfunction.

Five levels of learning

For purposes of analysis of the learning process, and remedial planning, Myklebust has developed a conceptualization of the verbal learning sequence, which he visualizes as having five levels. He calls these the hierarchies of experience and indicates that all humans go through these levels, if they are learning normally. Fig. 3 is a simplified graphic presentation of these five levels, and following is a condensed version of Myklebust's discussion of these five levels, including their implications for planning remedial efforts for learning disabled students.

Sensation is the lowest and most basic level. Those who have lost or never had the use of one of the sensory channels are deprived in the learning process. For purposes of consideration of the learning disabled youngster, adequacy at this level may be assumed for by definition these children have adequate sensory acuity.

Perception, the second level, is defined somewhat differently by different authors, but if it means the ability to accurately recognize sensory input, or information, then it is a relatively simple psychological process. However, it is important that the learning disability teacher know if the child has perceptual problems, for a deficit at this level interferes with all the higher, more complex processes in the hierarchy. A misdiagnosis at this level could lead to many faulty conclusions and wasted remedial procedures.

Imagery is the next higher process and has sometimes been confused with perception or perhaps, for the most part, overlooked. The imagery concept is necessary to explain the differences between perception and memory. Perception concerns the ability to differentiate between various similar, but different, ongoing sensations. Imagery pertains to information already received. When a child is exercising imagery, he is recalling aspects of a past experience or is relating to memory of past perceptions. If he describes what he saw on the way to school, he is exercising visual imagery of the earlier experience. If he explains the loud explosion he heard, he is utilizing auditory imagery, or memory. Myklebust cites the example of a child who

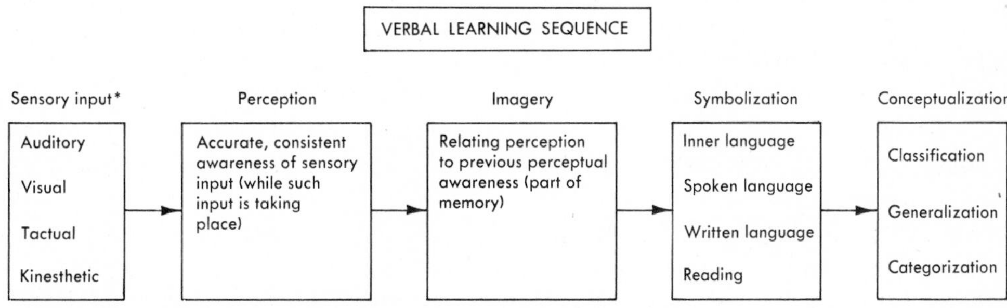

FIG. 3. (From Gearheart, B. R. *Teaching the learning disabled: a combined task-process approach.* St. Louis: The C. V. Mosby Co., 1976.)

could not recall the common features of his own bedroom or whether there were trees along the street on which he walked to school each day.

Symbolization is the fourth hierarchical aspect of experience among the learning processes. This next-to-the-highest level is sufficiently complex and all-inclusive to defy complete understanding. For example, it definitely includes both verbal and nonverbal categories of learning, and it may be called the ability to represent, or to trigger, the recall of experience. Myklebust views symbolization as the level in his hierarchy at which all forms of life lower than man drop out. That is, all forms of animal life engage in perception; some are apparently capable of imagery, but, as viewed by Myklebust, none but man is capable of or exercises symbolization. For purposes of discussion, symbolization may be thought of as the ability to acquire language, although, as will be pointed out later, both verbal and nonverbal symbolization are important in consideration of the learning disabled child.

Myklebust recognizes three major aspects of symbolization. The first, *inner language,* is a concept derived from the fact that people sometimes appear to say words but have no understanding of what they mean. If a word, by definition, is a vocal expression of meaning, then a word without meaning is not really a word. What gives a word meaning is experience, and inner language processes might be defined as those processes that permit experience and symbols to be related so as to give meaning to the symbols. Word-calling, or the vocalization of words without any knowledge of meaning, is one example of a lack of inner language. If taught the pronunciation guides and techniques, it is possible for a person to articulate a foreign language without the slightest understanding of what he is "reading." This is not a case of learning disability but an example of having no inner language in the language being verbalized. The individual who has serious difficulty in his own language may likely have this type of integrative learning problem.

Inner language is the result of basic integration of experience and can be developed only as the sensory and all other systems of the brain function effectively and simultaneously. It is this integration of experience, along with the capability to transfer freely among and between all the systems, that gives meaning and significance to language. The existence of a learning disability of this complex, integrative type must be recognized by those who work with learning disabled children.

Myklebust views inner language as the language in which an individual thinks. He suggests that bilingual individuals usually *think* in the language that is the native tongue. If faced by a particularly pressing problem, even though fluent in the second language and in the habit of using it daily, many such individuals revert to the native tongue to think through the problem. Because of his long association and considerable research with the deaf, Myklebust turns also to this area to illustrate inner language. He states that a number of his graduate students whose parents are deaf, who learned sign language from their parents as small children, still think in sign language when engaged in difficult mental tasks. This is the case even though the students hear adequately and use sign language only in conversing with their parents.

Because inner language is the first language to be acquired and must be learned before an individual can receive or express oral language, it may be very fixed and rigid. It is the foundation on which the rest of lan-

The development of more normal, age-appropriate language is a major goal for many learning disabled students.

guage acquisition and development is based.

A second aspect of symbolization is *receptive language,* which includes at least two major subparts—visual and auditory. Normally the auditory receptive is developed first, but, for example, in the normal reading process, both are required. Impairment of auditory-receptive language ability will have a reciprocal effect on the development of inner language, and both will then be retarded. A similar reciprocal relationship exists between the auditory receptive and visual receptive. If input (reception) precedes output (expression), any defect in receptive language will inhibit the development of expressive language, that is, written or vocal expression. At this level of the language development hierarchy, small deficiencies at a lower level, multiplied by any resultant higher-level deficiencies, become a major problem. For example, a deficiency in perception will result in additional deficiencies at the imagery level, and serious difficulties are likely at this symbolization level. If a child misperceives what he hears, he proceeds at the imagery and symbolic levels on the basis of this misperception, and his behavior seems inappropriate or bizarre. Or, with enough feedback of the reactions of others to his inappropriate behavior, he may tend to cut off any auditory perception except that of which he is absolutely certain, and he may appear to be hard-of-hearing or selectively deaf. The teacher may misunderstand the nature of the problem because, as in the previous example, a deficit may appear to be at one level of functioning (say, the imagery level) when in fact it is at a lower (perceptual) level. Myklebust is most concerned that this principle be understood, for otherwise the results may be inappropriate remedial attempts and failure for both the child and the teacher.

A key point to remember when considering apparent receptive language disabilities is that the development of adequate receptive language presumes adequate memory functioning. If memory span or memory sequence ability is impaired, symbolic functions cannot be developed in a normal manner. The most common evidence of memory sequence problems is the child's inability to follow instructions that involve three or four acts to be accomplished in a particular sequence. Since sequential behavior becomes increasingly important, particularly as the child grows older and is involved in more complex activities, this disability must be remediated.

The third major facet of symbolization is *expressive language.* This may take place when the child has developed inner language, when he has become competent in receiving language, and if other lower levels of the hierarchy are intact and functional. This expressive language, like the receptive, will be primarily either auditory or visual, with the auditory developing first in nearly all cases.

Often, defective expressive language is simply a direct indicator of defective receptive language. Expressive aphasia, one of the most common manifestations of a defect in expressive language, was the first of the language disorders to be separately identified and recognized as a specific condition. In many cases it is difficult to separate settings in which the output function alone is impaired from those in which output is defective, but the apparent cause, or at least a major related factor, is defective receptive language. Both expressive auditory (expressive aphasia) and expressive written (dysgraphia) language impairments are called apraxias. In apraxias, by definition, the motor system itself is not impaired, but rather the organism cannot use the motor system effectively to express language.

Conceptualization is the fifth and final level at which we must consider the possibility of learning disabilities. Although we may often see disabilities affecting perception, imagery, or symbolization, the conceptual ability, which man does not share with the other animals, is perhaps the most intriguing process. This behavior includes both the ability to abstract and the ability to categorize. Although abstraction can take place without conceptualizing, man cannot conceptualize without engaging in abstraction. Conceptual reasoning is somewhat difficult to explain and may be best shown through illustration. Development of the concept of the category of objects we call *dishes* will be considered as an example.

To the very small child, *plate* refers to the plate on which he eats. It may be highly distinctive in his life, have pictures of nursery rhyme characters, be divided into sections, and so forth, but it is plate to him. Later he learns that other objects on which he or others eat are called plates. In the meantime he has learned about cups and learned to distinguish between cups and glasses or perhaps mugs.

Then, although the word has been in his environment for some time, he becomes aware of the word *dishes*. Perhaps he first hears of it when Aunt Mary hands him a plate of food and calls it a dish. At any rate, he soon learns that all the plates, cups, bowls, and so on on the table are dishes. Through a group of experiences and through the language that has been used in these experiences, he has learned of the class of objects called dishes and that a plate may be called a plate or a dish. He has learned that all plates are not shaped alike, although they have similar uses (except for the decorative plates on the plate rail overhead), and he has learned that all plates are dishes. A plate is observable, but the category dishes is not, except as a group of experiences with a variety of items that others have called dishes. He has formed the *concept* of dishes.

It is important for the teacher to realize that some children may require specific assistance in forming even those concepts that appear to be quite simple and easily learned by other children. The concepts of *big* and *little* provide a good illustration. Some children may generalize from experience with, for example, the relative sizes of a big versus a little piece of cake, and a big as compared to a little pair of shoes, and be able to apply the big-little concepts to size (as in height or weight), amount, or degree (as in a "big hug" versus a "little hug"). Other children, those with disabilities in the conceptual area (or underdeveloped conceptual ability) may not be able to do this. It is often a matter of how *many* experiences are required for the child to be able to generalize and develop the concept in question. Ordinarily, developing the concepts that deal with more concrete experiences is easier for a child.

Myklebust notes that solid research evidence is not yet available about the precise manner in which language disorders and concept formation are related, but the existence of the relationship is generally accepted. For most teachers, awareness of this type of difficulty and that some children need specific assistance (usually a great deal more planned experience) to overcome it is a very good starting point toward remediation. Perhaps the most important fact for the teacher to understand is that *the class or category that forms the basis of a concept is not observable but depends on the individual's ability to relate a number of experiences, noting the "common denominator."* With this understanding, the teacher may proceed to assist the student to integrate and interrelate additional experiences, so as to eventually develop the concept.

A multidimensional approach to learning disability planning

In planning for a child with learning disabilities, the first step is an intensive diagnostic study. "This evaluation should yield a multidimensional definition of the disability because only then can the teacher proceed with the development of the remedial program" (Johnson and Myklebust, 1967, p. 51). The five multidimensional considerations are:

1. Is the disability within a single modality, or does it extend to more than one? Does it include intersensory functions? This information permits meaningful planning for remedial activities (for the defective functions) and selection of sensory channels to use to provide content input (the intact modalities).
2. What is the level of the involvement within the hierarchy of experience? Is it experienced first at the perceptual, imagery, symbolic, or conceptual level?

3. Is the deficiency one in which the sensations reaching the brain are meaningful or nonmeaningful? Is the problem basically verbal or nonverbal? For example, is the basic problem in auditory reception or visual imagery? Is it one of the abstracting-conceptualizing, that is, of gaining meaning?
4. Which of the subject matter areas does this disability affect most? Is it primarily a reading or an arithmetic problem, or does it also show up in art and physical education? This is important both in remediation planning and in guidance regarding course work, life planning, and so forth.
5. What are the effects, both present and potential, of the disability on the development of social maturity? If the goal of education includes development of independent, responsible, self-supporting citizens, this dimension is of prime importance.

Myklebust notes that educational/remedial planning will not be truly effective if these five dimensions of the problem are not considered and if provision is not made for coordination of the efforts of all who deal with the learning disabled student. He also notes the importance of careful consideration of what he calls the concept of *multiple states of readiness,* as outlined in the following section.

Multiple states of readiness

In addition to careful consideration of the five multidimensional considerations outlined above, it is important to consider the student's states of readiness in various subaspects of total readiness. For example, a student may be ready in terms of auditory, visual, and integrative functions but unable or unready to learn in the normal class setting because of social unreadiness or hyperactivity problems. He may be ready and able to function in class discussions at his chronological age level but be 3 years retarded in readiness for reading. The child must be approached and taught not at his *level* of readiness but at his *levels* of readiness. Teaching that follows and takes into consideration obtaining complete knowledge of the child—information regarding his various levels of functioning and understanding of the material to be taught—is what Myklebust calls *clinical teaching*. This, he believes, is the only acceptable procedure with the learning disabled.

When considering the implications for remediation that may be derived from an understanding of the five levels of learning, the five multidimensional considerations for educational planning, and the effects of readiness, one may generalize a number of major principles for remediation. Johnson and Myklebust have developed a list of these, and, although developed on the basis of their language-development-oriented approach, the principles are applicable to nearly all learning disabilities approaches. The 13 major principles for remediation that follow are condensed from their discussion of educational principles (1967, pp. 58-63) and provide a practical guide for remedial planning and implementation.

Major principles for remediation

1. *Individualize the problem.* The teacher must formulate an educational plan for *each specific child.* She should be aware of his deficits, his integrities, and his levels of language function, including reading, spoken, and written language. She should know him—his intelligence, his emotional status, his educational history. The program must be *his* program, not *a* program.

2. *Teach to the level of involvement.* Teaching must be aimed at the lowest level of involvement—perception, imagery, symbolization, or conceptualization.

3. *Teach to the type of involvement.* Does the disability involve intrasensory or intersensory learning? Does it involve verbal or nonverbal factors? Does it primarily relate to integrative functions? Whatever the case, teach appropriately for that type of involvement.

4. *Teach according to readiness.* Follow the principle of multiple readiness levels as presented in the preceding section.

5. *Remember that input precedes output.* Consider the fact that either input or output or both disabilities could be involved in the problem. Remember that output difficulties may actually reflect input problems.

6. *Consider tolerance levels.* Overloading is always a possibility. Certain types of stimulation may be distracting, either by themselves or by interfering with other modalities. The possibility that both psychological and neurological tolerance levels may be grossly abnormal in a learning disabled child must be carefully considered.

7. *Consider the multisensory approach.* The multisensory approach—teaching through several or perhaps all sensory channels—is always a possible alternative but must be approached with tolerance level and overloading potential in mind.

8. *Do not teach to deficits alone.* Teaching only to and through the deficient areas is a restricted, unitary approach and is unacceptable in the light of available evidence.

9. *Do not teach only to and through integrities.* This approach is insufficient when used alone. It presumes interneurosensory learning, which is not an acceptable assumption in many instances.

10. *Do not assume the need for perceptual training.* Perceptual training alone may be most inadequate. To stress perceptual training, except as diagnostic information so dictates, can be a waste of time or in some cases detrimental.

11. *Control important variables.* This principle calls for teacher control of variables such as attention (control elements that lead to distractions), proximity (to the teacher or to other children), rate (as in rate of presentation of materials), and size (of writing, objects, etc.).

12. *Emphasize both verbal and nonverbal learning.* Deliberately attend to both the verbal and nonverbal components of the learning problem with planned efforts to interrelate the two. (Myklebust recommends interweaving verbal and nonverbal components.)

13. *Keep psychoneurological considerations in mind.* The educator must attend to remediational needs in view of the behavioral components of the problem but should also consider the physical findings that indicate the status of the neurological system. The two must be incorporated into a single plan of educational remediation.

Visual and auditory dyslexia

Myklebust provides guidelines for remediation of specific types of learning disorders, including those he calls visual and auditory dyslexia. He notes that reading is a symbol system twice removed from the realities the symbols represent. The young child first integrates nonverbal experiences, then acquires an auditory system that is representative of the earlier nonverbal experience. Later, in learning to read, he acquires a visual verbal system that represents both the original nonverbal learning and the auditory symbol system. In this process, most children are able to differentiate one sound symbol from another and, later, one visual symbol from another. If such differentiation (auditory discrimination and visual discrimination) is faulty or very slow to develop, learning problems may result. In addition to the basic discrimination required, interpretive or memory problems may exist in relation to either modality.

A remedial plan for either the visual or the auditory dyslexic child must attend to the development of normal integration of (1) experience, (2) the spoken word, and (3) the printed word. The following descriptions of recommended remedial procedures for visual and auditory dyslexia are examples of the specificity provided by Myklebust for various types of learning disabilities.

Visual dyslexia. *Visual dyslexics* are viewed and approached as *auditory learners.* Myklebust believes that remediation of learning disabilities should circumvent the major deficit but must include simultaneous work on areas of weakness. For example, children with a visual deficit usually have difficulty in learning to read through a sight-word approach since they cannot hold a sequence of letters in mind. However, many of these children can learn sounds and sound blending. (In contrast, youngsters with auditory deficits may have difficulty in learning to read through phonics but may be able to learn by the sight-word approach.)

The remedial procedure used with visual dyslexics (auditory learners) is somewhat similar to that of Gillingham (see Chapter 6). It involves teaching isolated sounds and then blending them into meaningful words. Before initiating this approach, the teacher must evaluate the student's ability to blend sounds. If the child cannot blend sounds, the sight-word method should be used with emphasis on touch and kinesthesis. The following guidelines are used.

1. Teaching of letter sounds begins with consonants that are different in appearance as well as sound.
2. The child is asked to think of words beginning with each sound.
3. The child is taught to associate the sound with the letter having that sound. At first the youngster should be taught only one sound with each letter or letter combination.
4. One or two vowel sounds are presented after three or four consonants have been learned.
5. The child is taught to blend sounds into meaningful words. He then must tell what each word means and use it in a sentence.
6. Word families are taught (such as it, hit, sit, bit). The pupil learns how to change the initial and final consonants to form new words.
7. Two-letter consonant blends are introduced.
8. Long vowel combinations and consonant groupings representing a single sound are taught.
9. The teacher writes simple sentences, paragraphs, and stories using the child's reading vocabulary. Sentence structure should be similar to the pupil's spoken vocabulary.

Auditory dyslexia. *Auditory dyslexics* are approached as *visual learners.* Visual learners are taught to read by the sight-word approach since they generally have difficulty learning by phonetic methods. Therefore, a student is taught to make a direct association between the printed symbol and experience, or each new word is said for him. The auditory learner is taught from the part to the whole, whereas the visual learner works from the whole to the part. The procedures for visual learners follow.

1. The auditory-visual correspondence is taught by demonstrating to the student that words we say also can be written.
2. Nouns are selected that are in the child's spoken vocabulary and that are different in both auditory and visual configuration. The pupil matches the printed word with the corresponding object.
3. The printed word is matched with experience through labeling objects in the room such as the flag, chalk, and pencil. Action verbs also are associated with experience. First the child is asked to hop, walk, or run and then he is shown the printed symbol representing each action verb.
4. The child is introduced to simple phrases and sentences within his reading vocabulary. Prepositions and adjectives are presented at the same time. Pictures are used to illustrate the reading material.
5. As the child progresses, experience stories are integrated into the reading activities. Frequently a picture representing a new word is drawn below that word to aid the reading process.

Dyslexia with significant deficiencies in both the auditory and visual modalities may also exist. Myklebust suggests an approach that is somewhat similar to the simultaneous VAKT approach advocated by Fernald (see Chapter 6). In utilizing this general VAKT approach certain modifications should be made, depending on the child's pattern of strengths and weaknesses. One modification recommended in all cases is the use of a controlled vocabulary as opposed to the selected-by-student vocabulary recommended by Fernald. Other modifications are tailored to individual students.

A major strength of the Mykelbust language development approach is the recognition of and provision for a variety of different types of learning disabilities. These provisions take into account the strong and weak modalities and the level of readiness in all major areas of learning. Comprehensive assessment and regular reassessment are cornerstones of Myklebust's recommendations, regardless of the specific type of disability.

Other concepts growing out of Myklebust's efforts

Myklebust's basic ideas regarding learning disabilities are in many ways quite similar to those of other learning disabilities theorists even though he is proceeding from a somewhat different theoretical base than most of the others. Two concepts presented by Myklebust (and agreed to exist by other theorists) that may be of particular interest to teachers are overloading and nonverbal disabilities. These two concepts, and suggestions as to how they may apply in the teaching/learning process, are reviewed in this section.

Overloading may result when information moving through one sensory channel interferes or is in conflict with information moving through another sensory channel. This is one way to explain a phenomenon that may also be labeled interference. One example of overloading is what happens when someone tries to read a book and attend to an interesting television program at the same time. Another example is students who eventually learn that at times they can "listen better" with eyes closed than with eyes open.*

One final example of overloading may be

*I have observed such students in my classes regularly and have learned to be appreciative of their total attention rather than to improperly assume that they are asleep.

seen in the child who reads silently with good comprehension and little difficulty but when asked to read aloud has serious difficulty. For most adult application of reading, the need for the ability to read aloud is limited; however, it is the most practical way for the primary reading teacher to monitor a child's reading progress and so is generally required of young children. Let us take a look at the processes involved in reading silently and reading aloud.

In reading silently, the child moves his eyes across the printed page, recognizing the alphabetic symbols in groups called words and integrating these symbols with his memory to obtain meaning from the written page. When he scans a new word, he tries to ascertain its meaning, using whatever combination of word-attack skills he has found most practical (context clues, phonetic analysis, etc.). The child determines the speed with which his eyes scan the pages in relation to the difficulty of the concepts, the number of new words, and other such factors. This is not a simple process, but he is in control.

Reading aloud is much more complex. The reader must receive, interpret, and integrate two types of information simultaneously. He must not only visually take in symbolic information and therefore utilize visual receptive and integrative processes at the same time (as in silent reading), but he must also speak the words. Words spoken aloud to a teacher and classmates must be monitored by the child auditorily to make certain he is using proper intonation and inflection. Speed of reading must be paced so that what he is reading aloud makes sense to the listeners. He must actually divide his concentration between two complex processes. It is not surprising then that some children who apparently read silently with at least moderate success have serious difficulties when reading aloud. This simultaneous use of the intraneurosensory, interneurosensory, and integrative functions can be a cause of overloading in the process of reading aloud.

All teachers or prospective teachers should note that, for the younger child, who is most likely to be asked to read aloud, being forced to do so (to determine if he is in fact reading effectively) may be a deterrent to progress in reading. It would be wise for the teacher to investigate whether the child who has difficulty in reading aloud has a similar difficulty in reading silently. This can be done by assessing comprehension. Sometimes a child may simply need more time to develop his capability to process complex information through two sensory channels, and pressing him too hard can be a mistake.

Overloading may take many forms and lead to different types of problems. If the teacher is aware of the possibility of this type of difficulty, adjustments may be made, or, if the student has already made adjustments, these may be understood, not ridiculed. Anyone at times may "mask" or attempt to reduce certain kinds of incoming sensory stimuli. Many of the procedures recommended by Strauss, Lehtinen, and Cruickshank, outlined in Chapter 5, are directed at reducing incoming sensory stimulation. As long as such adjustments are essential to continued learning, they should be encouraged. However, in the long run, the student should be assisted to learn to cope with the more normal environmental distractions.

Nonverbal disabilities are recognized by a number of learning disabilities authorities, and Myklebust believes that there "is a neurology of learning that relates to verbal functions and a neurology of learning that relates to nonverbal functions" (Johnson and Myklebust, 1967, p. 45). He believes that one hemisphere of the brain serves mainly the verbal

Directed, properly sequenced language input through commercially prepared or teacher-developed audio equipment is a feature of many learning disability programs.

learning functions, whereas the other serves the nonverbal functions. He does not believe that one side, either the one represented by handedness or the one opposite established handedness, can be predicted to be the verbal hemisphere. He notes that apparently functions can be transferred from one side to the other and this is sometimes done naturally when, because of an accident, a person loses practical competence of one side.

An example of nonverbal functioning is recognition of the flag (as in patriotism) or of the cross (as in the Christian faith) at the symbolic level. Another example is the kind of recognition that most individuals give to such facial expressions as a smile or a frown. Although these may sometimes be misleading, social custom has resulted in general rules that provide a guide to the behavior that most children learn. This inability to properly interpret the social signals given by others can lead to embarrassment and misunderstanding, and, in some cases, such as in relation to employment, the end results may be disastrous. Children may eventually learn to "read" such signals, but, until this learning takes place, problems will inevitably result. The teacher may misinterpret the student's behavior that results from nonverbal disabilities and take inappropriate action based on such misinterpretation. In commenting on what he calls speechreading aphasia (an inability to associate meaning with movement of the lips), Myklebust notes that the problem may relate to the inability to perceive parts of one's own body and thus an inability to accurately perceive the body parts of others. In this instance, Myklebust definitely relates to some of the underlying thinking of perceptual-motor theorists.

SAMUEL KIRK

Samuel Kirk's involvement with language disabilities is not as total as that of Myklebust, and Hallahan and Cruickshank indicate that he "became deeply involved in the language disabilities of children at a rather late date in his career" (1973, p. 106). Special educators who were familiar with the field of special education prior to the emergence of learning disabilities as a recognized entity knew Kirk for his leadership at the University of Illinois, his efforts at the federal level, and his contributions in the area of mental retardation. As noted in Chapter 1, he is often recognized as providing the name and identity for the area of learning disabilities. Much of his interest was coincident with his efforts to develop an assessment tool that could determine the relative degree of development of what he called "psycholinguistic abilities." Most of this discussion of Kirk's contributions to language-development-related approaches relates to this assessment tool, the Illinois Test of Psycholinguistic Abilities (ITPA). This text's consideration of the ITPA involves two major sections. First, the test instrument, its origins, and some of the underlying theory are considered. Second, the manner in which it may be used to assist in the planning of educational programs is indicated.

The Illinois Test of Psycholinguistic Abilities was developed by Samuel A. Kirk and James J. McCarthy. It was the result of many years of work and particularly related to children who came from disadvantaged settings. Part of the authors' concern resulted from the wide discrepancies in the various abilities of these children. The need was apparent for a diagnostic instrument that could systematically differentiate and measure various facets of cognitive ability. As a result of this concern, Kirk enlisted the aid of others, and the ITPA, a test of communication abilities, was developed and put into use in 1961.

After experiencing both criticism and applause, the authors prepared a revised version, containing additions and modifications, for publication in 1968. The following account is concerned with the 1968 edition.

The Illinois Test of Psycholinguistic Abilities is based on a theoretical model of communications, developed by Osgood (1957), and is intended to be primarily diagnostic in nature. The Osgood model was modified, based on clinical observation and test construction problems, and the result became the ITPA model (Fig. 4).

The complete test is made up of 12 subtests that evaluate abilities in the two major channels of communication—visual-motor and auditory-vocal. Three types of psycholinguistic processes—receptive, organizing, and expressive—are recognized and evaluated. Two

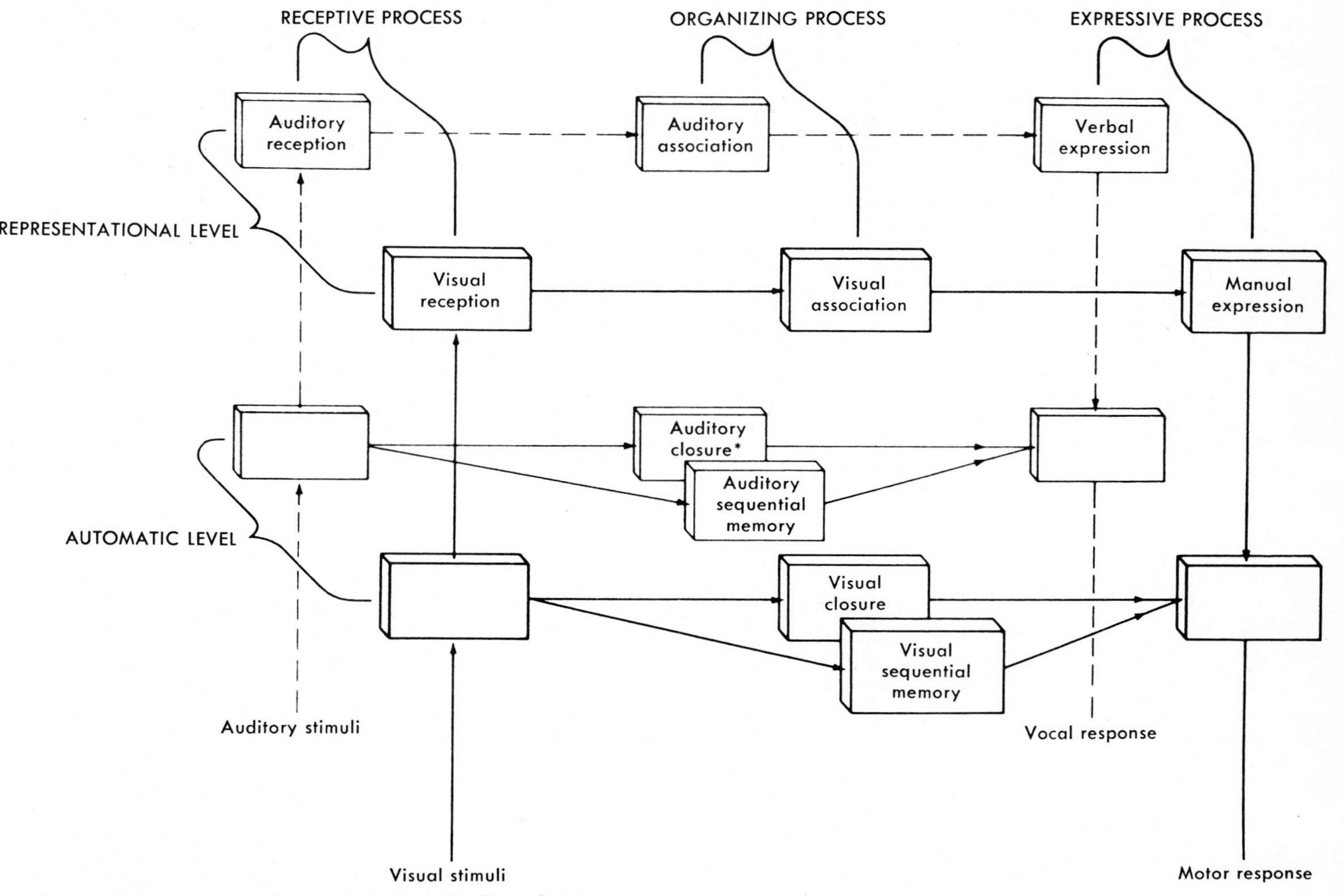

*Auditory closure, grammatic closure, and sound blending subtests

FIG. 4. ITPA three-dimensional model. (From Kirk, S., McCarthy, J., and Kirk, W.: Illinois Test of Psycholinguistic Abilities: Revised edition, examiner's manual, Urbana, Ill., 1968, University of Illinois Press.)

levels of organization are also recognized—the representational and the automatic (Fig. 4).

The following brief descriptions indicate the functions of the 12 subtests of the ITPA. They are described by levels—representational and automatic.

Representational level functions

Three general types of functions are tested at the representational, or symbolic, level—the receptive process, the organizing process, and the expressive process.

The *receptive process* may be defined as the process whereby children are able to comprehend symbols. Receptive process tests include the following:

1. *Auditory reception* test, which assesses ability to derive meaning from the spoken word. Fifty short, direct questions requiring only yes or no answers are included.
2. *Visual reception* test, which assesses ability to derive meaning from visual symbols. The child is shown a stimulus picture for 3 seconds and is told, "See this." Then a page of pictures, one of which is conceptually similar to the stimulus, is shown. Other choices may have structural instead of functional similarity to the stimulus, or they may be associated in some nonfunctional way with either the stimulus picture or the correct choice picture.

The *organizing process* may be defined as the ability to organize or relate symbols in a meaningful way and include the following:

1. *Auditory-vocal association* test, which assesses ability to relate concepts presented orally. Sentence completion is the technique used, including such statements as "I pound with a ______." This test contains 42 such analogies.
2. *Visual-motor association* test, which uses a picture-association technique. A single stimulus picture is surrounded by four optional pictures. The child is asked which of the optional pictures goes with the central stimulus picture.

The *expressive process* may be defined as the ability to transmit an idea through symbols and include the following:

1. *Verbal expression* test, which involves asking the child to tell about a number of different items. The score indicates the relevance and factualness of the concepts expressed.
2. *Manual expression* test, which assesses the ability to use manual expression in response to being asked "show me what we do with" questions. The child is to pantomime the response he wishes to give.

Automatic level functions

Two general types of functions are tested at this automatic, nonsymbolic level—closure and short-term sequential memory.

Closure may be defined as the ability to fill in the missing parts in an incomplete picture or expression, that is, to sense the whole. Closure tests include the following:

1. *Grammatic closure* test, which assesses the child's ability to fill in the missing parts of expressions. Items are presented orally along with pictures portraying the content of the expressions.
2. *Visual closure* test, which assesses the ability to identify common objects from an incomplete picture.
3. *Auditory closure,* supplementary test 1, which is a test of ability to fill in the missing parts of words, as might be heard in a faulty telephone connection.
4. *Sound blending,* supplementary test 2, which involves pronouncing the sounds

of a word, with intervals of silence between. This, like supplementary test 1, is a means of assessing the organizing process at the automatic level in the auditory-vocal channel.

Sequential memory may be defined as the ability to reproduce a sequence of stimuli. Tests include the following:

1. *Auditory sequential memory* test, which assesses the ability to reproduce sequences of digits that have been presented orally.
2. *Visual sequential memory* test, which assesses ability to reproduce sequences of figures from memory. Nonmeaningful figures are used, and the child has "chips" of these figures that he must place in the same sequence as those he has seen.

Interpretation of the ITPA

The major thrust of the ITPA is determination of discrepancies in scores for the various psycholinguistic functions measured. This was the original intent and motivation behind the development of the ITPA. The total pattern of discrepancies, rather than just individual subtest scaled score discrepancies, must be considered to obtain maximum interpretive capability from the ITPA.

Kirk has written a supplementary text, *Psycholinguistic Learning Disabilities: Diagnosis and Remediation* (Kirk and Kirk, 1971), which is recommended to increase the potential value of the ITPA. In addition, it may provide some valuable general insights about psycholinguistic abilities and the types of disabilities that may develop.

The ITPA has been overused and misused, but, given well-trained examiners and good judgment in interpretation, it provides valuable information with regard to various psycholinguistic abilities, on a basis that leads to important remedial implications. As with any other test, remediation should not proceed on the basis of a single test; verification of assessment results through multiple measurements is a primary rule and must be followed.

SUMMARY

The relationship between language development and learning is universally accepted and provides the basis for Johnson and Myklebust's recommendations for remedial efforts with children with what they call psychoneurological learning disabilities. Their theoretical concept of the verbal learning sequence—sensation, perception, imagery, symbolization, and conceptualization—provides a framework for assessing the level of development and determining the point at which remediation should originate.

Johnson and Myklebust provide a series of 13 principles for remediation and suggest 5 multidimensional considerations that must be applied in planning remediation. These guidelines are applicable to their suggested procedures for various types of disability and, with slight modification, may be applied when the remedial suggestions of other learning disabilities authorities are used as well. The efforts of Kirk in the development of the Illinois Test of Psycholinguistic Abilities were reviewed and suggestions were made regarding the strengths and limitations of this test. The ITPA is of value as a diagnostic tool, and Kirk's conceptualization of the interrelationships between the various psycholinguistic abilities assessed by this test may provide valuable insights for the learning disabilities teacher.

Programs and program components based on language development are important in the field of learning disabilities to provide balance for the earlier emphasis on perceptual-motor approaches. Programs that emphasize language development as directly related to the development of cognitive skills appear to be on the increase in the nation, along with those that emphasize direct remediation of academic deficits, with little concern for the probable basis of the disability. Predicting future trends in learning disabilities programming is difficult, but, because language permeates all of learning and educators are growing in awareness of this fact, emphasis on language development apparently will continue for some time. It seems to follow that concern with disabilities in language development will grow as a major concern for special educators who work with students with learning disabilities.

REFERENCES AND SUGGESTED READINGS

Bloom, B. (Ed.) *Taxonomy of educational objectives, handbook one: cognitive domain.* New York: David McKay Co., Inc., 1956.

Chalfant, J., and Scheffelin, M. *Central processing dysfunctions in children,* NINDS Monograph No. 9. Washington, D.C.: U.S. Department of Health, Education, and Welfare, 1969.

Frierson, E., and Barbe, W. (Eds.) *Educating children with learning disabilities.* New York: Appleton-Century-Crofts, 1967.

Gearheart, B., and Willenberg, E. *Application of pupil assessment information.* (ed. 3) Denver: Love Publishing Co., 1980.

Gillet, P. *Auditory processes.* San Rafael, Calif.: Academic Therapy Publications, 1974.

Hallahan, D., and Cruickshank, W. *Psycho-educational foundations of learning disabilities.* Englewood Cliffs, N.J.: Prentice-Hall, Inc., 1973.

Isgur, J. Establishing letter-sound associations by an object-imaging projection method, *Journal of Learning Disabilities,* 1975, *8,* 349-353.

Johnson, D., and Myklebust, H. *Learning disabilities: educational principles and practices.* New York: Grune & Stratton, Inc., 1967.

Karnes, M. *Helping young children develop language skills.* Washington, D.C.: Council for Exceptional Children, 1968.

Kass, C. Psycholinguistic disabilities of children with reading problems, *Exceptional Children,* 1966, *32,* 533-541.

Kirk, S., and Kirk, W. *Psycholinguistic learning disabilities: diagnosis and remediation.* Urbana, Ill.: University of Illinois Press, 1971.

Kirk, S., McCarthy, J., and Kirk, W. *Illinois test of psycholinguistic abilities* (rev. ed.); *Examiners manual.* Urbana, Ill.: University of Illinois Press, 1968.

Kirk, W. *Aids and precautions in administering the Illinois Test of Psycholinguistic Abilities.* Urbana, Ill.: University of Illinois Press, 1964.

Leakey, R., and Lewin, R. *Origins.* New York: E. P. Dutton, 1977.

McCarthy, J. J., and McCarthy, J. F. *Learning disabilities.* Boston: Allyn & Bacon, Inc., 1969.

Menyuk, P. Cognition and language, *The Volta Review,* 1976, *78,* 250-257.

Myklebust, H. *Auditory disorders in children.* New York: Grune & Stratton, Inc., 1954.

Myklebust, H. *Development and disorders of written language.* New York: Grune & Stratton, Inc., 1965.

Myklebust, H. Learning disorders: psychoneurological disturbances in childhood, *Rehabilitation Literature,* 1964, *25,* 354-359.

Myklebust, H. (Ed.) *Progress in learning disabilities.* New York: Grune & Stratton, Inc., 1968.

Myklebust, H., and Boshes, B. *Minimal brain damage in children.* Evanston, Ill.: Northwestern University Press, 1969.

Osgood, C. A behavioristic analysis. In Bruner, J. (Ed.) *Contemporary approaches to congition.* Cambridge, Mass.: Harvard University Press, 1957.

Osgood, C., and Sebeok, T. (Eds.) *Psycholinguistics.* Bloomington, Ind.: Indiana University Press, 1965.

Piaget, J. *The origin of intelligence in children.* New York: International Universities Press, 1952.

Smith, E., Goodman, K., and Meredith, R. *Language and thinking in school* (ed. 2) New York: Holt, Rinehart and Winston, Inc., 1976.

Stubblefield, J., and Young, E. Central auditory dysfunction in learning disabled children, *Journal of Learning Disabilities,* 1975, *8,* 89-94.

Wiig, E., and Semel, E. Productive language abilities in learning disabled adolescents, *Journal of Learning Disabilities,* 1975, *8,* 578-586.

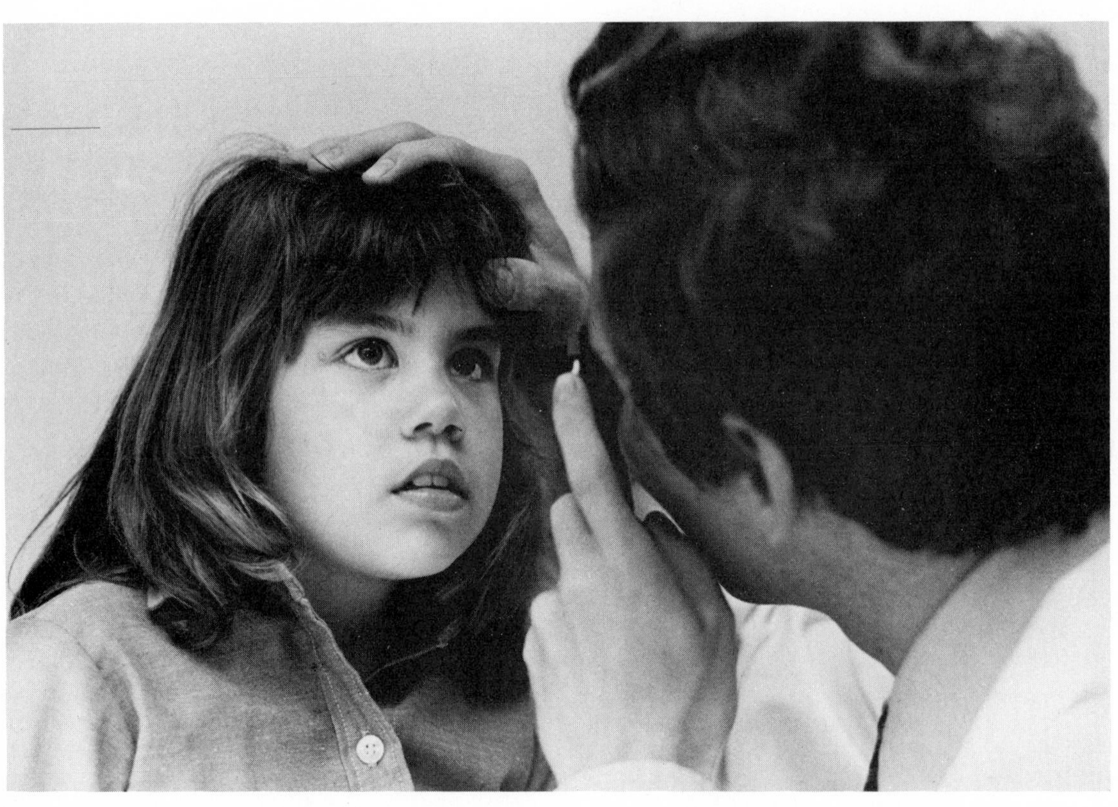

Chapter 8

The role of medicine and medical specialists in the field of learning disabilities

Not too many years ago the school was responsible for "readin', writin', and 'rithmetic," with perhaps a little history or literature thrown in. Teachers were supposed to be competent in teaching the basic skills or, at the secondary level, in some subject area; if these tasks were accomplished, they were successful. Teachers could not smoke or drink, and both their clothing and their language were required to be rather formal and "proper," but they were not questioned to any great extent about their pedagogical skills. That has all changed!

Today, in most parts of the nation, the matters of smoking, drinking, wearing apparel, and language are much less important than they were 50 years ago. A great deal of personal freedom has been won. Teachers are just "people," as far as societal mores are concerned; however, other things are expected. Parents regularly question teaching methods and expect the teacher to have various types of specialized knowledge. This is particularly true with special education teachers, and some of this specialized knowledge relates to the field of medicine.

The need for knowledge of drug treatments seemed to be sufficiently great that the Council for Exceptional Children recently published *Children on Medication: A Primer for School Personnel* (Gadow, 1979). Teachers need to know about drug treatment because many of their students require some type of pharmacotherapy. Teachers need to know how drugs may help or interfere with learning. They need to know about possible side effects and should understand the role that teachers may play in observing the effects of change of medication. If they are well informed about such subjects as allergies and dietary deficiencies as they relate to possible effects on learning, teachers may be able to assist parents through referral for additional medical evaluation. Because parents *do* expect more of teachers, especially teachers of learning disabled students, they should be informed about these topics, as well as such areas as megavitamin therapy and the possible effects of hypoglycemia.

Teachers must not attempt to play the role of physician! Teachers must be well trained and properly certificated; physicians must hold

George E. Marsh III prepared the chapter entitled "Medical practice and research in learning disabilities" in the second edition of *Learning Disabilities: Educational Strategies*, the chapter which this one replaces. Some of his ideas were used in this chapter in revised form. I gratefully acknowledge the assistance thus provided.

a medical degree and be licensed to practice medicine. These roles are quite distinct and separate. However, teachers can be more effective if they have some understanding of medicine and medical specialists as they relate to the unique needs of learning disabled students. This increased effectiveness may result from one or more of the following factors: (1) the teacher may assist in a team effort (along with the parent) in monitoring the effects of various types of pharmacotherapy; (2) the teacher may be more effective in urging the parent to check further with medical specialists regarding observations made in the classroom; and (3) the teacher will appear more *generally* knowledgable and thus educational recommendations are more likely to be respected and followed.

This chapter provides an overview of the various ways in which the professions of medicine and special education interrelate. The first concern is to briefly review the various types of medical or medically related specialists whom the teacher may contact. The next consideration is medical treatments that might be related to learning disabilities, and following is a review of some interesting developments relating to the expanding knowledge about the mysteries of the human brain.

MEDICAL SPECIALISTS AND ALLIED HEALTH CARE PROFESSIONALS

Medicine is a highly complex field, and the range of specialization is almost infinite. As recently as 50 years ago, many families went to "the doctor," meaning a general practitioner, for almost all medical problems. The doctor carried out all but the most specialized surgical procedures. He (the doctor was almost always a man) treated headaches and stomachaches; ear, nose, and throat problems; heart and lung problems; gastrointestinal and orthopedic difficulties; and rheumatism and skin problems. He delivered babies and treated them as children and then as adults. The doctor was a medical expert in the entire range of physical ills, an authority on nutrition, and an expert on most aspects of child rearing.

Today teachers must be aware of a wide variety of specialization to intelligently discuss medical roles and to understand what parents may ask or tell them. Usually the family physician makes actual recommendations for parents to see specialists, but parents may often ask teachers their opinion about seeing a particular type of specialist. At times parents may fully understand the role of the specialist and simply want another point of view; at other times they are really asking "what does this kind of special doctor do?" In either case the teacher should be able to respond in an intelligent, informed manner.

The following list of specialists includes those medical doctors with whom teachers are most likely to come into contact and certain other health care professionals who may play a significant role in the life of a child.The list is abbreviated, but it permits some understanding of the roles of each of these specialists and how their efforts may affect the students.

audiologist Audiology is an allied branch of medicine in which the audiologist, a nonmedical specialist, examines the integrity of the ear and its structures, measures hearing levels by use of an audiometer, and evaluates hearing defects. In recent years, audiologists have played an increasingly important role in various rehabilitative functions.

endocrinologist The endocrinologist is a medical doctor who specializes in the treatment of diseases involving secretions of glands of the endocrine system. As biochemistry and psychochemistry have become more important in the diagnosis and treatment of some children whose learning disorders seemed to be caused or worsened by endocrine imbalances, the endocrinologist has assumed a more important role in relationship to learning disabled students.

neurologist The neurologist is a medical doctor who evaluates the functioning of the central nervous system, determines seizure activity, and often employs the electroencephalograph (EEG). In recent years the numbers of children referred to the neurologist to assist in the diagnosis of learning disabilities and organic disturbances of the brain has increased significantly. With the obvious and unquestioned relationship between the integrity of the central nervous system and learning, this specialty likely will play an increasing role in diagnosis, remediation, and prevention of learning disabilities in the future.

occupational therapist The occupational therapist is a certified, nonmedical specialist who works with physicians on referral to provide treatment of mental and physical ailments by exercises designed to productively occupy the mind or correct physical impairments. The occupational therapist deals with physical functions that improve fine and gross motor activities relating primarily to upper body extremities. Recently, the occupational therapist has become increasingly involved in providing programs to improve or correct motor and visual-perceptual deficiencies in children.

oculist See ophthalmologist.

ophthalmologist The ophthalmologist is a medical doctor who specializes in the branch of medicine dealing with the structure, functions, and diseases of the eye. Children may be referred to the ophthalmologist for treatment of physical diseases of the eye, for surgery, or for determining the need for correction of visual acuity defects.

optometrist An optometrist is a licensed, nonmedical specialist who works with the measurement of the range and power of vision, examination of the eyes, and prescription of glasses. Some optometrists also practice orthoptics, which involves exercises to strengthen muscles of the eye by using prisms and various other techniques thought to improve functioning of the eyes.

otolaryngologist The otolaryngologist is a certified medical doctor who specializes in the branch of medicine dealing with diseases or malfunctions of the ear, nose, and throat.

otologist An otologist is a medical doctor who specializes in the branch of medicine concerned with care of the ear, including prevention and treatment of diseases and dysfunctions. Otologists may often utilize the services of an audiologist.

pediatrician The pediatrician is a medical doctor who specializes in the health care of infants and children. Of all the specialists listed here, pediatricians are the nearest thing to the old "family doctor," and, as such, they tend to be consulted by parents on a wide variety of problems, including whether or not a child is learning disabled, whether a child's language development is normal, and whether school practices and recommendations are of value. Some pediatricians are well informed on such matters, and some are not so knowledgeable. The pediatrician is the medical doctor whom the teacher is most likely to contact, and maximum cooperation between the school and the pediatrician is essential. Knowledge of the attitudes (toward the school and special education programming) of various specific pediatricians is of great value.

physical therapist The physical therapist, like the occupational therapist, is a certified, nonmedical specialist who works under the direction of a physician. The physical therapist deals with overall strengthening of the body and development of balance, ambulation, and independent motor functioning.

psychiatrist A psychiatrist is a medical doctor who specializes in the treatment of emotional disorders, especially psychoses and neuroses. Major differences exist in the manner in which various psychiatrists work, but all are involved in assisting the individual to better manage personal behavior, and, as such, they may be working with learning disabled students. Teachers of learning disabled children have come into more frequent contact with psychiatrists in recent years, as referrals have increased markedly.

psychologist The psychologist is a nonmedical specialist well known to most educators. The psychologist may treat emotional disorders in much the same way as a psychiatrist but without the use of medicine (clinical psychology), or he may be more involved with administering educational and psychological tests and treating school adjustment problems (school psychology).

The learning disabilities teacher is more likely to work with the psychologist in the assessment of learning disabilities and the management of school behavior.

The nature of the teacher's involvement with these various specialists will differ with individual circumstances, but knowledge of the special emphasis of many of these individuals will eventually be needed by most teachers. One can expect too much of medical tests, for example, the EEG, which cannot help in the choice of an instructional method. The most unrealistic expectations are those of parents who anticipate that learning disabilities will miraculously disappear after medical intervention. Any technique, from medication to behavioral management, must be clearly understood by all to avoid disappointment later. Some parents may initially object to medical intervention and then later relent. Unless spectacular results occur, some are quick to say "I told you so" or become upset with the school because of the lack of academic success.

A frequent problem is the administration of medication to children at school and home. Medications are prescribed to be taken at specific times of the day. If children are left to their own volition in taking medication, some troublesome or even dangerous consequences may ensue. Some children recognize that they perform better when taking medication so they decide that increasing the dose will help them more. Other children resent taking medicine and conveniently "lose" it. Children have been known to give pills to their friends, who consume them in the hope of becoming "smart." Parents have been known to assume authority in administering medication by increasing, reducing, or eliminating the dose, contrary to instructions.

These and other problems are common and will never be completely eliminated. However, it seems logical to assume that, with more specific information and better general understanding, school personnel can reduce problems that relate to medical information and can provide more effective programs for children in many cases. With this in mind, we will continue with a consideration of pharmacotherapy, the use of drugs to affect the student's behavior and general performance in school.

PHARMACOTHERAPY: GREAT PROMISE AND A NUMBER OF PROBLEMS

In *Children on Medication: A Primer for School Personnel,* Gadow notes that *pharmacology* (the study of the chemical and physical properties of drugs) has two major divisions: *"neuropharmacology,* which investigates the effects of drugs on the nervous system," and *"psychopharmacology,* the study of how drugs affect behavior" (1979, p. 5). "Behavior," in this definition, refers to ability to think or learn, feelings, perceptual abilities, motor activities, and the like. This discussion focuses on psychopharmacology.

Within the total group of drugs that may most often be used with children are two main categories—the *psychotropic* drugs and the *antiepileptic* drugs. Psychotropics influence behavior, cognition, and moods through their effect on the brain. The antiepileptic drugs are used to manage convulsive disorders. Some overlap exists in these two recognized categories, since a number of psychotropic drugs also affect convulsive disorders.

In addition to the confusion that may result from the overlap between antiepileptics and psychotropics, these same drugs may be used for still other purposes. And, as if this were not enough, any of these drugs may be referred to by registered trade name or by generic name. For example, Ritalin (the trade name) may also be called methylphenidate hydrochloride (the generic name). If a com-

Verification of the absence of medical and health problems is an important facet of the data gathering that precedes appropriate planning for learning disabled students.

pany patents a new drug, it is marketed under a registered trade name. The drug is almost always referred to by parents and in popular literature by the trade name, but medical journals use the generic name. The patented trade name is usually much easier to remember—for example, Dexedrine (the trade name), as opposed to dextroamphetamine (the generic name).

All of these sources of confusion cannot be eliminated; however, they can be noted and examples of the more commonly used drugs can be provided. (See Table 7 for a list of drugs commonly used to control hyperactivity. These specific medications have been chosen to illustrate the trade name versus generic name comparison and to show how basic classifications may differ. The drugs listed are those that are more likely to be known to teachers and therefore may be of greater interest than others.)

TABLE 7. Medications commonly used in treatment of hyperactivity

Trade name	Generic name	Classification
Cylert	Pemoline	Stimulant
Dexedrine	Dextroamphetamine	Stimulant
Haldol	Haloperidol	Antipsychotic
Mellaril	Thioridazine	Antipsychotic
Ritalin	Methylphenidate	Stimulant
Thorazine	Chlorpromazine	Antipsychotic

Whether they support or oppose the use of drugs, teachers and physicians must consider the fact that drugs always have some type of side effect. Some effects are inconsequential; others are quite serious. The obvious question when considering drug treatment is whether any desired, beneficial effects are worth more than the side effects.

One reason why stimulant drugs have been

used regularly is because "in moderate doses (they) produce few serious side effects and are generally considered to be quite safe" (Gadow, 1979, p. 24). Possible side effects include drowsiness, headache, stomachache, nausea, moodiness, irritability, and marked reduction in social interaction (Gadow, 1979). This listing may sound like something more than "few serious side effects," but more serious side effects might be expected with many other types of drugs. The fact that some of these effects are likely to occur is further support for the commonly held belief that medication should not be utilized unless the situation that the drug is designed to improve is relatively serious, with no viable alternatives.

The side effects indicated in the previous paragraph are often called *functional* side effects; they disappear when drug treatment is stopped. Other side effects are more serious and must be even more carefully monitored. One such possible effect is the reduction of overall body growth and development. Ritalin, one of the more popular stimulant drugs and regularly used to control hyperactivity, has been suspected of suppressing growth, but, according to Safer, Allen, and Barr (1975), after drug treatment is stopped, children experience a "growth rebound." Other stimulant drugs may have similar effects.

Even more serious side effects of certain drugs include reduction in the ability of the blood to coagulate and cardiovascular changes such as increased blood pressure and heart rate. Some antidepressant drugs may lower the seizure threshold. (Brown et al., 1973). In all cases, careful behavioral and medical monitoring and providing complete information to parents (regarding both potential benefits and side effects) are essential. Educators must be careful in advising parents regarding these matters for such advice is the prerogative of medical doctors, but providing sufficient information to permit the teacher to be reassuring or to advise the parent to ask more questions of the doctor is of value and importance.

Okolo, Bartlett, and Shaw conducted a study of the involvement of school personnel in the process of "referring, placing, educating, and monitoring the hyperactive child on medication" (1978, p. 648). They concluded that there tended to be a lack of involvement of teachers, which led to inability to provide the necessary feedback to physicians. This study disclosed that the communication problem was within the school, between the school nurse and the teacher, which indicates one way in which communications may break down. Since federal regulations require close, interdisciplinary efforts on behalf of the handicapped student, all settings in which medication is used dictate planned information exchange and close cooperation.

In conferences, workshops, and other gatherings of parents and professionals interested in the use of medication in the treatment of learning disabled students, I am regularly asked, "Do you believe in using drugs to treat hyperactivity?" The question is usually asked in a straightforward manner, and the apparent expected answer is a simple yes or no. *There is no simple answer to this question!* The needs of children and all of the variables of different situations are too complex to permit a simple answer. Some "experts" advocate drug treatment for nearly all hyperactive children, some believe that drugs should never be used and the opinions of others range all the way from one extreme to the other. Such strong beliefs are commonly found among educators, psychologists, and physicians. It would be quite easy to quote a number of "experts" who support either point of view;

however, rather than do this, let us consider a listing of "probable facts," which may be distilled from recent journal articles and which are as divorced from partisan opinion as possible.

1. Many authorities now believe that drug treatment should be avoided, if possible, for students who do not require medication to control a convulsive disorder. In other words, drug control of hyperactive behavior alone is a "last resort" treatment.
2. When students must have drug treatment (all other measures have failed), parents and students are advised to see physicians who have had extensive experience with this as well as other types of treatment (such as diet, megavitamin, or allergy-related treatment). During much of the 1970s parents pressured too many physicians into "trying out" drug treatments, even though the physicians had limited experience and information about such treatments.
3. The various programs in which relatively large numbers of students in certain school districts are given drug treatment in some type of experimental effort should not be approved by school authorities. Even though directed and monitored by physicians, the best educational procedure is *individualized planning;* if parents want to participate in drug treatment programs, they should arrange such treatment individually.
4. It is difficult, if not impossible, to accurately predict which type of medication will be effective with a given student, based on behavioral symptoms alone. Even when drug treatment is required, and accepted as desirable, trial and error is the only method to determine which drug will be most effective—a stimulant, a sedative, an anticonvulsant, or an antipsychotic.
5. Hyperactive children appear to respond more favorably to stimulant drugs than to other types of medication; there are, however, striking exceptions to this generalization.
6. All drugs have some side effects, and they must be carefully monitored.

Though a logical presumption is that some of the controversy surrounding drug treatment will decrease as more medical research takes place, the opposite may be happening. Perhaps this is because, as more evidence is compiled indicating good results with some children, additional evidence indicates negative effects with others. This should, however, not be too surprising in light of other medical controversies regarding questions such as determining which chemicals cause, or may lead to, the development of malignancies and how the chances of heart attack can be reduced. The complexity of the drug treatment problem is such that it may not be totally resolved for decades. (For further reading on this subject see the articles relating to drug control of hyperactivity in the References and Suggested Readings at the end of this chapter.)

Although basic research that relates to the functioning of the brain is further discussed later in this chapter, it is more appropriate to consider studies in which researchers have attempted to use chemicals to improve memory and general learning in this section. This research is controversial in part because of claims and counterclaims regarding the validity of related research efforts of the recent past. Following is a brief discussion of the thrust of some of these efforts.

Memory has been a subject of great interest to educational researchers. Numerous studies have been stimulated as a result of memory deficiencies in normally intelligent children. Many children who are diagnosed as having learning disabilities show characteristically low scores in tests of memory such as the digit span test of the Wechsler Intelligence Scale for Children and the auditory sequential memory test of the Illinois Test of Psycholinguistic Abilities. Most theories of memory conceive a model that consists of short- and long-term retention on a continuum from seconds or minutes to days or years (Atkinson and Shiffrin, 1968; Waugh and Norman, 1965).

Karl S. Lashley, an American psychologist, devoted years of intense study to the investigation of memory. He is well known for his studies of the effects of surgical removal of cortical tissue in rats in an effort to find the locus of memory in the brain. He did not accomplish his goal, and it is now known that memory incorporates large areas of the cortex and memory storage may remain relatively unimpaired even after extensive damage to the brain. Lashley also discovered that small amounts of strychnine enhanced learning performance in rats.

Pines (1975) has reviewed the research in this area and points out that the major emphasis in the study of the memory process has existed only for about 10 years. Lashley's research was not further pursued until Dr. Bernard Agranoff of the University of Michigan and Dr. James L. McGaugh of Irvine initiated their widely reported research. Agranoff worked with goldfish that had learned to cross an underwater barrier when a light flashed to avoid receiving a shock. Agranoff injected an antibiotic into the skulls of the fish immediately after they had been conditioned to the new skill and discovered that they no longer demonstrated the skill. The antibiotic apparently interfered with the transfer of initial learning to long-term memory; the process of transfer from initial learning to long-term retention must depend on some chemical integrity that was disrupted by the injection. It was later discovered that if injection occurred an hour or more after training, the fish remembered.

McGaugh, a psychobiologist following the lead of Lashley, further pursued the possibility of improving memory. He found that strychnine and amphetamines actually improved learning in rats. Rats so treated required fewer trials to learn tasks (as compared to control group rats), and rats receiving larger doses excelled in performance over rats with smaller amounts of chemical injection.

Wolf (1973) has reported the work of Robert Bowman of the Regional Primate Research Center of the University of Wisconsin who has extended the same line of research with monkeys. Through the use of Metrazol (pentylenetetrazol) as an injection, the learning of monkeys in a discrimination task was significantly improved.

The preceding examples of research on the effect of chemicals on the memory of animals are supported in part by results with humans from which it may be inferred that certain chemical compounds may in some way be related to intelligence. With humans, this is usually a matter of discovering some situation in which a chemical has been accidentally given in excess, such as has been with certain hormones, or where drugs have been given to those whose condition was such that experimental efforts were used as some sort of "last resort." The directions this research may take in the future are unclear, but it seems certain that progress will be made. Perhaps the results of basic brain function research (reviewed later in this chapter) will suggest further, fruitful avenues of investigation.

DIET-RELATED TREATMENT

One of the more popular of presently proposed treatments for hyperactivity, and thus for learning disabled students who exhibit hyperactivity, is diet control. If given a choice, many parents would likely prefer some sort of diet treatment as opposed to drug treatment, but when such a path is taken, they soon discover that diet treatment requires much more time and effort (and, at times, spin-off effects on other members of the family) than drug treatment. Managing and monitoring the taking of medication at given intervals of time is obviously much easier than managing and monitoring what a child eats at home, at a friend's home, on the way to and from school, at school, and elsewhere. To properly follow a prescribed diet takes effort and dedication, but it has some very obvious advantages over drug treatment when it works.

Many physicians tend to discount diet treatments, and advocates such as Feingold (1975) and others may appear to overstate some of their claims. Swanson and Kinsbourne (1980) indicate that stimulant therapy may be effective in about 60% of the cases, while diet therapy is effective in only about 15% of the cases. On the other hand, the continued existence of "Feingold Associations" (groups of parents who meet to discuss and reinforce one another about diet treatments and who strongly support its effectiveness for their own children) indicates some positive effects. Also, researchers have shown that ingestion of artificial food colors of the magnitude often taken by children can impair learning in some children.

Food and food additive allergies

A number of foods and food additives have been established as causes for allergic reactions. Among those suggested as immediately suspect are such foods as milk, chocolate, and cola drinks (Crook, 1975). These are recognized as *possible* sources of allergic reactions by most, if not all, physicians. The controversy relates to whether or not such reactions are as common as indicated by advocates of food elimination diets (diets in which certain foods are systematically eliminated during a test period to observe behavioral reactions) and whether they are as related to hyperactivity and learning problems as maintained by individuals such as Crook (1975), Powers (1974), and Feingold (1975).

We should all be very concerned about practitioners of any discipline who take advantage of parents of handicapped children, because they are vulnerable. However, I tend to agree with the logic of Allan Cott (a medical doctor who is president of the Academy of Orthomolecular Psychiatry and a physician in private practice in New York City) in his reply to criticism by another physician regarding controversial medical treatments for children with learning disabilities. Cott first noted that too many pediatricians, when confronted by parents of children showing early signs of learning difficulties, dismiss the problem as "a phase," which will likely be outgrown. Then, after the problem is so obvious that it can no longer be ignored, "the immediate solution is a prescription for either Ritalin or amphetamines" (1977, p. 161). In response to criticism of treatment based on theories that have not been established beyond a shadow of a doubt, Cott suggests that "an astute clinical observation has frequently in medical history led to important research findings, and is often far more valuable than a double-blind study which is poorly designed and executed" (1977, p. 162). The following review of reports by those (primarily medical doctors) who support various theories of hyperactivity and reduced learning ability resulting from reactions to foods or food additives presents one side of this story. The other side is caution with regard to procedures that cannot be proved to the satisfaction of all and concern about overacceptance of "miracle cures."

Sugar is viewed as a possible toxic agent by Dr. Hugh W. S. Powers, Jr. (1974), a physician in Dallas, Texas, who has conducted a variety of investigations into the relationship of blood sugar to brain metabolism. Powers (1975) examined 50 children who were referred with multiple nervous system problems including hyperactivity, psychosomatic complaints, irritability, inattention, poor memory, and declining school performance. It was found that the dietary intake of these subjects included 50 to 70 teaspoons of sugar per day from sweetened foods and drinks, huge intakes of carbohydrates (one 4-year-old was reported to consume 640 grams per day, when the requirement for a child his age is from 100 to 125 grams per day), and similarly large amounts of caffeine derived from cola drinks and chocolate candies. Sugar and sorbitol, an artificial sweetener in diet drinks, can act upon the blood sugar level as a stimulant or agitant causing various reactions such as excitement, irritability, and overactivity. Caffeine is also a stimulant, and Powers recommends its elimination or restriction in children who manifest these symptoms. This is particularly interesting because some investigators have maintained that caffeine may be effective in controlling hyperactivity in some cases.*

Powers reported on several case studies in which the school performance and psychological adjustment of children were dramatically improved by adherence to diets controlling the ingestion of caffeine, sugar, and carbohydrates. Cautioning that people just do not know what they eat, Powers noted that all the popular cola drinks as well as grape and orange drinks have the equivalent of six teaspoons of sugar in a single 10-ounce bottle. (Powers referred to the case of one teenage girl with serious learning and adjustment problems who consumed 4,000 calories and 510 grams of carbohydrates each day, derived mainly from soft drinks, pastries, and ice cream.) The cola drinks, including some diet brands, have caffeine amounts ranging from the equivalent of one-fourth to one-half cup of coffee in 10 ounces.

Dr. Clyde Hawley, a pediatrician, and Dr. Robert Buckley (1974), a psychiatrist, have treated children with hyperkinetic disorders by restricting dietary intake to substances free of aniline coal tar dyes (food dyes) and salicylates that occur naturally or as food additives. Soft drinks, ice cream, candies, hot dogs, and various fruits have been implicated by Hawley and Buckley as likely to cause hyperkinesis. In addition to extensive testing, which includes tests for allergies, these physicians recommend the elimination of all indicated foods from the diet followed by gradual introduction of some foods to establish tolerance levels.

Allergies will likely become targets of more intense medical investigation in the search for conditions that cause or contribute to learning disabilities. Although allergies are caused by innumerable substances, there are two general groupings: those caused by inhalants and those caused by food ingestion. Dr. William G. Crook (1974) has recently encouraged physicians to consider the "allergic tension-fatigue syndrome." The symptoms of this syndrome include fatigue, irri-

*The possibility that caffeine may *cause* (or be a contributing cause in) hyperactivity in some children and may serve to *control it* in others provides one more example of the differing ways in which different individuals may react to the same chemical compound.

tability, nasal stuffiness, headache, abdominal pain, and pains of the limbs. Crook believes this may be caused by an allergic reaction to foods that affect the nervous system. This syndrome is believed to be one cause of learning problems, hyperactivity, depression, and obsessive-compulsive behavior. Confirmation of the tentative diagnosis, according to Crook, depends on recognition of the possibility of the condition by the physician and remission and reappearance of symptoms after elimination and reintroduction of foods. Wunderlich (1973) has described a "neuro-allergic syndrome," which is said to be caused by various allergies, and its symptoms are similar to the condition described by Crook.

Berman (1974) has implicated middle ear effusion (fluid in the middle ear) as a cause of temporary hearing loss and a possible cause of poor academic achievement and social adjustment. The condition, caused by allergies, can adversely affect language development, speech discrimination, and attention, especially in young children. Research of this type is very limited but could disclose important facts that might aid in preventing learning disabilities.

Orthomolecular medicine

The term *orthomolecular* was coined by Dr. Linus Pauling, world-famed biochemist and twice a winner of the Nobel prize for his scientific accomplishments. For all practical purposes, orthomolecular medicine can be viewed as synonymous with *megavitamin treatment*, for this is the major thrust of orthomolecular medicine and is the more commonly used terminology in many parts of the nation. Orthomolecular medicine is based on the idea that a number of medical problems may be corrected if the body has the right combination of vitamins and minerals, assuming that different individuals may need vastly different amounts of these nutrients. The theoretical basis of orthomolecular medicine is quite complex and relates to the idea that there may be a dysfunction of one or more of the neurotransmitting processes in the brain. Medical problems that should become the target of megavitamin treatment (as viewed by advocates of orthomolecular medicine) are not those with a vitamin deficiency related to an acquired condition (for example, as in scurvy or pellagra). Rather, they are those with a genetic condition leading to biochemical abnormalities, which affect neurochemical balance (Hoffer, 1973).

One of the most frightening and debilitating psychotic disorders, schizophrenia, has been successfully treated by the control of diet and the administration of large dosages of vitamins (Ross, 1974; Hoffer and Osmond, 1966; Pauling, 1968). Graber (1973) described orthomolecular medicine as rejecting "the concept of mind-body duality, a basic premise of medicine since the Middle Ages. It rejects the notion that one's body operates autonomously in its environment, and that one internal organ is relatively independent of the other. It undermines the infection theory of disease, a pillar of modern medicine. And it minimizes the use of drugs or medications not naturally occurring in the human environment" (Graber, 1973, p. 10).

Advocates of orthomolecular medicine have conducted research with adults and children, following the lead of Dr. Pauling. Hoffer (1971) identified a group of 33 children who were described as having a "vitamin B_3 responsive syndrome" characterized by hyperactivity, poor school performance, perceptual changes, and poor school relationships. After receiving megadoses of vitamin B_3, 32 of the subjects were said to be free of the symptoms.

Cott (1971, 1972) has reported the treatment of 500 children who have been described as having a variety of disorders. Cott notes that, unlike drug treatment, which sedates or tranquilizes but does not cure, megavitamin treatment in many cases effects a cure. He maintains that sudden results cannot be expected since it takes 4 to 6 months before noticeable signs of positive change can occur, and the treatment must be used for years in order to bring about permanent changes. The age at which treatment is initiated is critical because children below the age of 7 respond better and more rapidly than those older than 7. Although some side effects are experienced by some subjects, Cott believes that they are far less severe than those experienced in drug treatment.

Cott treats children with orally administered pills, capsules, or liquids, which increase the effectiveness of substances normally found in the body that are believed to provide for optimum molecular composition of the brain. The principal vitamins used in treatment are niacin or niacinamide, ascorbic acid, pyridoxine, and calcium pantothenate. Furthermore, Cott contends that hyperactivity, a symptom found in many learning disabled children, may often be caused by ingestion of cereal grain and cereal grain products.

Cott states that in his experience "orthomolecular intervention with the hyperkinetic-learing disabled child can help better than 50%" (1977, p. 23). He also notes that megavitamins can, if necessary, be used in conjunction with drug therapy in most instances; however, he believes that drug therapy is not needed in many cases where it is presently used. In addition, Cott supports the use of controlled diets as an integral part of the treatment process. According to Cott, "failure to improve nutritional status can be responsible for achieving minimal results (and) removal of offending foods from the diet . . . can result in dramatic improvement in behavior, attention span, and concentration" (1977, p. 29). Although orthomolecular medicine and its use of megavitamin treatment originated in work with psychiatric patients, it is obviously now firmly entrenched in efforts related to the learning disabled.

Hypoglycemia and the narcolepsy complex

Another medical syndrome that may interfere with learning and involves nutrition in etiology and treatment is hypoglycemia. Hypoglycemia is often accompanied by the narcolepsy complex. In a paper presented to the 1968 annual conference of the Association for Children with Learning Disabilities, Dr. H. J. Roberts (1969) revealed the findings of medical research about hypoglycemia, its physiological consequences, effects on learning, and treatment.

His study involved 29 patients—24 children and 5 adults—who were referred to the clinic primarily as a result of severe reading problems. Of this group, all were reported to have adequate mental ability, most had a long-term reading disability problem, most had been given remedial reading instruction, and all were free of gross sensory impairments. Nearly 80% of the subjects were males.

Most of these patients were diagnosed as having narcolepsy complex (pathological drowsiness) secondary to hypoglycemia (an abnormally diminished content of glucose in the blood). Narcolepsy manifests itself in patients who experience a continual need for 14 or more hours of sleep, lethargy during the day, the need for naps, sleeping at inappropriate times, and sleeping after school in the case of children. Hypoglycemia causes the patient to experience attacks of hunger, nervousness, tremors, rapid heart action, and other signs of distress. Of the subjects in this group, Roberts found 66% with at least one first-order relative who had a history of narcolepsy. Diabetes mellitus or severe hypoglycemia was part of the family history in 68% of the patients.

Research findings indicate that disorders of reading are frequently related to these conditions. It is postulated that adequate central nervous system functioning depends on a sufficient supply of glucose in the blood. Children with limited glucose-storage ability may have a serious deprivation of glucose, which, subsequently, has neurological consequences for the act of reading. Obviously, if a child suffers from narcolepsy, attention is difficult and the somatic reactions of hypoglycemia can mean that a child simply does not feel well enough to learn.

Roberts treated 21 of these patients by requiring them to adhere to a strict dietary regimen that eliminated table sugar and foods containing simple sugar. The diet was high in protein and contained an adequate supply of fat. Roberts also prescribed "scientific nibbling" or frequent snacks during the day, at bedtime, and at least once during the night. All of the patients demonstrated noticeable improvement in reading at the end of 2 months of treatment. The reading programs were not changed in any way. Eighteen of the subjects experienced lessened drowsiness, 12 improved in other school subjects, and 5 experienced rapid growth in height. Two older subjects who had been school dropouts returned to school.

Powers' (1974) restricted diet programs are based, at least in part, on hypoglycemia treatment theory. In his study of 260 children and young adults with a variety of learning and behavioral problems, he prescribed a limited carbohydrate diet that entirely excluded sugar, coffee, tea, and cola drinks. Diets were supplemented with digestive enzymes to facilitate the utilization of proteins as a source of glucose, vitamin B, vitamin C, and adrenocortical extracts, and results were quite encouraging. Powers believes that his research provides strong support for his theories about the relationship between blood sugar and brain metabolism.

Summary: diet-related treatments

A number of diet-related treatments are presently advocated by various medical doctors and are in use. Each is predicated on one or both of the following ideas: (1) what is ingested may be a significant causal factor in learning problems and (2) vitamin and mineral needs of some are much greater than others, and without massive doses of such vitamins and minerals the brain may not be able to function properly. Diet treatments are based on the belief that the biochemical needs of individuals vary greatly; thus these specific treatments may be required.

In general, these approaches are not well accepted by many members of the medical community, but they are very popular with some parents. Their lack of acceptance by many physicians is because the research on their effectiveness does not meet usual medical research standards. Their acceptance by parents relates to their desire for non-drug-related intervention and apparent success in many instances. Additional research certainly will take place in the immediate future, and, unless specific health hazards connected with such treatment are discovered, parent interest will remain high.

BASIC BRAIN RESEARCH

In a special 1979 issue of *Scientific American* (Vol. 241, No. 3) devoted entirely to topics about the brain and internationally recognized scientists, the following comments precede the first article: "How does the human brain work? Although notable progress has been made, the question remains one of the profoundest confronting modern science" (1979, p.45). These comments succinctly summarize the present status of knowledge.*

However, another point of view may be taken. Despite the admitted complexity of the brain and the vast quantity of knowledge yet to be learned about its functioning, dramatic new findings have been made in the past 20 to 30 years, with the pace of progress quickening each year. This section includes some basic facts about the brain and its function for brain research may be the key to a better understanding of learning disabilities. According to the fundamental beliefs of the authorities reviewed in this text, learning disabilities are inextricably interrelated with brain function. Kephart's perceptual-motor match, Ayres' sensory integration, Fernald's multisensory learning, Myklebust's analysis of the levels of learning, and the medically related approaches presented earlier in this chapter—all involve the brain and central nervous system functioning. Educators must work directly with the resultants of dysfunction, and additional knowledge about the brain may be of great importance to future efforts. Following are a few known facts about the brain.

David Hubel, a neurobiologist at Harvard Medical School, states that "the brain is a tissue. It is a complicated, intricately woven tissue, like nothing else we know in the universe, but it is composed of cells, as any tissue is" (1979, p. 45). He further notes that, although these are highly specialized cells, they function according to the same laws that govern other cells. They can be investigated with regard to chemical and electrical signals, their chemical composition can be determined, and their interconnections can be mapped. Therefore, the brain can be studied, just like all other parts of the human body.

Rosenfeld and Klivington (1975) have summarized a variety of facts about the brain that should be of interest to the lay reader. The brain contains 100 billion cells, 10 billion of which are neurons. Neurons, or nerve cells, form the intricate mechanism for receiving, storing, and processing stimuli and neural transmission. These cells are packed into the brain with varying density, 100 million to the cubic inch in some parts. Each neuron may be connected with 60,000 other neurons and no two are identical in the circuitry of such connections. The brain appropriates 20% of the total blood supply and removes its nutrients before the blood delivers nutrients to other organs. Each neuron processes thousands of bits of information in controlling the body. Millions of RNA molecules transmit genetic instructions from DNA molecules to produce 100,000 types of protein.

Aberrant functions of the brain can occur for numerous reasons, many of which are not known. Genetic factors influencing chemical manufacture have been suspected of creating various adverse effects upon neurological functioning and development. Chemical imbalances can result from deficient dietary intake of needed nutrients, the ingestion of chemical substances that disrupt neurological functioning, or the improper secretion of chemicals by body organs. Chemicals can interrupt the transmission of signals in the brain, thereby impeding central nervous system functioning. Chemicals control our emotions, and the ingestion of certain chemicals, such as hallucinogens and alcohol, have well-known effects. In the same way, chemicals are known to impair perception and memory, which can have an impact on

*This valuable, single-topic issue of *Scientific American* is now published as a book, *The Brain* (1980). This provides an excellent source of up-to-date information for those who have further interest in this topic. (Publisher: W. H. Freeman and Company, San Francisco.)

learning. Chemical imbalances are also believed to cause schizophrenia and depression as well as other disorders. The syndromes recognized in learning disabilities may have many causes. The impact of actual brain damage to the lobes, to cortical tissues, or to the brainstem can cause learning disorders, or disorders can apparently result from imbalances of the many chemical agents that also interfere with proper brain functioning.

A wide variety of brain-related research with both animals and humans has provided implications for learning disabilities educators and guidelines for additional brain research. One example of animal research that, at the very least, provides some interesting *questions*, is that conducted by Kretch (1968). In this research, rats of weaning age were placed in two different environments, using littermate control groups. The enriched environment rats lived in large cages, in groups of eight to ten, where they could see out into the world and people could see in. The cage included a number of carefully designed toys, tunnels, swinging gadgets, and lever-controlled lights, which they soon learned to turn off and on. These cages were in large busy rooms, and, after a time, these rats were permitted to explore other environments for a period of time each day. They were given formal training on a number of tasks known to be possible for rats, and, all in all, led a good, upper-middle-class rat life, with maximum educational exposure. Their brother rats—those with the deliberately impoverished environment—lived in small cages in a quiet, dimly lit room. Each lived alone, where he could hear other rats but not see them. They did, however, have the same diet as their more fortunate brothers.

After 80 days, when the rats could be considered young adults, they were randomly numbered, taken to the laboratory, and decapitated. The technician who performed both this task and the analysis that followed had no way of knowing which rat came from which environment.

The results were as follows. Using brother-against-brother comparison, those rats that had lived in the enriched environment indicated (1) a much larger diameter capillary system supplying the cortex, (2) larger, deeper cortex (it literally weighed more), (3) larger neurons, (4) higher activity levels of acetylcholinesterase (the enzyme involved in the transsynaptic conduction of neural impulses), (5) an increase in cholinesterase (the enzyme found in the brain cells, which is believed to be involved in nutrition of the neurons and may assist in establishing permanent traces), and (6) a 15% increase in the number of the glial cells.

In summary, then, the rat who had lived the "good life" was a rat with a heavier, thicker, more efficient cortex and therefore was a better learner.

In a replication of this research, rats that had lived in the differing environments were not killed; rather the impoverished rats were taken out of their poor environment and placed with the others. The research that followed was detailed, but in summary it indicated that on simple problems, the formerly impoverished rats did as well as their more fortunate brothers, whereas on more difficult problems they remained less able.

Other animal research projects might also be noted, including those to determine, for example, which parts of the brain are concerned with position as opposed to shape and whether diet effects brain development. Often such experimental projects are suggested by observations of humans who have been injured in war or in accidents. Researchers cannot, and would not, want to further damage the brain of already injured individuals or remove parts of the brain of normal human subjects, but they can do so with animals. The results of such animal experiments cannot necessarily be translated into direct action with humans, but inferences and implications may be derived, which provide guidelines for action when a human has been injured and surgery must be performed.

In working with humans, researchers have accumulated the greatest amount of useful information from situations involving brain damage and in settings in which electrical stimulation can be used during brain surgery. One of the topics of recent interest to educators is the matter of left brain and right brain functions. This great interest resulted from surgery that was performed on an adult who suffered from severe epilepsy. In this surgery, the bundle of nerve fibers that normally connect the top of the brain were cut. The resulting "separate" hemispheres led to some very unusual reactions in the adult, verifying the very different functions of the two hemispheres. Since that time, similar surgical procedures have been completed with other humans, and much more is now known about the differing functions of the two hemispheres of the brain.

A brief review of some of the established facts about left-right functions may illustrate how further research in this area may be of great interest and potential value in the field of learning disabilities. For example, it has been established that, because of the manner in which the optic nerves are connected, the right visual field (what we see with both eyes as we look at an object to our right) is processed in the left hemisphere. Left visual field processing is handled by the right hemisphere. Sounds from the right ear are processed primarily in the left hemisphere, and sounds from the left ear are processed primarily in the right hemisphere. Smell is projected into the hemisphere on the same side as the nostril doing the smelling. Tactile information sensed by the left hand is perceived primarily by the right hemisphere, and, when the right hand is directed to write, the left hemisphere sends the signal. Many of these facts were fairly well established before the advent of split-brain research, but such research further confirmed them. In addition, it confirmed that, after the hemispheres are separated (though they are still connected through the brain stem), neither hemisphere has much knowledge of what has been learned through the other hemisphere.

The left hemisphere has most of the speech and language ability, but the right hemisphere has most of the geometric competence that is required for hand-eye-brain coordination. A great deal more has been learned from split-brain research, and exactly how this may be of assistance to learning disabled students cannot now be predicted. However, since learning disabled students apparently have difficulties with areas such as sensory-motor integration, visual, auditory, or tactile discrimination, and language development, this research will certainly provide additional information as to how such learning takes place. It may also provide information regarding how humans may be able to develop certain learning functions in the hemisphere opposite to that in which they are normally located.

Another type of brain research that may eventually have important implications for programs for the learning disabled has been reported by Sandra Witelson, a professor of psychiatry at McMaster University, Ontario, Canada. One basic finding of Witelson's work is that brains of males and females have certain basic differences that may explain other behavioral and educational differences (Witelson, 1976, pp. 425-427). This research concerns differences in the right hemisphere of the brain and indicates that males may achieve hemispheric dominance (at least for many functions) by the age of six, but females do not usually achieve such dominance until adolescence. This might help explain the generally recognized fact that males tend to have better spatial perception and organization at any given age (this is primarily a right brain function) and may also explain other phenomena of importance in learning disabilities. If the right hemisphere does not establish dominance until adolescence, this means that it remains more flexible or "plastic." Thus, if the left hemisphere is unable to carry out certain functions that are essential to learning (because of any of a variety of reasons), the right hemisphere may more likely be able to take over such functions up until age 12, 13, or even later. This would be true for females, but not for males, which might help explain, in part, the greater incidence of various types of learning disabilities among boys. Their lack of flexibility in brain function prohibits them from accomplishing this "hemispheric switching" in the same manner as girls. In this instance, earlier development of specialization may be a disadvantage if there is need for the right hemisphere to take over any of the usual functions of the left.

Additional work must be completed to further verify Witelson's findings, and then further research must be done on the various possible effects of this difference, if it does exist. This may be quite valuable information, once educators develop a greater understanding of its various implications for teaching the learning disabled individual.

Basic brain research, of which the preceding has been only a miniscule sample, will eventually lead to valuable information for all learners, not just the learning disabled. It is an exciting field, and, although educators will probably not be closely involved with the actual research, such involvement may increase as inferences of such research suggest modified teaching procedures or techniques. In any event, because learning disabilities are so closely related to brain function, this field is worthy of continued attention.

SUMMARY

To be better able to protect the rights of children, to be able to relate to and counsel parents, and to communicate, as required, with members of the medical profession, learning disabilities teachers must have certain basic information and understandings about a number of medically related matters. These include such areas as drug treatment prescribed by the physician and diet-related approaches to control hyperactivity. With respect to drug treatment, teachers, for example, should understand that stimulants are more often prescribed than any other category of medication, should be aware of some of the possible side effects, and should be able to recognize them, if they become evident at school. They should be aware of the various diet-related treatments to be able to cooperate with parents, when necessary, in attempts to maintain diet control. Teachers should also be aware of the different medical specialties and should not hesitate to suggest that parents consult further with their family physician when appropriate.

These various types of information and

Signs of unusual fatigue may be important indicators of various medically related causes of learning disabilities.

knowledge are essential for the teacher to play the proper role in the classroom and to maintain a proper "teacher image" for the parent. This latter consideration is important because of the need to maintain the confidence and support of the parent, which the parent will then more likely communicate to the child. Though the special educator may not be able to remain totally aware of all medical practices that hold promise, regular reading of the basic learning disabilities journals will go a long way toward remaining current in this most interesting field.

REFERENCES AND SUGGESTED READINGS

Adler, S. Behavior management: a nutritional approach to the behaviorally disordered and learning disabled child, *Journal of Learning Disabilities*, 1978, *11*, 651-656.

Atkinson, R., and Shiffrin, R. Human memory: a proposed system and its control processes. In Spence, K., and Spence, T. (Eds.) *The psychology of learning and motivation* (vol. 2). New York: Academic Press, Inc., 1968.

Berman, B. Hearing loss and allergic management, *Hearing and Speech News*, 1974, *42*(2), 14-16.

Brown, D., and others. Impramine therapy and seizures: three children treated for hyperactive behavior disorders, *American Journal of Psychiatry*, 1973, *130*, 210-212.

Conners, C. What parents need to know about stimulant

drugs and special education, *Journal of Learning Disabilities,* 1973, *6*(6), 349-351.

Cott, A. Megavitamins: the orthomolecular approach to behavioral disorders and learning disabilities, *Academic Therapy,* 1972, *7,* 245-259.

Cott, A. *The orthomolecular approach to learning disabilities.* San Rafael, Calif.: Academic Therapy Publications, 1977.

Cott, A. Orthomolecular approach to the treatment of learning disabilities, *Schizophrenia,* 1971, *3*(2), 95-101.

Cott, A. A reply, *Academic Therapy,* 1977, *13,* 161-171.

Cragg, B. Plasticity of synapses, *British Medical Bulletin,* 1974, *30*(2), 141-144.

Crook, W. *The allergic tension-fatigue syndrome: a paper.* New York: Insight Books, 1974.

Crook, W. *Can your child read? Is he hyperactive?* Jackson, Tenn.: Pedicenter Press, 1975.

Feingold, B. *Why Your Child is Hyperactive.* New York: Random House, Inc., 1975.

Gadow, K. *Children on medication: a primer for school personnel.* Reston, Va.: Council for Exceptional Children, 1979.

Graber, D. Megavitamins, molecules, and minds, *Human Behavior,* 1973, *2*(5), 8-15.

Hawley, C., and Buckley, R. Food dyes and hyperkinetic children, *Academic Therapy,* 1974, *10*(1), 27-31.

Hoffer, A. Mechanism of action of nicotinic acid and nicotinamide in the treatment of schizophrenics. In Howkins, D., and Pauling, L. (Eds.) *Orthomolecular psychiatry, treatment of schizophrenia.* San Francisco: W. H. Freeman and Co., Publishers, 1973.

Hoffer, A. Vitamin B-3 dependent child, *Schizophrenia,* 1971, *3*(2), 107-113.

Hoffer, A., and Osmond, H. *How to live with schizophrenia.* New York: University Books, Inc., 1966.

Hubel, D. The brain, *Scientific American,* 1979, *241*(3), 45-53.

Kinsbourne, M., and Caplan, P. *Children's learning and attention problems.* Boston: Little, Brown and Co., 1979.

Krech, R. *The frontiers of learning.* Dayton, Ohio: The Mead Corp., 1968.

McNeil, M., and Hamre, C. A review of measures of lateralized cerebral hemisphere function, *Journal of Learning Disabilities,* 1974, 7(6), 51-59.

Okolo, C., Bartlett, S., and Shaw, S. Communication between professionals concerning medication for the hyperactive child, *Journal of Learning Disabilities,* 1978, *11,* 647-650.

Page, J., and others. Pemoline (cylert) in the treatment of childhood hyperkinesis, *Journal of Learning Disabilities,* 1974, 7(8), 498-503.

Pauling, L. Orthomolecular psychiatry, *Science,* 1968, *160*(4), 265-271.

Pines, M. Speak, memory: the riddle of recall and forgetfulness, *Saturday Review,* Aug. 9, 1975, *58,* 16-20.

Powers, H., Jr. Caffeine, behavior, and the LD child, *Academic Therapy,* 1975, *11*(1), 5-19.

Powers, H., Jr. Dietary measures to improve behavior and achievement, *Academic Therapy,* 1974, *9*(3), 203-214.

Roberts, H. A clinical and metabolic reevaluation of reading disability. Selected papers on learning disabilities. Fifth Annual Convention, Association for Children with Learning Disabilities. San Rafael, Calif.: Academic Therapy Publications, 1969.

Rosenfeld, H., and Klivington, K. Inside the brain: the last great frontier, *Saturday Review,* Aug. 9, 1975, *58,* 13-15.

Ross, H. Orthomolecular psychiatry: vitamin pills for schizophrenics, *Psychology Today,* April, 1974, 7, 82-88.

Safer, D., Allen, R., and Barr, E. Growth rebound after termination of stimulant drugs, *Pediatrics,* 1975, *86,* 113-116.

Samples, R. Learning with the whole brain, *Human Behavior,* 1975, *4*(2), 17-23.

Shneour, E. *The malnourished mind.* Garden City, N.Y.: Doubleday and Co., Inc., 1975.

Sperry, R. Left-brain, right-brain, *Saturday Review,* Aug. 9, 1975, *58,* 30-33.

Stewart, M. Hyperactive children, *Scientific American,* 1970, *222*(4), 94-99.

Swanson, J., and Kinsbourne, M. Artificial color and hyperactive behavior. In Knights, R., and Bakker, D. (Eds.) *Rehabilitation, treatment, and management of learning disorders.* Baltimore: University Park Press, 1980.

Trites, R. (Ed.) *Hyperactivity in children.* Baltimore: University Park Press, 1979.

Waugh, N., and Norman, D. Primary memory, *Psychology Review,* 1965, *72,* 89-104.

Witelson, S. Sex and the single hemisphere: specialization of the right hemisphere for spatial processing, *Science,* 1976, *193,* 425-427.

Wolf, J. Chemicals to facilitate learning tested on Rhesus monkeys, *Primate Record,* 1973, *4*(2), 13-21.

Wunderlich, R. *Allergy, brains, and children coping. Allergy and child behavior: the neuroallergic syndrome.* St. Petersburg, Fla.: Johnny Reads, Inc., 1973.

Wunderlich, R. Treatment of the hyperactive child, *Academic Therapy,* 1973, *8*(4), 375-390.

chapter 9

Behavior modification and learning disabilities

In the consideration of learning theorists, Chapter 3 included a review of the frame of reference of the behaviorists, and in so doing, mentioned B. F. Skinner. Skinner, like other behaviorists, believes that the behavior of humans is composed of a complex series of responses that may be observed and related to other observable events. That is, behavior may be explained in relation to some sort of *activity* that affects the individual, a *response* that the individual makes, and a *connection* between the activity (stimulus) and the response. Skinner expanded the beliefs of earlier behaviorists to state that there were two general classes of responses: (1) *respondents* (those connected with a known stimulus) and (2) *operants* (those that are spontaneous). These operants can be viewed as examples of the individual acting *upon* the environment rather than reacting *to* the environment, as with respondents. Skinner has made much of his impact on the world in attempting to modify or condition this operant behavior.

Skinner and the work that has grown out of his theoretical postulations have had tremendous influence on the entire field of education. In the field of special education, Skinner's ideas were first applied to the mentally retarded and the emotionally disturbed and, more recently, to the learning disabled. This chapter focuses on the general principles of behavior modification with greater emphasis on operant conditioning and specific application to the field of learning disabilities. Behavior modification is viewed in a rather broad sense, and procedures such as contingency management, modeling (or behavioral modeling), role playing, and very simple reward systems are considered as important techniques for use with the learning disabled. For our purposes, *behavior modification is considered as any technique that provides for planned, systematic consequences to a given response that are designed to alter the response or its frequency.*

TYPES OF BEHAVIORAL CHANGE

Behavior modification is a procedure that most good teachers have used for decades; a number of education-oriented behaviorists have attempted to identify what makes behavioral approaches work and how to make them work better. In so doing, they have assisted educators to become much more effective in their application of behavioral techniques. Stated another way, education-oriented behaviorists have systematically studied a variety of school-related behavior, have explored the various ways in which such behavior can be influenced or changed, and have reported their findings for use in the classroom. These reports and the included recommendations take many forms and, at times, may employ somewhat unfamiliar terminology. These recommendations will be approached by first examining the types of behavioral change that may most likely be desired in the classroom setting.

Sulzer and Mayer (1972) suggest that desired behavioral change may be classified into a number of general categories. These are: (1) *increasing or strengthening* some behavior that is weak; (2) *extending* a good or desirable behavior to a new setting; (3) *restricting or limiting* a behavior to some specific setting; (4) *shaping or forming* some new behavior; (5) *maintaining* some existing behavior (particularly if it appears to be weakening); and (6) *reducing or eliminating* some very undesirable behavior. Most teachers could immediately relate to these categories by thinking of a number of practical situations in which these specific behavioral changes were precisely what they wanted to achieve. However, more than one of these types of behavioral change may apply in certain situations, and this is part of the reason why teachers should be fully aware of these different categories.

Educators should be able to readily relate these various goals and behavioral objectives to the Individual Educational Programs (see pp. 25 to 27) developed for each student who receives special education services. Such goals are required by both federal and state regulations, and most will fall within one of the six categories mentioned by Sulzer and Mayer. For example, consider Mike S., who is learning disabled, has difficulty in reading, and is moderately hyperactive and distractible. Goals for Mike may be written in a variety of ways but certainly might include: (a) increasing and strengthening behavior in which he is attending to his reading assignment; (b) restricting his loud vocalizations to outside playground activities; (c) maintaining the interest that he presently shows in science-related activities; and (d) reducing his physical abuse of other children. Behavior modification would then include procedures designed to facilitate desired changes in Mike's behavior.

To apply behavioral techniques, the teacher must learn to carefully observe behavior, find a way to measure it accurately, and be able to state just what behavioral changes are desired. It is not enough to say "I want Mike to learn how to behave better," or "I want him to learn to be a good citizen in the classroom." These statements are too subjective to permit effective application of behavior modification approaches. Teachers must learn to speak more precisely, especially in establishing behavioral objectives, to accurately determine progress toward ultimate goals. The categories of behavioral change outlined in this section provide a starting point. Further consideration of the nature of goals and behavioral objectives follows.

SPECIFYING GOALS AND BEHAVIORAL OBJECTIVES

As just indicated, it is quite important to be able to specify or establish meaningful goals. It is equally important to be able to establish more specific behavioral objectives. With such goals and objectives clearly established, it is much easier to implement behavioral approaches and to determine if progress is being made. Let us, therefore, further consider the matter of goals and objectives.

Goals are statements that indicate the broad, general outcomes that are desired.

They state what is desired in a manner that clearly indicates the direction of change and the general outcome but do not ordinarily indicate (in a behavioral sense) *precisely* what the learner will do or be able to do after the goal is accomplished. Goals may be expressed from the teacher's point of view or the learner's point of view. Usually, just a few goals are stated, and in some cases they may relate to something as nebulous as "developing an appreciation of classical music." More often, in the field of learning disabilities, the goal is somewhat more specific, such as "develop the ability to read, with understanding, the alternate second grade reader" or "accurately recognize all letters of the alphabet in both cursive and manuscript form."

Goals are important to establish the broad framework within which educators must identify specific behavioral objectives. Without goals, teachers may focus on objectives that are either (1) easier to recognize and achieve or (2) more attractive to them. They are then quite likely to overlook other objectives that are highly important. With goals, teachers should be able to establish objectives that, in composite, lead to accomplishment of the overall, broad purposes of instruction. Objectives are the units with which educators ordinarily work in behavioral approaches and are outlined in the following paragraphs.

Behavioral objectives are relatively specific statements of learning outcome on which one must focus on a day-to-day basis in the classroom. Without the statement of meaningful, attainable objectives, we cannot implement behavior modification procedures. Behavioral objectives may occasionally be expressed from the teacher's point of view but are usually expressed from the learner's point of view. Examples of specific instructional objectives are "John can consistently recognize and correctly use the consonant blend 'bl' at the beginning of at least twenty words," or "John can name the letters of the alphabet in correct order."

Behavioral objectives may be stated in many ways, and authorities often discriminate between *terminal behavior objectives* and day-to-day or week-to-week *instructional objectives,* with the latter being the intermediate learning outcomes necessary to obtain the terminal objectives. Perhaps the most important thing to remember is that to think in terms of behavioral objectives one must be able to clearly and specifically state the objective and accurately measure the extent to which it is being met. In the last analysis, behavioral objectives are needed to force the teacher to be more precise and scientific about what is to be attained and whether or not the student has attained it. Behavioral objectives are the fundamental tool of the behaviorist; some understanding of them is essential to understanding the remainder of this chapter.

OPERANT CONDITIONING

Operant conditioning is one of the most common types of behavior modification used in the schools. Operant conditioning principles grew out of experiments with animals that were a part of attempts to understand "trial and error" learning. One such experiment demonstrated that, through random exploration, cats placed in a box would eventually step on the pedal that would open a door, leading to an avenue of escape. When again placed in the box, "experienced" cats would find the escape pedal more quickly. Eventually, these cats would go immediately to the pedal and to freedom. In related experiments with pigeons, in which a release button was the means whereby food was dispensed, similar results were obtained. After first pecking randomly and accidentally causing the release of food, the pigeons eventually "learned" that, by pecking a particular place, they would receive food.

The results of these and numerous similar experiments were eventually recognized as a major type of conditioning. It was named *operant conditioning,* because it required the learner to actively operate on the environment and then to respond to the results. This is quite different from classical conditioning, in which the learner is passive and simply responds to a particular stimulus. It was verified that responses (activities) that are reinforced by environmental contingencies are more likely to be repeated; thus the basis for operant conditioning, as used in the schools, was established. In operant conditioning, the teacher will often reinforce that which approximates the desired behavior in an attempt to establish new operant behavior. Sometimes it is necessary to reward behavior that is somewhat different from what is desired, just to establish the reinforcement principle, and then to reinforce only those behaviors that are in the desired direction. This is sometimes called "shaping," and the movement in the desired direction is through successive approximations of the desired goal. Considerable research has led to the development of much information about such procedures, both in lower animals and in human beings, but the following generalizations will be sufficient for purposes of this review.

There are two general types, or schedules, of reinforcement—continuous and intermittent. Continuous reinforcement means reinforcement after each desired response. *This is where most reinforcement programs must start.*

Intermittent schedules may be any one of four types:

1. *Fixed-interval schedule.* An example is providing reinforcement every 10 minutes. Fixed interval refers to fixed *time* intervals and does not relate to how many responses have occurred during that time interval. The subject may reduce response rate soon after reinforcement, since no reinforcer is immediately forthcoming.

2. *Variable-interval schedule.* This may be used when fixed-interval schedules lead to low probability of response. When this is initiated, the subject cannot predict when reinforcement may come. It may come after 2 minutes, then not for 12 minutes, then 4 minutes, and so on. The tendency is for higher probability of response than with fixed-interval, along with less likelihood of extinction of response.

3. *Fixed-ratio schedule.* In this schedule, reinforcement comes after every x number of responses. This may lead to long time periods between reinforcement and is inefficient.

4. *Variable-ratio schedule.* This tends to be a highly efficient procedure. With this schedule, reinforcement may come after 3 responses, then after 50 responses, then after 13, and so on. The subject cannot predict when the reinforcement will come and tends to continue the desired response so as to take no chances on missing reinforcement. *A variable ratio schedule is usually the most effective if the purpose is rapid, steady response and high resistance to extinction.*

In all cases the reinforcement must truly represent a "reward" to the subject involved, or the system fails. What is a reward to one 7-year-old boy may not be a reward to another 7-year-old boy. This is even more the case when considering boys versus girls, different age groups, and different socioeconomic backgrounds.

Other variations of behavior modification are in common use in the classroom and will be briefly considered. These include contingency management and behavioral modeling.

CONTINGENCY MANAGEMENT AND CONTINGENCY CONTRACTING

Contingency management is the management of a situation so that the child knows that a particular reward is contingent on certain other desired behavior or completion of a certain task. As in all behavior modification approaches the reward must be of sufficient value to the individual to motivate the attempt to complete the task. *Contingency contracting* is a form of contingency management in which a "contract" with the child is established so that he has assurance of a given reward if he fulfills his part of the contract.

In discussing contingency contracting, Lloyd Homme (1971) speaks of "Grandma's Law" (clean up your plate, then you may have dessert) as the principle after which contingency contracting is modeled. He provides 10 rules for contingency contracting:

1. The contract payoff (the reward) should be immediate.
2. Initial contracts should call for and reward small approximations.
3. Rewards should be frequent with small amounts.
4. The contract should call for and reward accomplishment rather than obedience.
5. The performance should be rewarded after it occurs.
6. The contract must be fair.
7. The terms of the contract must be clear.
8. The contract must be honest.
9. The contract must be positive.
10. Contracting as a method must be used systematically.

Contingency contracting is one of several accepted forms of behavior modification and follows the same basic principles as all other forms. Homme's rules are so simple that some may wonder if they can really work. The first five rules relate to the reward and are generally applicable to other types of behavior modification. The last five rules directly relate to the contract and thus are not applicable except when using some type of contract. In my experience, such contracting *will* work, if applied consistently (as Homme recommends) and if the objectives under consideration are realistic for the student.

One additional type of behavior modification that involves contingency management should be mentioned in concluding this consideration. *Cost contingency* is a term sometimes applied to a procedure in which rewards or reinforcers are subtracted if specific, undesirable behavior is observed. This too is implemented in accordance with an established procedure or, in some cases, a contract.

BEHAVIORAL MODELING

Modeling, or *behavioral modeling*, involves the use of reinforcement (rewards) to promote the copying of behavior of those who are indicated as "models." This method, or approach, assumes that most (if not all) behavior is imitative and that children who are imitating socially unacceptable behavior must be shown that it is more rewarding to imitate socially acceptable behavior. This technique is practiced by most teachers but is not necessarily done in a systematic manner. Like all behavior modification techniques, it works better if systematized.

The use of behavioral modeling, contingency management, or operant conditioning means rejection of the medical model and its dependence on the concept of a deep-seated cause for maladaptive behavior. This is particularly true when these behavioral approaches are used to change acting-out behavior, for the behavioral theorist believes that, if the undesirable behavior is gone, the problem is gone. The use of rewards to in-

Although reward systems may include the use of noneducationally related activities, it is often possible to reward educational or behavioral achievement through the use of activities that are directly applicable to the child's learning needs.

crease motivation, and thus to increase academic performance, is not such a clear-cut rejection of the medical (causative) model, but, since it is based on the beliefs of behavioral scientists, it too is anticausation oriented. A number of other behavioral approaches exist, but it is not consistent with the purposes of this chapter to attempt to outline all variations of applied behaviorism. Instead we will consider certain principles that relate to effective implementation of almost all behavioral approaches.

PRINCIPLES FOR IMPLEMENTATION

Before the discussion of certain examples of *application* of behavior modification procedures with the learning disabled student, several important basic principles should be noted.

1. *Behaviorists are concerned with behavior that is observable, measurable, and controllable.* Unless the desired outcome can be reduced to behavior that can be viewed by a number of independent observers with considerable agreement on what was observed, and unless that behavior can be measured, it is not appropriate for behavior modification techniques. Whether or not it can be controlled can be determined theoretically, but, in actual application, practical ability to control is a more important consideration.

2. *Behaviorists do not attempt to accomplish the academically or physiologically impossible.* Because of the deliberate departure of

behaviorists from the medical, causal frame of reference, some individuals with limited information have mistakenly concluded that the behavior modification theorist does not become involved in diagnostic work or search for background information and therefore may not be aware of physiological or psychological limitations. Brady and Lind (1965) reported an interesting case study in which behavior modification procedures were of great value in assisting in remediation of blindness. However, this was *hysterical* blindness, and the experimenters would not have attempted this procedure if neurological and ophthalmological examinations had not indicated the absence of physiological cause for blindness. That is, if the subject had been diagnosed as blind because of known ophthalmological causes, there would have been no case study to report. In a similar manner, if a child is not able to read and a carefully conducted educational/psychological study indicates he is severely mentally retarded, behavior modification theorists would not expect him to become a proficient reader. They might, using behavior modification techniques, try to teach him to accomplish some other task, if it is within the realm of possibility.

3. *Behavior modification techniques in learning disabilities should be used in parallel with other learning disability methods, but the influence of these methods should not be allowed to reduce the effectiveness of the reinforcer or the preciseness and systematization imposed by the behavior modification framework.* This principle is closely related to the second.

For example, if the child is known to have problems in auditory discrimination, this should be carefully considered by those establishing the program of behavior modification. The child should continue to have whatever learning disability programming seems to be appropriate for his age, academic level, interests, and so forth, with behavior modification techniques utilized to promote the accomplishment of specific educational objectives.

One of the major problems with some learning disabled children is inability to attend to any specific task, particularly an academic one. Nonattending behavior is one fruitful target area for behavior modification methods and is an excellent example of how behavior modification can work along with other learning disability approaches. Even though, for example, a careful assessment-based approach is used, modality weaknesses are known, present level of functioning is established, and appropriate materials are available, unless the child will attend to these materials, all the other efforts may be essentially wasted. In such a case, use of behavior modification techniques *in parallel with the planned, methodologically appropriate approach* is the best way to proceed. Care must be taken so that the specific approach components are complementary to the behavior modification techniques, or, at the very least, not detrimental to them. This requires carefully thought out, planned-in-advance procedures, including planning for various alternative happenings and consequences. Because many learning disabled children have some degree of hyperactivity, nonattending behavior, or both, behavior modification techniques have been used to a considerable extent to attempt to improve attendance to the learning task.

4. *Without careful explanation, which will hopefully lead to understanding and cooperation, behavior modification procedures may fail, even though the project might have been successful with the understanding and cooperation of professional peers.* This principle relates to the fact that a number of educators, includ-

ing both teachers and administrators, are not familiar with behavior modification techniques. Parents, too, must be a part of the total plan, or failure is a definite risk because of their misunderstandings.

These four principles, if carefully followed, will lead to success in many cases. One final word of caution is: *Behavior modification is both simple and complex; it is important to understand both its potential and its limitations.* Behavior modification can easily be seen as a simple reward system, and little more. It is, in fact, much more. The section Recommendations for Practitioners, near the close of this chapter, provides further practical insights, but the reader of this brief chapter is not ready to implement a behavior modification program. The only acceptable method is for one to study behavior modification approaches in some depth and then to establish the first program with the advice and assistance of another educator who has had successful experience with behavior modification. Then, one may receive the reward of reasonable success and will be encouraged to proceed further with this interesting approach.

ILLUSTRATIVE CASE STUDIES

The term *survival skills* has come into accepted use by behavior modification researchers and includes such behavior as attending to schoolwork and complying with the teacher's instructions. The term *survival* refers to survival in the classroom environment as it is typically structured. The survival skills, particularly the ability to ignore most of the distracting stimuli in the classroom and attend to the learning task, provide a high priority focus for behavior modification techniques. Three studies in which such survival skills (attending behavior) were obtained through behavior modification procedures are reviewed next.

The first is the study of a preschool youngster who was not actually diagnosed as a learning disability child, but, had his nonattending behavior continued, there seems little chance that he would have learned in a normal manner in the formal school setting. The methods used in dealing with him, with only slight modifications, can be applied with many nonattending youngsters in the primary grades. This study was reported by Allen and co-workers in 1967.

In this study the investigators believed that the ultimate goal of the preschool was to develop the child's skill in using material constructively and creatively. To do this the child had to become engaged in meaningful activity. The 4-year-old subject of this study tended to move so rapidly from activity to activity that meaningful results were nearly impossible.

Attending behavior was operationally defined for this study, and social reinforcement was used after a minimum period of time in any one activity. Withholding reinforcement from the child meant turning away from him, not looking or smiling at him, not speaking to him, and so on. One teacher was responsible for the reinforcement and was trained to be able to do so consistently.

Baseline data were gathered that indicated the child averaged 56 activity changes every 50 minutes. After completion of the initial procedure, the subject averaged 20 activity changes in 50 minutes. He frequently spent 15 to 20 minutes in a single activity, which was highly satisfactory in this preschool setting. No ill effects were noted; only the inappropriate behavior was diminished. His acceptable behavior was maintained, except on those occasions when his mother visited the preschool. Because she did not reinforce him on the same basis as the preschool teachers, his behavior deteriorated in her presence.

A second study of interest was designed to increase attending behavior of third- and fourth-grade children in an elementary school remedial room (Wolf et al., 1970).

The experimenters noted that, although ability to maintain order in the classroom does not necessarily result in increased academic achievement, a certain degree of orderliness and attendance to the learning task is necessary for an effective group learning situation. Therefore a number of behavioral researchers have focused on management of out-of-seat behavior. One method for such management has been the use of a kitchen timer, set by the teacher for various intervals, with the children either receiving some type of tokens by being in their seats when the timer rings or avoiding loss of tokens by being in their seats. A variable time schedule, with time intervals unknown to the children, is used in this type of setting, and the procedure has been called the *timer game.* This study is an application of that game.

The 16 subjects in this study were low-achieving third- and fourth-grade children from an urban, low-income school. This remedial class met for 3 hours every afternoon, and a token (points) reward system was used. These points were given for correct answers and were backed up by such primary reinforcers as candy, clothing, and field trips. The remedial program was based on an assessment of each child's present educational level, as well as his abilities and disabilities.

A trained observer was employed in observing out-of-seat behavior. The out-of-seat definition required that the "seat" portion of the child's body not be in contact with any part of the seat of his chair.

To establish baseline data, two different observers recorded behavior on the basis of 30-second intervals, observing each student in a predetermined order and counting the number who met the criterion for being out of their seats. Interrecorder agreement was 93% and 94% on two observation sessions.

The experiment proceeded in the following manner: (1) Baseline rate was established for each child for seven sessions. Then the timer game was introduced. The timer rang on intervals ranging from 0 to 40 minutes averaging 20 minutes between rings. (2) Every student who was in his seat when the timer rang was given 5 points. It should be noted that the average student's point accumulation for all activities was 400 points a day, so this represented a relatively small proportion of his total daily effort. (3) The timer game was continued for six sessions; then the baseline condition was reinstated for seven sessions.

Results of the study indicated the effectiveness of the timer game in reducing out-of-seat behavior. During the first baseline period, on the average, 17 intervals containing out-of-seat behavior per child were recorded. Use of the timer game reduced the average to about 2 intervals per child. Return to the baseline condition (after six sessions with the timer game) resulted in a return to the average of 17 intervals per child.

Results of this study also demonstrate a principle that has been receiving increasing attention from various researchers in behavior modification. Although the timer game did dramatically reduce out-of-seat behavior (from 17 to 2 intervals per child), after the timer game was discontinued, the out-of-seat behavior returned to the original level. In this instance, only six sessions with the timer game were used, but treatment gains obviously must be maintained after intervention has been terminated, or the whole procedure is little more than an experimental exercise. A variety of posttreatment behavior-maintenance approaches are now under investigation, and several show real promise. These posttreatment procedures may be initiated during the course of the original behavioral intervention and will likely use a variety of reinforcers. The planning of the posttreatment environment may prove to be the most important single feature in the entire process, as such methods are applied to the practical classroom setting.

Although most children in the class modified their behavior while exposed to the timer game, some showed little change. One such child was the subject of a further, separate experiment. This student was called Sue in the experimental report.

In this second experiment, focused primarily on Sue, classroom setting and the token reinforcement system were the same as in the total class experiment. Out-of-seat behavior was recorded by an observer for a 1½-hour period each day, during a baseline period and under two different contingency conditions, both using the timer game.

In the first of the new settings, Sue was told she could earn extra points under a new set of conditions. (The assumption was that the timer game as played with the entire group was not sufficiently rewarding to Sue, hence it made little difference in her behavior.) A piece of construction paper with the numbers 10, 20, 30, 40, and 50 drawn on it was attached to the wall. Sue was told that she would start with 50 points but that each time she was out of her seat when the timer rang she would lose 10 points. When this happened, the teacher would mark off the highest remaining number, thus leaving a visual reminder of points remaining and points lost. The timer was set on a varying time schedule, averaging one ring every 10 minutes.

In the second of the new settings the rules were changed so that peers were involved. These peers were the four students who sat nearest to Sue, and all were made a part of the expanded game. The 50-point starting place remained, and Sue lost points—10 each time she was out of her seat when the timer rang, just as before. However, the points that remained at the end of the session were divided equally between Sue and her four classmates. For example, if 20 points remained, each would receive 4 points.

The results of these two settings, directed specifically at Sue, are interesting. In the first of the individual point games, an immediate decrease in her out-of-seat behavior occurred. Even more interesting was the result involving the four peers. Even though Sue received only one fifth as many points in this situation, her out-of-seat behavior was reduced even further.

This timer-game approach has been presented in considerable detail for several reasons. First, it is effective in a group setting as a complement to other methodological approaches. Second, it can be administered without continuous monitoring by the teacher. In the experimental setting, continuous monitoring was required to establish the worthwhileness of the approach, but, for use in the classroom, the teacher is involved only in setting the timer and observing the children's behavior when it rings. Third, the variable-interval contingency effectively reduces the likelihood that children will discriminate when the timer will ring, and it greatly enhances the effectiveness of the procedure. Fourth, and last, the various possibilities for individual adaptations, such as that reported with Sue, make this an ideal approach. Many of the various behavior-modification methods are applicable and effective with some children but are not effective and not readily adaptable to others. They are therefore difficult to "sell" for use in the public school classroom, simply because of this factor. The timer game is a happy exception.

A third study, not typical of the nonattending behavior type, may be of interest. This study concerns a special class of teenage students who were severely retarded educationally. Their major problem was almost total lack of motivation, as far as any type of academic task was concerned.

This study involved 24 Navajo children, ages 14 to 16, who were performing at a very low level in both reading and mathematics (mid-first-grade level to low-third-grade level in reading; mid-first-grade level to upper-second-grade level in mathematics). All had been in school less than their chronological age would indicate. Their primary language was Navajo; English was their second language. As best could be measured through a variety of instruments, they were within the normal range of intelligence. They would not fit the definition of learning disabilities used by some, but, because they were learning considerably less than their peers, many of whom had received no more formal education than they, and because they did not have sensory acuity deficits or significantly low intellectual ability, they could be considered learning disabled. They became part of a special project in which they attended a resource room in four groups, 90 minutes per group. During this 90-minute period they were given special assistance by a resource room teacher (who was an Anglo male) and an aide (who was a Navajo female) in developing arithmetic skills. Prior to initiation of this project, extensive achievement testing and diagnostic work-ups had been completed. Special materials were obtained, which were appropriate regarding achievement level but were of higher interest level. All students in this class were Navajo; the school was a Navajo boarding school. An effort had been made to obtain materials that were closely related to the American Indian cultures, but such materials are not in great supply.

Sufficient standardized data and personal/social information had been gathered on these 18 boys and 6 girls to lead to the belief that the following general description fit all 24:

Intellectual level—normal range or above
Visual and auditory acuity—normal
Achievement level—very low, even as compared to peers who had no more known opportunities to learn than they
Attendance record—very low for the past 2 years, even though this was a boarding school; some known truancy
Known process disabilities—none that could be definitively established, except that auditory discrimination was low in some
Interest in extracurricular activities sponsored by the school—very low
General motivation in school—very low
Known interests—some obvious interest in members of the opposite sex in some; some of the boys had an interest in sports; all were interested in western music; all had at least limited appreciation of the value of money; most (particularly the older ones) were interested in quitting school (several had tried at least once)

Although it would have been better if more diagnostic information were available, about all that was known was that some students did not have normal auditory discrimination.* Therefore it was decided to utilize materials with as much interest as possible and to provide strong positive incentives for the subjects to attend to the learning task. Be-

*With younger Navajo children we believed that we were achieving meaningful results with testing of auditory discrimination. With these older, very unmotivated children we were not certain whether we were finding discrimination problems or "I don't care" problems.

cause of an apparent interest in music and interest in having their own radio, a system of points was established whereby students could receive credits toward some significant prizes including radios and record players. Rewards such as boots and others selected by the subjects were also included, thus following the principle that rewards must be true rewards in the eyes of the subjects under consideration.

A system was established whereby points were awarded for work completed with the likelihood that many might earn a significant reward in 3 to 4 months. In addition, when work was completed each period, students were permitted to listen to western music tapes of their own choosing through headsets, which permitted them to listen without leaving class. Leaving students in the class where others could see that they were listening seemed to provide motivation for others to finish their work so that they too could listen.

Arrangements were made so that there was sufficient budget to cover the costs of the incentives, and the system apparently worked well for 2 to 3 weeks. The Navajo aide indicated that there was genuine interest in earning enough points to get the rewards, and the students were apparently motivated by the western music. Teachers who had worked with the students before were impressed. It appeared that we had found the "key" to improved achievement.

Then the project began to fall apart. The music still provided some incentive, but students completed barely enough work to get to listen to the music, then slipped back into their nonattending, nonachieving ways. The desire to gain points toward prizes in which they had seemed so interested melted away. A series of conferences was held to try to save the project, with those university consultants who earlier felt so smug now feeling baffled.*

Project personnel turned to the Navajo aide for help. She was a most insightful individual and had been invaluable in assisting with the learning tasks, so she was now asked to help discover what was wrong. She said she had an idea but needed to think about it. She indicated she would watch carefully for a day or two. After a day she said she knew the answer.

It seems the class members jointly decided that it was too much work just to earn points. They felt that *maybe* they would receive prizes, but what if they quit school? Or what if the prizes were not available later? They had little faith in school authorities and (as we knew but had not been sufficiently sensitive to) were not very future oriented. They wanted rewards *now*.†

In further discussions as to what might prove a meaningful reward, the aide suggested the *big* chocolate candy bars to be given on Friday based on points earned. Parents were contacted by school personnel and all agreed.

As mentioned previously, one of the principles of establishing an effective reward system is that the rewards should be personalized—they should fit individual desires, for what is a reward to one student may not be to another. In this case, our desire to "personalize" led us to overlook the principle that we should not establish a system in which rewards are too far in the future.

---

*I played a major role in this project and must take credit for the miscalculation. We had tried to combine immediate reward (the music) and long-term reward (the radios, boots, etc.) and thought this would work. It did not!

†It should be noted that this lack of future orientation had been discussed, but after initial conversations with the class, the aide had felt that they did understand the longer-term reward system and did understand and like this plan. Perhaps they did, but it took less than 3 weeks for this type of motivation to become ineffective.

This story does have a happy ending. Our major emphasis in this program was mathematics, and the combination of western music (daily) and the oversize candy bars (on "payday," Friday) apparently was the major contributing factor to growth in arithmetic achievement, which averaged almost two grade levels and included three boys who gained more than three grade levels. Methods and materials used to attempt to promote learning of arithmetic concepts were undoubtedly a part of the reason, but some of these same methods and materials had been used earlier to no avail. The low teacher-pupil ratio was also undoubtedly a factor, but low teacher-pupil ratio had not been the answer in other, similar efforts. All connected with the project felt the main two factors were the western music and the big chocolate candy bars. We did a great deal of planning and theorizing, then stumbled onto the right combination. *These boys and girls were motivated to achieve in school in a way they had not been for years, perhaps never had been.*

In this case, success came only after a reassessment of earlier plans that did not proceed as scheduled, but this may happen with behavioral techniques just as it does with other educational efforts. The important fact is that, when we eventually arranged a set of circumstances in which these students felt real motivation to try to learn, excellent results were obtained. Behavioral approaches cannot assist children to do something for which they do not have the ability or cause them to skip over large segments or steps in the learning process. Blind children cannot be made to see, and the severely retarded cannot be taught to read at the grade level of their normal peers. Children can be effectively encouraged to attend to academic tasks and to try much harder than they ever have before, if we give them a reason that is important to them. Positive reinforcement, carefully planned and implemented, can be a powerful tool in the hands of learning disability teachers.

RECOMMENDATIONS FOR PRACTITIONERS

Tom Lovitt provided the following recommendations in concluding a two-part journal presentation (*Journal of Learning Disabilities, 8* [*7* and *8*], September/October, 1975). He notes that most of the 13 steps are applicable, regardless of which behaviors are involved. In this instance, Lovitt is speaking of what he terms applied behavior analysis (ABA).*

(1) Identify the precise behavior that should be taught—e.g., naming letters, writing numerals.

(2) Determine the level to which that behavior should be taught—e.g., 20 correct letters per minute, 35 correct numerals per minute.

(3) Arrange a situation whereby the identified behavior can occur. That is, schedule a time and prepare performance sheets or stimulus materials that provide many opportunities for the identified behavior to be expressed.

(4) Obtain a few days of base line data (e.g., correct and incorrect rates) in regard to the identified behavior. During this diagnostic phase the instructional conditions should be "normal." If praise is ordinarily given for every other correct answer, that practice should continue during the base line period.

(5) Throughout the base line phase, in addition to keeping correct and incorrect rate data, study the error patterns of the pupil. Ordinarily there is only one way to say correctly the word "dog," or compute the problem "2 + 2 = [ ]." There are, however, many ways the pupil can incorrectly respond to these stimuli.

(6) Following the base line phase, determine first whether instruction is necessary. If the behavior should be changed, some teaching technique

*Reprinted by special permission of Professional Press, Inc.; from *Journal of Learning Disabilities*, 1975, *8*, 515-517. Copyright by Professional Press, Inc.

must be scheduled. In order to increase the probability that the technique will postively affect the behavior, the base line data *and* the patterns of responding must be analyzed, and a technique accordingly selected.

(7) Two general types of techniques are available: contingent and noncontingent events. Contingent events are those which have a direct cause and effect relationship with the measured behavior. For example, if recess is granted when a pupil's correct reading rate is faster than 90 words per minute, he would be allowed recess only if this rate exceeded the specified amount. Noncontingent events happen regardless of the quality of the behavior. For example, if flash card drill was noncontingently scheduled to increase oral reading rate, drill would be administered whether the pupil's rates were high or low.

(a) There are several ways contingent events may be arranged. An event may be given or taken away for correct responding, or given or taken away for incorrect responding. Other combinations could be arranged; for example, an event could be given for correct responding and taken away for incorrect responding.

(b) There are many types of noncontingent events and several ways they may be arranged. Some of the types include modeling (showing the pupil how to do something); informing (telling the pupil how to do something); cueing or prompting (showing or telling the pupil a part of what he should do); using mnemonic devices (e.g., the ABC song to remember the alphabet); using aids (e.g., the abacus or Cuisinaire rods). Noncontingent events, unlike contingent events which must be scheduled to follow the identified behavior, can be scheduled to appear before, during, or after the behavior.

(8) In addition to studying the behavior rates and error patterns in order to select the best teaching technique, there are two factors about the performance of a child that should be considered:

(a) If the child does not do something, is it because he cannot, or because he will not? If the former is true, perhaps it would be better to select a noncontingent event to aid performance. If the latter were indicated, a contingent event should probably be selected.

(b) In respect to developing a certain behavior, is the pupil in the "acquisition" or "proficiency" stage? If the pupil is beginning to acquire a behavior, it would perhaps be better to schedule a noncontingent technique. If, however, the child is familiar with the behavior, yet not proficient, it might be preferable to schedule a contingent event.

(9) Whichever noncontingent or contingent technique is selected, it should be as natural and simple as possible. A natural event is one which is indigenous to a particular environment. A simple technique is one that is readily available, easy and quick to administer, and inexpensive. There are two obvious reasons for selecting such events:

(a) No more time than necessary should be spent teaching a particular skill. The more time required to teach a pupil a skill, the more he will be delayed in developing a more advanced skill. Meanwhile, time spent teaching a skill to one pupil is time deprived from another child.

(b) Once the behavior is developed to a certain level using a teaching technique, that technique, generally, must be removed. The teaching of most behaviors is complete only when the behavior can be performed at a specified level without props. Ordinarily, behaviors maintain better after the techniques have been withdrawn when those techniques are natural and simple.

(10) Whichever technique is selected for initial instruction, that technique should remain in effect for a few days. A decision must then be made whether to continue using the technique or to replace it with another. In order to arrive at such a decision the data from the two phases (base line and first intervention) must be compared in respect to central tendencies and trends. If adequate progress is being made, the technique should remain in effect; if not, a different technique should be chosen.

(11) When the performance level of the behavior, with the instructional technique in effect, has reached the criterion mark, the technique should be removed. When the third phase of the project commences, one of two happenings could occur:

(a) The rate of the behavior could continue at a satisfactory level, or even improve. In such instances a new behavior should be selected for instruction. Meanwhile the newly acquired behavior should be measured intermittently in order to be informed as to the pupil's ability to retain the behavior. If, after a time, the performance level of the previously learned behavior deteriorates, teaching should be rescheduled.

(b) The rate of the behavior might not continue at a satisfactory level. In instances of this type, either the first instructional technique should be rescheduled or a different technique should be arranged.

(12) Along with assisting pupils to acquire and retain specific behaviors, concern should be directed toward certain generalizations. There are at least two types of generalizations: situation and response.

(a) Situation generalization would be indicated if the pupil acquired a behavior in one setting and was able to perform the same behavior in another setting.

(b) Response generalization would be indicated in instances where the pupil was taught to respond to certain problems and be learned to respond to other (nontaught) problems at the same time.

Data in regard to either type of generalization could be obtained while the principal behavior is being taught or after the behavior was acquired.

(13) Self-management behaviors should be taught. Students should be allowed to manage various aspects of their programs for at least three reasons:

(a) When they help obtain performance data, the teacher is assisted.

(b) Often, pupils are motivated by being allowed to attend to their own matters; and they then perform other academic tasks more satisfactorily.

(c) Pupils should be taught to manage several of their behaviors in order that they will emerge from schools as independent persons.

SUMMARY

Many of the procedures recommended by educators who are also behaviorists are used by educators who "do not believe in behavior modification." The practical use of rewards, the use of unwritten, but nevertheless existing, contracts, and many other behavioral techniques have been used by teachers for decades. Lovitt's recommendations for practitioners, presented in the immediately preceding section of this chapter, provide an excellent summary of how to implement behavior management approaches and serve as a fitting summary of this chapter.

The four major principles for implementation, as presented in this chapter, may be of importance to the teacher who has limited experience with behavioral approaches, and consideration of the use of arranged events as an alternative to programmed events should be of value to all teachers.

Behavior modification (or management) systems can work and, when dealing with very simple behaviors, may be relatively easy to establish and implement, but many attempts have failed because of the naiveté and lack of knowledge of teachers. Learning disabilities teachers must develop a good command of behavior modification techniques to be maximally successful. This chapter provided a starting point—it is now up to the teacher, or prospective teacher, to carry through.

REFERENCES AND SUGGESTED READINGS

Allen, K., and others. Control of hyperactivity by social reinforcement of attending behavior, *Journal of Educational Psychology*, 1967, *58*, 231-237.

Brady, J., and Lind, D. Experimental analysis of hysterical blindness. In Ullman, L., and Krasner, L. (Eds.) *Case studies in behavior modification.* New York: Holt, Rinehart & Winston, Inc., 1965.

Buckley, N., and Walker, H. *Modifying classroom behavior* (rev. ed.) Champaign, Ill.: Research Press Co., 1970.

Fauke, J., and others. Improvement of handwriting and letter recognition skills: a behavior modification procedure, *Journal of Learning Disabilities*, 1973, *6*, 296-300.

Fine, M., Nesbitt, J., and Tyler, M. Analysis of a failing attempt at behavior modification, *Journal of Learning Disabilities*, 1974, *7*, 70-75.

Forness, S., and MacMillan, D. The origins of behavior modification with exceptional children, *Exceptional Children*, 1970, *37*, 93-99.

Haring, N. *Attending and responding.* San Rafael, Calif.: Dimensions Publishing Co., 1968.

Haring, N., and Schiefelbusch, R. (Eds.) *Methods in special education.* New York: McGraw-Hill Book Co., 1967.

Haring, N., and Whelan, R. (Eds.) *The learning environment; relationship to behavior modification and implications for special education.* Lawrence, Kan.: University of Kansas Press, 1966.

Homme, L. *How to use contingency contracting in the classroom.* Champaign, Ill.: Research Press Co., 1971.

Lovitt, T.: Part II: Specific research recommendations and suggestions for practicioners, *Journal of Learning Disabilities*, 1975, *8*, 504-517.

Lovitt, T., and others. Using arranged and programmed events to alter subtraction performance of children with learning disabilities. In Keller, F., and Ribes-Inesta, E. (Eds.) *Behavior modification: applications to education.* New York: Academic Press, 1974.

Novy, P., and others. Modifying attending-to-work behavior of a learning disabled child, *Journal of Learning Disabilites*, 1973, *6*, 217-221.

Patterson, G. An application of conditioning techniques to the control of the hyperactive child. In Ullman, L., and Krasner, L. (Eds.) *Case studies in behavior modification.* New York: Holt, Rinehart & Winston, Inc., 1965.

Reynolds, G. *A primer of operant conditioning.* Glenview, Ill.: Scott Foresman & Co., 1968.

Skinner, B. *The behavior of organisms.* New York: Appleton-Century-Crofts, 1938.

Skinner, B. An operant analysis of problem solving. In Kleinmuntz, B. (Ed.) *Problem solving: research, method, and theory.* New York: John Wiley & Sons, Inc., 1966.

Skinner, B. *Science and human behavior.* New York: The Macmillan Co., 1953.

Skinner, B. *The technology of teaching.* New York: Appleton-Century-Crofts, 1968.

Smith, K., and Smith, M. *Cybernetic principles of learning and educational design.* New York: Holt, Rinehart & Winston, Inc., 1966.

Stephens, T. *Directive teaching of children with learning and behavioral handicaps.* Columbus, Ohio: Charles E. Merrill Publishing Co., 1970.

Stillwell, R., and others. Educationally handicapped and the engineered classroom, *Focus on Exceptional Children*, 1970, *2*(1), 1-14.

Strong, C., and others. Use of medication versus reinforcement to modify a classroom behavior disorder, *Journal of Learning Disabilities*, 1974, *7*, 214-218.

Sulzer, B., and Mayer, R. *Behavior modification procedures for school personnel.* New York: Holt, Rinehart & Winston, Inc., 1972.

Ullman, L., and Krasner, L. *Case studies in behavior modification.* New York: Holt, Rinehart & Winston, Inc., 1965.

Walker, J., and Shea, T. *Behavior modification: a practical approach for education.* (ed. 2). St. Louis: The C. V. Mosby Co., 1980.

Wolf, M., and others. The timer game: a variable interval contingency for the management of out-of-seat behavior, *Exceptional Children*, 1970, *37*, 113-118.

SECTION THREE

Teaching approaches for reading, arithmetic, and language difficulties for grades K through 12

This final section of *Learning Disabilities: Educational Strategies* emphasizes teaching strategies that are valuable in assisting students to improve basic skills or performance in specific subject areas. Learning disabilities, by definition, relate to educational deficits in basic skills or academic areas. Therefore improvement in educational deficits must be the major concern of learning disabilities practitioners.

In this section we will consider the teaching of reading in more detail than other areas of the school program. We will emphasize practical methods, without concern as to whether they represent perceptual-motor-related, language-development-related, or other approaches, since in many cases these methods cross theoretical boundaries.

Also included in this section is a review of teaching strategies that may be used in assisting learning disabled students whose academic difficulties relate to arithmetic or to written language. These two areas of the traditional school program appear to be second only to reading, as measured by the concern expressed by regular educators. Finally, to complete the consideration of practical teaching strategies, guidelines for secondary school programs are given. Because secondary programming appears to require a somewhat different emphasis than elementary programming, it is discussed in a separate chapter.

In total, this section provides information regarding methods through which both the regular class teacher and the learning disabilities teacher may more effectively teach learning disabled students. Since success for the learning disabled student is the focus of this text, it is only fitting and proper that this final section be dedicated to this goal.

How fast does the earth travel around the sun?
Why don't you feel the earth moving?

chapter 10

Reading methods for students with learning disabilities

Difficulties in reading have been associated with learning disabilities to a much greater extent than difficulties in any other single academic area. This fact may be established by reading the works of the major authors in the field, by observing students in organized educational programs for the learning disabled, or by analyzing the implications of the accepted national definition of learning disabilities. A considerable debate may be generated by the question "What is the difference between the student who needs remedial reading and the one who is learning disabled, with major difficulties in reading?" Answers to the question might include: (1) little or no difference, (2) it's a matter of semantics, (3) it's a matter of degree, (4) it's a matter of type (of reading problem), (5) it's a matter of state (special education) regulations, (6) it depends on whether we have indications of minimal brain dysfunction, or (7) some combination of the preceding. These suggested answers do not exhaust the wide range of possible responses, but they do indicate the variety of interpretations. Responses to this question may relate to the background or training of the respondent, the state or local guidelines or regulations in effect, or the available resources in any given setting. Only one fact appears to remain undisputed—more of the students among those called learning disabled were referred because of reading problems than because of any other single academic difficulty. This does not mean that no other difficulty is a matter of concern but rather that reading was the major academic problem. Thus, any focus on learning disabilities methods might logically begin with a consideration of reading methods.

The purpose of this chapter is to consider a variety of reading methods that may be of value. Detailed recommendations regarding when to use certain methods, how long to try them before concluding that they will not work, and other such considerations are not included here. They may be more meaningfully approached after the teacher has achieved a greater understanding of how to use various types of assessment data and how to develop effective individual educational prescriptions. These considerations are more properly approached as part of planned college or university "methods" courses, in training programs that should include specific course work in remedial reading along with supervised experience in teaching students with learning problems. This review of various reading methods is provided so that those who plan to pursue further formal course work in learning disabilities may have some idea of the variety of methods that may be considered and as a guide to further reading and investigation of these methods. This review is also provided for those for whom this text may be the one and only contact with "learning disabilities."* Preceding the review of reading methods is a consideration of certain basic controversies that for the past 150 years have surrounded the question "What is the best way to teach children to read?" This may provide a more meaningful perspective for the review of specific methods, which immediately follows the discussion of reading controversies.

BASIC CONTROVERSIES IN HOW TO TEACH READING†

Since learning theorists cannot agree on how learning takes place (as discussed in Chapter 3), it is not surprising that there are disagreements on how to teach reading. The most familiar controversies are probably related to what type of phonic approaches are most effective (assuming some type of "phonics" should be used), how much phonics should be included in the standard reading program, or both. During the past 150 years, the "phonics" versus "whole-word" pendulum has swung back and forth many times, and each time the change in direction has been "supported by research." One might wonder about the nature of such investigations, but research on the complex set of skills and abilities related to the process of reading is admittedly subject to a number of variables that are difficult, if not impossible, to control effectively. One of the major problems in attempting to sort out conflicting points of view among reading experts is the vested interest that each tends to have with regard to his or her beliefs.

Another major problem is how to measure success in reading. Does success mean speed in reading, the ability to analyze new words, the number of words learned, or the ability to understand or draw inferences from what is read? Does it mean abilities measured immediately after completion of research, or is it more important to measure long-term effects 2, 3, or 4 years later? These questions, difficulties in establishing truly "controlled" control groups, effects of parental instruction at home, and many, many other problems have led to controversies about which is the most successful method for teaching reading. And, this controversy may never be settled with certainty, given the complexity of the human subjects with which this question deals.

Given these problems, how should teachers approach the question of how to teach children to read? Perhaps the first step is to attempt to maintain an open attitude and refuse to accept any highly touted method proposed as the "final solution" or the "only way" by any supposed authority. Teachers should remember that, for as long as there have been formal programs in the teaching of reading, certain individuals have believed (or wanted teachers to believe) that they were going to "save" all of these unfortunate children who had difficulties developing ac-

*Conversations with instructors from other universities and experience in our own university indicate that as many as one half of those students who enroll in an introductory course in learning disabilities are majors in other areas (early childhood, elementary education, etc.) and this will be their only course related to learning disabilities.

†Significant sections of the remainder of this chapter are adapted from Gearheart, B. *Teaching the Learning Disabled: A Combined Task-Process Approach*, 1976, pp. 73-111.

ceptable reading skills. In earlier years some of these individuals were "remedial reading experts." Today some call themselves "learning disabilities experts." And, throughout all this period of time, significant numbers of students did not or could not learn to read efficiently. So, what are teachers to do? First, it may help to examine, as objectively as possible, those reading approaches that have had some success over the years.

One attempt to sort out the conflicting ideas and arrive at objective conclusions regarding how children may most effectively be taught to read was through a study supported by the Carnegie Corporation in the 1960s. Although this study was conducted more than a decade ago (Chall, 1967), many of the findings may be relevant today. This study had the following advantages: (1) adequate financial support, (2) not being supported by textbook companies (with possible vested interest) or a given university (with possible philosophical bias), and (3) the major investigator was not a firmly entrenched advocate of a specific point of view. The following findings from this study are an important consideration, regardless of frame of reference or philosophical bias, and it seems most appropriate to consider them prior to reviewing actual approaches. Because the point of view espoused in this text is that *there is no single, most-effective approach for teaching reading to learning disabled students* (because of the variety of types of learning problems and the effects of earlier educational efforts), no attempt is made to discover the *best* way to teach reading. Rather, a number of reading methods more, or less, effective with given students are considered. As teachers and prospective teachers review the following findings, their concern should be relevance to planning an appropriate reading program for learning disabled students.

Significant findings of Chall's study*

1. *Interest in reading may be determined more by what a teacher does with a particular method than by which method is used.* What is done with the method should be interpreted to include what is done with materials, with boys and girls, and with space and time parameters. Interest appears to be highly related to pacing, to how well the teacher can sense and manipulate the time and materials so that children are challenged but not presented with impossible tasks. Children who find the basic work too easy or the pace too slow should be provided more challenge through additional work of interest, not busywork.

2. *The story–the content of what is read–does not seem to be a major factor in the child's interest,* contrary to what has been believed by many reading specialists for years and promoted by authors and publishers. It was observed that children were as interested in words, in spelling, and in rules for learning reading as in the stories. Basal readers were exciting to most children if they were in fact learning successfully. It was concluded that children can become interested in almost anything if the atmosphere is conducive of such interest.†

3. *Systematic phonics programs, while not necessarily inherently "dull," have a potential*

---

*Chall observed more than 10 different classes and teachers for each of the many reading methods reviewed in her investigation. These numbered findings are based on her observations as abstracted from the reports of her study.

†Note that Chall is referring to children who are learning *along with other children at the same grade level.* These generalizations may not apply to, for example, 10-year-old children who are presented second grade material to which they have already been exposed many times. Also note that the general assumption is that these children have the visual and auditory acuity and perception to learn through the methods used.

for such dullness if the words sounded out and defined are too abstract or too far removed from the real world of the child. Although the teacher's use and presentation of materials seem to be important, certain hazards that relate to specific methods seem to be subject to generalizations. Some systematic phonics programs are so structured and the teacher is so strongly admonished against deviation from format that commonsense judgment may be ignored and the teacher may push ahead with the program even though children are sending clear signals that they have been "turned off." Basal reading programs have a similar problem with teacher questions to determine whether the material read has been understood. *Extended questioning about a story—a part of many basal reader programs—may be too much for many children.* As in phonics, an element of common judgment should be applied to interpretation of the teachers' guides that commonly accompany basal readers.

4. *Any extensive use of workbooks or teacher-made worksheets tends to produce apathy, leads to bad practice effect (copying of the work of others with little or no understanding), and has a number of other negative effects.* A few children may work independently for relatively long periods of time, but for most the worksheet is something to avoid. Some types of programmed materials or the use of educational hardware may reduce this effect, but these should be carefully monitored.

5. *Although some success factors can be attributed to method, the most important factor seems to be whether the method is preceived as "new" or "old" by teachers using it.* Apparently, at times, a "new" method is thought by those using it to be solving nearly all reading problems; that is, they are reluctant to admit that it does not work with all children. However, other schools or individuals using this same method who view it as old (if it has been in use for several years) are much more likely to admit its shortcomings.

Factors other than perceived newness may be in effect in many of these settings—such as more workshops, more discussion with other teachers, and perhaps more self-examination as to the various other aspects of the teaching-learning process that may contribute to success with new methods. Another factor that may be in operation is some type of self-selection of teachers who are willing to innovate. Within a given school unit it may be that the more able teachers and those who are more imaginative and questioning of the system are those who become involved in new methods and approaches. Differences between school units may exist because teachers may seek employment in school districts on the basis of knowledge (or hearsay) regarding that district's tendency to use or permit the use of new methods.

Paradoxically, one of the factors that may limit the effectiveness of any new method is the inability of those using it to see its shortcomings. Seldom is an old method discarded unless it can be demonstrated that it has serious limitations or shortcomings. These are usually analyzed and documented, and of course the new method takes these problem areas into account. What is sometimes forgotten is that the old method was once new and that it is the responsibility of those initiating a new method to investigate seriously for shortcomings as well as strengths both before and after adoption. The publisher who is promoting the new method most likely will not document these problem areas; therefore, the searching professional educator must find them.

6. In some cases *teachers using a "new" method, although enthusiastic about its advantages, tend to use discarded components of the*

old method that common sense indicates important. Chall reported that, several times during her observations, proponents of a specific method were embarrassed to find teachers doing a number of things "not permitted" by the method. She further suggested that this may in some cases be part of the strength of many new methods.

Based on this observation and on the history of the effectiveness of new methods, an interesting theory may be postulated. If teachers tend to use new methods as they are adopted, but add some of the components of the old that are missing in the new, the result may be a viable combination of old and new applied in a manner that is compatible with observed success on the part of children. This combination of methods developed by practitioners who actually work with children may provide the best of both approaches. After many years of theoretical acceptance of the new method, as children grow up through more and more "pure" application of the new approach and teachers who have never used the old approach, come into the field, the method becomes more pure and perhaps less effective. This could explain the apparently greater effectiveness of the initial move away from phonics programs in the late 1920s and the 1930s, with the new program receiving more and more ciriticism until the mid-1950s (just prior to Chall's investigation) when a countermovement back to phonics began.

7. As a result, *the mingling of old and new approaches often carried out by the teacher when the classroom door is closed makes the results of any large-scale research efforts highly suspect.* This is a factor to consider carefully when attempting to interpret research results.

8. *As times passes, the innovators who helped initiate the presently used approach become the greatest force against change.* This is because of a combination of many of the factors outlined above and must be considered if additional change is contemplated.

9. As a broad generalization, it could be stated that *reading programs that emphasize a more systematic teaching of the sound-symbol relationship tend to achieve better results.* This for the most part means systems that used such programs in addition to the basal reading program. It must be noted that the authors of basal reading series have moved in the direction of more planned inclusion of some sort of phonic component in all or nearly all of the major basal reading series published since that time.

10. Many school programs were observed as a part of this broad-scope, comprehensive investigation. This included low-income districts, high-income districts, and some private schools with very low teacher-pupil ratios and children from backgrounds that should have provided optimum preparation and readiness for school. *All programs included children who did not read with success; that is, no system, regardless of optimistic promise, was totally successful.* In even the best programs the need for remedial instruction remained.

This conclusion, apparently still valid, is the reason for present-day programs of remediation. It appears that, despite overwhelming evidence that one approach will not work with all children, the problems of large class size and the high rate of attrition among primary teachers have left most public and private schools with but one major methodological approach in most classrooms. Talk of real individualization continues but is seldom factual. Different learning styles, varying preschool experiences, and differing rates of growth and development in addition to a variety of specific learning problems are facts of life. One role of the learning disabilities teacher is to assist children who do not succeed in reading, regardless of which reason or reasons apply.

It must be noted here that subsequent review and analysis of the manner in which Chall drew certain of her conclusions has led to a number of questions about her study. As noted by Spache and Spache, "many reviewers . . . did not feel that Chall had proved her theory (in this case relating to phonics), particularly when she depended so strongly upon studies over a long period of time, . . . sources which often differed in their instructional practices from Chall's definition" (1977, p. 364). Similar criticisms have been directed at some other parts of her work, but it is likely that many of the general conclusions reached by Chall (as outlined in the preceding paragraphs) have continued implications for the field of reading. In addition, even with respect to the critical comment of Spache and Spache, these same authors note that Chall's book "triggered a tremendous amount of attention to contrasting phonics systems which enlivened the field of reading for some time" (1977, p. 364). With the apparent need for continued research into various aspects of teaching reading, it seems educators should be grateful for honest attempts to shed further light upon this highly complex educational concern.

Keeping in mind the conclusions reached in Chall's study, we will proceed to a review of the major types of reading approaches in use in the schools today. These are the methods by which learning disabled students have been taught and that, for some reason or reasons, have not been effective with some students, although quite effective with others.

MAJOR READING APPROACHES

The major reading approaches considered here are those in most common use in the schools. This discussion is concerned mainly with those approaches in use in teaching reading in the English language, in the United States and Canada. Other approaches are mentioned in a later section of this chapter, but for now we will focus on four major approaches: (1) the *basal reader* approach, (2) *linguistic* approaches, (3) *language experience* approaches, and (4) *individualized* approaches. In addition, we will consider *phonic components* in reading, following the present trend to consider phonics as a technique, not as a total approach. It is important to remember that these approaches often overlap and that they are considered separately here only for purposes of comparison. Before the actual review of these approaches is a discussion of certain reading skills that must be included in *any* comprehensive reading sequence. Various authors categorize these skills differently from the classification indicated (adapted from Karlin, 1971), which is a simple listing that is generally consistent with the thinking of many reading authorities today.

Classification of reading skills*

1. Word recognition skills
   a. Contextual clues
   b. Phonic analysis
   c. Structural analysis
   d. Dictionary
   e. Sight vocabulary
2. Word meaning skills
   a. Contextual clues
   b. Structural clues
   c. Dictionary
   d. Multiple meanings
   e. Figurative language
3. Comprehension skills
   a. Literal meaning
   b. Inferred meaning

*As the learning disabilities teacher may attempt to develop skills such as comprehension in children who are reading at the upper elementary grade levels or above, a more detailed guide must be obtained. This may be found in several of the reading texts listed at the end of this chapter.

   c. Critical evaluation
   d. Assimilation
4. Study skills
   a. Location of information
   b. Selection of information
   c. Organization and retention of information
   d. Graphic and typographical aids
   e. Previewing
   f. Flexibility
5. Appreciation skills
   a. Language of literature
   b. Forms of literature

Basal reader approach

Use of the basal reader has been accepted practice in a majority of elementary schools since the late 1920s. Although there have been variations, the following characteristics seem to be common to most of the major basal reading series:

1. Reading is defined broadly to include word recognition, comprehension, interpretation, and application of what is read.
2. Children should go through a readiness period, and those who are not prepared for reading after the prescribed length of time (usually as determined by a standardized readiness test) should spend more time in the readiness program.
3. Actual reading begins with whole words—words that are intended to be meaningful in the life of the reader. Reading should be related to both the experiences and interests of the reader whenever possible. Because many basal readers in use up until the 1960s tended to feature the white, middle-class culture, this intent was not realized for many minority racial and ethnic groups. There also tended to be a great deal of traditional sex-role stereotyping. These two problems have been at least partially corrected in many basal readers in use in the 1980s. Silent reading is stressed from the start, with discussion and teacher's questions the means of checking for understanding.
4. When the child is able to recognize at sight (without pausing to analyze, sound, etc.) a given number of words (different series recommend different numbers), he then begins to learn the basic elements of phonetic analysis. At about the same time he learns to identify new words by picture or context (meaning) clues. Structural analysis such as separating compound words or using a knowledge of prefixes and suffixes begins at about the same time, or perhaps somewhat later. One difference in various basal reader series, which may be featured prominently in "sales pitches," is the time and manner in which certain of these identification skills (especially phonics) are introduced.
5. Word-attack skills, although introduced in the first grade, are presented throughout the first 3 or 4 years of schooling, or in some cases throughout the first six grades.
6. Words appearing in basal readers are presented often, and it is expected that children will learn to recognize them on sight through repetition. These words are related to the theoretical speaking, usage, and listening vocabulary for children at various ages. Except for the names of characters in stories, the words at the beginning levels tend to be short, and the sentences are short and simple in construction.
7. Nearly all basal readers are accompanied by workbooks in which children are expected to find the planned opportunity for additional practice with words introduced in the readers. All have teachers' manuals that include precise instructions; however, in contrast to

teachers' manuals of the 1940s through the 1960s, the instructions now tend to advise teachers to deviate from the manual as required to make the program interesting and applicable to the students under consideration. (This use of the teachers' manual as an "idea book" rather than as a rigid guide to be followed explicitly evolved as a result of strong criticism of the earlier procedure. It also permits the use of other complementary approach components or techniques, in accordance with the unique needs of the students.)

Spache and Spache (1977, p. 55), in commenting on the *positive* aspects of basal readers, noted the following:

Basal reading programs provide:

1. A sequential, planned program for the development of recognition, comprehension, and vocabulary skills.
2. Materials based on common experiences, thus providing a common core of experiences for the entire group.
3. Techniques, procedures, and materials for determining readiness for reading and for movement from stage to stage in the reading program.
4. A basic core vocabulary, based on extensive research.
5. Materials that are carefully scaled according to difficulty, presented in a sequence that is consistent with available knowledge about learning, and a semicontrolled vocabulary.
6. Materials that are carefully constructed with regard to such considerations as format and typography.
7. A selection of reading experiences that includes poetry and prose, factual and fictional reading, and informational and entertaining materials. This combination of recreational and primarily informational reading expands the students' information base, but through balance maintains the concept of reading for fun.

Obviously, no reading series can provide for the wide range of interests and experiences of all children who attend the schools today, but the basal reader series, according to Spache and Spache, represent the best available attempts, given our need for group teaching. In further comments regarding the basal reading series, Spache and Spache noted a number of shortcomings of such programs, but most appear to be related to lack of understanding or expertise of the teacher or extreme rigidity. (A fairly safe assumption is that such teachers might not do a particularly effective job of teaching with *any* approach.) Another shortcoming that applies to varying degrees to the various basal reader series is that phonics instruction does not always correlate well with words used in stories and may not follow an adequately structured sequence.

The basal reader approach is undoubtedly quite effective with students who are learning normally. However, learning disabled students are, by definition, not learning normally; therefore, alternate procedures may be required.

Linguistic approaches

In 1961, the book *Let's Read* (Bloomfield and Barnhart, 1961) provided the initial impetus to what was to become the linguistics movement. This book is primarily the work of Bloomfield, a linguistic scientist who left at his death some unpublished works relating linguistics to reading. Barnhart, a friend of Bloomfield, felt an obligation to get these ideas published; the resulting text was the beginning of what was to become a popularly acclaimed answer to how reading might be most effectively taught.

In 1963, Charles Fries published his book

Linguistics and Reading. Fries' book brought new converts to the movement that was already under way and tended to focus additional attention on the possible role of linguistics in reading. Some authorities would liken linguistic approaches to phonic approaches, although a number of linguists who have commented on the topic are opposed to phonics methods just as much as they are opposed to the sight method. If authorities were to search diligently for an acceptable definition for a linguistic approach, they would probably conclude that *a linguistic approach is one that applies the science of linguistics and the knowledge held by linguistic scholars to the problems of teaching reading.* The problem is that, even if authorities could agree on a given set of linguistic knowledge, it has been demonstrated that various linguistic scholars would interpret and apply this knowledge to reading in different ways.

One of the early linguistics-related theses was that sounding and blending (as recommended by many phonics enthusiasts) should not be taught. Early authorities such as Bloomfield believed that words should be learned as wholes, although he did believe that the "code" (the alphabet) had to be learned very early. He would suggest spelling (not sounding) a word that a child could not learn as a whole. Linguists who comment on beginning reading recommend starting with words that have regular spelling and leaving the irregularities of the English language until later. Most of them also have suggestions as to the use of word families (for example, ran, fan, and man), but the child is to discover for himself the relationship between these words *as whole words,* not to sound them out letter by letter.

Matthes (1972) suggested that the ideas of linguists as related to teaching of beginning reading may be condensed to a few basic statements of recommended procedure.

1. Initiate the formal teaching of reading by teaching children all of the letters of the alphabet by name (not by sound).
2. Start with simple, three-letter words that follow the consonant-vowel-consonant pattern. At the beginning use only words in which each letter represents just one phoneme (phonetic value). Avoid words with silent letters.
3. Use word families, those in which only one letter is changed, such as fan, ran, man.
4. Do *not* teach letter-sound correspondence rules. Allow the children to develop the correct responses as a natural outgrowth of the regularity of the words used.
5. Use words in sentences after they are learned.
6. At all times teach words only as wholes. Spell out the entire word, speak of it as a word, and emphasize the wholeness of words in reading to build recognition that reading is "talk" written down.

Like others who have reviewed reading approaches, Matthes indicates that it is difficult to describe *the* linguistic approach because linguists do not agree on how to teach reading. She thinks that a major advantage to the emphasis or popularization of approaches called linguistic is that teachers have been encouraged to explore the science of linguistics and to place more emphasis on language activities.

In conclusion, a number of approaches to reading called linguistic have been influenced considerably by the ideas of various linguists. The authors of many of these approaches speak as negatively about phonic approaches as they do about sight-recognition approaches, but linguistics and phonics appear to be growing closer together. However, linguistics advocates strongly prefer that children learn words as a whole; in this respect they are somewhat closer to the sight-recognition approach.

Many of the major recognized reading authorities seem to agree with Spache and Spache when they indicate that some linguists have propounded "conflicting and naive theories of the reading process" (1973, p. 103), because of their lack of knowledge of the area of reading. They do indicate that one school of linguists, that concerned with psycholinguistics, has made highly important contributions to such areas as the meaning of children's oral reading errors, the relationship between decoding and encoding, and the influence of context on comprehension. However, others have produced programs that are "not discernibly different from approaches discarded many years ago" (Spache and Spache, 1977, p. 103) and are making little real contribution.

Language experience approach

In the language experience approach, reading is considered only one part of the total communication development spectrum; it is thoroughly integrated with listening, speaking, writing, and spelling. In fact, reading grows out of what the child is thinking and talking about rather than following a set pattern of development designed for all children. According to Aukerman (1971), the language experience approach is built on the belief that a child can most effectively learn to read if reading is presented so that the child goes through the following thinking process:

1. What I am thinking, I can talk about.
2. What I talk about, I can write (or someone else can write).
3. What is written, I can read, and so can others.
4. I can read what I have written and what others have written for me to read.

Thus through logical steps the child views reading as just another language activity, an extension of what is thought and what is talked about.

Durkin (1974) indicates that a language experience approach is based on three assumptions:

1. Children have had, and will continue to have, experiences.
2. Children are able to tell about their experiences.
3. If children can learn to write down what they tell, this may be used as an instructional tool to teach them to read.

The language experience approach is highly individualized, with each child reading what he wants. This means that the experiential background of the child is a major determinant of his reading material, and some would note that this may also be a limiting factor.

The role of the teacher is to broaden and enrich the child's experiences so that he will have a broad base from which to think, speak, and read. Organized language experience programs include such daily activities as painting and artwork, the experiencing (by the teacher reading to the class) of children's literature, practice in printing, discussion of interest topics (including those that develop as a part of the evolution of the day), and practice in developing sight vocabulary (a specified common core of words). During the week the activities may include films, planned sensory experiences (tasting, smelling, feeling things, etc.), field trips, and other similar experiences.

In summarizing the results of the available research on the effectiveness of the language experience approach as compared to the basal reader approach, Spache (1977) noted that in at least some of the studies the language experience approach was equal or superior to the basal reader approach in promoting general reading performance. Al-

Telling stories may be an important activity in relation to learning to read, and creative activities that involve the simulated use of the telephone may be used to encourage such story telling. (From Gearheart, B. R. *Teaching the learning disabled: a combined task-process approach.* St. Louis: The C. V. Mosby Co., 1976.)

though results were mixed in many areas, quality of writing was definitely superior in children taught by the language experience method. An unexpected result was a definite trend toward better performances in other academic areas by children in the language experience group. All writings about the language experience approach, both by proponents and opponents, agree that a less structured, more individualized classroom atmosphere is required.

Certain generalizations about the language experience approach may be made. Unlike some other so-called approaches, the language experience approach is considered by many reading authorities as a total approach. When considering quantity, quality, and diversity of vocabulary in writing, the language experience approach appears to be superior to other approaches. Although recognized more widely as a method for teaching reading in primary grades, it has been used with success with all ages, including adults. It has also been used successfully with individuals with normal intelligence, with the mentally handicapped, and with the gifted.

A disadvantage is the possibility that a teacher who feels secure with the planned, sequential activities and detailed instructions of the basal reader may be confused and insecure with the language experience approach. The innovative teacher who is personally secure, is certain enough about reading goals to attempt to achieve them through an unstructured vehicle, and believes in the inherent inseparability of the various communication skills, will probably be effective with the language experience approach.

Because the language experience approach has the potential to personalize reading for each child, some components of it should be considered for inclusion as a part of the primary reading program no matter which basic approach is used.

Although some of the results obtained through the use of the language experience approach suggest that it may be better than most, if not all, other approaches, its effectiveness is limited by the degree of knowledge and effort required of the teacher. In the hands of less able teachers, it may produce much less desirable results than, for example, the basal reader series approach. If learning disabilities teachers are more than usually knowledgeable and willing and able to expend extra effort, then it may be well for such teachers to consider carefully the use of such an approach.

Individualized reading approach

The individualized reading approach, like the language experience approach, requires a teacher with a comprehensive knowledge of reading goals and objectives who is able to teach without the step-by-step structure of the basal reader or structured phonics program. Most programs that are identified as individualized reading programs are, in fact, a combination of programs; they include some basal readers and some planned phonics instruction. Individualized reading may not be started in some cases until after 6 months or a year of the more traditional basal reading program.

In all cases the individualized approach requires a large supply of books of varied reading levels with many areas of interest represented at each level of difficulty. The cost of such a collection of books may be a significant factor in considering the possible adoption of such a program. The individualized reading approach attempts to provide for a variety of levels and types of readiness, reading ability, and interest. However, rather than elicit reading material from the children, it provides for such differences through a wide variety of reading material and permits self-selection. Almost always included are a number of group activities, a checklist of skills for the teacher, and grouping for certain types of planning and interaction.

A wide variety of programs have been described as individualized reading, a situation that makes it extremely difficult to comment on researched effectiveness. In fact, it is fairly safe to say that, although the principles of individualized reading may be stated in such a manner as to find agreement among authorities who support it, actual public school classes that are allegedly individualized reading classes may be highly dissimilar.

It is expected that individualized reading programs will promote wide differences in achievement in children, as will any truly individualized system. Thus the more traditional attitudes toward group achievement goals, standardized testing, and accountability may have to be revised if individualized reading is used.

Individualized reading, like the language experience approach, is not likely to take the nation by storm, but each has significant contributions that may be made as a part of the overall program of teaching reading to children.

Phonic components in reading approaches

No discussion of reading approaches would be complete without a careful consideration of the potential contribution of phonics in teaching reading. Phonic elements are a part of the multisensory approaches outlined in Chapter 6 and the language-related approaches discussed in Chapter 7. According to Spache and Spache, in the preface to *Reading in the Elementary School,* "The move to earlier and stronger phonic programs in the primary grades, now called 'decoding,' has gone beyond a trend to become almost universal practice in our beginning reading programs" (1977, p. ix).

Emans, in a historical review of phonics, noted that phonics has been "in" and "out" as a technique in reading since the 16th century (1968). Noah Webster included the *Elementary Spelling Book* in his *Grammatical Institute of the English Language* (a three-part publication), completed during 1783, 1784, and 1785. In this speller, popularly called the "Blue-backed Speller," Webster attempted to teach Americans to pronounce words correctly through phonics. The reader was used by much of the nation, and "by 1850, when the total population of the United States was less than 23,000,000, the annual sales of Webster's spelling book were about 1,000,000 copies" (The New Columbia Encyclopedia, 1975, p. 2948). Through the history of phonics, the question of when and how much to use phonics has stirred debate. During the 19th century, national educational leaders like Horace Mann were reminding teachers that children must learn to read whole words, and psychologists were demonstrating that children reacted primarily to whole words. At the same time, readers, like the McGuffey Readers, that emphasized phonics were among the most popular in the schools.

The variable nature of educators' concern with or belief in the value of phonics can be traced to many factors, but, throughout the entire period of time since the early emphasis by Webster, the use of phonics in beginning reading has had supporters. Historically, educators have tended to move away from phonics on the basis of published research or acceptance of certain learning theories (such as Gestalt learning theories) and back toward phonics in reaction to reports that children were not learning to read. While it is likely that most school district officials today would report that they are "using phonics," they may be doing so in very different ways. According to Spache and Spache, in 1965 none of the major basal reader programs "attempted to teach pupils how to use letter sounds at the readiness or preprimer stages" (1977, p. 366). By the mid-1970s, it was common to teach children "to use the sounds of all 21 initial consonants, some final consonants, and some vowel sounds during the readiness-preprimer levels" (1977, p. 366). This illustrates the speed with which the educational pendulum can swing.

So, with the need for some type of phonics instruction apparently established today, an important question to consider is "Just what is phonics?" In her text *Phonics and the Teaching of Reading,* Durkin stated that "phonics . . . is the end-product of an attempt to select from the findings of the phonetician whatever is useful for reading and spelling" (1965, p. 2). She further indicated that phonics was concerned with the common sounds in the (English) language and syllabication. Durkin noted that the major value of phonics was in identifying written words, but that it was only one tool for such identification. Spache and Spache indicated that "phonics, the practice of using letter sounds as an aid to word recognition, is a minor element of the field of phonetic analysis" (1977, p. 362). Most other authorities seem to agree that phonics is a procedure whereby knowledge regarding letter sounds (including letter combinations, syllabication, and accent) are used as a part of the total arsenal of word-recognition techniques. Whether this procedure should be formally pursued at the preschool level or later, after or concurrent with training in auditory discrimination, before or after learning to recognize a basic core of words as part of a whole-word sight vocabulary, and so forth remains a matter of debate.

Much of the value of a phonic approach depends on the degree of consistency within the language; that is, a phonic approach obviously is most valuable if most letters or letter combinations are always "sounded" the same. According to Durkin (in a statement following examples of sounds represented differently in different words, for example, her and fur, and letters with no corresponding sound, for example, debt, gnat) "these kinds of inconsistencies, plus the frequency with which they occur, have led linguists to conclude that of all the great languages in the world, English is the most erratic from a phonetic point of view" (1965, p. 2). This statement from an author writing about the *value* of phonic approaches emphasizes one of the major shortcomings, as applied to the English language. It also illustrates why phonics teaching must be carefully planned and sequenced, with adequate emphasis on situations in which the sample rules of letter-sounds do not apply and sufficient training and practice regarding these unusual situations.

Aukerman (1971) emphasized two psychological bases that relate to and undergird phonic (he calls them phonemic) systems. The first is that phonic systems require rote memorization of which sounds relate to which letters. This requires good auditory and visual memory, a particularly important consideration in dealing with children with learning disabilities. The second psychological base is that of *part learning,* learning through individual elements and then assembling these elements into a whole. The synthetic phonic approach (see p. 219) depends more totally on the part-learning principle, although both synthetic and analytic phonics depend on it to a considerable extent.

One element of phonic systems may be viewed as both a strength and a weakness. Advocates note that the normal American child has developed an oral vocabulary of thousands of words by the time he enters school. If a system can be used that maximizes this learning, certainly it will be advantageous. Phonic system enthusiasts believe that once the child learns to recognize the letters of the alphabet and to respond to the visual stimulus of these letters with the sound they represent, he has mastered the one most efficient way to enter the world of reading. Because children already have this comparatively large oral vocabulary, comprehension (of what is on the printed page) will automatically come as a result of pronunciation. The one serious problem to this simple theorem is the irregularity of the English language.

By now is should be clear that, although phonics should be used in the teaching of reading, there is no clear consensus as to *how.* Additional information that might clarify, rather than further confuse, the issue includes the following statements, which seem to represent the thinking of a number of reading authorities who believe in the value of phonics but are not of the "phonics is the only way" school of thought.

1. Phonics' major value is in the identification of new words.
2. Phonics is most valuable at the primary grade levels. (It may also be needed at higher age levels for students with reading disabilities.)

3. Teaching the initial sounds of familiar words appears to be the most effective way to initiate phonics instruction with very young children.
4. Synthetic phonics instruction means the direct teaching of phonic generalizations with the hope that the pupils will be able to apply these generalizations to specific, new words they need to identify. This approach means, for example, learning the sounds of single letters or blends, then synthesizing the new word. A similar procedure applies in learning generalizations about syllabication, then applying them to new words.
5. Analytic phonics instruction means, for example, learning to recognize words by a whole-word approach, then, after learning several words with similar phonic elements, recognizing that each has a given letter that has the same sound. A similar analytic approach would be used to discover common rules for syllabication.
6. Some combination of synthetic and analytic phonics is usually more valuable than the rigid use of one or the other alone. Moving back and forth between the two types of phonics may be the most effective procedure, if accomplished with an understanding of the processes involved.
7. Phonics should be systematically taught, and specific practice is important.
8. Students must learn to use phonological cues along with others (for example, semantic, syntactic, and structural).
9. Although there is disagreement on the role of auditory discrimination in phonics instruction and to what extent it should be taught separately, extremely poor auditory discrimination makes most traditional types of phonics instruction almost useless.
10. Phonics instruction may be of very limited value to students of significantly lower than average mental ability.
11. The proper use of phonics requires that the teacher do more than apply the prescribed sequential steps of phonic instruction. As with other instructional procedures, it requires "classroom diagnosis" to permit individualization in the use of phonics instructional elements and to assist the teacher to determine when to use phonics elements in combination with other techniques.
12. Certain words, at any grade level, are more appropriately taught by a whole-word method than through the use of phonics.
13. Although the situation apparently has improved since the 1960s, too many teachers who indicate that they believe in and use phonics seem to have very limited knowledge about phonics.

In conclusion, although some allegedly "pure" phonics approaches may still be advocated by some, upon investigation these approaches are found to include components or facets that must be considered to be related to other approaches. Certainly, phonics will be regularly used, along with basal reader series, in conjunction with linguistic approaches, or simply as a primary word identification technique for the immediate future. This does not mean that significant questions no longer remain. The matter of how and when to use deductive (synthetic) as opposed to inductive (analytic) phonics remains an open debate for many phonics advocates. Other questions such as when to initiate formal phonics instruction, how much formal training in auditory discrimination is necessary, and how valuable phonics may be for culturally different children remain to be further researched. However, the general value of phonics is no longer an issue; it is accepted as an important part of the reading program, with major application in the first three grades. It is also a part of several of the specialized learning disabilities approaches discussed earlier in this text.

Reading approaches—a summary

Four reading approaches and one approach component have been reviewed and discussed. Although all four are sufficiently well recognized by some educators to be called approaches, the *basal reader* approach appears to be by far the most widely used. The *linguistic* approach, is felt by a number of authorities in reading not to be a unique approach at all, but "linguistic reading series" continue to exist. The two remaining approaches, the *language experience* and the *individualized* appear to have considerable merit but require a greater degree of knowledge and understanding of the process of teaching reading and more individual effort by the teacher. These requirements have apparently retarded the growth of these two approaches; however, elements of these approaches are now in use along with the basal reader approach in many parts of the nation. One approach component, phonics instruction, was considered separately because of the great amount of discussion it has engendered throughout the years. It appears that a fair amount of phonics instruction is now a part of nearly all basal reader programs.

In concluding this overview of major reading approaches, we must recognize that in the 1980s a "pure" approach is used in few, if any, school systems. Even if such an approach were dictated, it is almost certain that some teachers in the system would use their own combinations of methods in spite of school district policy. However, most children have been initiated into the mysteries of reading through some procedure that is determinable and describable, and comparative information on reading approaches may be of significant value in planning alternate approaches to remedy or compensate for reading difficulties. In the following major section we will consider the selection of a reading approach for use with students who are learning disabled.

READING APPROACHES FOR STUDENTS WITH LEARNING DISABILITIES

The preceding description of reading approaches illustrates major variations in what is felt to be the best way to teach the child who is learning "normally," that is, in accordance with what might be expected in consideration of his age, ability, environmental opportunities, and the like. If authorities cannot agree on how normal students should be taught to read, it would certainly seem ridiculous to indicate that they know one specific approach that is generally effective in teaching reading to the learning disabled. However, certain guidelines may be used to select an appropriate approach. The guidelines that follow, a good understanding of the basic skills and the abilities required in reading, plus some knowledge of the approaches that may be used to teach reading will permit meaningful planning for individual students.

Basic guidelines for remediation

1. *There is no single "right method" to use with learning disabled children.* Children are referred for assistance in learning disabilities programs because they are *not* learning by the approach used in the classroom with the general population of boys and girls. If, for example, three 9-year-old, third-grade boys of average intelligence, all reading at the

Electronic equipment may be successfully used to promote interest in reading activities.

early first-grade level were placed in the same learning disabilities resource room, it would be unlikely that all would require the same educational program, either for remediation or to build reading skills through utilization of their existing abilities.

All three might have learned to read more effectively if the school had recognized their learning strengths and weaknesses and approached them appropriately at an earlier time. However, they were probably taught by a general "most acceptable for the average" approach and are now in trouble academically.

It would be the height of absurdity to move from one "right" approach (that was not right for them) to another "right" approach that might be equally inappropriate. Present assessment techniques cannot always indicate exactly how to approach each child with learning disabilities, but teachers can avoid the error of belief in a single approach and can know that they may need to try a number of approaches and methods in certain difficult cases.

2. *All other factors being equal, the newest* possible method should be tried first.* If certain approaches have been used with little or no

*"Newest" means newest to the child.

success, they simply may have been inappropriate. This is not always true; the approaches may have been poorly implemented or the child may not have developed certain requisite abilities at an earlier date and may possess them now. However, teachers must also recognize the possibility that the student may have developed a failure syndrome when, after trying to accomplish a task, he was only to be met by repeated failure. In initiating new efforts, *teachers should make a deliberate attempt to use a method that "looks" and "feels" different to the child.* The more severe the learning problem and the longer it has been recognized and felt by the child, the greater the need for this procedure. This principle dictates that, when many approach paths appear possible and all other factors are approximately equal, the most different approach (from earlier methods used) is likely to be the most effective. It also dictates that teachers gather information as to which methods have been previously used in both the regular classroom and in any earlier remedial attempts.*

3. *Some type of positive reconditioning should be implemented, if at all possible.* Pioneers in the learning disabilities field, such as Fernald and Gillingham (Chapter 6), recognized the value of positive reconditioning, a value that remains today. This effort is important to convince the child that he is OK—to boost his self-concept to the point that he will approach the learning task with increased confidence and thus maximize his chances of success.

*The importance of checking on previous remedial attempts may be seen in cases in which poorly implemented attempts have tended to cancel out the effectiveness of a particular approach even though all other clues and evaluative results indicate the probable effectiveness of such an approach.

A good deal has been written about the "self-fulfilling prophecy" effect on teachers when they are told that a given child is mentally handicapped and therefore will not learn as well or as much as a normal child. The result may be even more devastating when the child becomes convinced through painful experience that he cannot learn. This then becomes a self-imposed limitation that must be overcome. Various ways are available to overcome this, and such efforts must be tailored to the individual. No matter how it is accomplished, it is essential to encourage renewed motivation to learn.

4. *Complete, accurate information about learning strengths and weaknesses is essential.* An appropriate educational plan for the child with learning disabilities must be based on recent, complete, accurate information. This information is used to determine which areas require maximum remedial efforts and which solid abilities may be used as approach avenues in attacking the disabilities. Accurate assessment of strengths indicates those abilities that may be utilized in the continuing attempt to teach content and concepts during the major part of the day, when remedial efforts are not the point of focus.

A single assessment tool is insufficient to determine strengths or weaknesses. Even if several assessment tools and techniques are used, every effort should be made to use at least two different measures to verify the existence of each area of dysfunction or low-level functioning. It also is important to remember that *when teachers discover one problem area, they should not automatically assume that it is the major cause of the academic retardation.* For example, in certain learning disabilities programs educators were so concerned with visual-perceptual problems and so intent on providing programming in this one area of remediation that, for all intents and purposes, they looked for only this type of disability. In many cases, even if such a problem could be documented, it was a less significant problem than others that were eventually discovered through additional assessment.

Complete, accurate information requires a comprehensive investigation of all possible causal factors, the compilation of accurate historical information, and an objective attitude on the part of those interpreting such data. It means not accepting the first evidence of problem areas as the final answer and also means a structured system whereby continual assessment and scheduled reevaluation are accomplished. Both common sense and existing federal regulations require such a system of assessment and reevaluation.

5. *Educational time and effort must be carefully maximized; teachers must be concerned with both process- and task-oriented assistance and remediation.* The learning disabled child is already educationally retarded in comparison to what his intelligence indicates he should be learning; therefore time is of the essence. A number of major variables must be considered in educational planning for each child; the mere placement of a child in a learning disabilities program is an insufficient solution. Teachers should attempt to pinpoint specifically the learning abilities to be developed (for example, auditory discrimination appropriate to age and general development level). In addition, they must consider academic skill areas to be emphasized and the effect of the disability on them. These areas may be broadly defined as reading, for example, or more narrowly defined as the ability to hear specific phonemes accurately so as to use phonetic approaches to reading effectively. Finally, the content, concepts, or both that are of prime importance at this point in educational planning must be identified.

How to balance these major variables most effectively for each student depends on such things as how and where the student is served by the educational system. If he is in a resource room for only 90 minutes each day, the major focus of the resource room teacher may be remedial efforts. It is important to note, however, that remedial efforts must be closely related to and coordinated with content and activities in the regular classroom. When a student spends the major part of the day with the special program teacher, some time will likely be spent on content learning, regardless of whether those efforts directly contribute to remedial efforts. Program planning for the student with learning disabilities that does not take into account both remedial efforts and continued application of the student's intact learning skills to the problem of learning content and developing concepts and understandings is shortchanging the student.

• • •

The preceding guidelines may be applied in nearly all cases when approaching *initial* program planning. After several weeks or a few months of classroom experience with the student, the diagnostic implications of this experience may dictate certain program changes.

In planning for any given student, teachers must remember the basic learning abilities that are presumed to be intact and normally operational for any of the more standard reading approaches to be effective. If reading includes accuracy in word recognition, ability to comprehend a series of words in sequence, and ability to apply what is read in personal, practical situations, then certain basic abilities and previous learnings are presumed by most reading approaches.

Some of these abilities are required to a greater extent by some approaches than others, and relating the child's apparent abilities and disabilities to the approach or system is absolutely necessary. An example of the different degrees of previous learning that may be required by various approaches may be illustrated by considering the degree of development of vocabulary and language ability. A pure language experience reading approach would theoretically be able to take whatever limited language the child had and (if all other abilities and learning factors permitted) build his reading program on present language. A basal reader approach and some phonic approaches might assume too much language ability and thus be ineffective.

Understanding of the basic abilities, experiences, and previous learning of children is necessary to implement the best possible individualized programs for students with demonstrated learning problems. The list that follows is not all-inclusive but includes most of the basic abilities, experiences, and previous learning that must be considered in planning a modified, individualized reading approach.

1. Gross motor development
2. Gross motor experience (This is usually consistent with No. 1, but not always.)
3. Fine motor development
4. Experience (practice) in using fine motor skills
5. Sensory-motor integration (directionality, laterality, etc.)
6. Visual acuity
7. Auditory acuity
8. Visual perception
   a. Discrimination
   b. Figure-ground perception
   c. Closure
9. Auditory perception
   a. Discrimination
   b. Figure-ground perception
   c. Closure
10. Visual memory
11. Auditory memory
12. Experience in using visual perception skills (Usually this is consistent with developed ability, but if not [for example, if a child has much experience but little ability], then knowledge of the amount of experience is essential)
13. Experience in using auditory perception skills
14. Language development
    a. Opportunity to have learned English
    b. Opportunity to have learned another language (where applicable)
    c. Articulation
    d. Spoken vocabulary (both in English and in any other language)
    e. Words and phrases understood even if not in spoken vocabulary
15. Motivation to succeed (in this case, to read)
    a. Parental attitude
    b. Other early environmental data
16. Health and nutritional status (Does condition of health contribute or detract from readiness or motivation to learn?)
17. Attention to task (Many of the above factors contribute to attention to task, but it must be considered carefully and in many cases separately from other factors.)
18. Level of intelligence (This is especially important if the student's I.Q. is near the lower end of the range eligible for assistance and in many cases will be important if it is unusually high.)

Some of the abilities and factors listed are required to about the same degree or are of about the same importance in most reading approaches. All should be considered when completing individual planning for a child with a reading disability. Careful consideration of these abilities and factors may have an important bearing on where to start, how to proceed, and the eventual success of the program.

SPECIFIC APPROACHES TO BE CONSIDERED

The following listing of approaches is not in order of preference, and with the variety of learning needs of learning disabled students, the most important consideration is to find an appropriate program for each student. The first of the following sections indicates major approaches that have been previously described. Other descriptions, which follow, are presented in alphabetical order. Each appears to be of value to some students and thus deserves recognition.

Major approaches (previously described)

Approaches that might be called *language development oriented*, such as those described in Chapter 7, and approaches that might be called *multisensory*, such as those described in Chapter 6, are among those that appear to be in most common use. There are many variations of such approaches, and because they were discussed in some detail in the two previous chapters they are not further considered here.

Language experience approaches, patterned after the description provided on pp. 214 to 216, are also in fairly common use, and seem to have practical application for many learning disabled students. Because language experience approaches can be highly individualized and many of the ideas included in language-development-oriented and multisensory approaches can be easily incorporated in language experience approaches, this combination and integration is preferred by many teachers. If the regular classroom teacher can combine various programs and approaches with a full reading group, certainly the learning disabilities specialist should be able to do so with a much smaller group or with individuals. However, in each case such program combinations should be the result of careful analysis of the students' needs.

Ideas taken from the perceptual-motor approaches (see Chapter 4) may become part of a total program, and in preschool, first, or second grade programs such ideas may be a significant part of overall planning. These are less likely to be applicable with older students.

All of the preceding approaches have been described at some length earlier in this text; therefore they are not further discussed here. The following approaches should not necessarily be considered as *major* ones, but they have been used in some places in the nation and apparently have value for some students. They are presented in alphabetical order.

Color-coded phonetic approaches

Reading approaches have been developed that use color cues to assist the reader to identify phonetic elements in words. One such system, the *Psycholinguistic Color System*, was developed by Alex Bannatyne (1971), known for his work in learning disabilities and for the Bannatyne Children's Learning Center in Miami. This system is called psycholinguistic because it involves planned sensory input and motor output, sequencing of phonemes and graphemes, and the use of words sequenced in meaningful context.

The Psycholinguistic Color System is a phonetic system in which the child learns the shape of each individual letter as a phoneme, with the color names serving as cues to the sounds that the colors represent. The core of the color-coding aspect is the use of the 17 vowel phonemes that are color coded. The set of materials includes 24 wall charts in color, flash cards, workbooks, and colored pencils. Bannatyne believes that traditional orthography must be used. Thus all symbols are the traditional letters; only the color coding is different from what the child may see in any usual reading material.

The whole program includes four major stages that are to take the student from the introduction to color-coded letters to reading and writing in black and white. The stages are as follows:

Stage 1: The student learns the shapes of letters of the alphabet *as phonemes.*

Stage 2: The student learns the sounds of both consonants and vowels. (Bannatyne believes in "overlearning" the color coding, which is emphasized at Stage 2.) Cursive writing is started.

Stage 3: The program is extended to phonetically irregular words, and the child builds his own stories. Blending and syllabication are begun. Rhyming plays an important role.

Stage 4: The student starts (or restarts) the use of vowels in black and white. A set of rules to assist in spelling is taught. Entrance to Stage 4 is based on the assumption that the child has learned the various vowel sounds represented by the color coding and therefore no longer needs color.

The Bannatyne system was developed for dyslexic children and thus is undoubtedly most applicable where considerable visual-perceptual problems exist. For such children or for those who have adequate visual-perceptual abilities but significant problems in sorting out the various phonetic possibilities of the vowels, this is a system to consider.

Informal color-coding system. Another possibility that deserves mention is the use of some variety of informal color-coding system. Master teachers have used color coding to varying degrees for years, and Frostig indicates that, although a number of specific color-coding systems are advocated, her experience at the Frostig Center has shown that "a relatively informal, flexible system is often best for teacher and child" (Frostig, 1973). Frostig suggests, for example, that short vowels might be colored red (for *stop* short) and long vowels colored green (for *go* long). She notes that this color coding directs the child's attention to sound-graphic symbol relationships and may assist in recognition and learning of phonetic rules. She also points out that this type of word analysis should always be followed by word synthesis (the child should see the word that was written in color also written in black and white).

A suggestion for application of color coding for more advanced readers is the use of different colors for prefixes, root words, and suffixes. Another idea is writing syllables in different colors. Some type of informal color-coding system may be easily used in conjunction with other established approaches. Color coding is used only until the student begins to read in a manner consistent with normal expectations. It is then discontinued.

DISTAR program

DISTAR, an acronym for Direct Instruction Systems for Teaching Arithmetic and Reading, is difficult to characterize as anything but what the name implies. This program was developed as an outgrowth of work carried out at the Institute for Research on Exceptional Children at the University of Illinois. Carl Bereiter and Siegfried Engelmann provided the original thrust for this program, which was established primarily as a compensatory effort to prepare disadvantaged black children for entrance into the traditional middle-class, white-oriented school program. Engelmann continued these efforts, which culminated in the DISTAR program.

The DISTAR program has received considerable criticism from more child-centered early childhood authorities because it is admittedly very fast paced and seems (to some at least) to ignore the interests and feelings of the child (Moskovitz, 1968).

The authors admit that theirs is not a child-centered method in the usual sense of the term but rather a method whereby a good teacher can help children be ready to compete in school. They call their program highly structured and intensive and make no apologies. They think that such fast-paced, directive programming is essential to the children for whom this program was designed.

Teachers are given a detailed guide as to what to teach and the order in which it should be taught. No readiness assumptions are made; the program is designed to develop the skills necessary for reading. The teacher is very much in charge and children learn this quickly. DISTAR includes a special alphabet (used in initial teaching only) and practice in sequencing, blending, rhyming, and, most important, in following instructions implicitly. Training in what might be called visual-perceptual skills and auditory skills is included—all in a specific sequence. A training film is provided for in-service or preservice training. Unless teachers have seen a DISTAR teacher in action, this film is quite important if the materials are to be used in the most effective manner.

Reading I (the beginning level) starts with sound-symbol identification, left-to-right sequencing, and oral sound blending. Children learn to read by sounding words, then to read groups of words as complete thoughts. Reading I provides a highly structured, fast-paced approach to the skills usually developed in the first grade.

The DISTAR system includes take-home stories and exercises, recycling lessons, and specific teacher instructions. Reading II is an expansion of the skills emphasized in Reading I, and each level comes in a teacher's kit that contains all necessary materials. Student materials for Reading I and Reading II come in sets of five.

Reading III is advertised as a basal reader program for grade three or for use as a remedial reading program. It is designed to teach reading skills within the framework of factual material and to provide new concepts and concept applications. Like Reading I and II it may be purchased in a complete teacher kit, but unlike Reading I and II much of Reading III is designed for use with 30 children at one time. (Beginning DISTAR program materials can be used for an entire class, but the materials are designed for use with small groups [five children] at a time.)

DISTAR must be experienced to be understood and appreciated and is sometimes "too much" for some teachers. Unusually high rates of progress in reading are reported in a variety of DISTAR literature, and teachers who try DISTAR appear to have fairly strong feelings one way or the other as to its value.

Words used in the DISTAR sales literature —"disciplined," "fast-paced," "immediate feedback," and "logical sequence"—may well be used to characterize and summarize the DISTAR approach.

Montessori-related approaches

Montessori's ideas would seem to have potential value to learning disabilities specialists because of the nature of the children with whom she originally worked and the indication that such approaches have been valuable in developing reading skills in children who were not learning effectively in the regular school program. Montessori's original educational efforts were directed toward teaching the mentally retarded. Historical accounts indicate that she was so successful with some children who were thought to be mentally retarded that they were able to pass national examinations that entitled them to primary certificates. Her early work with the retarded (who were likely pseudoretarded who had been denied an opportunity to normal environmental stimulation and learning) led to efforts with children in some of the worst slums of Rome. Here she experienced more remarkable success, which led to the formal development of the method that now carries her name, a method known and used to varying degrees all over the world. There are many components of the Montessori method; only a few are described here. (For an interesting account of an American approach to the Montessori method, see Rambusch, 1962.)

Montessori often refers to preparing children for learning, a reference to her version of readiness for reading. One of the ways in which children are prepared for reading is through use of sandpaper letters written in script. The child is directed to look carefully at the letters and then to trace them with his eyes closed. Later a stick is used to trace letters as preparation for use of the pencil (in earlier times, a pen). The purpose of the first tracing of sandpaper letters is to reinforce the visual image and, of course, as early training for writing. As Montessori saw it, reading is preceded by writing, and writing is preceded by preparation for writing. Montessori believed that if a child could write, he could read.

Another activity in which children participate in preparation for reading is matching letters of the alphabet that can be picked up, handled, and compared with exact copies of these letters in a partitioned box. The child manipulates these letters (although they are not learned as letters of the alphabet but as sounds) and in so doing receives additional reinforcement. Vowels and consonants are separated, and children learn to recognize them all before they start to read. In the initial tracing stage, children trace and say the sound of the letter. In the next stage the teacher asks the child to "give me an i" (using the short vowel sound for the i) and the child responds by finding and handing the teacher an "i." In the third stage the teacher holds up a letter (in this case it is more properly called a phonogram) and asks, "What is this?" The child then gives the letter sound.

Montessori used an earlier version of this multisensory initial approach to teach the Italian slum children and achieved excellent results. Her observations there and in later application of her evolving method led her to believe that children can write if they are prepared in three areas: (1) how the letter feels (kinesthetically), (2) how it is pronounced, and (3) how to move a pencil to properly form the letter. Then, following her educational logic, they will be able to read.

In Montessori's work with Italian children the development of ability to write and the transition to reading came very quickly in many cases, but we must remember two things in comparing her results and efforts in the United States. Many of the children in Italy were older than children we have attempted to teach through Montessori methods in the United States; thus they had more fully developed fine motor ability. In addition, the Italian language is more phonetic in nature and has fewer irregularities than English, so more rapid learning might be expected.

The transition to reading is accomplished

by the teacher preparing slips of paper on which the names of toys (toys available in the room) have been written; by various means the children take the slips, read the name of the toy, and get to play with it. For underprivileged slum children this undoubtedly had high motivational value; for some more privileged children this might have little motivational impact.

After words are learned through word games, phrases and sentences are learned. The sentences direct the children to perform some action, such as "go to the door and close it." As soon as children are able to read the more simple directions, sentences are lengthened and made to include directions that require sequential compliance. The emphasis on active gamelike teaching is an important part of much of the Montessori method.

Original Montessori methods did not proceed through a reading-aloud stage. Montessori thought that, except for the game periods, which did include activity and oral participation of the children, much of the day should be spent with the child working alone and in silence. American Montessori schools have modified this concept in practice over the past 20 or 30 years.

The educational continuum, according to Montessori, does not require a timetable—children will learn when they are ready. If properly prepared, the child will soon begin composing words with his movable alphabet letters, and that is the start of reading. Although some work can be done in small groups, much must be done individually, and rate of progress is the most individual aspect of all.

Rambusch is one of several spokespersons for the Montessori method as adapted in the United States. In *Learning How to Learn* (1962) she provides more specific suggestions on using an adapted Montessori approach. Although Montessori started with the retarded and with underprivileged children, Montessori schools in the United States tend to enroll children from the other end of the social and intellectual spectrum. Montessori materials are a good source of ideas and techniques for teachers searching for new or modified approaches. The emphasis on kinesthetic skills as a prerequisite to formal reading is similar to ideas previously discussed in several other systems and might be reviewed by those looking for more ideas in this area.

Open Court Correlated Language Arts Program

The Open Court basic readers provide an alternative to other basal reader programs and, in fact, are considerably different from many of the other basal reader series. The Open Court program has a strong phonic element and has more kinesthetic-tactile emphasis than any other of the major basal reader series. It provides one viable alternative for teachers who feel the need for this kinesthetic-tactile input but find the Fernald approach too unstructured.

The Open Court Correlated Language Arts Program has three main components or program goals. The first is to teach children to read and write independently by the end of the first grade. The second is to provide reading selection of "literary quality and rewarding content." The third is to provide a total, correlated language arts program for use through the sixth grade. Our focus here is on the first two components.

Much of the first half of the first-grade program is multisensory, with more kinesthetic-tactile emphasis than many programs that are advertised as multisensory. The entry to this multisensory emphasis is through sounds, and in learning the sound the child hears, says, sees, and writes the letters being learned. Much of this can be accomplished in large groups, an advantage over Fernald-related approaches, which require a one-to-one setting. The intent of the program is for the child to discover inductively the basic relationships of the English language. Writing at the board, proofreading, and listening activities are all used from the beginning. Anagram cards and games, poems, and songs are a part of this comprehensive program.

The teacher's guide to the foundation program is very detailed and comprehensive and provides suggestions for children who are moving more slowly than the rest of the group. Aukerman (1971) suggests that the teacher's guide provided with this program is "probably the most complete teacher's guide available for any system outside of the traditional basal reader series."

The Open Court program features a "workshop" concept that is unique among the various approaches. Workshop is the term for all activities in the Open Court program in which children participate independently. The teacher guides these activities discreetly and indirectly, provides instructions, and establishes limits. Although no set time is regularly allotted for workshop, the teacher is admonished to see that time is available in which the children are to pursue independent reading activities. In some respects this aspect of the Open Court program is an individualized reading program. A separate guide for *Reading Activities in Workshop* is provided, complete with many illustrations, materials lists, general suggestions, and detailed instructions.

Significant parts of the Open Court series were initially supported in part by the Hegeler Foundation, and research reports relating to this support sound favorable, but reports provided for public consumption do not provide sufficient data to permit careful evaluation. The literature provided with this series includes stories such as "The Little Red Hen" and others in which perseverance, self-sacrifice, and other traditional American virtues are promoted.

Although some may not wish to use the entire program, there are many strengths to this approach to early reading, and the teacher's manual and the suggested activities for workshop contain many ideas and specific suggestions that will be valuable for some children with learning disabilities. The flexibility of the program, the inclusion of specific suggestions for a multisensory approach, and the provision for a variety of individualized work make it a program to investigate.

Programmed instructional systems

Programmed instructional systems have been used with students of various levels of learning ability and may be of value for some students with learning disabilities. Two different systems are described to exemplify this type of approach.

Programmed reading approach. Programmed reading, associated with the work of Cynthia Buchanan (1968), is a linguistic-phonics approach in which students experience a sequence of learnings in which they must write their responses; this alledgedly reinforces what is learned. In *Programmed Reading* (published by the Webster Division, McGraw-Hill), certain prerequisite learning must take place so that each child in the class is at a given starting point. To be able to use these materials effectively, children must know and recognize the alphabet and be able to print both lowercase and uppercase letters.

In the first books of the first series the child must read simple sentences and respond with a "yes" or "no." The teacher works through this procedure, instructing the children in the manner in which they are to read, enter their responses, and move the "slider" into position so that they may see the correct answer. This positive reinforcement of correct answers and immediate knowledge of wrong answers is a major feature of programmed material.

Regular testing is provided to correct or compensate for the possibility (or likelihood) that some children may look for the correct answer *before* they record their choice of answers and to make certain learning is taking place.* This type of material is supposed to be self-pacing, which means (at least theoretically) that 30 different children in a given class can proceed at 30 different speeds according to their own readiness, ability, and motivation. Programmed Reading and other similar programmed materials have been used with entire classes, with subgroups within classes, or with just one or two children with whom the teacher cannot work effectively in existing class reading groups. The immediate feedback system, the small, planned sequential steps, and the fact that this system frees the teacher from most "paper correcting" are featured advantages of this and other programmed systems.

Disadvantages include the fact that this type of programming assumes that required content and skills can be learned effectively by being broken down into small segments. There is also a question as to how well this system provides for higher-level integrative and conceptual skills. Still another problem is the reduction and sometimes near elimination of class interaction when skills or topics are learned in this manner.

This type of programming lends itself to use of various types of educational hardware, the so-called teaching machines. These too are organized to provide immediate feedback and to permit the student to proceed at his own pace.

The major value of this type of reading system for children with learning problems may be in the newness of the approach. It is necessary before attempting to place a child in such a program to make certain he has the necessary process abilities to utilize the system and that there is sufficient motivation to keep him going once he starts. Proceeding through such a program may be valuable to the teacher in determining the areas in which learning, in effect, breaks down. This will require close observing and monitoring of the child and his performance with the materials.

Individually Prescribed Instruction. A second system that may be considered in this section is Individually Prescribed Instruction (IPI). IPI, introduced in the early 1960s at the Oak Leaf School in Pittsburgh by Glaser and Bolvin (Dallmann and others, 1974), is a highly individualized program. From the outset, emphasis is placed on the use of comprehensive diagnostic tests to assess the learning abilities of each child at each instructional level. As soon as the student demonstrates a satisfactory degree of competency in a particular skill, he progresses to a more difficult instructional level. Master files composed of materials collected from commercial sources, the teacher's files, and newly constructed materials are set up for the entire program. These files are used to develop reading prescriptions for each child based on diagnostic test results and daily progress.

This system is similar to Programmed Reading in providing for self-pacing and indi-

*A potential problem with any programmed reading approach, particularly for use with a learning disabled child who is likely to be anxious and eager to have the "right answer," is the difficulty in controlling the child's "peeking" at answers to be right. This must be carefully monitored.

vidual modes of problem solving. At least part of the program has the immediate feedback provision for supplementary materials, experiences, and learnings, as indicated by the teacher's assessment of work completed. This is in contrast with some other programmed materials in which each child goes through the same steps as every other child. This system has about the same advantages and disadvantages as other programmed materials except as specifically noted.

Rebus approaches

A rebus is a picture that stands for a word. Rebus reading approaches are picture-word systems in which pictures are substituted for the traditional orthography. To the extent that a picture has only one obvious mean-

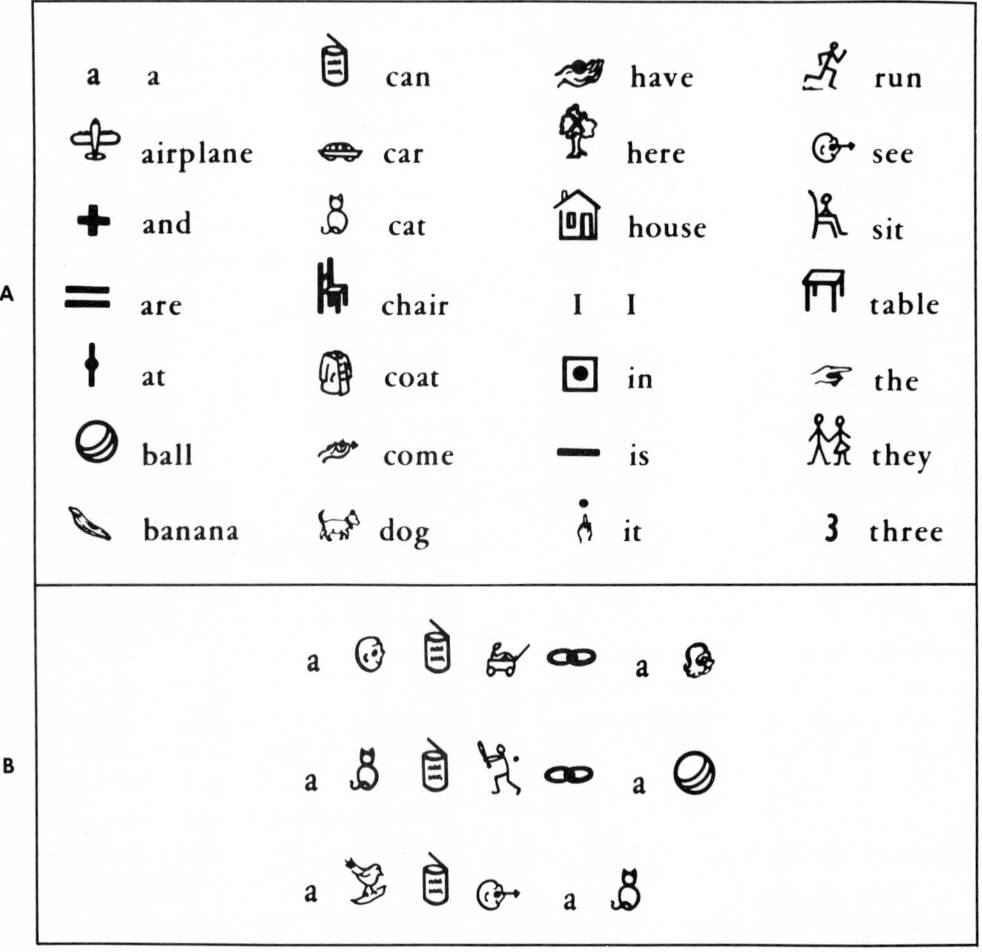

FIG. 5. A, Sample vocabulary and, **B,** sample sentences from *Introducing Reading: Book Two* of the Peabody Rebus Program. (From American Guidance Service, Inc., Circle Pines, Minn.)

ing, reading is quite easy; the child does not have to learn to interpret symbols that are at the start quite abstract and meaningless but rather can "read" a much nearer representation of the real thing. For example, "horse" is simply a picture of a horse.

Some type of picture-word stories have been around since cavemen used this method to record events of their day. There has been some limited use of pictures to substitute for letters in the kind of storybooks designed for parents to read to children (and for them to "read" at ages 2 and 3 years) for many years. But the first systematic application of this principle that led to commercial publication and wide use was that made by Woodcock in 1967, an effort that produced the *Peabody Rebus Reading Program.* This program, in addition to its carefully planned use of rebuses, includes the advantages of a programmed text format.

The Peabody Rebus Program includes three programmed workbooks and two readers. The content and emphasis of these five books are as follows:

Introducing Reading: Book One includes a rebus vocabulary of 35 words and introduces the child to the basic skills required in the reading process. There is an emphasis on the use of context clues in identifying new words.

Introducing Reading: Book Two extends the rebus vocabulary to 68 words. Structural analysis skills are introduced, and experience and practice with use of context clues and general skills of the reading process are continued. (See Fig. 5 for a sample of vocabulary and sentences.)

Introducing Reading: Book Three is correlated with the two rebus readers. There is further extension of comprehension skills and introduction of phonic skills for six consonants and for 10 vowel-consonant combinations.

Red and Blue Are On Me: Rebus Reader One and *Can You See A Little Flea: Rebus Reader Two* are used with *Introducing Reading: Book Three.* The reading vocabulary is extended to 172 words; 122 of these are known as spelled words. Twenty-nine of these words are taught through phonic approaches presented in *Introducing Reading: Book Three.*

Without going into detail as to the specific procedure used in the Peabody Rebus Reading Program, it may be noted that such basic reading skills as left-to-right, down-the-page, and page-to-page progression as well as use of pictorial and textual context clues are taught effectively by rebus reading. Children develop an understanding of the facts that written language is made up of words combined to make sentences and that there is variety in sentence structure.

The Peabody Rebus Program may be used as a complete program of beginning reading; children may be started at any level (consistent with individual needs), and the program may be terminated at any level. The teacher's guide is well done, and the program has been used enough to demonstrate its usefulness for a variety of purposes.

For beginning readers who have not been successful in the more traditional approaches, the rebus approach may bring success and motivation to learn to read. With the exception of mentally retarded or bilingual children who have never read in any language, the rebus system is primarily for younger children. Certain older learning disabled children who need immediate success to provide a stepping-stone to other methods may also benefit.

SUMMARY

The development of reading skills more consistent with a given student's age and experiential opportunities continues to be the most frequent major objective for those who have been identified as learning disabled. In many cases this means improving the basic reading ability of students who can already read to some extent, but it may mean developing the skills that are recognized prerequisites to reading or, at the other end of the continuum, developing some of the more complex reading abilities. Pursuit of these tasks is made more difficult by the fact that many questions remain regarding how normal children may best be taught to read; however, the considerable research into alternative reading methods has provided a number of potentially beneficial approaches.

This chapter included a review of questions that reading authorities have posed with regard to their own efforts and has outlined four recognized reading approaches: the basal reader approach, linguistic approaches, language experience approaches, and individualized reading approaches. Also included was a brief historical look at phonics and an attempt to summarize present consensus as to its strengths and weaknesses.

In addition to these major approaches, there are certain more specific approaches that might be considered in planning for learning disabled students. These include language-development-related approaches, multisensory approaches, and perceptual-motor approaches, all discussed in some detail in earlier chapters. This chapter has also considered the following additional approaches: (1) color-coded phonetic approaches, (2) the DISTAR program, (3) Montessori-related approaches, (4) the Open Court program, (5) Programmed Instructional Systems, and (6) Rebus approaches. Each may have some value with certain students, and most have the possibility of being used (in part) along with some other organized system or in the development of some type of eclectic approach.

Also considered were five basic guidelines for reading remediation that apply directly to planning for the learning disabled student. In addition, this chapter included a listing of certain basic abilities and experiences that are recognized as highly important to success in reading. There are no quick answers or conveniently packaged solutions to the question "What is the most effective reading method for the learning disabled student?" but understanding of the information and concepts presented in this chapter plus good diagnostic teaching ability on the part of the learning disabilities teacher should lead to the desired results for many learning disabled students.

REFERENCES AND SUGGESTED READINGS

Aukerman, R. *Approaches to beginning reading.* New York: John Wiley & Sons, Inc., 1971.

Bannatyne, A. *Language, reading, and learning disabilities.* Springfield, Ill.: Charles C Thomas, Publisher, 1971.

Bereiter, C., and Hughes, A. *Teacher's guide to the Open Court Kindergarten program.* La Salle, Ill.: Open Court Publishing Co., 1970.

Bloomfield, L., and Barnhart, C. *Let's read.* Detroit: Wayne State University Press, 1961.

Buchanan, C. *Programmed reading, A decade of innovations.* Newark, Del.: International Reading Association, 1968.

Carter, H., and McGinnis, D. *Diagnosis and treatment of the disabled reader.* New York: The Macmillan Co. Publishers, 1970.

Cazden, C. *Child language and education.* New York: Holt, Rinehart and Winston, Inc., 1972.

Chall, J. *Learning to read: the great debate.* New York: McGraw-Hill Book Co., Inc., 1967.

Dallmann, M., and others. *The teaching of reading* (ed. 4). New York: Holt, Rinehart & Winston, Inc., 1974.

Dechant, E. *Linguistics, phonics, and the teaching of reading.* Springfield, Ill.: Charles C Thomas, Publisher, 1969.

Durkin, D. *Phonics and the teaching of reading.* New York: Teachers College, Columbia University, 1965.

Durkin, D. *Teaching them how to read.* (ed. 2). Boston: Allyn & Bacon, Inc., 1974.

Emans, R. History of phonics, *Elementary English,* 1968, *45,* 602-608.

Fernald, G. *Remedial techniques in basic school subjects.* New York: McGraw-Hill Book Co., 1943.

Fries, C. *Linguistics and reading.* New York: Holt, Rinehart & Winston, Inc., 1963.

Frostig, M. *Selection and adaptation of reading methods.* San Rafael, Calif.: Academy Therapy Publications, 1973.

Gattegno, C. *Words in color.* Chicago: Encyclopaedia Britannica, Inc., 1962.

Gearheart, B. Teaching the learning disabled: a combined task-process approach. St. Louis: The C. V. Mosby Co., 1976.

Guszak, F. *Diagnostic reading instruction in the elementary school.* New York: Harper & Row, Publishers, 1972.

Hall, M. *Teaching reading as a language experience.* Columbus, Ohio: Charles E. Merrill Publishing Co., 1970.

Harris, A. *How to increase reading ability* (ed. 5). New York: David McKay Co., Inc., 1970.

Johnson, D., and Myklebust, H. *Learning disabilities: educational principles and practices.* New York: Grune & Stratton, Inc., 1970.

Jongsman, E. *The cloze procedure as a teaching technique.* Newark, Del.: International Reading Association, 1971.

Karlin, R. *Teaching elementary reading.* New York: Harcourt Brace Jovanovich, Inc., 1971.

Kaufman, H., and Biren, P. Cursive writing: an aid to reading and spelling, *Academic Therapy,* 1979, *15,* 209-219.

Lane, A. *Severe reading disability and the initial* teaching alphabet, *Journal of Learning Disabilities,* 1974, 7(8), 23-27.

Lerner, J. *Children with learning disabilities: theories, diagnostic, and teaching strategies.* Boston: Houghton Mifflin Co., 1976.

Matthes, C. *How children are taught to read.* Lincoln, Neb.: Professional Educators Publications, Inc., 1972.

Money, J. (Ed.) *The disabled reader: education of the dyslexic child.* Baltimore: The Johns Hopkins University Press, 1966.

Montessori, M. *The Montessori method.* New York: Schocken Books, Inc., 1964.

Moore, O., and Anderson, A. The responsive environments project. In Hess, R., and Bear, R., (Eds.) *The challenge of early education.* Chicago: Aldine Publishing Co., 1967.

Moskovitz, S. Some assumptions underlying the Bereiter approach. *Young Children,* 1968, *24*(1), 24-31.

Rambusch, N. *Learning how to learn—an American approach to Montessori.* Baltimore: Helicon Press, Inc., 1962.

Richardson, E., and Bradley, C. ISM: a teacher-oriented method of reading instruction for the child-oriented teacher, *Journal of Learning Disabilities,* 1974, 7(6), 19-27.

Robins, D. *Special education guide to the Open Court Program.* La Salle, Ill.: Open Court Publishing Co., 1970.

Robinson, H. *Teaching reading and study strategies: the content areas.* Boston: Allyn & Bacon, Inc., 1975.

Robinson, R. *An introduction to the cloze procedure, an annotated bibliography.* Newark, Del.: International Reading Association, 1971.

Spache, E. *Reading activities for child involvement.* Boston: Allyn & Bacon, Inc., 1976.

Spache, G. *The teaching of reading: methods and results.* Bloomington, Ind.: The Phi Delta Kappa Educational Foundation, 1972.

Spache, G., and Spache, E. *Reading in the elementary schools* (ed. 3). Boston: Allyn & Bacon, Inc., 1973.

Spache, G., and Spache, E. *Reading in the elementary school* (ed. 4). Boston: Allyn & Bacon, Inc., 1977.

Woodcock, P. *Peabody Rebus reading program.* Circle Pines, Minn.: American Guidance Service, Inc., 1967.

Work:
75
-23
53802

chapter 11

Teaching arithmetic and written language to students with learning disabilities

Two major areas of the curriculum that have received considerable attention from learning disabilities specialists, although certainly less emphasis than reading, are arithmetic and written language. In this chapter we will discuss arithmetic and written language, including handwriting, spelling, and the ability to effectively express oneself through writing. Although arithmetic and written language have received some limited attention from learning disabilities specialists, they have not received the attention that they deserve. It may be that early educational activities are so focused on reading (the emphasis of kindergarten and the primary grades) that this has tended to mask many learning disabled children's needs for assistance with arithmetic. In addition, the fact that written language is so interwoven with reading (some teachers have difficulty in separating them when first asked to do so) may have retarded further focus on this area. At any rate, learning disabilities in arithmetic and written language can have very negative effects in later life if proper assistance is not provided. In this chapter a number of approaches are reviewed that may be of value in assisting students with learning disabilities in these areas.

LEARNING DISABILITIES THAT AFFECT ARITHMETIC

Arithmetic disabilities of students with normal mental ability have been recognized since early in the century, and various authors have developed remedial programs to assist such students—for example, Grace Fernald, whose work in the application of multisensory teaching methods with students in her clinic (starting in the early 1920s) provided guidelines for remedial arithmetic in her classic text *Remedial Techniques in Basic School Subjects* (1943). However, her work in arithmetic did not receive the acknowledgment that her efforts in reading have been accorded. Other authors have provided analyses of the types of errors that often lead to lack of achievement in arithmetic, but among the first who definitely related learning problems in arithmetic to what we now call learning disabilities were Strauss and Lehtinen in another well-known work, *Psychopathology and Education of the Brain-injured Child* (1947). Another recognized learning disabilities authority, William Cruickshank, devoted more space to the teaching of arithmetic than to the teaching of reading in *A Teaching Method for Brain-injured and Hyperactive Children* (1961). Still another description of arithmetic problems of learning disabled students was provided by

Kaliski, in a paper that was first published by the Orton Society in 1961 but gained more attention as a contribution to Frierson and Barbe's *Educating Children with Learning Disabilities: Selected Readings* (1967). Kaliski's effort also concerned arithmetic problems of the *brain injured* and related to the types of disabilities that are associated primarily with students who are known to be brain injured.

Among the earliest of the presently recognized authorities in learning disabilities who provided specific educational suggestions for learning disabled students, *without emphasizing the characteristics of brain injury,* were Johnson and Myklebust, in their text *Learning Disabilities: Educational Principles and Practices* (1967). Since that time many authors of general texts relating to learning disabilities have provided a section or a chapter on the types of arithmetic or mathematical problems the learning disabled may experience and how to teach arithmetic skills, but no full-length text was written specifically on arithmetic problems manifested in learning disabled students until 1979. A book entitled *Arithmetic and Learning Disabilities: Guidelines for Identification and Remediation* by Stanley Johnson (1979) is now available and is further described later in this chapter.* The preceding texts, plus a few texts in remedial or diagnostic arithmetic that are not specifically addressed to arithmetic as related to learning disabilities, represent the present state of development in this area.

In one of the earlier descriptions of problems in arithmetic as they relate to learning disabilities (as defined today), Kaliski (1967) outlined the following characteristics of learning disabled students:

1. Difficulties in spatial relationships (up, down, high, low, far, near)
2. Size relationships (big, small, more, less)
3. Motor disinhibition ("driven" behavior)
4. Left to right confusion (disorientation with regard to number sequence)
5. Perseveration (difficulty in shifting from one process to another, in a problem that requires such shifting)
6. General difficulty with language symbols (Arithmetic is a special language system.)
7. General difficulty in abstract thinking (in conceptualization or in understanding cause-effect relationships)

The notations following each characteristic are simply examples; many others may apply in specific cases.

Other authors have generally agreed that the preceding difficulties do, in fact, exist. In addition, however, various authorities have emphasized such factors as difficulties with memory, closure, sensory-motor integration, auditory-visual association, one-to-one correspondence, and others that are essentially subparts of the difficulties outlined in the preceding paragraph. In total, the types of specific disabilities that are ordinarily associated with learning disabilities seem to provide *a priori* evidence that many learning disabled students will have unusual difficulties with arithmetic. The rest of this consideration of arithmetic deals mainly with teaching procedures to be used in the remediation of arithmetic difficulties.

TEACHING APPROACHES FOR USE WHEN ARITHMETIC DIFFICULTIES RELATE TO LEARNING DISABILITIES

A diagnostic-remedial approach

In the preceding section we recognized that a number of authors that have provided some guidelines for determining the type and degree of learning problems in arithmetic and

*This book by Johnson and *A Guide to the Diagnostic Teaching of Arithmetic* (ed. 2), by F. Reisman (1978), are recommended to readers who require more information than is available in this chapter.

suggestions for remediation; however, Johnson (1979) was the first to address the topic of arithmetic and learning disabilities in depth. His text is organized in such a manner that the first part (approximately one fourth of the text) explains learning disabilities and suggests a strategy through which the teacher can implement a prescriptive-remedial process. He noted that "it is virtually impossible to isolate the diagnostic procedure from the prescriptive remediation process" (1979, p. 58). The majority of Johnson's text is devoted to methods and materials to use in the classroom, paired with diagnostic activities that may be used to determine the types of materials that are needed.

Johnson recognizes eight different types of learning disabilities that directly affect the learning of arithmetic, although he notes that "different theorists would establish different hierarchies of importance for the areas included" (1979, p. 93). These eight types are (1) memory disabilities, (2) visual-auditory discrimination disabilities, (3) visual-auditory association disabilities, (4) perceptual-motor disabilities, (5) spatial awareness and orientation disabilities, (6) verbal expression disabilities, (7) closure and generalization disabilities, and (8) attending disabilities.

Johnson has divided the arithmetic curriculum (for purposes of his diagnostic-remedial scheme) into three major *curriculum-content levels:* (1) preschool readiness level, (2) introductory level, and (3) postintroductory level. These levels are then subdivided into curriculum areas as shown in Table 8, and diagnostic activities, methods, and materials are keyed to specific curriculum areas and types of learning disability.

The diagnostic process (which also includes the preparation and use of remedial materials) is outlined as follows:*

1. The teacher or diagnostician should *look for specific indications of problems in*

*Adapted from Johnson, 1979, pp. 62-75.

TABLE 8. A diagnostic-prescriptive format in which learning disabilities may be related to deficits in the learning of arithmetic content and skill areas

Learning disability	Curriculum-content level	Content and skill areas
Memory	Readiness level	Number recognition
Visual-auditory discrimination		Counting
Visual-auditory association		Grouping
Perceptual motor		Relationships (vocabulary)
Spatial orientation		Verbal expression
Verbal expression	Introductory level	Vocabulary
Closure and generalization		Relationships (sets)
Attending		Operations (addition and subtraction)
		Grouping
		Problem solving
		Verbal expression
	Postintroductory level	Operations (multiplication and division)
		Rule application
		Written problem solving
		Nonwritten problem solving

Adapted from Johnson, S. *Arithmetic and learning disabilities: guidelines for identification and remediation.* Boston: Allyn & Bacon, Inc., 1979.

regular classwork. These problems are called "deficit behavior" and this step involves the development of hypotheses that may or may not be later confirmed. Johnson provides examples of "problem-free behavior" in relation to each type of learning disability and curriculum area and suggests sample tasks that may be used to check out any preliminary indications or hypotheses (see pp. 241-242).

2. Based on the indications or hypotheses formed in Step 1, the teacher should *use material specifically designed to check out the type of behavior believed to be "deficit behavior."* Johnson provides "do-it-yourself diagnostic activities" in relation to each learning disability type and curriculum area and indicates that each hypothesis must be checked out carefully (see pp. 241 and 243). This means devising other tasks similar to the one provided to attempt to verify the particular problem area.
3. The teacher should *search for non-arithmetic-related deficit behavior that may suggest that the behavior indicated in Step 2 may have generalized to other areas of functioning.* Johnson provides in his guide to each curriculum area and type of learning disability a suggestion as to how to initiate this search. These suggestions are under the heading of "non-arithmetic situations where similar behaviors are required" (see pp. 241 and 243). These are specific suggestions and are intended to provide teacher insight regarding other similar situations that should be tailored to the student's age, interests, and so forth.
4. After completing the first three steps of this diagnostic process, the teacher should *decide whether or not to seek additional outside help.* This applies to the regular classroom teacher who may be attempting to provide remediation without asking for extensive additional evaluation and the services of a learning disabilities specialist. If there is sufficient diagnostic information to permit the identification of specific deficit behavior and to establish remedial objectives, then the teacher may proceed, at least until it is discovered that the procedures are not working. Since the learning disabilities specialist *is* the "additional outside help" this step would ordinarily not apply to him or her.
5. After the deficit behavior has been pinpointed, the teacher should *establish a specific remedial objective (or objectives).* In his text, Johnson provides examples of "remedial objectives for confirmed problems" for each curriculum area and learning disability type (see pp. 241 and 243). These are only samples of the type of objective that might be established but in many instances could be used with little modification.
6. Next, the teacher should *prepare and use remedial materials.* At least one "sample remedial activity" is provided for each curriculum area and learning disability type. The sample activities are relatively simple, and teachers are encouraged to search for other similar activities that will satisfy the stated remedial objective (Step 5) (see pp. 242 and 243). This may include either teacher-made or commercial materials; the important thing is that the materials match the remedial objective.
7. The final process may or may not be required. If the remedial materials do not appear to be effective, the teacher must *revise and rework the diagnostic process.*

Depending on the circumstances, this may mean moving back to Step 5, Step 2, or perhaps back to the very beginning. This may also mean reconsidering Step 4, whether or not to seek additional outside help.

The framework for diagnostic-remedial efforts recommended by Johnson is particularly practical as related to his suggested remedial activities that are based on a prescribed series of diagnostic activities and keyed to 15 curriculum areas and 8 types of learning disability (see Table 8). The pages reproduced from Johnson's text (see pp. 241 to 243) indicate the manner in which he has organized his approach. His work is of practical value to both regular classroom teachers and learning disabilities teachers and specialists.

CURRICULUM AREA: VOCABULARY

LEARNING DISABILITY TYPE □ MEMORY

Problem-free behavior

The child is able to recall newly learned vocabulary in direct relationship to the specific arithmetic use of each term.

Sample task where deficit child may display difficulty

Shown a one-step number sentence, ask the child to remember the labels for the different parts, such as, addend, plus, equals, sum, and so on.

Do-it-yourself diagnostic activities

Following a lesson about telling time or the use of the clock, the child can name, describe, or tell about the parts or functions of the clock which have arithmetic relevance if this area presents no problems. Hence, questions such as the following are diagnostically useful:

1. "What does the '3' on the face of the clock tell us?"
2. "What numbers do we find on a clock?"
3. "Which number is used when we talk about one-half of an hour?"

Non-arithmetic situations where similar behaviors are required

Though misnaming is an obvious clue to such deficits, the child having problems remembering labels usually quickly develops compensating mechanisms or substitute words. Using colloquial stand-by phrases such as "you know" and resorting to positional descriptions instead of labels (the "bottom number" instead of "subtrahend") is typical. Use of backdoor descriptions such as describing a glass as "only a little empty" instead of staying it is "almost full" can be a warning sign.

Remedial objective for confirmed problems

The child will be provided with practice in remembering and then correctly identifying use of arithmetic labels and terminology.

From Stanley W. Johnson, ARITHMETIC AND LEARNING DISABILITIES: GUIDELINES FOR IDENTIFICATION AND REMEDIATION.

Continued.

CURRICULUM AREA: VOCABULARY—cont'd

Sample remedial activity

Play "Memory Tic-Tac-Toe" or "Bingo." Give the child a plating board with nine compartments. Each compartment should contain an arithmetic word or symbol. Briefly show the child flashcards with similar words or symbols, one to a card. After the card is exposed, a brief waiting period follows varying from a second or two up to ten seconds. Then ask the child to point to the word or symbol he has seen. If the remembered identification is correct, the child is allowed to cover that word on his card with a marker or poker chip. The important variable here is memory; therefore, the words and symbols should be known or easily identifiable ones.

6	add	3
=	subtract	−
sum	+	two

LEARNING DISABILITY TYPE □ SPATIAL ORIENTATION
Problem-free behavior

The child is able to recognize and produce temporal, spatial, or orientational vocabulary appropriate to observed concrete relationships.

Sample task where deficit child may display difficulty

The child can correctly produce positional vocabulary, as in answering, "What word describes the position of the ball to the square in each example?"

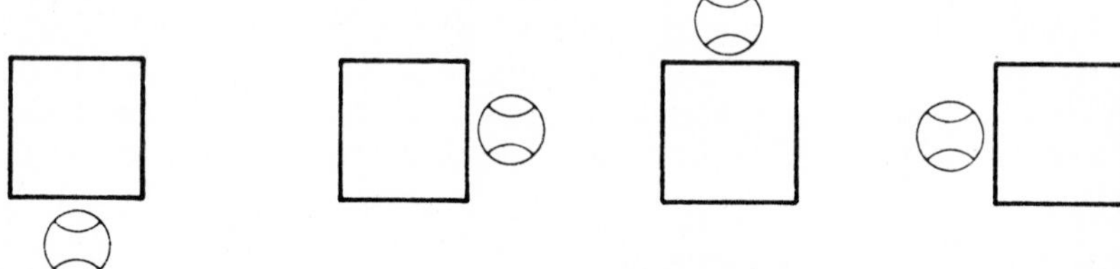

Do-it-yourself diagnostic activities

Superimpose object drawings on a clock-like circle. Ask the children questions such as:

1. "What word describes the cat's and dog's position?"
2. "The cat is ______ than the dog."
3. "Is the ball or the drum on the right side of the circle?"

Non-arithmetic situations where similar behaviors are required

A common behavioral example of deficit learning in a child of this age is failure to learn to tell time, despite thorough knowledge of numbers and obvious interest in time concepts.

Remedial objective for confirmed problems

The child will be provided with practice in using and applying spatial, temporal, and orientational terms in arithmetic relationships.

Sample remedial activity

Remedial worksheets should require the child to match or produce the correct terminology to demonstrated relationships. For example:

1. Where is the ball? Circle the right word.

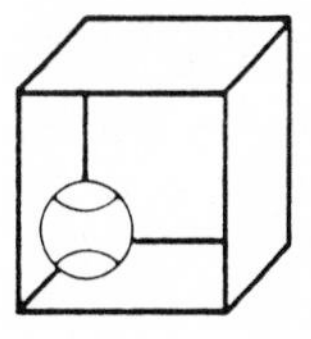

Inside
Outside

2. Which way is the arrow pointing?

3. The dog is sitting ______ the cat.

Other teaching ideas

Various remedial mathematics authorities have provided useful ideas, and teachers of learning disabled students should review existing remedial programs to determine which will likely be most advantageous with the students under consideration. However, observation of the student actually attempting to complete arithmetic problems or exercises, supplemented by carefully phrased questions, may be one of the best ways to evaluate what will be effective with a given student. The following teaching ideas illustrate methods that *may* work, but there is no assurance that any one will be effective with any given student.

The use of concrete, manipulative materials may encourage the "doing" of activities that lead to arithmetic understanding. This could include a wide variety of materials, both commercial and teacher made. It is most practical to investigate what materials are available

Accurate information about the student's ability is an important factor in developing remedial strategies.

as part of the regular school program. If the school district has a mathematics consultant, in most cases he will be available for assistance to the learning disabilities personnel and his help should be sought. The following are sample ideas and activities.

1. *Cuisenaire rods* are available in many school districts. The 291 Cuisenaire rods are of varying lengths and colors and are made of wood. Accompanying booklets provide suggestions regarding how they may be used to promote equivalence, sequences, patterns, and other mathematical concepts. Cuisenaire rods are useful for developing original understanding of certain aspects of arithmetic, and the tactile and visual reinforcement provided appears to be effective with some learning disabled students. Their concrete nature is a definite plus factor, and the instructional suggestions provided with the complete set help the teacher who is unsure of where to begin with certain students.
2. *Sets of solid cubes, rods, cylinders, and the like* may be of value if this is the stage of development at which the student needs assistance. If the sets include two or three sizes of each geometric shape and form-boards into which they are to be placed, they may be used (depending on complexity of the set) to promote the learning of shape and size and appropriate terminology.
3. *Beads, counting boxes, counting frames* and other similar materials may be of value to certain students. Counting, seriation, addition, subtraction, and other skills or concepts may be learned through these concrete materials.
4. *Various common games such as dominoes, Chinese checkers, and playing cards* may be used to teach counting, fractions, or other concepts. These may require considerable teacher involvement at times to get the process started, or peer tutoring may work in certain situations.
5. *Yardsticks, meter sticks, play money or real money,* and any other everyday device or material that has to do with measuring or counting can be of value if properly used. Poker chips or something similar may also be of value for teaching basic arithmetic concepts.

It is important with all of the above to attend to the question of the verbal interaction, arithmetic terminology, and related concepts that must be learned. The student may be able to say "one half" or "one fourth" with ease and memorize when the teacher wishes him to say it in a standard situation. However, the goal must be for him to understand the meaning of *one half* and *one fourth* as applied in various situations. Therefore, in the use of concrete, manipulative materials, teachers must be careful to verify that the concept can be applied in a variety of situations. In a similar manner, a student may be taught with some success to add four and five (4 + 5) by counting blocks or other concrete objects, but the final goal is that he understand the concept involved and be able to add 4 + 5 by rote memory.

The use of number cards and process sign cards may help in the transition from concrete material to the more abstract symbols. Ordinary flash cards may be of value and should not be overlooked as a potential resource. However, it is more likely that another intermediate step might be needed. For this we may write the various numbers on 3 by 5 cards and write the process symbols (+, −, ×, ÷) on other 3 by 5 cards of a different color. Then the student can be directed to engage in whatever level activity is appropriate. One activity might be to arrange the cards in numerical order. Any addition, subtraction, multiplication, or division problems that the existing cards make possible can also be accomplished. For reasons that are not fully understood, moving the cards into place appears to reinforce learning for some students. (An "immediate feedback" version of such activities involves smaller cards that present a problem to the student—for example, 3 + 6—and directs him to match the 3, the +, and the 6 on the desk in front of him. He then either writes the answer or finds it among other available cards. The answer is on the back of the card that directed him to do the original problem.) A wide number of possibilities exists through use of this simple, teacher-made card system.

The use of teacher-dictated problems may assist the student to learn the meaning of the nomenclature of arithmetic. This permits a teacher-monitored setting in which words such as *plus, added to, minus, take away, subtracted from, more than, less than, equals,* and so forth may be used in dictated form to see if the student can relate the auditory form of these mathematical processes to the visual forms. In addition to determining where discrepancies exist between visual and auditory recognition, this procedure permits the teacher to observe the child's thinking processes at work and pinpoints where to focus remedial attention.

Although many of these teaching ideas may appear to be very fundamental in nature and therefore applicable only to very young children, one report of arithmetic problems in college students indicates that some learning disabled students of college age have extremely low arithmetic ability and need some basic remediation. This study (Tarnopol and Tarnopol, 1979) indicates that some community college students in remedial mathematics programs have severe difficulties in visual figure-ground and visual-motor integration that seem to relate to the difficulties in arithmetic. Causal relationship was not definitely established in this report, but preliminary findings seemed to indicate the value of visual-perceptual training, even at this age.

In closing this consideration of teaching ideas and before proceeding to a brief review of the potential contributions of Piaget to the teaching of arithmetic to the learning disabled, let us consider the conclusions of Harry Chandler, an experienced learning disabilities teacher who launched a review of existing research and expert opinion regarding methods for teaching arithmetic to learning disabled students. Chandler concluded that research results were contradictory with regard to how to teach arithmetic to normal students and even more so with regard to teaching the learning disabled (Chandler, 1978). In his conclusion, Chandler noted, "If concrete materials and attempts to strengthen weak sensory modalities don't work, something else must be tried." He further noted, in a statement that may be most profound in its simplicity, "It makes sense to find out what students are doing wrong in solving problems, find out what they need to learn to solve the problems, and then teach the students that" (1978, p. 368).

Piaget and the development of arithmetic and mathematical skills

A number of authors who have provided guidelines for the development of remedial efforts in arithmetic have suggested some sort of relationship to the work of Piaget (Hammill and Bartel, 1975; Marsh, 1976; Johnson, 1979). Piaget, in *Science of Education and the Psychology of the Child* (1974), indicated that mathematics is an extension of logic and, as such, the two cannot actually be separated. However, as noted by Marsh, "It seems paradoxical that there are students who are well endowed with logical thinking but unable to perform adequately in mathematics" (1976, p. 121). In practice, the work of Piaget (see pp. 51 to 56 for a brief outline) may be of most value as teachers attempt to understand why some students have so much difficulty when they reach the stage of synthesizing and hypothesizing in mathematics. Knowledge of the stages through which Piaget believed all individuals must move to reach adult levels of ability may assist the teacher to see that a given student simply has not progressed to the stage of learning required to handle a given type of problem. If this is the case, the more drill on mathematics may not be appropriate until the required level is reached.

Piagetian thinking does not directly contribute practical, programmed methods for remediation but may provide a useful frame of reference when teachers attempt to think through cases where programmed approaches are not working.

ARITHMETIC AND LEARNING DISABILITIES—AN EVOLVING ISSUE

Some students have had unusual difficulty in learning arithmetic or mathematics ever since these academic areas became organized fields of study, and specific suggestions for remedial efforts via published textbooks or teachers' guides have existed for at least the past century. Most of the earlier efforts to assist students who were having such difficul-

Arithmetic may be "logical" and "systematic" to some, but others will require very special assistance and encouragement. (From Gearheart, B. R. *Teaching the learning disabled: a combined task-process approach.* St. Louis: The C. V. Mosby Co., 1976.)

ties were discussed in terms of "diagnostic studies," "remedial arithmetic," or "remedial mathematics." Some of these early efforts, for example, *Diagnostic Studies in Arithmetic* (Buswell and John, 1926), are still cited regularly by authors who are reviewing remedial ideas in arithmetic.

Beginning in the 1940s, special educators (who are now called learning disabilities specialists) working with brain-injured students observed certain patterns of learning problems with respect to the learning of arithmetic and mathematics and began to develop remedial procedures based on their understanding of the effects of brain injury. They used existing knowledge in the teaching of arithmetic, including remedial procedures developed over the years, adapting these ideas and procedures to fit the characteristics of brain-injured students. During the 1940s, 1950s, and 1960s, the term *dyscalculia* at times was applied to students who exhibited unusual difficulties in mathematics, but most educators today believe that such a label has very limited value.

As the learning disabilities field began to emerge as a recognized subarea of special education in the 1960s, it was known that some learning disabled students had difficulties in mathematics, but the major points of focus were reading disabilities and, to a lesser extent, a broad range of language development difficulties. Mathematics did not receive primary attention probably because reading was viewed as much more important. Certain authors, such as Johnson and Myklebust (1967), provided both theoretical rationale and practical teaching suggestions, but the emphasis remained on reading and language disorders.

Beginning in the mid-1970s, as the field of learning disabilities was beginning to take a more generally recognized shape and focus and a national definition (including the mention of arithmetic as one of the specific areas in which a disability might be manifested) became more widely accepted and understood, it became apparent that more attention must be given to the area of arithmetic. Authors of introductory learning disability texts began to include more prominent mention of arithmetic, and "methods" texts in learning disabilities often included a chapter on teaching arithmetic. Recommended procedures included the work of various earlier authors and programs such as DISTAR, which was developed primarily to assist students who were not learning because of lack of opportunity or cultural disadvantage. Certain programmed arithmetic materials have also been highly recommended by some.

This is not a "methods" text, but a review of some of the methods that have worked with learning disabled students has been included to assist in a more accurate overall conceptualization of learning disabilities. In that spirit, two texts are mentioned that may be of value for further consideration. One, *Arithmetic and Learning Disabilities* (Johnson, 1979) relates arithmetic to learning disabilities within a framework that is consistent with the manner in which authorities have come to describe learning disabilities. A second text, not actually described in this discussion of arithmetic and learning disabilities but recommended for further investigation, is *A Guide to the Diagnostic Teaching of Arithmetic*, ed. 2 (Reisman, 1978). This text was not written to fit the learning disabilities frame of reference but is highly applicable and is used by learning disabilities practitioners.

Given a broad understanding of the major characteristics that interfere with learning of learning disabled students, it is probably safe to say that most remedial programs in mathematics may have some value and applicability. The necessary ingredients to maximize the likelihood that the program will be effective are an understanding of the manner in which learning disabilities may interfere with learning in general, an understanding of the nature of arithmetic and mathematics, including the manner and sequence in which they are usually learned, and accurate information regarding the learning strengths and weaknesses (abilities and disabilities) of the student under consideration.

LEARNING DISABILITIES AND WRITTEN LANGUAGE DISORDERS

All major, recognized definitions of learning disabilities relate specifically to language disorders, and the federal definition (see p. 12) mentions language disorders first in its listing of types of disabilities or deficits that are included as learning disabilities. Although there are a number of ways to define and subdivide language disorders, one of the most common is to consider two major areas—*spoken* and *written*. The concern here is with written disorders, more specifically those of handwriting, spelling, and the ability to express thoughts or ideas through writing.

Handwriting disabilities

Handwriting disabilities among certain segments of the adult population are so common that a well-accepted joke is that one of the earliest courses in medical school relates to how to write illegibly. It is important, however, to differentiate between the poor handwriting exhibited by many adults and the type of difficulty referred to here. The handwriting problems of many adults can be dramatically reduced by their decreasing the speed of handwriting, increasing the size of letters, concentrating more on the task, or combining some of these efforts. Deficits in handwriting skills of learning disabled students usually mean that the skill was never learned and that certain more basic learning deficits are major contributing factors. For many school-age individuals, undeveloped (or underdeveloped) handwriting skills have carry-over effects in the areas of spelling and reading. Retardation in spelling and reading may then have the effect of further slowing the development of adequate handwriting, and a vicious cycle is established. Therefore, acceptable handwriting must be considered important not only as a means of communication but also as part of the total area of language development.

Critics of modern education often point to a reduction in the amount of time spent in the lower grades on the development of near-perfect (highly consistent with models provided in workbooks) cursive writing during the past 20 to 30 years. It does appear that, in terms of actual classroom time spent on the development of handwriting, such a reduction in emphasis has taken place. It is not clear, however, whether learning disabled students would benefit from more of the *traditional* handwriting procedures or whether they may have additional, unique needs resulting from underlying deficits in motor coordination, inability to concentrate, or perhaps visual-perceptual difficulties. Various authors in the area of learning disabilities have provided suggestions as to why writing is so important and how it may be taught; these suggestions are the point of focus here.

Handwriting instruction for the learning disabled is important for the following reasons:

1. *Writing can be therapeutic.* Cruickshank and others (1961) indicate that "the physical activity of writing channels [the child's] restless energy and gives him the rare experience of using that energy as a way which calls forth praise" (p. 191).
2. *Writing can help to develop improved visual-perceptual abilities.* This idea is suggested by many authors in learning

disabilities who directly approach the question of the value in teaching handwriting to the learning disabled student.

3. *Writing can help to improve visual-motor integration.* Visual-motor integrative problems are the basic reasons for the extremely poor handwriting of some learning disabled students according to certain writers. Johnson and Myklebust, for example, indicate that *dysgraphia* is a condition in which the individual "has neither a visual nor a motor defect, but he cannot transduce visual information to the motor system" (1967, p. 199). This inability to *copy* differentiates dysgraphia from the other written language disorders, according to this point of view.
4. *Writing can help the student to see wholes (gestalts).* This concept is supported by Fernald (1943) and Cruickshank (1961) and inferred by those who believe that the *cursive writing* of a *whole word* helps build an understanding that letters, grouped together, form a word with real meaning and help tell a story (communicate meaning).
5. *Writing can aid in reading and spelling.* The belief that writing, especially cursive writing, is an important aid to the development of reading and spelling skills is basic to the methods advocated by Fernald and Gillingham (see Chapter 6) and to a great extent is the final effect desired by those who support reasons (1) through (4) above. In concluding their discussion of "Cursive Writing: an Aid to Reading and Spelling," Kaufman and Biren state that "the striking simplicity of cursive writing for the spatially disoriented child has not been fully recognized" (1979, p. 218). They believe that a program they espouse (which depends heavily on accurate cursive writing) can help learning disabled students with a number of different types of basic learning deficits and should be more fully appreciated and utilized.

The potential value of and the need for particular attention to handwriting in learning disabled students who have often been called dysgraphic is generally recognized, and the goal of most learning disabilities authorities who advocate special assistance in this area relates to the final reason outlined above—to aid in the development of reading and spelling. Many adults function quite adequately with very little actual handwriting, but most have already learned to read and spell and *could* write if necessary. On the other hand, writing may be an essential tool for learning to read and spell for some learning disabled students, and thus its importance is considerably greater than if it were to be learned for writing alone. In addition, however, the normal school program requires a good deal of written work that is seldom duplicated in need in adult life but nevertheless required in school. Thus it is generally agreed that for this combination of reasons educators must attend to the development of adequate writing skills in the learning disabled student.

Methods for developing handwriting skills. A number of approaches may assist the student to develop handwriting skills. In all likelihood certain of the commercial, workbook-format programs will be of value, *if* teachers begin at a sufficiently basic skill level and pay close attention to clues as to a given student's specific needs. For example, some younger children may have difficulty in holding the pencil or other writing tool correctly. Teachers may assume that this is the case for many 5-year-old children and thus provide primary (large-diameter) pencils or crayons. They must remember that some 7- or 8-year-old children may not have developed motor skills appropriate for their chronological age and it is critical that they have prerequisite motor skills before initiating specific programs of remediation.

If, then, a child does not know how to hold a pencil or crayon properly, remediation should start here. It may be a matter of the child not seeing how to hold the pencil or of inability to motorically imitate what he sees. He may hold the pencil too tightly, too loosely, too far from the point, or (more often) too close to the point. He should have large-diameter pencils; short pencils (which might encourage holding too close to the point) should be avoided.

How to hold the pencil should be demonstrated and explained carefully, and then the instructor should make certain that the proper grasp is taken. When these steps are not enough (repeated attempts should be made before concluding that they are not effective), the child should be asked to close his eyes, grasp the pencil softly, and then make large, sweeping movements as though he were writing very large letters. This may be necessary when the visual input is somehow leading to confusion. In this case, the teacher may guide the movements, thus encouraging and reinforcing large, sweeping motion.

Some children cannot replicate curved lines in such a manner that their reproduction is curved in the same direction as the letter or form that they are trying to copy. In such cases, copying of straight lines, shading within a large-copy figure, or similar preschool-type activities may be needed. At times children may be assisted by a cutout stencil that guides them. Copying very large patterns on the chalkboard or other such activities may be of value if this type of large-muscle training is needed. The use of colors may be of value in some cases, as are oversized teacher-made ditto sheets that permit a great deal of repetition. In addition to these types of activities, Johnson and Myklebust suggest other specific techniques that may be used to reinforce newly formed or developing writing patterns. These include:

1. *Tracing folds.* Paper is folded into various patterns: squares, rectangles, and triangles. After unfolding, the child is directed to trace with his index finger the remaining traces of the folds. He then traces the "folds" with crayon or pencil. The tactile impression derived from tracing is viewed as beneficial.
2. *Drawing roads.* Various patterns that might represent straight or curved roads are cut from stencils or drawn on paper. At first these can be relatively wide patterns (perhaps as much as one inch) but are narrowed as the child's ability increases. The child must trace between the lines.
3. *Tracing with copy paper.* Various figures may be drawn with dark, felt-tipped pens on standard-size paper or heavyweight construction paper. Onionskin paper (or anything through which these patterns will show) is placed over the copy form, and the child traces on the copy paper. Successively more difficult patterns are used as skill improves.
4. *Dot-to-dot figures.* First a complete figure is drawn. Then a dot-to-dot figure is provided that the child may complete to develop a similar figure. After the child learns the technique, the complete or "model" figure can be discontinued.

The preceding activities exemplify the type that may be used to develop prewriting skills and may be particularly important with learning disabled children in that they may not develop skills that other children develop naturally. Without these prerequisite skills, it is almost impossible for a student to learn actual writing skills.

After the development of these basic, prewriting skills, it may be practical for teachers to first attempt to teach writing just as they would with children with normal abilities. (If the preceding skills are learned well, normal writing skills may develop in a relatively normal manner.) If the normal or "standard" approaches do *not* work, then special methods must be applied at the writing level also. This may include tracing of embossed letters, tracing over letters that have been written with felt-tipped pen, completing dot-to-dot letters (in this case, direction of movement must be indicated), or the teacher moving the hand of the child through the form of various letters. Generally speaking, larger-than-normal letters may be needed for initial learning.

There is some debate about whether initial teaching of the letters should be accomplished through manuscript or cursive writing. Strauss and Lehtinen (1947) suggested cursive but Johnson and Myklebust (1967) recommended manuscript. In practice, I suggest that this may be determined by the age of the child, the type of writing to which he has already been exposed, and motivation. Johnson and Myklebust indicated that manuscript movements are "less complex and there are fewer reciprocal movements and changes of letter forms" (1967, p. 213). Strauss and Lehtinen (1947) and Fernald (1943) believed that the "wholeness" involved in teaching cursive writing of words, plus the fact that children learning cursive words automatically learn about spacing (small space between letters, large space between words), make cursive a better procedure. In addition, Fernald would see a better carryover to reading (that is, learning that a series of letters make a word) when cursive is used. Whichever is used, teachers must remember that the process may take a great deal of practice, that they often err on the side of assuming prewriting skills, and that copying, tracing, and other kinesthetic methods that must be closely monitored to assure the greatest success seem to be the key.

Most of the preceding suggestions relate more to young children than to secondary school students. At the secondary level, serious handwriting disabilities that cannot be greatly improved through a process of slowing down or writing larger are usually more difficult to deal with than for younger children. This is because the defective pattern of functioning, whatever the cause, has been practiced for so long and thus is so well established. Some of Fernald's suggestions regarding tracing may be of value in severe cases; however, some secondary-aged students may reject such activities because they are so "babyish." If properly motivated, students may follow such procedures with good results or may try such things as going back to carefully printed manuscript, which may then later be "connected" to produce cursive writing. In extreme cases, if an older student can print legibly and can be taught to write his name (as for signatures), that may be the most reasonable goal. One other technique that appears to work in some cases is to teach the student to reduce the slant of his cursive writing (make it more perpendicular to the line on which it is written). In any event, remediation of handwriting difficulties is much more likely if such attempts are initiated long before the student enters the secondary schools.

Spelling disabilities

Spelling disabilities are the second general type of written language disorder for consideration here. According to Johnson and Myklebust, "Spelling requires more auditory and visual discrimination, memory, sequentialization, analysis and synthesis, and integration simultaneously than perhaps any other skill" (1967, p. 239). In other words, spelling is a most complex ability requiring a combination of skills and abilities that are not fully understood by many, or perhaps most, teachers who are responsible for teaching spelling.

In a statement regarding the remedial teaching of written language disorders, Johnson and Myklebust noted that the objective is "to assist the child in revisualizing letters and words, hence making it possible for him to write and spell properly" (1967, p. 222). In the discussion from which the previous quotation was taken, Johnson and Myklebust were speaking of students who can read successfully but cannot revisualize for purposes of spelling. (Most readers of this text can undoubtedly *read* some words that they cannot later *spell* correctly. This situation may exist to a limited degree in many individuals with respect to certain less common words, but with some learning disabled students it exists to an unusually great extent. In these extreme cases the students are considered to have spelling disabilities.) The type of revisualization referred to by Johnson and Myklebust may be called *total recall* (as opposed to partial recall), and they suggest that teachers attempt to work from (1) recognition, to (2) partial recall, to (3) total recall. One of the ways to approach this task is through some system of cues, and the use of auditory or tactile-kinesthetic cues often seems to be of value.

The Fernald VAKT (visual-auditory-kinesthetic-tactile) approach (see pp. 120 to 125) may be of great value in the remediation of spelling disabilities. The addition of the kinesthetic and tactile sensory modalities apparently develops an awareness of the "feel" of various words, and these tactile and kinesthetic cues help the student learn to spell correctly. In fact, most remedial spelling methods appear to involve the use of learning channels other than visual to assist in developing accurate visual memory.

Some students have spelling difficulties with nearly all words, while others have difficulties only with nonphonetic words. Analysis of the type of spelling errors is an important first step if teachers are to achieve remediation with a minimum of time and effort. If the errors fit some obvious pattern (for example, difficulties in spelling nonphonetic words or words that include letters that are more often reversed because of visual-perceptual problems), then teachers know where to direct their major remedial efforts.

In summary, spelling is in many ways more complex than reading, and this fact is not always fully appreciated. The basic difficulty (and this is an oversimplification) is that, even though the student can recognize a word auditorily and can read a word (using various types of word attack skills), he cannot revisualize it precisely. He may be able to remember or determine through analysis the beginning letter (if it is standard phonetically) but is unable to exercise total recall. In some cases, however, he may not even be able to remember the first letter.

Whatever the degree or type of spelling difficulty, the objective is to develop the ability to accurately revisualize words. One way to assist the student to accomplish this task is through training and experience that will provide the necessary additional cues. Since the difficulty lies primarily with efficient use of the visual channel, it is only logical that teachers use some combination of the other major learning modalities, the auditory, kinesthetic and tactile, as temporary support for the visual. The *final* goal, however, is to develop adequate *visual* recall, if at all possible.

One final note of practical importance: Even though teachers may have a broad repertoire of alternate approaches whereby they should be able to provide the needed support for underdeveloped or defective revisualization abilities, they must remember the role of attention with respect to memory. Given the fact that learning disabled students are more likely than the normal population to have attention difficulties, teachers may need to use any of a variety of attention-getting techniques along with other procedures. They must remember that many learning disabled students are distracted to an unusual extent by sounds and movements that are of little consequence to other children. Teachers may need to reduce this type of distraction to achieve success with other efforts. It may also be necessary to use verbal cues such as "Ready!" or "Let's look now!" to start each new learning task. In addition, pointers, tachistoscopic-like devices, or other means may be necessary to direct attention. A number of commercially developed methods for teaching spelling are of value with the learning disabled student, but teachers must always remember and provide for the "other" difficulties that may exist. Keeping these possible difficulties in mind and applying what they know about the learning, teachers may be able to assist the student to achieve much greater success in spelling, which will in turn lead to greater success in other language-related areas. This overall, generalized success should be the final goal.

Written expression

An individual's ability to adequately express thoughts, ideas, and feelings through writing, an ability that might simply be called written expression, is the final area of concern in this section. Clearly, the first two types of written language, handwriting and spelling, are prerequisites to the development of adequate written expression. (One exception is individuals who do not have and cannot develop motor skills required to write or print by hand. They will probably be taught to type, as a substitute for cursive or manuscript writing.) Once the student can write and spell with at least moderate success, he must learn to use these two abilities to express thoughts, ideas, or feelings. Then, in addition to learning the rules of punctuation and grammar, the student must learn to convert thoughts and ideas (which he can express orally) to the written form. Johnson and Myklebust (1967) suggest that the following sequence may be of value when a learning disabled student is having little or no success with writing but is able to discuss various topics successfully.

First, the student must progress from *experience,* to *auditory language,* to *written language.* To move through this sequence, a student must be encouraged to engage in oral discussion of his experiences, preferably those that are of considerable interest to him. Then, using whatever assistance is necessary, he should learn to put down in writing what he said orally. This second step may involve a great deal of individual assistance from the teacher or teacher aide, including writing down many of the words for the student. The end result must be that the student can see what he said (which he earlier experienced) in written form.

Once the student learns that he can produce written language, the task becomes that of moving through the following concrete-to-abstract progression:

1. Concrete-descriptive
2. Concrete-imaginative
3. Abstract-descriptive
4. Abstract-imaginative

The starting place with any given student depends on the level at which he is presently operating. This must be determined from observation and analysis of whatever written work he can produce. *Teachers must note that the student may be able to speak or discuss at the abstract-imaginative level, but written work may be obviously at the concrete-descriptive level.* This is what a *written* language disability is all about. Brief suggestions on how to proceed to assist the student through this sequence follow.

1. If the student cannot write even the simplest sentence or phrase, start by showing him common objects (for example, a ball, a pencil, a jacket, or whatever seems appropriate) and asking him to write the name of each. Then ask him to describe it in one word (round, yellow, warm, or any accurate description that comes to the student's mind). Combine these words (a round ball, a yellow pencil, a warm jacket), thus showing a complete thought.

   Move from this to asking the student to tell how each is used (thrown, used to write with, worn). Then ask the student to develop short sentences about these and other common words that relate to concrete situations with which he is familiar. He is thus utilizing concrete-descriptive language. Other activities, such as the use of pictures of common objects and events, may be used to stimulate more sentences that represent concrete objects in real settings. In each case, the student should be provided whatever help is necessary to permit him to develop a meaningful sentence.
2. At the concrete-imaginative level, the student must learn to develop ideas based on inference or imagination. For example, instead of responding to the picture of a boy throwing a ball by simply "The boy is throwing a ball," he might respond, "The boy is throwing the ball to third base." For some students this is relatively easy with teacher assistance. For others (such as the learning disabled student who would be called "stimulus-bound" by Johnson and Myklebust) it may take a great deal of effort to assist the student to be able to make assumptions regarding what he cannot see directly. In addition to being of value in relation to writing ability, developing this type of freedom from complete dependence on what can be actually seen may have spin-off value in other areas of functioning.
3. At the abstract-descriptive level, the use of *time* and *sequence* concepts should be encouraged (Johnson and Myklebust, 1967, p. 236). The keeping of a simple diary or the use of simple plays that involve going through some action sequence may be of value. The situation can be talked through or acted out, then the action recorded in writing.
4. At the abstract-imaginative level, stories that require the use of figures of speech, imaginative settings, and the like should be used. The idea of using words (written language) to "paint a picture" may be utilized here. For example, in telling about a big, very bright airport spotlight, the idea of comparing it to the sun and evolving the phrase "bright as the sun" might be meaningful. For some students, it may require much practice and it may literally take many months or years of planned experience to develop a satisfactory level of written language ability.

The preceding brief description of how written language development might be encouraged was provided to give some idea of practical approaches to this complex problem; those who eventually teach the learning disabled will learn many approaches, each of which will require adaptation in relation to a specific student.

SUMMARY

In this chapter we have reviewed certain difficulties that learning disabled students may have in learning arithmetic and a sample of how one author suggests that teachers approach remedial mathematics for learning disabled students. Stanley Johnson's diagnostic-prescriptive approach format was designed specifically for learning disabled students and appears to be consistent with general remedial mathematics procedures. Other potentially useful sources or ideas were also suggested.

Three aspects of written language disorders were presented and discussed. The first, handwriting, is more obvious and is more simple to remediate than the other two, spelling and written expression. A number of practical suggestions as to how handwriting skills might be developed were given, but, because of the complexity of disabilities in spelling and written expression, only a sample of possible remedial activities were provided in each of these areas. These samples should illustrate what may be done, but it is beyond the scope of this introductory text to go into detail in these two areas. Those who become full-time professionals in learning disabilities will become involved in a great deal of additional reading and investigation of written language disorders before launching their professional careers.

REFERENCES AND SUGGESTED READINGS

Buswell, G., and John, L. *Diagnostic studies in arithmetic.* Chicago: University of Chicago Press, 1926.

Capps, L., and Hatfield, M. Mathematical concepts and skills, *Focus on Exceptional Children,* 1977, *8,* 1-8.

Cawley, J., and others. *Project MATH.* Tulsa: Educational Programs Corp., 1976.

Chandler, H. Confusion confounded: a teacher tries to use research results to teach math, *Journal of Learning Disabilities* 1978, *11*(6), 361-369.

Connolly, A., Nachtman, W., and Pritchett, E. *Key math diagnostic arithmetic test.* Circle Pines, Minn.: American Guidance Service, 1971.

Cruickshank, W., and others. *A teaching method for brain-injured and hyperactive children.* Syracuse, N.Y.: Syracuse University Press, 1961.

Dunlap, W., and House, A. Why can't Johnny compute? *Journal of Learning Disabilities,* 1976, *4,* 210-214.

Englemann, S., and Carnine, D. *DISTAR arithmetic* (Levels I, II, and III). Chicago: Science Research Associates Inc., 1972, 1975, 1976.

Fernald, G. *Remedial techniques in basic school subjects.* New York: McGraw-Hill Book Co., 1943.

Hammill, D., and Bartel, N. *Teaching children with learning and behavior problems.* Boston: Allyn & Bacon, Inc., 1975.

Haring, N., and Bateman, B. *Teaching the learning disabled child.* Englewood Cliffs, N.J.: Prentice-Hall, Inc., 1977.

Johnson, D., and Myklebust, H. *Learning disabilities: educational principles and practices.* New York: Grune & Stratton, Inc., 1967.

Johnson, S. *Arithmetic and learning disabilities: guidelines for identification and remediation.* Boston: Allyn & Bacon, Inc., 1979.

Kaliski, L. Arithmetic and brain-injured child. In Frierson, E., and Barbe, W., (Eds.) *Educating children with learning disabilities: selected readings.* New York: Appleton-Century-Crofts, 1967.

Kaufman, H., and Biren, P. Cursive writing: an aid to reading and spelling, *Academic Therapy,* 1979, *15*(2), 209-219.

Lerner, J. *Children with learning disabilities* (ed. 2). Boston: Houghton Mifflin Co., 1976.

Marsh, G. Teaching arithmetic and mathematics to the learning disabled. In Gearheart, B. *Teaching the learn-*

ing disabled: a combined task-process approach. St. Louis: The C. V. Mosby Co., 1976.

Otto, W., McMenemy, R., and Smith, R. *Corrective and remedial teaching.* Boston: Houghton Mifflin Co., 1973.

Piaget, J. *The growth of logical thinking in the child.* New York: Basic Books, Inc., Publishers, 1958.

Piaget, J. *Science of education and the psychology of the child.* New York: Grossman Publishers, 1974.

Reisman, F. *A guide to the diagnostic teaching of arithmetic* (ed. 2). Columbus, Ohio: Charles E. Merrill Publishing Co., 1978.

Strauss, A., and Lehtinen, L. *Psychopathology and education of the brain-injured child.* New York: Grune & Stratton, Inc., 1947.

Tarnopol, L., and Tarnopol, M. Arithmetic disability in college students, *Academic Therapy,* 1979, *14*(3), 261-266.

chapter 12

Secondary school programs for the learning disabled

Learning disabilities are defined in precisely the same way at the secondary school level as at the elementary school level, but the procedure for serving secondary level students with learning disabilities may be significantly different. The need for this difference in approach begins to develop at the upper elementary grades, takes on greater importance at the junior high school level, and becomes critical at the senior high level. The difference, which is actually a change in emphasis, relates to a number of factors, but the end result is that much more time must be spent at the secondary level on accommodation and compensatory teaching, with less time spent on direct remedial efforts. The percentage of emphasis of accomodative/compensatory teaching versus remedial teaching varies from student to student, based on individual variables, but appears to be a nationwide phenomenon, based on experience that indicates that it is the more effective approach.

This chapter considers the factors that seem to support the need for this modification in emphasis and the program elements required to make secondary programs for the learning disabled effective. Those who are considering the possibility of teaching the learning disabled adolescent will find it necessary to pursue this topic in more detail, but the contents of this chapter provides a frame of reference for further study.*

THE NATURE OF THE SECONDARY SCHOOL AND THE SECONDARY SCHOOL STUDENT

One major reason for differences in serving the secondary school learning disabled student may be seen when the structure and organization of the secondary school is compared with that of the elementary school. There are wide variations throughout the nation, but in general the emphasis in elementary schools is on mastery of basic skills, while in secondary schools the emphasis is on subject content. Elementary school teachers are more likely to be educational "general-

*Although there are dozens of texts about learning disabilities, few systematically consider the teaching of learning disabled students at the secondary level in any great detail. Two such texts are recommended for those who have further interest in this area. The first, *The Learning Disabled Adolescent: Program Alternatives in the Secondary School* (Marsh, Gearheart, and Gearheart, 1978) was a major source of information for this chapter. The second, *Teaching the Learning Disabled Adolescent: Strategies and Methods* (Alley and Deshler, 1979) provides another useful source of information.

ists," with more emphasis on understanding child growth and development and more training in individualization of instruction. Secondary school educators are more likely to be "specialists" (for example, in history, biology, and literature) and tend to attempt to teach the entire class through use of the same general methods, assuming that students have mastered basic skills. In addition, in elementary school a child is more likely to spend most of the day with one teacher, while students at the secondary level often see a different teacher every hour, all day long.

As a result of the above differences, it would be difficult to apply the remedially oriented learning disability approaches in use in the elementary schools to the secondary schools, even if such were totally desirable. The resource room teacher has not just one teacher with whom to plan, but four or five, and many techniques that may work with an 8-year-old in third grade are basically unworkable with a 16-year-old in the 10th or 11th grade. In addition to these factors, secondary schools are usually much larger in size, and other complicating factors such as emphasis on departments, protection of departmental domain, and a demand for "scholarship" cause most learning disabled students a great deal of difficulty. Also, because secondary schools have recently been under a great deal of criticism for not demanding higher academic standards, it is easy to see why secondary school educators do not always welcome learning disabled students with open arms.

When teachers consider the characteristics of adolescence, efforts to serve secondary level learning disabled students take on an additional dimension of difficulty. Elementary and secondary schools are obviously different, and differences between the students enrolled at these two levels are equally obvious. The following description of differences between younger children and adolescents and the problems that are generated when adolescents have learning difficulties in school may provide valuable insight into the reasons for different emphases in secondary level learning disabilities programming.

Each [the young child and the adolescent] is a *Homo sapiens* who has moved through only part of the physical, social, and emotional sequence that leads to maturity, but in many ways the period of adolescence is quite different from earlier childhood (Powell and Frerichs, 1971). Dictionary definitions characterize adolescence as the period between puberty and maturity, but this leaves a great deal unsaid. The length of the period of adolescence varies throughout the world, with the Western world having a longer period of adolescence because of the lengthy time required in preparation for employment. Although adolescents have certain characteristics similar to those of younger children, we must focus on their unique interests, needs, abilities, and problems if we are to plan effective modified educational programs.

In addition to their general involvement with developing a workable self-concept and the stresses that sexual maturation may impose, there is, according to authorities such as Colemen (1971), an adolescent subculture, which has a value system quite different from that of adults. The adolescent usually is greatly influenced by the immediate peer group and by the larger peer subculture. This influence is often in direct conflict with the goals of parents and school authorities. In the case of secondary students who are achieving satisfactorily, the school may receive its share of attention, at least during class periods. Parents and teachers may be satisfied by acceptable grades, leaving the student to focus on what is immediately important in the remainder of his or her life. Life is segmented, and if academic requirements do not interfere too much with social requirements, this is an acceptable arrangement. Adolescents may feel that the most useful function of the school is to provide opportunities for varied social contact.

In the case of the secondary student who is not

learning effectively within the normal school framework, another picture emerges. There is little satisfaction in the inability to complete school assignments, and if teachers use ridicule or sympathy to handle their part of the relationship, this is likely to lead to loss of prestige in the peer subculture. One reaction (which is accepted by some peers) is to become the class clown. Another is to become very belligerent. These do not promote learning and often lead to other difficulties with school authorities, but may be of value within the peer subculture. In many states, it is possible to drop out of school with few, if any, complications or repercussions. In fact, if a student begins to be a behavior problem, this may be encouraged by school authorities. In some instances, if the school cannot or will not adapt or modify the school program, the dropout may simply be reacting to the "facts of life." The school is in effect saying, "We provide a number of different programs; you must select among these and conform to our structure." The student is saying, "You don't really have anything to offer me—at least anything I find of value."

Adolescents, particularly those who are unsuccessful in school and can see little value in what is offered, are most interested in the approval of their peers and may not be particularly future oriented. They are not interested in having more failure experiences and they find little need to attend school to please adults. They have not developed the attitude (accepted by many persons with more maturity) which holds that we must take some routine, uninteresting, and perhaps even unfair events in life to be able to benefit from the more positive elements. They are interested in the here-and-now, and if school has little immediate value, the best plan is to drop out.*

The end result of school differences and differences that may be generalized to the adolescent subculture is that teachers must modify their thinking as they plan for secondary school students with learning disabilities. As indicated in the introduction to this chapter, one main modification in planning has to do with the relative amount of time spent on remedial activities. The following descriptions of remediation and accomodation (or compensatory teaching) may be of value to provide a basis for further discussion of a framework for secondary school planning.

Remediation (remedial teaching) includes those activities, practices, and techniques that are directed toward a strengthening of specific areas of functioning that are viewed as weak or deficient. The focus is on academic and skill areas that may be identified and demonstrated to be weak or underdeveloped, according to some type of established criteria. This might mean remediation in reading, mathematics, spelling, or specific subskills in these areas or with respect to identified processing abilities. The underlying assumption is that if these "low" or "weak" areas can be improved so that they are more consistent with the student's other abilities, he or she will become a more proficient learner. Hopefully, more effective learning in one area may also carry over to other areas. Finally, it is assumed that if sufficient improvement takes place the regular school program may become more feasible.

In contrast, "*accommodation and compensatory teaching refer to a process whereby the learning environment of the student, either some of the elements or the total environment, is modified to promote learning. The focus is on changing the learning environment or the academic requirements so that the student may learn in spite of a fundamental weakness or deficiency*" (Marsh, Gearheart, and Gearheart, 1978, p. 85). Accommodation may involve the use of a number of techniques or procedures, including (1) modified instructional techniques, (2) modified academic requirements, (3) more flexible administrative practices, or (4) some combination of these and other

*From Gearheart, B. *Special Education for the 80's*, St. Louis: The C. V. Mosby Co., 1980, pp. 419-420.

The secondary level learning disabled student may often be misunderstood, but, with appropriate assistance, success and satisfactory achievement are possible. (From Marsh, G. E., Gearheart, C. K., and Gearheart, B. R. *The learning disabled adolescent: program alternatives in the secondary school.* St. Louis: The C. V. Mosby Co., 1978.)

modifications. The goal is to evolve a system in which the student may use existing strengths and experience genuine success. Older students quickly recognize contrived success; therefore academic accomplishments must be real.

The goal in accommodation or compensatory teaching is the same as in remediation; it is academic success. In many instances, the use of both remedial and accommodative/compensatory techniques may be needed. Accommodative and compensatory practices and procedures are the focus of the remainder of this chapter, for these are the "new" techniques, as compared to the primary emphasis of most elementary programs.

ACCOMMODATION AND COMPENSATORY TEACHING: A VARIETY OF PROCEDURES

It is important to understand that accommodation and compensatory teaching do not usually mean an alternative curriculum. Rather, they are a matter of applying, in a very individualized manner, a series of steps that make it possible for the learning disabled student to find success within the regular classroom whenever possible. All of these steps are not possible in all school settings and all are not necessary, or appropriate, with all students. *Individualized planning is the key to success and must be based on an evaluation of the student's strengths and weaknesses and the conditions (both positive and negative factors) that exist within the school environment.* The listing of factors that follow are condensed from a discussion of accommodation and compensatory teaching in *The Learning Disabled Adolescent: Program Alternatives in the Secondary School* (Marsh, Gearheart, and Gearheart, 1978, Chapter 5).

Special information and communication from "feeder" schools is particularly important for students with unusual learning needs. This applies to both the elementary schools that "feed" any one junior high school and the junior high schools that send students on to the senior high. In other areas of the curriculum, for example, competitive sports, the senior high school coaches certainly attempt to learn more about potential basketball or football talent and the junior high coaches provide information. This sharing of information is in the interests of the students involved and reflects a strong professional concern for the specialized area (football, basketball) in question. Special educators must provide information in the same manner, a practice that certainly is in the best interests of the students involved. This allows for planning and preparation for various types of accommodation and compensatory practices and permits the students to get off to a good start in the new school setting. The central administrative office for each school district should establish a procedure whereby this information is provided during the school year prior to the time when any learning disabled students will be enrolling in a new school, thus permitting time for the necessary planning.

Enrollment assistance from secondary level special education personnel and counselors can provide for enrollment of students with those teachers who have indicated an interest in working with the learning disabled and whose earlier efforts have indicated their ability to provide adapted programs. With the variety of electives that may be possible after the first year, assistance from school personnel who understand the unique academic requirements of various courses, plus the abilities and liabilities of individual learning disabled students, can be invaluable. The wrong courses, an overly heavy course load, or a teacher with little or no understanding of students with learning problems can make or break the school year.

Course equilibrium should grow out of the enrollment assistance just discussed. This is a matter of avoiding too many "heavy" courses during any one quarter or semester and, when possible, clustering courses so that a number of them are related. These procedures benefit most students, but the learning difficulties of the learning disabled student may make them particularly important for continued success. In some cases, in planning sessions with the student and his parents, it may be decided that an extra semester or an extra year may be required to finish school. Balancing courses and providing reasonable pacing through the school program is much better than repeated failures, even though it may take an extra year. *It is most important to assist the student to have continued success, particularly after he becomes old enough that he could legally drop out of school.*

Course substitution or supplantation may be required as the total secondary program is implemented. Substitution involves obtaining special permission for one course (usually one that requires, for example, less reading ability) to substitute for another in the core of required courses. Supplantation means that the learning disabilities teacher serves a direct teaching role within a special setting. In some states, this substitute course could be listed under the regular course title; in others, it would require special provisions to be counted toward graduation. In all instances, it should approximate as closely as possible the content of the course supplanted.

Modified or special texts may be used at times for a given subject. An increasing number of these are available, designed to meet the objectives of other basic texts (cover the same material and concepts) but with reduced complexity in reading material. This procedure works in a limited number of subject areas and requires teacher understanding and cooperation.

Special preparation for participation in regular classes provided in the resource setting may be one of the best ways to increase the chances that the learning disabled student will succeed in the secondary school. This special preparation is normally provided by the resource room teacher but requires the cooperation of regular classroom teachers. It includes many possible facets but emphasizes preparation for the aspects of the regular class that the student's disabilities or his underdeveloped basic skills make most difficult. Examples of such preparation include the following:

1. *Advance learning of technical vocabulary.* Ordinary reading is often a problem for the learning disabled student, but the technical vocabulary of areas such as biology and certain other required courses may become the proverbial straw that broke the camel's back. If the regular classroom teacher provides a list of specialized vocabulary ahead of time so that it can be approached on an individual or small group basis in the resource room, then the learning disabled student may be able to function with greater success in the regular class.
2. *Abstract concepts.* Like technical or specialized vocabulary, abstract concepts may be a serious roadblock to some students. This is a particularly difficult problem when the student must learn such concepts purely through reading. If this is the case and the resource teacher has sufficient information ahead of time, written material can be taped so that the student may receive the basic information in this manner. He may listen to the tape several times (if necessary) and the resource teacher can provide further explanation, using concrete materials. Then when the concept is considered in the regular class, the student can participate with much greater understanding.
3. *General class content preparation.* This type of advance preparation is effective but depends on having accurate information about course outlines, sequence of topics, and the like. The intent is to prepare the student ahead of time, usually

through oral consideration of what is to be taught, so that he may be better able to understand class lectures. This is not a matter of special, abstract concepts but rather a general conceptualization of the direction in which the course will proceed and the major goals of the instructor. Like all other such assistive measures, this requires close cooperation with the regular classroom teacher—one who is relatively secure and not reluctant to share such information with the special education teacher. The use of peer tutors has seemed to be of value in implementing this approach; they can help prepare the learning disabled student ahead of time and review materials and ideas after class. This procedure works, but requires a great deal of organization and coordination from the learning disabilities resource teacher.

4. *Study skills.* Study skills are a multifaceted concern and may include specific assistance to the student in such areas as notetaking, preparing for tests, use of the library, use of different reading rates for different types of reading, and techniques for taking both multiple-choice and essay tests. Certain of these skills can be taught in the resource room in small group instruction but some must be accomplished on an individual basis.

In composite, the preceding preparatory steps may assist the learning disabled student to function in the regular class, despite his disability. He is not likely to be an "A" or perhaps even a "B" student, but he may be able to learn and, if properly motivated (a crucial factor), to earn an average grade. Actually *earning* an acceptable grade may prove to be one of the most motivating factors to be found; thus a pattern of success may be established. This can be the real payoff for the special preparation and all the time that it required.

SECONDARY PROGRAMMING: A TUTORIAL EMPHASIS

In an article entitled "Secondary Special Education: A Practical Tutorial Approach for High School Students with Learning Disabilities," Wiens, a high school teacher in Ontario, Canada, describes an approach that contains most of the components that have been previously described in this chapter (Wiens, 1980, pp. 9-11). Wiens notes that his philosophy is to assist the student to use existing strengths so as to remain a part of the regular program to as great a degree as possible. He includes such activities as the teaching of study techniques, and test-taking skills. Wiens indicates that the resource room teacher must play a student-advocacy role, conduct ongoing in-service for members of the staff, assist the regular classroom teachers in behavior modification techniques, work with parents and community agencies, and provide a variety of additional support activities. Although some might not think of *tutorial* as being specifically different from *remedial,* Wiens' description of tutorial efforts as those including "multiple task analyses employing alternative means of instruction rather than . . . simple reteaching of material already presented in the regular class" (p. 11) aptly describes the philosophy of the procedures that have been outlined in this chapter. His report seems to indicate that some Canadian special educators have arrived at about the same conclusions regarding secondary programs for the learning disabled that have been reached in the United States.

Tutorial efforts as suggested by Wiens are primarily those carried out by the teacher. It is also possible that *peer* tutoring, under the direction of the teacher, may be quite valuable at the secondary level. Selection of tutors must be accomplished with care, and monitoring procedures must be established. When working effectively, peer tutoring can greatly multiply the efforts of the learning disabilities teacher and reduce the problem of the high cost of learning disabilities programming at the secondary level. It is certainly worth a try.

SPECIAL MODIFIED PROGRAMS

Although the ideal program for the learning disabled in secondary schools permits students to remain in regular classes (through adaptation and accommodation), some apparently require additional modifications. This may mean a program in which many of the basic courses are taught by learning disabilities teachers or in which other secondary teachers teach special class sections in which only learning disabled students are enrolled. This may be required for only part of the school day or may be a totally separate curriculum. Certain students may spend approximately half of the school day in a core program designed especially for them. This is usually a rather small group, perhaps 10 to 15 students, and may be taught by one teacher in a self-contained class setting. This requires special planning and the emphasis is usually on maximizing practical learning, with minimal remedial efforts. The manner of recording such courses on the high school transcript varies from school to school and from state to state. If the program is realistic and meaningful goals are established and met, these courses can usually apply toward graduation (accrediting agencies will usually accept them) but state education agencies vary in their acceptance of such programs.

Some of these modified curricula are similar in content to standard high school programs; others are designed to be more like the work-study programs used with some other handicapped students and therefore are quite different from standard programs. In some cases, these programs are part of some "alternative school" arrangement, although the alternative school is usually established for students other than the learning disabled. The manner in which work-study programs or the alternative school may be used to serve the learning disabled is considered in the following section.

Work-study programs

Work-study programs first received positive attention as apparently viable alternative secondary school programs for the educable mentally retarded. The fact that they had been used with students with less-then-average intellectual ability at first may have discouraged their use with the learning disabled, but this appears to have been at least partially overcome in the past few years. In one way or other, some type of strong vocational component seems to be used in many programs, and one that emphasizes the development of work skills on the job would seem to have obvious face validity. This is not to indicate that all learning disabled students plan to enter the work force on completion of high school or that they cannot be successful in college. Some find success in college programs, but a larger percentage probably go into post-high-school vocational programs or directly into the work force. Because of this, work-study programs have been implemented in a number of school districts and are often received with enthusiasm. In such programs, the student typically prepares for off-campus work assignments for a 1- or 2-year period (along with more academic pursuits) and then is placed on the job on a half-time basis for the last 1 to 2 years. Close monitoring is maintained on these selected job sites, and class sessions related to the job are used to share experiences and to attempt to develop a better understanding of topics such as job attitudes, withholding tax, insurance, social security, and unions. Further information and discussion related to these topics then become an integral part of the class content. Some work placements for learning disabled students may be similar to those for the educable mentally retarded, but, because of their higher level of intelligence, learning disabled students also find success in much higher-level employment. These higher-level work placements should be obtained whenever possible.

Students who are part of a work-study program usually continue to study both job-related areas of concern and various other subjects that should contribute to successful participation in adult society. These subjects might be related to government (the voting function, how individuals participate in the American form of democracy, and so forth), practical economic considerations, family-related courses, and applied mathematics. At times these are taught as a special class section by teachers who normally teach these subjects; in other instances they are taught by teachers of the learning disabled. In all cases, various adaptive procedures are used as required.

The variations in how work-study programs for the learning disabled are implemented are numerous. They relate to amount of time spent on the job, job location, when (at which grade) this on-the-job experience is initiated, which courses are taught by special education teachers and which by regular class teachers, whether the program is formally associated with outside agencies (for example, rehabilitation services), how grading is accomplished, how high school credits are assigned, type of diploma, and others. But no matter how these variables are worked out, many of these programs are best described as work-study or special vocational preparation programs, and, apparently, some of these programs are quite successful.

Alternative schools

Alternative schools were not organized for learning disabled adolescents, but in some communities they may be attended by a number of such students. Alternative schools were organized to be deliberately "different from" the traditional high school and thus to provide an alternative. These schools do not fit any set pattern except that they are nontraditional—*not* like the ordinary high school. Most were organized to attempt to keep dropouts in school, and, inasmuch as learning disabled students are at risk with respect to dropping out, some learning disabled students eventually find themselves enrolled in an alternative school as a sort of "last chance" type of enrollment.

Although I do not recommend the alternative school as the most desirable setting for most learning disabled adolescents (the best place is in the regular secondary school), sometimes it is the best *available* program. It may actually be for some learning disabled students the *best* program, because of unique individual needs. Two strengths of the alternative school are: (1) it is obviously different, a factor that is quite important motivationally to some students, and (2) the teachers tend to be accustomed to and comfortable with the idea of teaching in a nontraditional manner. As for this latter factor, the ability to be comfortable with nonstandard, nontraditional teaching procedures may be the major reason why some secondary school teachers cannot successfully teach learning disabled students. The alternative school should not be thought of as the best placement for learning disabled students simply because of their learning disabilities. However, if other factors such as behavioral difficulties are part of the reason why students are enrolled in alternative schools, this might be a viable placement for some learning disabled students.

SUMMARY

Educational practices and procedures for learning disabled students in the secondary schools must be considerably different from elementary programs because of differences in the organization and structure of the school and the needs and characteristics of the adolescents being served. This difference is a matter of emphasizing adaptation, accommodation, and compensatory teaching strategies, rather than remedial efforts. In such efforts, the learning environment is modified so as to assist the student to learn, despite fundamental weaknesses or deficiencies.

Accommodation and compensatory teaching include (but are not limited to) such elements as modification of instructional techniques, modification of academic requirements, and institution of more flexible administrative practices. Specifically this may mean course substitution or supplantation, use of special texts, special planning of schedules so as to balance "heavy" subjects, reduced course loads, and other similar procedures. One important facet of accommodation is special, advance preparation for the learning disabled student that may increase his likelihood of success in the regular classroom. This may include advance learning of technical vocabulary, individual instruction relating to abstract concepts, tutoring with regard to study skills, and any other assis-

High school students may seem very poised and self-assured, but the learning disabled adolescent has great need for specialized assistance. (From Marsh, G. E., Gearheart, C. K., and Gearheart, B. R. *The learning disabled adolescent: program alternatives in the secondary school.* St. Louis: The C. V. Mosby Co., 1978.)

tance that provides the student a "head start." The emphasis and intent of adaptation, accommodation, and compensatory efforts are to help the student remain in the regular class. This should be the initial goal in all student planning, but in some cases more modified, restrictive programs may be required.

The most common of the special-program emphases (for students who are not able to function successfully in regular classes, despite our best efforts) is some type of modified vocational-preparation program, with work-study efforts being among the more common. this program may be not too different from that planned for the educable mentally retarded, except that the learning disabled student often is able to undertake employment that requires a higher level of intelligence. However, the goals in relation to learning more about work habits, requirements of employers, and getting along with other employees, while in an environment that permits guidance, feedback (from employer and school supervisor), and the right to "fail," but benefit from such failure, are quite similar to those of other work-study programs. These programs may be integrated with a limited amount of more standard academic classes or may be a total program, depending upon individual needs.

The present focus of most secondary school programs for the learning disabled was developed after unsuccessful attempts to apply the elementary model. It is primarily a matter of different emphasis, and if this difference is understood, the innovative teacher (with administrative support) may find that a wide variety of techniques are effective. In all cases, it is important to complete a survey of existing programs and facilities, determine which teachers may be willing to attempt to modify their programs and teaching practices, and then build a program for each student, based on his needs and these available resources. Often the secondary level learning disabilities teacher may spend about half of his time working directly with students and the rest in arranging other program components and assisting regular classroom teachers.

REFERENCES AND SUGGESTED READINGS

Alley, G., and Deshler, D. *Teaching the learning disabled adolescent: strategies and methods.* Denver: Love Publishing Co., 1979.

Ausubel, D. P., and Ausubel, P. Cognitive development in adolescence. In Powell, M., and Frerichs, A. H. (Eds.) *Readings in adolescent psychology.* Minneapolis: Burgess Publishing Co., 1971.

Colella, H. V. Career development center: a modified high school for the handicapped, *Teaching Exceptional Children,* 1973, *5,* 110-118.

Colemen, J. S. The adolescent subculture and academic achievement. In Powell, M., and Frerichs, A. H. (Eds.) *Readings in adolescent psychology.* Minneapolis: Burgess Publishing Co., 1971.

Gearheart, B. *Special education for the '80s.* St. Louis: The C. V. Mosby Co., 1980.

Marsh, G., Gearheart, C., and Gearheart, B. *The learning disabled adolescent: program alternatives in the secondary school.* St. Louis: The C. V. Mosby Co., 1978.

Powell, M., and Frerichs, A. H. (Eds.) *Readings in adolescent psychology.* Minneapolis: Burgess Publishing Co., 1971.

Schloss, E. (Ed.) *The educators' enigma: the adolescent with learning disabilities.* San Rafael, Calif: Academic Therapy Publications, 1971.

Schweich, P. D. The development of choices—an educational approach to employment. *Academic Therapy,* 1975, *10,* 277-283.

Scranton, T., and Downs, M. Elementary and secondary learning disabilities programs in the U.S.: a survey. *Journal of Learning Disabilities,* 1975, *8,* 394-399.

Wiens, E. Secondary special education: a practical tutorial approach for high school students with learning disabilities, *Special Education in Canada,* 1980, *54*(2), 9-11.

Appendixes

appendix A

Pupil Behavior Rating Scale

The Pupil Behavior Rating Scale reprinted here first appeared in *Learning Disabilities: Educational Strategies* (Gearheart, 1973). It is an adaptation of a scale developed under a U.S. Public Health Service research grant and used in the Aurora Public Schools, Aurora, Colorado. Since 1973 it has appeared in other publications and has demonstrated its value in continued use. It is similar to other rating scales in use in the elementary schools and is to be completed by the classroom teacher. Children are "rated" in five major areas of learning and behavior in comparison to their classmates. Thus the scale is most effective after a teacher has worked with a group of children for several weeks or, preferably, several months.

Completion of this scale leads to an objectification of the classroom teacher's observations of children in the class; the student screening profile indicates relative performance in 5 major areas and 24 subareas. Low ratings on this scale *do not* indicate the presence of a learning disability. They do indicate that the pupil's performance should be further investigated and evaluated. The various possibilities that might be indicated by low ratings may be illustrated by the case of a first-grade child who was rated quite low in section I, auditory comprehension and listening, and section II, spoken language.

This girl appeared more capable in other areas of first-grade work than in reading and, in contrast to the low ratings in sections I and II, had high ratings in parts of section III, orientation, and all of section V, motor. Her school performance was erratic; that is, she did very well in some tasks and scored relatively low in others. In many ways she seemed to be a learning disabled child, perhaps one with auditory-perception problems. However, after completing the rating scale and noting the low scoring areas, her teacher discovered that she had been absent during the week in which the audiologist had completed hearing screening with her class. On referral it was learned that she had a borderline mild to moderate hearing loss, but because she was quite intelligent (a fact discovered by individual intelligence testing) she was able to compensate for her loss to a considerable extent, and it had not been discovered. It was also discovered that her hearing loss was slowly becoming more severe, but medical intervention helped reduce the loss and stopped the deterioration.

In this case the Pupil Behavior Rating Scale was a "failure" in discovering a learning disability but a success in assisting in educational assessment and (in this instance, medical) amelioration. The Pupil Behavior Rating Scale and others like it have been used most commonly in screening for children with learning disabilities, but in the process they have been highly valuable in providing a meaningful point of focus for further investigative efforts on behalf of children other than the learning disabled. Low scores on such scales indicate that teachers should look further (with certain children), and they tell where to focus the investigation.

PUPIL BEHAVIOR RATING SCALE*

Instruction manual

One of the most important techniques for diagnosis in learning disabilities is the Pupil Behavior Rating Scale. This scale is used to assess areas of behavior that cannot be measured by standardized group screening tests. Therefore your careful rating of individual pupils is necessary.

You are asked to rate each child on these five areas of learning and behavior:

I. Auditory comprehension and listening

In this section, you evaluate the pupil as to his ability to understand, follow, and comprehend spoken language in the classroom. Four aspects of comprehension of language activities are to be evaluated.

II. Spoken language

The child's oral speaking abilities are evaluated through the five aspects comprising this section. Use of language in the classroom and ability to use vocabulary and language in story form are basic to this ability.

III. Orientation

The child's awareness of himself in relation to his environment is considered in the four aspects of learning that make up this section. You are to rate the child on the extent to which he has attained time concepts, knowledge of direction, and concepts of relationships.

IV. Behavior

The eight aspects of behavior comprising this section relate to the child's manner of participation in the classroom. Self-discipline in relation to himself (i.e., ability to attend) as well as in relation to others is critical to your rating in this section.

V. Motor

The final section pertains to the child's balance, general coordination, and use of hands in classroom activities. Three types of motor ability are to be rated: General Coordination, Balance, and Manual Dexterity. Rate each type independently because a child may have no motor difficulties, only one type of difficulty, or any combination of those listed.

*Adapted from a project developed under Research Grant, USPHS Contract 108-65-42, Bureau of Neurological and Sensory Diseases.

Name ______________________ No. ____ School ______________________ Grade ____

Sex ____ Date ______________________ Teacher ______________________

PUPIL BEHAVIOR RATING SCALE*

1	2	3	4	5
I. Auditory comprehension and listening				
Ability to follow directions				
Always confused; cannot or is unable to follow directions	Usually follows simple oral directions but often needs individual help	Follows directions that are familiar and/or not complex	Remembers and follows extended directions	Unusually skillful in remembering and following directions
Comprehension of class discussion				
Always inattentive and/or unable to follow and understand discussions	Listens but rarely comprehends well; mind often wanders from discussion	Listens and follows discussions according to age and grade	Understands well and benefits from discussions	Becomes involved and shows unusual understanding of material discussed
Ability to retain orally given information				
Almost total lack of recall; poor memory	Retains simple ideas and procedures if repeated often	Average retention of materials; adequate memory for age and grade	Remembers procedures and information from various sources; good immediate and delayed recall	Superior memory for both details and content
Comprehension of word meanings				
Extremely immature level of understanding	Fails to grasp simple word meanings; misunderstands words at grade level	Good grasp of grade level vocabulary for age and grade	Understands all grade level vocabulary as well as higher level word meanings	Superior understanding of vocabulary; understands many abstract words
II. Spoken language				
Ability to speak in complete sentences using accurate sentence structure				
Always uses incomplete sentences with grammatical errors	Frequently uses incomplete sentences and/or numerous grammatical errors	Uses correct grammar; few errors of omission or incorrect use of prepositions, verb tense, pronouns	Above-average oral language; rarely makes grammatical errors	Always speaks in grammatically correct sentences

*Adapted from a project developed under Research Grant, USPHS Contract 108-65-42, Bureau of Neurological and Sensory Diseases.

Continued.

PUPIL BEHAVIOR RATING SCALE—cont'd

1	2	3	4	5
II. Spoken language—cont'd				
Vocabulary ability				
Always uses immature or improper vocabulary	Limited vocabulary including primarily simple nouns; few precise, descriptive words	Adequate vocabulary for age and grade	Above-average vocabulary; uses numerous precise descriptive words	High level vocabulary; always uses precise words to convey message; uses abstraction
Ability to recall words				
Unable to call forth the exact word	Often gropes for words to express himself	Occasionally searches for correct word but adequate for age and grade	Above-average ability; rarely hesitates on a word	Always speaks well; never hesitates or substitutes words
Ability to formulate ideas from isolated facts				
Unable to relate isolated facts	Has difficulty relating isolated facts; ideas are incomplete and scattered	Usually relates facts into meaningful ideas; adequate for age and grade	Relates facts and ideas well	Outstanding ability in relating facts appropriately
Ability to tell stories and relate experiences				
Unable to tell a comprehensible story	Has difficulty relating ideas in logical sequence	Average ability to tell stories	Above average; uses logical sequence	Exceptional ability to relate ideas in a logical meaningful manner
III. Orientation				
Promptness				
Lacks grasp of meaning of time; always late or confused	Poor time concept; tends to dawdle; often late	Average understanding of time for age and grade	Prompt; late only with good reason	Very skillful at handling schedules; plans and organizes well
Spatial orientation				
Always confused; unable to navigate around classroom or school, playground or neighborhood	Frequently gets lost in relatively familiar surroundings	Can maneuver in familiar locations; average for age and grade	Above-average ability; rarely lost or confused	Never lost; adapts to new locations, situations, places
Judgment of relationships: big, little; far, close; light, heavy				
Judgments of relationships very inadequate	Makes elementary judgments successfully	Average ability in relation to age and grade	Accurate judgments but does not generalize to new situations	Unusually precise judgments; generalizes them to new situations and experiences

PUPIL BEHAVIOR RATING SCALE—cont'd

1	2	3	4	5
III. Orientation—cont'd				
Learning directions				
Highly confused; unable to distinguish directions as right, left, north, and south	Sometimes exhibits directional confusion	Average; uses R vs L, N-S-E-W	Good sense of direction; seldom confused	Excellent sense of direction
IV. Behavior				
Cooperation				
Continually disrupts classroom; unable to inhibit responses	Frequently demands spotlight; often speaks out of turn	Waits his turn; average for age and grade	Cooperates well; above average	Cooperates without adult encouragement
Attention				
Is never attentive; very distractible	Rarely listens; attention frequently wanders	Attends adequately for age and grade	Above average; almost always attends	Always attends to important aspects; long attention span
Ability to organize				
Is highly disorganized; very slovenly	Often disorganized in manner of working; inexact, careless	Maintains average organization of work; careful	Above-average ability to organize and complete work; consistent	Always completes assignments in a highly organized and meticulous manner
Ability to cope with new situations: parties, trips, unanticipated changes in routine				
Becomes extremely excitable; totally lacking in self-control	Often overreacts; new situations disturbing	Adapts adequately for age and grade	Adapts easily and quickly with self-confidence	Excellent adaptation, utilizing initiative and independence
Social acceptance				
Avoided by others	Tolerated by others	Liked by others; average for age and grade	Well liked by others	Sought by others
Acceptance of responsibility				
Rejects responsibility; never initiates activities	Avoids responsibility; limited acceptance of role for age	Accepts responsibility; adequate for age and grade	Enjoys responsibility; above average; frequently takes initiative or volunteers	Seeks responsibility; almost always takes initiative with enthusiasm
Completion of assignments				
Never finishes, even with guidance	Seldom finishes, even with guidance	Average ability to follow through on assignments	Above-average ability to complete assignments	Always completes assignments without supervision

Continued.

PUPIL BEHAVIOR RATING SCALE—cont'd

1	2	3	4	5
IV. Behavior—cont'd				
Tactfulness				
Always rude	Usually disregards other's feelings	Average tactfulness; occasionally socially inappropriate	Above-average tactfulness; rarely socially inappropriate	Always tactful; never socially inappropriate
V. Motor				
General coordination: running, climbing, hopping, walking				
Very poorly coordinated; clumsy	Below-average coordination; awkward	Average coordination for age	Above-average coordination; does well in these activities	Exceptional ability; excels in this area
Balance				
Very poor balance	Below-average; falls frequently	Average balance for age; not outstanding but adequate equilibrium	Above average; does well in activities requiring balance	Exceptional ability; excels in balancing
Ability to manipulate utensils and equipment; manual dexterity				
Very poor in manual manipulation	Awkward in manual dexterity	Adequate dexterity for age; manipulates well	Above-average manual dexterity	Almost perfect performance; readily manipulates new equipment

STUDENT SCREENING PROFILE

Date of birth ____________

Name ______________________________ Sex _____ Date ____________

School ____________________ Grade or level _____ Teacher ____________

For office use only—do not write on this side

I. Auditory comprehension and listening

A. Ability to follow directions — A. ________
1 2 3 4 5

B. Comprehension of class discussion — B. ________
1 2 3 4 5

C. Ability to retain information — C. ________
1 2 3 4 5

D. Comprehension of word meanings — D. ________ TOTAL I ________
1 2 3 4 5

II. Spoken language

A. Ability to speak in sentences — A. ________
1 2 3 4 5

STUDENT SCREENING PROFILE—cont'd

II. Spoken language—cont'd

B. Vocabulary ability — B. ________
1 2 3 4 5

C. Ability to recall words — C. ________
1 2 3 4 5

D. Ability to formulate ideas — D. ________
1 2 3 4 5

E. Ability to tell stories — E. ________ — TOTAL II ________
1 2 3 4 5

III. Orientation

A. Promptness — A. ________
1 2 3 4 5

B. Spatial orientation — B. ________
1 2 3 4 5

C. Judgment of relationships — C. ________
1 2 3 4 5

D. Learning directions — D. ________ — TOTAL III ________
1 2 3 4 5

IV. Behavior

A. Cooperation — A. ________
1 2 3 4 5

B. Attention — B. ________
1 2 3 4 5

C. Ability to organize — C. ________
1 2 3 4 5

D. Ability to cope with new situations — D. ________
1 2 3 4 5

E. Social acceptance — E. ________
1 2 3 4 5

F. Acceptance of responsibility — F. ________
1 2 3 4 5

G. Completion of assignments — G. ________
1 2 3 4 5

H. Tactfulness — H. ________ — TOTAL IV ________
1 2 3 4 5

V. Motor

A. General coordination — A. ________
1 2 3 4 5

B. Balance — B. ________
1 2 3 4 5

C. Manipulative skills — C. ________ — TOTAL V ________
1 2 3 4 5

appendix B

Alaska Learning Disabilities Ranking Scale (ALDRS)

The Alaska Learning Disabilities Ranking Scale (ALDRS) was developed as part of an effort to provide an early identification and prevention program for children who would likely have academic problems in the primary grades without specific additional educational assistance. This was intended as a screening procedure that could easily be completed by a kindergarten or first-grade teacher without the expenditure of many hours of time and effort and without the need for expensive test materials. It has been in use in Anchorage, and it is hoped that it may be of use throughout Alaska, including rural villages.

The first part of this process, *Teacher Ranking,* provides for the identification, in rank order, of those children whom the teacher considers as "high risk." This requires that the teacher indicate the specific difficulties that children are having. This first step tends to eliminate a large majority of students from further consideration.

Part two, use of the *Individual Checklist,* involves a compilation of behaviors, skills, and preacademic tasks that are considered as highly important prerequisites for academic success in a typical first-grade class. This part encourages objective evaluation of discrete, specific skills that a child may or may not have mastered.

The third part, entitled *Letter Identification Test,* provides for an assessment of the child's already developed knowledge of the alphabet. The bottom half of the page is removed and used by the student, with the teacher recording responses on the remaining portion of the page.

ALASKA LEARNING DISABILITIES RANKING SCALE

School ______________________ Date ______________________

Teacher ______________________ Grade ______________________

No. of children in class ______________________ ______________________

I. Based on your professional judgment, please list those children in your class whose progress to date is such that you think they would *not* be likely to succeed in the regular first-grade program. Rank them in order of severity, beginning with the *most* severe case first. Please provide complete information for each child you identify.

II. State at least two specific reasons that you think a child will be likely not to succeed in grade one. State the *major interference* to the learning process *first*.

I. Name of child	Checklist score	Alpha. rec.	Sex (M or F)	Birthday	II. Specific reason(s) for identification
1.					
2.					
3.					
4.					
5.					

ALASKA LEARNING DISABILITIES RANKING SCALE (INDIVIDUAL CHECKLIST)

III. On completion of the preceding ranking scale, please complete a copy of the accompanying checklist for each child you identified. Complete every question for each child that you can answer from memory. After this take each checklist with unanswered questions and take the child aside and determine whether he/she has mastered those specific skills or behaviors. Please answer *all* questions.

Master score table

1 = 3%	6 = 20%	11 = 36%	16 = 53%	21 = 70%	26 = 86%
2 = 6	7 = 23	12 = 40	17 = 56	22 = 73	27 = 90
3 = 10	8 = 26	13 = 43	18 = 60	23 = 76	28 = 93
4 = 13	9 = 30	14 = 46	19 = 63	24 = 80	29 = 96
5 = 16	10 = 33	15 = 50	20 = 66	25 = 83	30 = 100

Student ______________________________ Birth date __________

Teacher ______________________________ Date __________

School ______________________ Raw score ________ Percentage ________

	Yes	No
1. Can this child count by rote to 10?	☐	☐
2. Can this child say the alphabet by rote?	☐	☐
3. When compared with his/her classmates, can this child listen attentively and follow oral directions without frequent repetitions or failure to complete them?	☐	☐
4. When shown a picture of a single, common object (an animal, building, utensil, etc.) and asked to name it and use it in a complete sentence, can the child do so as well as the majority of his/her classmates?	☐	☐
5. When shown a story picture (for example a picture from a basal reader), can the child make a story of at least three sentences to describe it?	☐	☐
6. Can this child match any eight randomly selected pairs of lowercase letters of the alphabet? (For example, b, d, g, p, q, m, n, w and w, q, n, b, m, g, d, p.)	☐	☐
7. Does this child demonstrate the ability to imitate letter sounds when requested to do so by the teacher?	☐	☐
8. Does this child know two of the three following facts: first and last name, address, and telephone number?	☐	☐
9. When shown the eight basic colors (red, yellow, blue, green, orange, purple, black, brown), can the child identify at least seven of them?	☐	☐
10. Can this child present from memory the nursery rhymes, songs, and stories learned in class as well as the majority of his classmates?	☐	☐
11. Does this child demonstrate a level of understanding comparable to the majority of his/her classmates for the concept of position and direction? (For example, can he/she describe the position of people and objects in the room and describe the location of his home or how to get there?)	☐	☐
12. Can this child grasp a pencil properly in a three-finger position preparatory to writing or drawing?	☐	☐
13. Can this child print his/her first name from memory?	☐	☐

ALASKA LEARNING DISABILITIES RANKING SCALE (INDIVIDUAL CHECKLIST)—cont'd

	Yes	No
14. Can this child reproduce a circle, square, and triangle from visual stimulus without serious distortion? (The triangle and square should possess three and four clearly defined sides and angles, respectively.)	☐	☐
15. Can this child write letters, numbers, and words without frequent reversals and/or rotations?	☐	☐
16. When presented with any 12 lowercase letters of the alphabet, can this child correctly identify at least 11 of them?	☐	☐
17. Can this child recognize at least two sight words (for example, red, yellow), excluding his name?	☐	☐
18. When utilizing concrete objects (blocks, tokens, rods, etc.), does this child demonstrate an understanding of the concepts of "one less" and "one more"?	☐	☐
19. Can this child manipulate concrete objects to add and subtract from 1 to 5?	☐	☐
20. Can this child match and recognize numerals and sets out of sequence from 1 to 10?	☐	☐
21. Does this child wash his/her hands and face properly without assistance (uses soap, uses and disposes of towel in wastepaper basket, etc.)?	☐	☐
22. Does this child usually put on and take off his/her coat, boots, etc. without assistance?	☐	☐
23. Is this child responsible for his/her own belongings (hangs up his/her coat, keeps his work area clean, etc.)?	☐	☐
24. Does this child display the ability to function independently outside the classroom (goes directly to get a drink and returns promptly, carries a message, etc)?	☐	☐
25. Is this child's behavior average or better than the majority of his/her peers (minimal crying, pouting, withdrawal, and temper outbursts)?	☐	☐
26. Does this child demand or require *only* his fair share of attention (no more than the majority of his classmates)?	☐	☐
27. When compared with his/her classmates, would this child's behavior be termed typical in regard to hyperactivity (inability to sit still) and distractibility (inability to attend the task at hand)?	☐	☐
28. When compared with his/her classmates, does this child exhibit relatively consistent performance from day to day and/or subject area to subject area?	☐	☐
29. Does this child demonstrate the ability to cooperate with peers and follow rules?	☐	☐
30. Does this child display an understanding of the concepts of left and right equal to his/her classmates?	☐	☐

TOTAL NUMBER OF YES RESPONSES ________

IV. After answering the 30 questions on the checklist, count the number of Yes responses. This is the raw score; write this on the first page of the checklist. To obtain the percentage score, use the table on the first page; enter this in the appropriate place. The lower the percentage, the more likely it is that this child will experience problems during the first grade and should be considered for special intervention.

LIST OF MATERIALS NEEDED TO COMPLETE CHECKLIST

The following numbers correlate with the items on the checklist. (In order to assess item No. 4 you need the item described after No. 4 below.)

4. Picture of one common object (example: animal, vehicle)
5. Picture depicting an activity that would encourage use of sentences for description
6. Two sets of letters for matching
9. Crayons for identification of eight basic colors
14. Circle, triangle, and square drawn on paper to provide the stimulus for the child to reproduce with a pencil or crayon
16. Use alphabet recognition test for this item
18. Blocks, tokens, rods
19. Blocks, tokens, rods
20. Set of cards with numerals 1 to 10 on one side and sets on the other

Stopwatch for letter identification test

ALASKA LEARNING DISABILITIES RANKING SCALE
LETTER IDENTIFICATION TEST

Cut along the dotted line and present to the student the student letter identification list. Determine the number of letters he/she can correctly identify in a timed *1-minute* interval. If the child cannot identify a letter in 5 seconds, instruct him/her to omit it and proceed to the next one. Should he/she identify all the letters on the page before the time limit is expended, instruct him/her to continue by proceeding again from the first line.

Use the following teacher's letter identification recording score sheet to score and record each student's performance. Please list all requested information for each student tested.

Student's name ______________________ Number correct (1 min). ________

Teacher's name ______________________

ALASKA LEARNING DISABILITIES RANKING SCALE
Teacher's letter identification recording and score sheet

n	w	y	k	d	o	a	s	x	z	(10)
f	b	e	l	p	c	v	m	j	p	(20)
t	u	i	r	g	h	n	w	y	k	(30)
d	o	a	s	x	z	f	b	e	l	(40)
p	c	v	m	j	q	t	u	i	r	(50)

- -

ALASKA LEARNING DISABILITIES RANKING SCALE
Student letter identification list

n	w	y	k	d	o	a	s	x	z	(10)
f	b	e	l	p	c	v	m	j	p	(20)
t	u	i	r	g	h	n	w	y	k	(30)
d	o	a	s	x	z	f	b	e	l	(40)
p	c	v	m	j	q	t	u	i	r	(50)

appendix **C**

Chart of normal development of motor and language abilities

This chart of developmental milestones in the areas of gross and fine motor abilities and language development may be of value in conceptualizing the manner in which learning normally progresses. It is important to remember that the developmental milestones represented here are *averages* and that some variation from average development is normal. It would be an error to interpret normal variations in growth as indicative of handicaps, but when a child varies significantly from these milestones, additional investigation should be undertaken.

Age	Motor (gross and fine)	Language (understood and spoken)
0-1 yr	Sits without support Develops one- and two-arm control Crawls Stands Walks with some aid Begins to indicate hand preference Pincer grasp develops Loses sight of object and searches Transfers objects from one hand to other	Responds to sound (loud noises, mother's voice, familiar or unfamiliar) Turns to sources of sound Babbles vowel and consonant sounds Responds with vocalization after adult speaks Imitates sounds Responds to words such as "up," "hello," "bye-bye," and "no" if adults use gestures
1-2 yr	Begins scribbling in repetitive, circular motions Holds pencil or crayon in fist Walks unaided Steps up onto or down from low objects Seats self Turns pages several at a time Throws small objects Turns doorknobs	Begins to express self with one word and gradually increases to 50 words Uses several successive words to describe events Understands phrases such as "Bring it here," "Take this to Daddy." Uses "me" or "mine" to indicate possession Can identify parts of the body such as eyes, ears, foot, tummy Is able to follow simple two-part directions such as "Come here and bring the ball."

Adapted from National Institute of Neurological Diseases and Stroke. *Learning to talk: speech, hearing and language problems in the preschool child.* Washington, D.C.: U.S. Department of Health, Education, and Welfare, 1969; Cratty, B. J. *Perceptual and motor development in infants and children.* New York: The Macmillan Co., 1970; *Developmental characteristics of children and youth,* compiled for the Association for Supervision and Curriculum Development, 1975; and *Mainstreaming preschoolers: children with learning disabilities.* Washington, D.C.: U.S. Department of Health, Education, and Welfare, 1978.

Age	Motor (gross and fine)	Language (understood and spoken)
2-3 yr	Begins a variety of scribbling patterns in various positions on paper Holds crayon or pencil with fingers and thumbs Turns pages singly Demonstrates stronger preference for one hand Is able to manipulate clay or dough Runs forward well Can stand on one foot Can kick Is able to walk on tiptoe	Can identify pictures and objects when they are named Joins words together in several word phrases Asks and answers questions Enjoys listening to storybooks Understands and uses "can't," "don't," "no" Is frustrated when spoken language is not understood Refers to self by name
3-4 yr	Pounds nails or pegs successfully Copies circles and attempts crosses such as + Runs Balances and hops on one foot Pushes, pulls, steers toys Pedals and steers tricycle Can throw balls overhead Can catch balls that are bounced Jumps over, runs around obstacles	Uses words in simple sentence form such as "I see my book." Adds "s" to indicate plural Can relate simple accounts of previous experiences Can carry out a sequence of simple directions Begins to understand time concepts such as "Tomorrow is the day we'll go to the store." Understands comparatives such as bigger, smaller, closer Understands relationships indicated by "because" or "if"
4-5 yr	Copies crossed lines and/or squares Can cut on a line Can print a few letters of the alphabet Can walk backward Is able to jump forward successfully Is able to walk up and down stairs alternating feet Draws human figures including head and stick arms and legs	Can follow several unrelated commands Can listen to longer stories but often confuses them when retelling Asks "why," "how," and "what for" questions Understands comparatives such as "fast," "faster," and "fastest" Uses complex sentences such as "I like to play with my tricycle in and out of the house." Uses relationship words such as "because" or "so" Generally speech is intelligible; however, there may be frequent mispronunciations
5-6 yr	Can run on tiptoe Is able to walk on balance beam Skips using alternate feet Is able to jump rope May be able to ride two-wheel bicycle Can roller skate Copies triangles, name, numerals Has firmly established handedness Cuts and pastes large objects or designs Includes more detail in drawing humans	Generally communicates well with family and friends Spoken language still has errors of subject-tense agreement and irregular past-tense verbs Is able to take turns in conversation Receives and gives information With exceptions, use of grammar matches that of the adults in family and neighborhood
7-10 yr	Continued development and refinement of small muscles such as those used in writing, drawing, and handling tools Masters physical skills necessary for game playing Physical skills become important in influencing status in peer group and self-concept	Develops ability to understand that words and pictures are representational of real objects Understands most vocabulary used; however, continues to learn and use new words Begins to use language aggressively Can verbalize similarities and differences Uses language to exchange ideas Uses abstract words, slang, and often profanity
11-15 yr	Adolescent growth spurts begin May experience uneven growth resulting in awkwardness or clumsiness Continued improvement in motor development and coordination	Has good command of spoken and written language Uses language extensively to discuss feelings and other more abstract ideas Uses abstract words discriminately and selectively Uses written language extensively

Glossary

acalculia Loss of ability to calculate. Inability to successfully manipulate number symbols.

agnosia Receives information but is unable to comprehend or interpret it. Inability to recognize objects, events, sounds, etc., even though the sense organ is not basically defective. Usually a specific rather than general agnosia as in:

- **auditory agnosia** Cannot differentiate between various common sounds.
- **form agnosia** Form discrimination difficulty, for example, geometric forms.
- **tactile agnosia** Does not recognize common objects by touch alone.
- **visual agnosia** Difficulty in recognition of objects or people, even though they should be easily recognized (old acquaintances, etc.).

agraphia Cannot relate kinesthetic pattern (required motor movements) to visual image of a word or letter.

alexia Loss of ability to read or an initial inability to learn to read because of brain damage.

alternative school An academically, remedially, or skill-oriented program for adolescents that is markedly different from traditionally organized secondary schools.

anomia Difficulty in recalling names of persons, objects, etc.; difficulty in nouns.

anoxia Deficiency in oxygen carried by the bloodstream resulting in deficiency of available oxygen to any particular part of the body so affected.

aphasia Loss of ability to use language symbols, as in speech.

- **auditory aphasia** Cannot comprehend spoken words (also may be called *receptive aphasia* or *receptive dysphagia*).
- **expressive aphasia** Cannot speak, even though he knows what he wants to say.

May also include inability to express language through signs. Some authorities also list a number of other specific types of aphasia.

apraxia Loss or partial loss of ability to move purposefully; not the same as paralysis or cerebral palsy. (Sometimes called *dyspraxia.*)

assessment A process employing mental, social, psychological, or educational tests and observations to determine an individual's strengths and weaknesses.

astereognosis Object, or form, agnosia.

asymbolia Cannot understand or use symbols, as in chemistry or mathematics.

ataxia Condition in which central nervous system deficits lead to incoordination in motor activity —jerky movements, balance problems, and sometimes speech and writing problems.

audiometer A hearing screening device, either a pure-tone audiometer or a speech threshold audiometer.

auditory association Ability to relate concepts presented orally.

auditory closure Ability to recognize the whole from the presentation of a partial auditory stimulus.

auditory discrimination Ability to distinguish auditorily between slight differences in sounds.

auditory memory Ability to recall words, digits, etc., in a meaningful manner; includes memory of meaning.

auditory perception Ability to receive sounds accurately and to understand what they mean.

auditory reception Ability to derive meaning from orally presented material.

auditory sequential memory Ability to reproduce a sequence of auditory stimuli.

body concept In general the same as body image; may mean how one *thinks* he looks.

body image Combination of knowledge of how one's own body and position in space relates to other objects in space and how one's movements affect that relationship.

brain damage Any actual structural (tissue) damage resulting from any cause or causes. This means verifiable damage, not neurological performance that is indicative of damage.

brain dysfunction Term used to describe a suspected malfunctioning of the brain.

brain injured Refers to one who before, during, or after birth has received an injury to the brain. The injury can be the result of trauma or infections. Usually affects learning.

central nervous system (CNS) That part of the nervous system to which the sensory impulses are transmitted and from which motor impulses pass out; in vertebrates, the brain and spinal cord.

cerebral dominance Assumption that one cerebral hemisphere generally leads the other in control of bodily movements. In most individuals, the left side of the brain controls language and is considered the dominant hemisphere.

cerebrum Major portion of the brain—the two cerebral hemispheres considered together.

channels of communication The sensory-motor pathways through which language is transmitted (e.g., auditory-vocal, visual-motor, among other possible combinations).

closure Ability to recognize a whole or gestalt, especially when one or more parts of the whole are missing or when the continuity is interrupted by gaps.

cognition Activities or mental behavior that are *not* feeling or affectively oriented. Analytical, or logical, thinking, as opposed to emotional thinking, is cognitive.

cognitive strategies Those strategies by which an individual monitors the internal process of attending, thinking, and remembering.

cognitive theory That which is characterized by attention to perception, problem solving, information processing, and understanding.

conservation In Piaget's theory, the ability to retain a concept of area, mass, length, etc., when superficial changes are made in the appearance of an object or scene.

contingency contracting Use of an agreement indicating positive and negative consequences for specific behaviors. Usually established between the teacher and the student, and a major type of behavior modification.

continuum of educational services The full range of services available for handicapped students. The range extends from full-time residential placement, which is the most restrictive, to full-time placement in regular classrooms, which is least restrictive.

Council for Exceptional Children A national professional organization for all who work for and with gifted and handicapped persons. Included within the broad organization are divisions for each area of exceptionality.

decoding The receptive habits in the language process (e.g., sensory acuity, awareness, discrimination, and vocabulary comprehension).

developmental aphasia Impairment or loss of the ability to comprehend written or verbal language.

directionality Awareness of laterality (the two sides of the body) and verticality (vertical axis awareness), as well as the ability to translate this discrimination within the organism to similar discrimination among objects in space.

discrimination Process of detecting differences between and/or among stimuli.

- **auditory discrimination** Identification of likeness and differences between sounds.
- **visual discrimination** Ability to recognize differences between similar but slightly different forms or shapes, as in alphabetic letters.

disinhibition Lack of ability to refrain from response to what is perceived, often resulting in hyperactivity and distractibility.

dissociation Inability to integrate, to see the "wholeness" of objects. Tendency to see small segments without relation to the total configuration of which they are a part.

distractibility Tendency to be easily drawn away from any task at hand and to focus on extraneous stimulus of the moment.

dyscalculia Synonymous with acalculia for many authorities. May mean partial or less severe acalculia.

dysgraphia Inability to express ideas in writing, even though motor ability is present.

dyskinesia Poor coordination, clumsy, inappropriate movements in an individual without detectable cerebral palsy, etc.

dyslexia Reading difficulty not attributable to ordinary causes; generally, but not always, attributed to some sort of brain impairment. Though some would make a case for differences in meaning between alexia and dyslexia, in practice they are often used synonymously. Some authorities would delineate as many as eight to ten types of dyslexia, including congenital, constitutional, affected, and partial.

dysphasia For the most part, accepted as synonymous with aphasia, although some authorities prefer one term to the other.

dyspraxia Generally accepted as the same as apraxia, at least in common usage.

echolalia Meaningless "echoing" or repetition of words, or sometimes of sounds.

electroencephalograph (EEG) Records electrical currents (or *brain waves*), which are developed in the cerebral cortex as a result of brain functioning.

encoding The expressive habits in the language process (i.e., response formation including word selection, syntax, grammar, and the actual motor production of the response).

engram Pattern, or trace, that is (theoretically) left in the brain after a mental process takes place.

etiology The origin, or cause, of a particular condition; usually used in relation to an unusual or abnormal condition.

expressive language skills Skills required to produce language for communication with other individuals. Speaking and writing are expressive language skills.

feedback The sensory or perceptual report of the result of a somatic, social, or cognitive behavior.

figure-ground Tendency of one part of a perceptual configuration to stand out clearly while the remainder forms a background.

figure-ground disturbance Inability to discriminate a figure from its background.

finger agnosia Inability to recognize the name or identify the individual fingers of one's own hand.

gestalt A term used to express any unified whole whose properties cannot be derived by adding the parts and their relationships; an entity that is more than the sum of its parts.

global Perceived as a whole without attempt to distinguish separate parts or functions.

grammatic closure Ability to make use of the redundancies of oral language in acquiring automatic habits for handling syntax and grammatical inflections.

gustatory Pertaining to taste.

handedness Refers to hand preference of an individual.

hand-eye coordination Ability of the hand and eye to perform effectively together.

hemispherical dominance Refers to the fact that one cerebral hemisphere generally leads the other in control of body movement, resulting in the preferred use of left or right (laterality).

high-risk children General term used to describe children who, because of various environmental deficiencies, delayed normal development, or other factors, may experience a more-than-normal likelihood of future handicaps.

hyperactivity Unusual activity, particularly for an individual of a given age in a given setting. Usually also denotes disruptive activity.

hyperkinetic One who typically exhibits hyperactivity.

hypoactivity A condition characterized by lethargy and lack of activity. Opposite of hyperactivity.

hypoglycemia A condition in which there is an abnormally low glucose content in the blood.

imagery Representation of images.

impulsivity Initiation of sudden action without sufficient forethought or prudence.

incoordination Lack of coordination.

individualized education program A written plan of instruction that includes a statement of the child's present level of functioning, specific areas needing special services, annual goals, short-term objectives, and method of evaluation. Required for every child receiving special educational services under the conditions of PL 94-142.

inner language The process of internalizing and organizing experiences so that they may be represented by symbols. It is the language in which an individual thinks.

interneurosensory That which involves more than one system in the brain.

intraneurosensory That which involves only one system in the brain.

itinerant services Those services provided by specialists who travel among schools, homes, hospitals. The services may include academic instruction, counseling, or therapy.

itinerant specialists Those who travel from school to the home or hospital to provide special services for the handicapped.

juvenile delinquency Law-breaking behavior, as defined by statute, on the part of minors.

kinesthetic The sense by which muscular motion, position, or weight are perceived; thought of as being in muscles and joints.

language The ability to communicate thoughts and feelings through sounds (primarily words), gestures, and written symbols.

laterality The internal awareness of the two sides of one's body. A sense of sidedness that includes the tendency to use one hand for specific tasks.

learning A process through which an individual develops or acquires knowledge, skills, or attitudes.

learning disabilities see **learning disabled.**

learning disabled A general term used to describe individuals who demonstrate a discrepancy between the expected level of achievement and their actual achievement. Usually implied is lower-than-average ability to understand or use spoken and written language.

least restrictive environment A concept dictating that a handicapped student should be educated within the environment that is most like that in which he or she would be educated if *not* handicapped. In laws and legal opinions, this refers to the least restrictive environment in which an *appropriate* or *effective* educational program can be provided. For example, a child in a wheelchair, with no intellectual disabilities, should be educated with peers in a regular classroom with physical accommodations made for the wheelchair.

locomotion Movement from one location to another (walking, crawling, rolling, etc.).

mainstreaming The practice of providing handicapped persons an education with their nonhandicapped peers to the greatest extent possible.

medulla oblongata Part of the brain immediately above the spinal cord.

megavitamin Refers to various types of treatment consisting of large doses of vitamins.

memory The ability to store and retrieve upon demand previously experienced sensations and perceptions, even when the stimulus that originally evoked them is no longer present; also referred to as imagery and recall.

memory span Degree of immediate recall, often tested by determining the number of unrelated numbers, words, or other symbols that can be immediately remembered.

metabolism A general term referring to all the chemical processes and changes involving cells and tissue that maintain life.

midbrain Part of the brain immediately above the pons.

minimal brain dysfunction A general term referring to a diagnosed or suspected mulfunction in the central nervous system. Usually related to children who may also be called learning disabled.

mixed (cerebral) dominance Name applied to the theory that certain learning disorders, particularly language functions, are caused in part by the fact that neither side (hemisphere) of the brain is dominant. (See *Cerebral dominance.*)

mixed laterality or lateral confusion Tendency to perform some acts with a right-side preference and others with a left, or the shifting from right to left for certain activities.

modality The pathways through which an individual receives information and thereby learns. The modality concept postulates that some individuals learn better through one modality than through another. For example, a child may receive data better through the visual modality than through the auditory modality.

modeling Providing a demonstration of a particular behavior.

movigenics The motor-based curriculum developed by Barsch for children with specific learning disorders.

multisensory A term referring to training or teaching procedures that simultaneously utilize more than one sensory modality. Often means the use of three or more modalities.

neurological examination An examination of sensory or motor responses, especially of the reflexes, to determine presence of localized impairments of the nervous system.

neurologically impaired A general term referring to a number of conditions that result from an injury to or a dysfunction of the central nervous system.

neuron Basic unit of the nervous system.

neurophrenia Refers to the behavioral symptoms resulting from central nervous system impairment.

ontogeny How an individual organism develops—its developmental history.

operant conditioning A type of behavior modification in which rewards are provided or withheld based on the child's actions.

ophthalmologist A physician who has additional training in treatment of diseases of the eyes. Can prescribe medication or perform surgery in addition to measuring refraction and prescribing lenses.

optometrist A nonmedical person trained in the functioning of the eyes. Can measure refraction and prescribe lenses.

overattention The act of focusing attention on one particular object or task and the seeming inability to break the focused attention.

patterning Specific set, or sequence, of movement exercises prescribed (particularly in the Doman-Delacato method) to treat learning problems.

perception Mechanism through which the organism recognizes sensory input, or information. This involves an ability to differentiate between various similar but different sensory stimuli.

perceptual constancy Ability to accurately perceive the invariant properties of objects (shape, position, size, etc.) in spite of the variability of the impression these objects make on the senses of the observer.

perceptual disorders Inability to interpret or organize information received through any one or combination of the senses.

perceptual-motor approaches Those approaches to learning disabilities that focus on the interaction of perception and motor activities. Most common of the perceptual areas utilized are visual, auditory, kinesthetic, and tactual.

perseveration Continuing with a particular response after it is no longer appropriate. Inability to shift from one center of focus to another. (Note that this is not like *echolalia* because in perseveration the first response may well have been appropriate.)

phylogeny Evolutionary development of an entire species. (Contrast with *ontogeny.*)

pneumoencephalogram Result of taking an electroencephalogram after first injecting gas into the ventricular spaces of the brain.

pons Portion of the brain immediately above the medulla oblongata.

preliminary review Refers to the introductory or first examination of the information collected regarding a child experiencing some difficulty in school.

proprioceptor Nerve ending that relays the perception of the movement or position of the body; found in the ear, muscles, tendons, and joints.

psychoeducational diagnostician A specialist who diagnoses and evaluates a child who is having difficulty in learning. A variety of psychological and educational testing instruments are used.

psycholinguistics The field of study that blends aspects of two disciplines, psychology and linguistics, to examine the total picture of the language process.

psychomotor Pertaining to the motor effects of psychological processes. Psychomotor tests are tests of motor skill that depend on sensory or perceptual-motor coordination.

psychoneurological learning disabilities Refers to learning problems that are related to central nervous system dysfunctions.

receptive language Language that is spoken or written by others and received by the individual. The receptive language skills are listening and reading.

referral The process of informing the appropriate specialist(s) about an individual for the purpose of collecting further information and considering the possible need for special educational services.

reinforcer Reward that increases the likelihood of a behavior being repeated. May be food, free time, or other activity.

residential school A facility in which an exceptional individual resides for 24 hours each day. The mentally retarded and mentally ill may at times need this type of service.

resource room A service delivery model characterized by the provision of assistance to a child by a specialist for some portion of the school day. The room in which this assistance takes place is usually referred to as the resource room.

resource teacher A specialist who works with children with learning problems and acts as a consultant to other teachers, providing materials and methods to help children who are having difficulty within the regular classroom. The resource teacher may work from a centralized resource room within a school where appropriate materials are housed.

reversal A transposition of letters or other symbols.

revisualization Ability to retrieve a visual image of a letter or word that is heard from one's memory so that it can be written.

right-left disorientation Inability to distinguish right from left; having no awareness of directionality.

rigidity Maintaining an attitude or behavioral set when it is no longer appropriate.

rotations The turning around of letters in a word; for example, *p* for *d*.

sensorimotor A term applied to the combination of the input of sense organs and the output of motor activity. The motor activity reflects what is happening to the sensory organs such as the visual, auditory, tactual, and kinesthetic.

sequential development A step-by-step plan of development wherein one skill is built upon another.

shaping A procedure of reinforcing responses resembling the desired one, providing reinforcement for increasingly closer approximations, until the final desired response is attained.

soft neurological signs Behavioral symptoms that suggest possible minimal brain injury in the absence of gross or obvious neurological abnormalities.

spatial orientation Awareness of space around the person in terms of distance, form, direction, and position.

special class Class organized, usually by a particular diagnostic label (such as emotionally disturbed or learning disabled), that has a full-time teacher and in which the students receive most of their instruction. Students are integrated into the regular class for only short periods of time or not at all.

special day school Provides day-long educational experiences for children. Often private; may be limited to one handicap, or may accept children with various handicaps.

specific language disability A term usually applied to those who find it very difficult to learn to read and spell but who are otherwise intelligent and usually learn arithmetic readily. More recently, this term has been applied to any language deficit—oral, visual, or auditory.

splinter skills Highly specific isolated physical skills that develop to satisfy academic demands that lie beyond a child's regular skill development.

staffing A term commonly used to describe an officially scheduled meeting of various concerned persons regarding the placement or education of a particular child.

Strauss syndrome The cluster of symptoms characterizing the brain-injured child; includes hyperactivity, distractibility, and impulsivity.

strephosymbolia Reversal in perception of left-right order especially in letter or word order; twisted symbols.

syndrome Characteristic grouping, or pattern, of symptoms that usually occur in a particular disability.

tactile Pertaining to the sense of touch; also *tactual.*

tactile perception Ability to interpret and give meaning to sensory stimuli that are experienced through the sense of touch.

verbal expression Ability to express one's concepts verbally.

visual acuity How well one sees. Can refer to close or far vision as well as clarity in distinguishing various characteristics.

visual association The organizing process by which one is able to relate concepts presented visually.

visual closure Ability to identify a visual stimulus from an incomplete visual presentation.

visual discrimination Ability to visually discern similarities and differences.

visual fusion Coordination of the separate images received through the two eyes into one image.

visual memory Ability to retain and recall what is seen.

visual motor Ability to relate visual stimuli to motor responses in an appropriate way.

visual-motor coordination Ability to coordinate vision with the movements of the body or parts of the body.

visual perception The identification, organization, and interpretation of sensory data received by the individual through the eyes.

visual reception Ability to gain meaning from visual symbols.

visual sequential memory Ability to reproduce sequences of visual items from memory.

visuomotor model Term used to describe the manner in which higher-level intellectual abilities develop from lower-level motor systems. Conceptualized by Gerald Getman.

Index

A

Abstract, descriptive, 254
Abstract concepts, 264
Academic functioning, measures of, 36-37
Accommodation, 261, 262
Accommodation and compensatory teaching, 263-265
  course equilibrium, 263
  course substitution, 264
  enrollment assistance, 263
  individualized planning, 263
  modified or special texts, 264
  special information, 263
  special preparation, 264-265
Acquiring expressive auditory language, 145
Acquiring receptive language, 144
Adaptive behavior, 36
Advance learning of technical vocabulary, 264
Agranoff, B., 174
AKT approach, 135
Alaska Learning Disabilities Ranking Scale (ALDRS), 22, 280-285
Alertness, levels of, 87
Allen, K., 194
Allen, R., 172
Allergic tension-fatigue syndrome, 106
Allergy, 106
  from food and food additives, 175
Alternative school, 266, 267, 268
American Association on Mental Deficiency (AAMD), 35-36
American Psychiatric Association, 101, 104
Animal brain research, 181-182
Antiepileptic drugs, 170
Apples, bananas, and candy approach, 138-139
Applied behavior analysis, 199
Arithmetic, 237-249
  factors that affect, 237-238
  teaching approaches, 238-247
Arithmetic disabilities, 237-247
Assessment of Children's Language Comprehension (ACLC), 37-38
Assessment procedures
  how influenced by P.L. 94-142, 32-33
  planned behavioral observation in, 41
  tests used in, 33-41
Assessment process, 19-25
  parent permission for, 23, 33
Atkinson, R., 174
Attention Deficit Disorder, 104
Attitudes, 58-59
Audiologist, 168
Auditory closure, 162
Auditory Discrimination Test (Wepman), 38
Auditory dyslexia, 155-156
Auditory-integration system, 84
Auditory language, 254
Auditory learners, 156
Auditory perceptual problems, 15
Auditory reception, 162
Auditory sequential memory, 163
Auditory-vocal association, 162
Aukerman, R., 214, 218, 230
Automatic level functions, 162-163
Ayres, J., 88-90, 180

B

Balance, 74, 79-80
Bannatyne, A., 225-226
Barbe, W., and Frierson, E., 238
Barnhart, C., 212
Barr, E., 172
Barsch, Raymond, 7, 85-86
Bartel, N., 246
Bartlett, S., 172
Basal reader approach, 211-212
Baseline data, 194-195

Basic Concepts Inventory (BCI), 38
Behavior, adaptive, 36
Behavior analysis, applied, 199
Behavior modification, 187-201
  behavioral modeling, 191-192
  contingency contracting, 191
  contingency management, 191
  illustrative case studies, 194-199
  operant conditioning, 189-190
  principles for implementation, 192-194
  recommendations for practitioners, 199-201
  specifying goals and behavioral objectives, 188-189
  types of behavioral change, 187-188
  use with hyperactivity, 105-106
Behavioral change, 187-188
Behavioral modeling, 191-192
Behavioral objectives, 189
Behavioral observation (as an assessment procedure), 41
Behaviorism, 48-49
Bender Visual-Motor Gestalt Test, 39
Bereiter, C., 226
Berman, B., 177
Bhatara, V., 114
Bilateral movement, 74
Binet (Stanford-Binet), 34
Biofeedback to reduce hyperactivity, 113-114
Biren, P., 250
Blau, Harold and Harriet, 135
Bloomfield, L., 212
Bloom's taxonomy of educational objectives, 144-145
Body control, 74
Body image, 78-79, 81
Boehm Test of Basic Concepts (BTBC), 39
Bowman, R., 174
Brady, J., 193
Brain, phylogenetic development of, 94
Brain damage, 102, 107
Brain functioning, 181-182
  semiautonomous systems of, 147
Brain injured, 111
Brain research, 179-183
Braud, L., 113
Braud, W., 113
Brigance Diagnostic Inventories, 37
Brown, D., 172
Brown, Rita, 138-139
Bruner, Jerome, 47, 48, 51
Buchanan, Cynthia, 230
Buckley, R., 176
Buswell, G., 248

C

Case studies
  in behavior modification, 194-199
Case studies—cont'd
  in Fernald VAKT approach, 125-130
Categories (period of), 53, 54-55
Central nervous system functions, 147
Chaining, 56, 60
Chalfant, James, 144
Chall, J., 207-210
Chandler, H., 246
Characteristics
  of hyperactive students, 101-103
  of learning disability students, 14-15
  of secondary students, 260-261
Class content preparation, general, 264, 265
Closure, 162, 239
Cognitive strategies, 58
Coleman, J. S., 260
Color-coded phonetic approaches, 225-226
Color Progressive Matrices, 39
Columbia Mental Maturity Scale, 35
Communication from "feeder" schools, 263
Compensation, 261-262
  applied in compensatory teaching, 263-265
Concept development, 152-153
Concept learning, 56, 62-63
Conceptualization, 152-153
Concrete descriptive level, 254
Concrete-imaginative level, 254
Concrete manipulative materials for arithmetic, 244-245
Concrete operations, 53, 54-55
Conditioning, operant, 189-190
Connors, C., 102
Conservation, principle of, 54-55
Consultive programs, 31-32
Contact, 79
Contingency contracting, 191
Contingency management, 191
Continuous reinforcement, 190
Contracting, 191
Coordination, lack of, 15
Cost contingency, 191
Cott, Allan, 175, 178
Counting boxes, 245
Course equilibrium, 263
Course substitution, 264
Cove Schools for Brain-injured Children, 107
Cratty, Bryant, 86-88
Crook, William, 106, 175, 176, 177
Cross-lateral movement, 74
Cross pattern movement, 94
Cruickshank, William, 7-8, 73, 82, 91, 96, 110, 111, 112, 113, 249, 250
Cuisenaire rods, 245

D

Dallman, M., 231
Decision process hypothesis, 104-105
Deficit behavior, 239-240
Delacato, Carl, 93-96
  concerns about approach, 96
Dember, W., 5
Developmental milestones, 74
Developmental Test of Visual-Motor Integration (VMI), 39
Developmental Test of Visual Perception (DTVP), 37, 91-92
Diet-related treatment, 175-179
  food and food additive allergies, 175-177
  hypoglycemia and the narcolepsy complex, 178-179
  orthomolecular medicine, 177-178
Directionality, importance of, 76-77, 78
Disabilities
  arithmetic, 237-247
  learning; *see* Learning disabilities
  spelling, 252
Discrepancy requirements, 36
Discrimination learning, 56, 61-62
DISTAR program, 226-228, 248
Doman, Glen, 93
Drugs, antiepileptic, 170
Durkin, D., 214, 217, 218
Dyscalculia, 248
Dysgraphia, 250
Dyslexia, 155-156

E

Educational objectives, taxonomy of, 144-145
Electromyographic biofeedback (EMG), 113, 114
Emans, R., 217
Endocrinologist, 168
Engelman, Siegfried, 226
Enrollment assistance, 263
Environmental control approach, 106-113
  Cruickshank, 110-113
  Strauss and Lehtinen, 106-110
Expression, written, 254-256
Expressive language, 152
Expressive process, 162
Eye-motor coordination, 91-92

F

Fay, Temple, 94
Feingold, B., 175
Fernald, Grace, 6, 113, 120-125, 180, 222, 237, 250, 252, 253
  case studies, 125-130
  modified versions of approach, 136-137
Figure ground, 92
Fine motor skills, 74-75
Finger movements, 74-75
Fixed interval schedule, 190
Fixed ratio schedule, 190
Flemings, D., 113
Food additives, 175
Form perception, 81
Formal operations, period of, 53, 55-56
Frierson, E., and Barbe, W., 238
Fries, C., 212
Frostig, Marianne, 7, 91-93, 226
Fund for Perceptually Handicapped Children, 9

G

Gadow, K., 167, 170
Gagné, R. M., 46, 56-65
Gall, Franz, 4, 5
Games
  to promote learning, 87-88
  for use in arithmetic, 245
Garry, R., 46, 50
Gearheart, B. R., 27, 29, 261, 263
Gearheart, Carol, 27, 261, 263
General class content preparation, 264, 265
Getman, Gerald, 7, 82-85
  visuomotor model, 83
Gillingham, Anna, 6-7, 131-135, 222, 250
Gittleman-Klein, R., 106
Goals in behavior modification, 188-189
Goldman-Fristoe Test of Articulation, 39
Goldman-Fristoe-Woodcock Test of Auditory Discrimination (GFW), 39
Goodman, K., 143
Graber, D., 177
Grammatic closure, 162
Gross motor skills, 74
Guthrie, Edwin, 47, 48

H

Habilitation, 112
Hallahan, D., 73, 82, 91, 96
Hammill, Don, 246
Handwriting disabilities, 249-250
Handwriting skills, methods of developing, 250-252
Harris Tests of Lateral Dominance, 39-40
Hawley, C., 176
Hayden, Alice, 74
Head, H., 4
Hebb, D. O., 47, 48, 49
Hinshelwood, James, 5
Hoffer, A., 177
Homme, L., 191
Hubel, David, 180
Hull, Clark, 47, 48, 49

Hyperactivity, 14-15, 101-114, 118
  approaches to reduce
    behavior management, 105-106
    biofeedback, 113-114
    environmental control, 106-113
    medical, 105-106
  causal hypothesis of, 103-105
  characteristics of, 101-103
  definition of, 101-102
Hyperkinetic; *see* Hyperactivity
Hypoactivity, 15
Hypoglycemia, 178-179
Hysterical blindness, 193

I

I.E.P.; *see* Individualized educational program
Illinois Test of Psycholinguistic Abilities (ITPA), 40, 160-163, 174
  interpretation of, 163
  subtests of, 162-163
Imagery, 149
Imitation, 147
Implementation of behavior modification, 192-194
Inattention, 15
Individualized educational program, 21, 25-27, 188
  outline of content of, 26
Individualized planning, 263
Individualized reading approach, 216
Individually prescribed instruction, 231-232
Informal color-coding system, 226
Information acquisition hypothesis, 103-104
Innate responses, 82
Inner language, 150
Instructional objectives, 189
Integrative learning, 148
Intellectual development, 85
Intellectual skills, 57-58
Intelligence, measures of, 34-36
Intermittent reinforcement, 190
Internalization, 147
Interneurosensory learning, 148
I.Q., 34-35
Itinerant teacher program, 31
I.T.P.A.; *see* Illinois Test of Psycholinguistic Abilities

J

John, L., 248
Johnson, Doris, 145-146, 238, 248, 250-255
Johnson, S., 238-239, 240, 246

K

Kaliski, L., 238
Kaufman, H., 137-138, 250
Keogh, Barbara, 102, 103, 104
Kephart, N., 7, 76-82, 113, 180
Kerr, James, 5
Kinesthetic learning, 118-119
Kingsley, H., 46, 50
Kinsbourne, M., 175
Kirk, Samuel, 8, 9, 10, 160-163
Klivington, K., 180
Kretch, R., 181

L

Language
  auditory, 254
  expressive, 152
  expressive auditory, acquiring, 145
  inner, 150
  receptive, acquiring, 144
  written, 254-256
Language abilities, normal development of, 286-287
Language-development-related approaches, 143-164
Language experience approach, 214-216
Lashley, Karl, 174
Laterality, 78
Law of effect, 49
Law of exercise, 49
Leakey, Richard, 143
Learning
  concept, 56, 62-63
  definition of, 46
  discrimination, 56, 61-62
  integrative, 148
  interneurosensory, 148
  kinesthetic, 118-119
  levels of, 149-153
  major theories of, 47-66
  nature of, 46-47
  normal, 45-46
  rule, 56, 63-64
  signal, 59-60
  stimulus-response, 60
  tactile, 118-119
Learning disabilities
  characteristics of students with, 14-15
  criteria for determining existence of, 12
  definition of, 9-14
  history of, 4-12
  I.E.P.s for, 25-27
  legislation for, 10, 11
  multidimensional approach to, 153-154
  placement alternatives for, 27-32
  screening procedures for, 21-22
  tests used in, 33-41
Learning disabilities and written language disorders, 249-255
  handwriting disabilities, 249-250

Learning disabilities and written language disorders —cont'd
methods for developing handwriting skills, 250-252
spelling disabilities, 252-254
written expression, 254-255
LeFrancois, G. R., 48, 50
Lehtinen, L., 7, 107, 108, 109, 110, 113
Levels of alertness, 87
Levels of learning, 149-153
Leviton, Harvey, 31
Lind, D., 193
Linguistic approaches, 212-214
Lip movements, 75
Locomotion, 79
Loney, Jan, 101, 104, 106
Lovitt, T., 199
Lupin, M., 113

M

Major principles for remediation (Myklebust), 154-155
Manual expression, 162
Marsh, George, 27, 246, 261, 263
Mayer, R., 188
McCarthy, James, 160
McGaugh, J., 174
Maslow, Phyllis, 92
Matthes, C., 213
Medical specialists, role of, 167-183
Medication
effects on children, 167, 170, 172
for hyperactivity, 103
Medicine, orthomolecular, 177-178
Meeting Street School Screening Test (MSSST), 40
Memory, 173-174, 239
disorders and, 15
sequential, 163
Memory-for-Designs Test (MFD), 40
Meredith, R., 143
Methods for developing handwriting skills, 250-252
Metrazol, 174
Miccinati, J., 136-137
Midline, crossing of, 74
Modality blocking approach, 135
Modeling, 191-192
Modified or special texts, 264
Monroe, Marion, 6-7
Montessori, M., 227-229
Montessori-related approaches, 227-229
Morgan, W. P., 5
Motor abilities, normal development of, 286-287
Motor bases of learning, 77-79
Motor development
general, 82-83
special, 84
Motor-Free Test of Visual Perception, 40
Motor skills, 57
fine, 74-75
Motoric/linguistic method, 137-138
Movement generalizations, 79
Movigenics, 85-86
Multidimensional approach to learning disabilities, 153-154
Multiple states of readiness, 154
Multisensory methods and approaches, 117-140, 229-230
Myklebust, Helmer, 7, 47, 145, 146-160, 180, 238, 248, 250, 251, 252, 253, 254, 255
levels of learning, 149-153
principles for remediation, 154-155

N

Narcolepsy complex, 178-179
National Advisory Committee on Handicapped Children, 10
National Association for Retarded Children, 8
Nature of secondary school, 259-263
Nature of secondary school student, 259-263
Nelson, A., 106
Neobehaviorism, 49-50
Nervous system functions, 147
Neurological impairment hypothesis, 103
Neurological organization theory, 93-94
Neurologist, 169
Nomenclature of arithmetic, 246
Nonverbal disabilities, 158-159
Normal development, 286-287
Normal learning, 45-46
Norman, D., 174
North Carolina, discrepancy requirements in, 36
Number cards, 245
Numbers, period of, 53, 54-55

O

Occupational therapist, 169
Ocular control, 81
Ocular motor development, 84
Oculist, 169
Off-campus work assignments, 266, 267, 268
Okolo, C., 172
On-the-job experience, 267
Ontogeny, 94
Open Court Correlated Language Arts Program, 229-230
Operant conditioning, 49, 189-190
Operants, 187
Ophthalmologist, 169
Optometrist, 169
Order and structure, 111-112, 113
Organizing process, 162
Orthomolecular medicine, 177-178

Orton, Samuel, 6, 131-135
Osgood, Charles, 47, 48, 49, 160
Osmond, H., 177
Otolaryngologist, 169
Otologist, 169
Overattention, 15
Overloading, 157-158

P

Parent conferences, 30
Parent permission or involvement
  in assessment, 20, 23, 33
  in I.E.P., 21, 33
  in program placement, 21, 33
  in staffing, 21, 33
Pauling, Linus, 177
Peabody Individual Achievement Test (PIAT), 37
Peabody Rebus Reading Program, 233
Perception, 84-85, 149
Perceptual disorders, 15
Perceptual-motor authorities
  Ayres, 88-90
  Barsch, 85-86
  basic beliefs of, 75-76
  Cratty, 86-88
  Delacato, 93-96
  Frostig, 91-93
  Getman, 82-85
  Kephart, 76-82
Perceptual-Motor Survey, Purdue, 79-80
Peripheral nervous system functions, 147
Perseveration, 15, 109
Pharmacotherapy, 170
Phonetic approaches, color-coded, 225-226
Phonetic components in reading, 216-220
Phonics, 218-219
Phrenology, 4
Phylogenetic development of brain, 94
Physical therapist, 169
Piaget, Jean, 47, 48, 51-56, 246, 247
  table of periods of cognitive development, 53
Picture Story Language Test (PSLT), 40
Pines, M., 174
Placement alternatives for the learning disabled, 27-32
Placement decision, 32
Position in space, 92
Posture, 77-78, 79-80
Powell, M., 269
Powers, Hugh, 175, 176, 179
Preliminary review, 22
Problem solving, 56, 64
Programmed instructional systems, 230-232
  individually prescribed instruction, 231-232
  programmed reading approach, 230-231
Programmed reading approach, 230-231
Propulsion and receipt, 79
Psychiatrist, 169
Psychodynamic factors, 147
Psycholinguistic Color System, 225-226
Psychologist, 169
Psychoneurological learning disabilities, 146
Psychotropic drugs, 170
Public Law 91-230, 10
Public Law 94-142, 11, 19
  guidelines for assessment, 19, 32-33
Pupil Behavior Rating Scale, 22, 273-279
Purdue Perceptual Motor Survey, 40, 79-81

R

Rambusch, N., 228
Rapp, D., 102
Raven, J. C., 39
Reading approaches, 210-220
  basal reader, 211-212
  individualized, 216
  language experience, 214-215
  linguistic, 212-214
  phonetic components, 216-217
Reading controversies, 205-210
Reading methods for learning disabled
  color-coded phonetic, 225-226
  DISTAR program, 226-227
  individually prescribed, 231-232
  informal color-coding, 226
  Montessori-related, 227-229
  Open Court Correlated Language Arts Program, 229-230
  programmed instructional systems, 230-231
  rebus, 232-233
Reading remediation, 220-226
Rebus approaches, 232-233
Receipt and propulsion, 79
Receptive language, 151-152
Receptive process, 162
Recommendations for practitioners in using behavior modification, 199-201
Reduced space, 111
Reduction of environmental stimuli, 110
Referrals, 19-20
Reinforcement schedules, 190
Reisman, F., 248
Relations, period of, 53, 54-55
Remediation
  major principles for, 154-155
  for secondary student, 261
Representational level functions, 162
Residential settings, 27

Resource rooms, 28-31
guidelines for, 29-31
Respondents, 187
Revisualizing, 253
Roberts, H. J., 178-179
Rogan, Laura, 7
Rosenfeld, H., 180
Ross, H., 177
Rule learning, 56, 63-64

S

Safer, D., 172
Scheffelin, M., 144
School, alternative, 266, 267, 268
Screening, 21, 22
scales for, 273-285
Secondary programming, a tutorial emphasis on, 265-266
Secondary school programs, 259-268
Self-contained classes, 27-28
Semiautonomous systems of brain functioning, 147
Sensation, 149
Sensorimotor evolution, 52-54
Sensorimotor period, 52-54
Sensory integration, 88-90
Sequential memory, 163
Shaw, S., 172
Shiffrin, R., 174
Signal learning, 56, 59-60
Simpson, D., 106
Skinner, B. F., 47, 48, 49, 187
Slossen Intelligence Test for Children and Adults, 35
Smith, E., 143
Smith, F., 46
Sound blending, 162
Southern California Sensory Integration Tests (SCSIT), 40, 88-89
Spache, E., 212, 214, 217
Spache, G., 212, 214, 217
Spatial awareness, 239
Spatial orientation, 74
Spatial relations, 92
Special motor development, 84
Special preparation for participation in regular classes, 264-265
abstract concepts, 264
advance learning of technical vocabulary, 264
general class content preparation, 264-265
study skills, 265
Special schools, 27
Specifying goals and behavioral objectives, 188-189
Speech-motor system, 84
Spelling disabilities, 252
Spence, Kenneth, 49
Staffing, 21, 33
Standardized Road Map Test of Direction Sense, 40-41
Stanford-Binet, 34
Stillman, Bessie, 6-7
Stimulus-response learning, 56, 60
Stimulus-response psychology, 49
Stimulus value of teaching materials, 112
Strauss, Alfred, 7, 101, 107, 108, 109, 110, 111, 113, 237, 252
Strephosymbolia, 6
Structured school program, 111-112
Study skills, 265
Sulzer, B., 188
Swanson, J., 175
Symbolization, 150

T

Tactile defensiveness, 90
Tactile learning, 118-119
Tarnopol, L., 246
Tarnopol, M., 246
Taxonomy of educational objectives, 144-145
Teaching materials, stimulus value of, 112
Technical vocabulary, advance learning of, 264
Templin-Darley Tests of Articulation (TDTA), 41
Tests used in identification of learning disabilities, 33-41
Texts, modified or special, 264
Thorndike, Edward, 47, 48
Tolman, Edward, 47, 48
Tongue movements, 75
Tonic neck reflex, 82
Tutorial emphasis on secondary programming, 265-266

V

VAKT approach, 120-125, 253
Variable interval schedule, 190
Variable ratio schedule, 190
Variable reinforcement, 190
Verbal association, 56, 60-61
Verbal expression, 162
disabilities in, 239
Verbal information, 58
Visual-auditory association disabilities, 239
Visual closure, 162
Visual discrimination disabilities, 239
Visual dyslexia, 155-156
Visual learners, 156
Visual memory, 253
Visual-motor association, 162
Visual-motor integration, 250
Visual-perception, 249
Visual perceptual problems, 15
Visual perceptual skills, 91-92
Visual recall, 253
Visual reception, 162

Visual sequential memory, 163
Visualization, 84
Vocabulary, technical, advance learning of, 264

W

Wadsworth, B. J., 51
Watson, John, 47, 48
Waugh, N., 174
Webster, Daniel, 217
Wechsler, David, tests developed by, 34-35
Wechsler Adult Intelligence Scale (WAIS), 34
Wechsler Intelligence Scale for Children-Revised (WISC-R), 34-35, 174
Wechsler Preschool and Primary Scale of Intelligence (WPPSI), 34
Wepman, Joseph, 38
Werner, Heinz, 7
Wertheimer, Max, 47
Wide Range Achievement Test (WRAT), 36-37
Weiderholt, L., 4
Wiens, E., 265
Witelson, S., 182
Wolf, J., 174
Wolf, M., 195
Woodcock, P., 233
Word blindness, 5
Work-study programs, 266-267
Wrist movements, 74-75
Written expression, 254-256
Written language, 254-256
  abstract-descriptive, 254-255
  abstract-imaginative, 254-255
  concrete-descriptive, 254-255
  concrete-imaginative, 254-255
Written language disorders, 249-255
Wunderlich, R., 105